STRONG IN WILL: WORKING FOR THE AMERICAN EMBASSY IN PARIS DURING THE NAZI OCCUPATION

MARIE-LOUISE DILKES

Edited by
VIRGINIA A. DILKES

CASEMATE
Pennsylvania & Yorkshire

Published in the United States of America and Great Britain in 2024 by
CASEMATE PUBLISHERS
1950 Lawrence Road, Havertown, PA 19083, USA
and
47 Church Street, Barnsley, S70 2AS, UK

Copyright © 2024 Virginia A. Dilkes

Hardcover Edition: ISBN 978-1-63624-378-8
Digital Edition: ISBN 978-1-63624-379-5

A CIP record for this book is available from the British Library

Printed and bound in the United Kingdom by CPI Group (UK) Ltd, Croydon, CR0 4YY
Typeset in India by DiTech Publishing Services

For a complete list of Casemate titles, please contact:

CASEMATE PUBLISHERS (US)
Telephone (610) 853-9131
Fax (610) 853-9146
Email: casemate@casematepublishers.com
www.casematepublishers.com

CASEMATE PUBLISHERS (UK)
Telephone (0)1226 734350
Email: casemate@casemateuk.com
www.casemateuk.com

Cover image: The Digital Collections of the National WWII Museum, "American embassy. Paris." Paris, France. Circa May 1945.

Contents

1. Baden-Baden   Germany
2. Berchtesgaden   Germany
3. Berlin   Germany
4. Bern   Switzerland
5. Besançon   France
6. Biarritz   France
7. Bordeaux   France
8. Brussels   Belgium
9. Caen   France
10. Candé   France
11. Cerbère   France
12. Danzig   Poland
13. Dinard   France
14. Dunkirk   France
15. Fresnes   France
16. Hendaye   France
17. Limoges   France
18. Lisbon   Portugal
19. London   England

20. Lourdes   France
21. Lyon   France
22. Madrid   Spain
23. Monte Carlo   Monaco
24. Munich   Germany
25. Nantes   France
26. Orléans   France
27. Paris   France
28. Portbou   Spain
29. Prague   Czechoslovakia
30. Reggio Calabria   Italy
31. Rome   Italy
32. Sedan   France
33. Versailles   France
34. Vichy   France
35. Vienna   Austria
36. Warsaw   Poland

Europe before World War II

Preface

"Quand Même" is how Marie-Louise Dilkes expressed her joy. It was her motto inscribed on a nameplate on her desk. She loved America, she loved France, and she enjoyed working for the American Embassy in Paris. She was willing to do whatever it took to keep these three loves alive in her heart and in her soul.

Personal Background

Marie-Louise Dilkes was born in Philadelphia, Pennsylvania, on March 12, 1886, and died in Paris on March 30, 1964. She was educated at the Holy Child Academy in Sharon Hill, Pennsylvania. She was a follower of Christian Science in the last 30 years of her life.

In 1917 through family connections, she volunteered to join the Emergency Aid of Pennsylvania,[1] which sent her to Paris to help establish the American Soldiers' and Sailors' Club,[2] a retreat for American soldiers from the stress of battle of the Great War. When her brother, a combat engineer in WWI, was on leave, he went to see her in Paris.[3]

She was the secretary for the American Soldiers' and Sailors' Club and worked under Dean F. W. Beekman of the American Episcopal Cathedral of the Holy Trinity in Paris.[4] Marie-Louise Dilkes fell in love with Paris and stayed on after the Great War to work as a code clerk for Colonel T. B. Mott,[5] Military Attaché for the American Embassy in Paris. At the conclusion of these duties, she returned to the United States and worked for the Embassy of Belgium in Washington, D.C. She was the personal secretary to the Belgian Ambassador to the United States, initially Baron de Cartier de Marchienne[6] and later Prince Albert de Ligne,[7] who awarded her the Croix de Chevalier de l'Ordre de Léopold II. All four of these men would recommend her for appointment as receptionist for the American Embassy in Paris. To further support her application for appointment, it is worth noting that Marie-Louise's sister, Dolores, was married to Richard Morin[8] who was Vice Consul for the American Embassy in Paris (1929–1933) and a Foreign Service officer at the U.S. Department of State in Washington, D.C. (1933–1935).

Historical Background

When Nazi Germany invaded France in June 1940, members of the French cabinet fled Paris to the Château de Cangé, then to Bordeaux, and ultimately established the French government in Vichy, which became the de facto seat of government of unoccupied France. The American Embassy stayed in Paris until May 1941 when some staff members were reassigned to establish the American Embassy in Vichy. In June 1941 the German authorities ordered all French and all foreign employees of the Embassy, including Americans, to vacate the American Embassy in Paris.[9] The United States knew it still had to have a presence in Paris to address the needs of five thousand American citizens caught in the turmoil. Through negotiations with Berlin, on June 4, 1941, the American Embassy closed its main entrance on 2 Avenue Gabriel and opened the facility on June 10 as the American Consulate in Paris using the side entrance on rue Boissy d'Anglas. Twelve men and three women were assigned as staff for the now American Consulate in Paris. Marie-Louise Dilkes was one of the three women.[10]

This book is of her experiences as a member of the American Embassy in Paris during the dark years of 1939–1941, the American Consulate in Paris (1941), the American Consulate in Lyon (1941), and the U.S. Legation in Bern, Switzerland (1942–1944), where she was assigned after Nazi Germany took over all of France. With the success of the Allied landings in Europe in 1943–1944, the Nazi scourge was diminishing across Europe, and Germany surrendered Paris to the Allies in August 1944. At the end of August, Marie-Louise Dilkes received orders to be part of a team to reopen the American Embassy in Paris. She wrote of the triumphant reentry into France, with the help of the U.S. 7th Army, and the reestablishment of the American Embassy in Paris on October 14, 1944.

The history of the American Embassy in Paris and the splintering of its staff in 1941 into the American Consulate in Paris and the American Embassy in Vichy are outlined. Through the trials and tribulations of war, both of these components of the American Embassy were able to come together to reestablish the American Embassy in Paris by the end of 1944.

American Embassy in Paris Splintered in 1941

Consular Operations

Embassy Operations

Embassy facility in Paris changed to consulate: June 4, 1941	Embassy moved to Vichy: May 1, 1941
Entrance on Rue Boissy d'Anglas: Consul Laurence Taylor	Ambassador Admiral William Leahy
Staff: 12 men + 3 women*	

Paris, France	**Vichy, France**
Consulate expelled from Paris: July 20, 1941	Ambassador Leahy called back to the U.S.
Paris consulate travelled to Biarritz to Hendaye to Biarritz to	Chargé d'Affaires S. Pinkney Tuck
Hendaye to Lisbon to Portbou to Cerbère to Lyon	May 22, 1941–May 1942

Lyon, France	**Lourdes, France**
Paris consulate ordered to Lyon	American Embassy in Vichy seized by German troops
(Diplomatic pouch service to Vichy: October. 12–14)	American Embassy staff interned in Lourdes
September 3–December. 26, 1941	November 1942–February 1943

Bern, Switzerland	**Baden-Baden, Germany**
Paris consulate ordered to U.S. Legation in Bern	American Embassy staff interned in Germany
December 29, 1941–October, 10, 1944	February 1943–February 1944
	Released in diplomat exchange

Paris, France	**Paris, France**
Paris consular staff ordered to Paris: Oct. 11, 1944	American Embassy reopened to the public
American Embassy reopened for diplomatic purposes:	Ambassador Jefferson Caffery
Chargé d' Affaires Selden Chapin	November 25, 1944
October 14, 1944	

American Embassy Reestablished in Paris
October–November 1944

*Marie-Louise Dilkes

The splintering of the American Embassy in France (1941–1944)

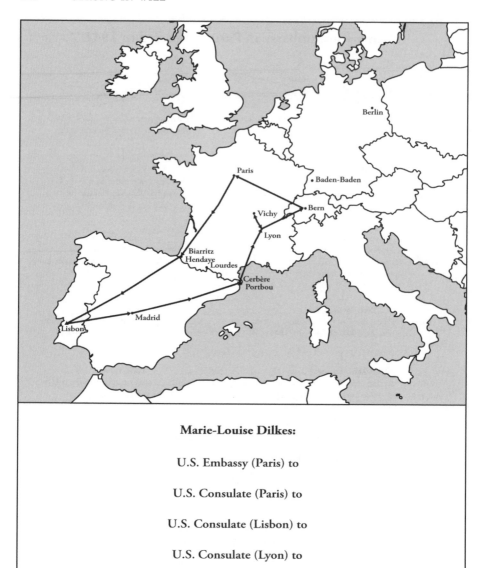

Marie-Louise Dilkes:

U.S. Embassy (Paris) to

U.S. Consulate (Paris) to

U.S. Consulate (Lisbon) to

U.S. Consulate (Lyon) to

U.S. Legation (Bern) to

U.S. Embassy (Paris)

1941–1944

Assignments for Marie-Louise Dilkes in WWII

Introduction

Marie-Louise Dilkes worked for the American Embassy in Paris from 1933–1954. As the American Embassy receptionist, she experienced the chaotic times in Europe with the rise of Hitler and all that followed. While her career as a member of the Embassy staff spanned 21 years, her writing focused on the years 1939–1944. She wrote her manuscript, which she titled *Paris Notes*, in Paris in 1955.[1]

Marie-Louise began her *Notes*: "Monsieur Pierre Audiat[2] has written in the preface of his interesting book *Paris Pendant la Guerre*[3] that no one, no matter how learned he is or how great his intuition or imagination, is able to feel or evoke the atmosphere of Paris during the German Occupation unless he himself had breathed it. Even memory would not be adequate nor would material facts be sufficient."

She wrote, "One must indeed have lived in occupied France during those eventful days to have felt and experienced that atmosphere. From the hearts and souls of the French, there was a surge of fierce passions, of strong emotions strongly controlled, and so often unhappily uncontrolled, as those great, bitter waters closed over them and their country. There were scorn, hatred, distrust, resentment, mockery, defiance and a sullen acceptance of the rules of Occupation as days moved into months and months into four long, unhappy years."

While she endeavored to describe the atmosphere of Paris during the Occupation and to relate some of the facts of the war as they came into her experience, she did not focus on what made her contribution to this part of history so unique: her role as receptionist to the American Embassy in Paris during World War II. Using subtitles, I have extracted her experiences as a member of the Embassy staff, which drew out how much the Embassy impacted the lives of Americans, Parisians, and all who passed through the door to the American Embassy in Paris.

The writings of Marie-Louise Dilkes are very much a portrait of a woman born in the 1880s, 1886 to be exact, and who lived to experience the tragedies of two world wars. In her focus on detail, she emerges as a woman who was educated, elitist, and emotional. She enjoyed seeing France through the architecture that surrounded her and the writings through the ages that inspired her. She was well-read and often cited literature in her writing. Marie-Louise would quote from the Bible and from French, British, and American literature, especially poetry; from the classic

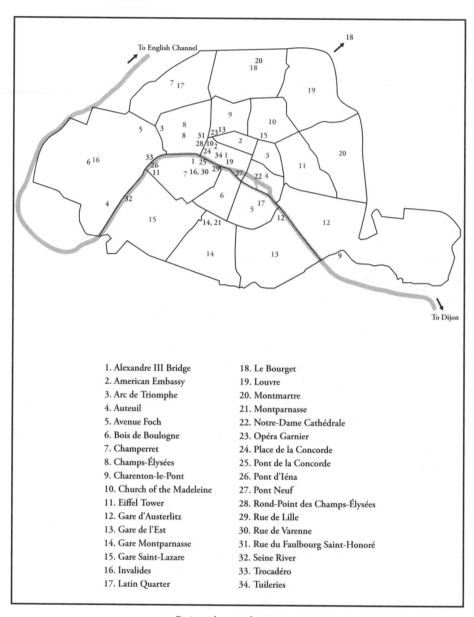

1. Alexandre III Bridge
2. American Embassy
3. Arc de Triomphe
4. Auteuil
5. Avenue Foch
6. Bois de Boulogne
7. Champerret
8. Champs-Élysées
9. Charenton-le-Pont
10. Church of the Madeleine
11. Eiffel Tower
12. Gare d'Austerlitz
13. Gare de l'Est
14. Gare Montparnasse
15. Gare Saint-Lazare
16. Invalides
17. Latin Quarter

18. Le Bourget
19. Louvre
20. Montmartre
21. Montparnasse
22. Notre-Dame Cathédrale
23. Opéra Garnier
24. Place de la Concorde
25. Pont de la Concorde
26. Pont d'Iéna
27. Pont Neuf
28. Rond-Point des Champs-Élysées
29. Rue de Lille
30. Rue de Varenne
31. Rue du Faulbourg Saint-Honoré
32. Seine River
33. Trocadéro
34. Tuileries

Paris with arrondissements

or bestseller books of the times; and from American, French, Belgium, German, Italian, and Swiss newspapers.

She hobnobbed with the elite, from dukes and duchesses of the United Kingdom to European royalty to people of high position. Marie-Louise was comfortable among the elite since she was born into a family of privilege. The Dilkes family was a member of Main Line Philadelphia society. Her father, George R. Dilkes,[4] had owned the Southern Steamship Lines[5] in Philadelphia, Pennsylvania. She carried her privileged life and society friends to Paris and tried to live her life in France accordingly. The war interrupted her lifestyle, and she wrote about her frustrations. While she adjusted to the sparse war-time life, her thoughts never did. Throughout her writing the reader will recognize her elitist thoughts. Her society friends in turn sought her out because of her appointment at the American Embassy. Whether in social settings or at the Embassy, her friends often inquired of her if or when the U.S. was going to enter the war, whether she could offer visa advice, or how they could protect their assets. Her friends found her wherever her journey with the U.S. State Department took her.

She made no bones about her support for the Allies, especially the Americans, the French, and the British, and her hatred for the Nazis. She hated those who would destroy the France she loved. Her manuscript is filled with her thoughts on what the world should be or what she wished it could be. The engaged reader will not have a problem discerning Marie-Louise Dilkes' thoughts and opinions from what is happening in the world around her.

Mary-Louise Dilkes is my aunt. I never met her. Readers first met her in the writing of Charles Edward Dilkes, her brother and my father, which related his experiences as a combat engineer in World War I in his book *Remembering World War One: An Engineer's Diary of the War*. Marie-Louise and her brother were able to get together in Paris in April 1919 when he was on leave while serving with the U.S. Army of Occupation.

Through her World War II memoir, I have come to understand the love Marie-Louise had for America and France. Through her writing it was interesting to visit the places that were a part of her life—and then to research those places today. It would have been nice to have known my Aunt Marie-Louise. She was a woman of her times and one for the generations to come.

Virginia Dilkes, 2023

To the Modern Reader

Editorial adjustments were made for the modern reader. I addressed Marie-Louise Dilkes' use of punctuation, her long chapters, her footnotes, and her spelling of some words.

Marie-Louise liked to use punctuation to bring the reader in, especially through her use of exclamation points and ellipses. I changed some of her exclamation points to periods to save the emphasis of her emotion to when it mattered most. One of the challenges as editor was how to retain her emotions yet keep with what she was trying to evoke. She liked to end her sentences with ellipses as if her writings of those dark years went beyond words.

Her long chapters are kept intact although I segmented them through subtitles. Her footnotes are kept as original footnotes while I used endnotes to clarify and explain the background history. Some of the endnotes and words in the glossary will seem trivial to the older generation or those versed in European World War II history. The spelling of words is kept as the common form used in the 1940s. Spellings may differ based on how the British spell the words in contrast to the American way of spelling: phoney or phony; rumour or rumor; despatch or dispatch; enquire or inquire; armour or armor; grey or gray.

Even though the world had recognized Russia as one state in the Soviet Union since 1922, Marie-Louise never referred to Russia as the Soviet Union in her writing. The reader will be able to discern when she is referring to the Soviet Union as Russia.

I hope *Strong in Will* gives the reader insight into how her position as receptionist to the American Embassy in Paris made her a part of the unfolding events of World War II.

Virginia Dilkes

Dedication

To my father who shared his history and that of the Dilkes family and their contributions to America's history through their participation in two world wars ...
To my mother who kept the Dilkes legacy alive ...
To my brothers and sisters who supported telling the story ...
To my children, Jim, Judy, and Anne, who encouraged me ..., and
To my grandchildren, Rachel, Robert, and Caroline, who are the future.

Virginia A. Dilkes, Editor

Marie-Louise Dilkes

CHAPTER I

August 25, 1939–June 14, 1940

Serving with the American Embassy
in Paris in Turbulent Times

Paris, August 25, 1939

Dear D.[1]

War seems imminent tonight. All day tanks and camions have been passing through the city toward the frontier. Few taxis find their way about the streets, autobuses are scarce—the drivers are being called to the colors. Posters noting the different classes that are being called up have been affixed through the city. The stations are filled with soldiers starting on their long journey from which thousands shall never come back. Tonight, the Prime Minister, M. Daladier,[2] spoke over the radio urging the men, women, and children of France to be strong and united in the defense of *La Patrie* before the German menace that is threatening all Europe. All day the newsstands have been surrounded by people frantic for the latest news. From the *École Militaire* near my apartment house on the Avenue de la Bourdonnais come the vibrant strains of "La Marseillaise." With it ringing in my ears I close my shutters with a heavy heart and turn to my bed certain that my sleep will be troubled.

The morning broke with rain over the city. I walked to the [American] Embassy, found the large reception hall at the entrance crowded with Americans seeking information and help of various kinds. Most of them were registering and making desperate efforts to have aid in finding places on already crowded boats for America. Some U.S. battleships are waiting at Villefranche in the south of France to repatriate United States citizens. The French are calm and resolute. They try not to think of Munich almost a year ago when the Arc de Triomphe was alight with hope, and when cheers resounded for Daladier as the savior of the country.

I sailed for home, you remember, on October 6, 1938. I recall the dinner party at the home of one of my friends the evening before my departure and the day after the conference of Munich. There were about ten guests: some Americans, two British subjects, a few French, and a German who was seated on my right—a young blond Nazi, married to a French girl. The girl was not in Paris at the time, but as memories went back to another gathering when I had met her, I could hear her deep voice as she turned to me and in admiring tones exclaimed, "Hitler and Mussolini! They are the greatest statesmen in Europe, in the world perhaps today, and there is not another man intelligent enough to negotiate with them." At the time I wondered at these words coming from a French citizen and was not surprised, a few months later, to find a card announcing her marriage to a German.

As dinner proceeded on this evening after Munich, there was a feeling of trouble pending, or if not trouble, certainly of something disturbing. I turned to answer a trivial question asked by my German partner. There was a certain insolence in his bearing, a sureness in his attitude. For a moment there was tense silence. Suddenly the Englishman opposite me, his features taut, leaned toward the German and asked: "How did you feel after Munich? Did you feel that you were the victors? Did you feel that you had lost, or were you of the opinion that you were standing pat?"

The reply had a patronizing tone: "I think that the German leaders felt they had gone far enough." Our host hastily changed the subject, and the dinner proceeded with no further incident.

That was a year ago. Today France is taking no chances. She is preparing for war. At home, in America, as I write this, you are peacefully going about the daily routine. France is so far away....

American Embassy Families Ordered to Dinard

August 26, 1939

Dear L.[3]

The tension seems lighter today as the papers announce that Hitler has called the American, British, French, and Japanese ambassadors in Berlin for a conference—after pressure had been put on him by President Roosevelt, the King of Belgium, and the Pope—in an effort toward peace.[4]

German merchant ships en route to America had been ordered, in mid ocean, to return to Germany. One such ship was the SS *Bremen*[5] of the German line, which also carried tourists. United States tourists with return passage had feared to take it. The SS *Bremen* however proceeded to New York where its passengers safely disembarked. I frequently wondered why our compatriots took the risk of coming to Europe in all this turmoil, a condition that has existed for months.

The German–Soviet Pact of Nonaggression[6] was signed yesterday as, of course, you saw by the press. The French Communist newspapers, *L'Humanité* and *Le Soir*,[7] upholding the Soviets for making the pact with the Nazis, were withdrawn from circulation by the Government.

The rapidity with which one event follows another is little less than astounding.

I dined tonight at the restaurant Chez Francis on the Place de l'Alma.[8] My host was a retired U.S. Colonel whom I had known for many years and whose love for

France had brought him back to this country from his home in America. He had joined the American Field Service[9] recently organized in the United States.

Tonight was the first time since the end of the last war that I saw French officers and soldiers of the army and navy in large numbers. They are beginning to fill the streets and cafés. It was very warm on the crowded terrace where we were seated. The Place de l'Alma was dimly lighted, and the traffic of camions, taxis, official and private cars went swiftly through the streets giving the city a warlike air. After dinner we wandered up the Avenue George V toward the Champs-Élysées. We went into the cinema house Le Paris[10] where they were playing an excellent film entitled *Toward His Destiny*,[11] the early life of Abraham Lincoln, beautifully interpreted by Henry Fonda. It was a sad picture and I thought, as I left the cinema, of this "rail-splitter, tree chopper and the greatest man that history ever made," of his love for humanity and the dignity of human life. How largely it was due to him that the United States is so great and united today. And I thought that Lincoln will live in the hearts of men through all ages while Hitler, as the heartless brigand that he is, will be reviled.

Today the Department of State ordered the wives and children of the Embassy staff to proceed to Dinard, in Brittany, as it is thought they will be safer there should events be precipitated.

August 27, 1939

My window looks out over the broad Avenue de la Bourdonnais. This morning as I leaned out from it, I saw seated at tables, spread from the corner of my street along the pavement to the next street, officers and soldiers requisitioning or taking numbers for the requisition of private cars, trucks, and wagons of all kinds.

All Germans are leaving or being ordered to leave the country; Italian organizations are swearing allegiance to France; stained glass windows from the different churches, notably Chartres,[12] are being removed and, although there is still optimism in the French spirit and press, the Government is preparing for any eventuality. Gradually French children are being evacuated. American citizens in great numbers are leaving for different French ports to await ships.

My spirits went higher as I passed Smith's Bookshop[13] in the corner of the rue de Rivoli and the rue Cambon today. I purchased a book called *Hitler's Last Year of Power*.[14] The author is an astrologer and has made a study of the horoscope of Europe and the leaders of the nations. He states that there will be no general war; negotiations will continue, and local wars will take place. I know very little about astrology, but I grasp at anything that might point to peace, and I insist on thinking that nothing so devastating as a general war will happen. You will think that I am living in a fool's paradise. Perhaps I am. But I cannot, I shall not believe that we, in this twentieth century, are not able to find a way to prevent a conflagration that would put the progress of the world back for centuries.

I cannot write more. I am tired and depressed thinking that this fair land of France will again....

September 1, 1939

August passed into September. Just think of it! The world tremblingly held in uncertainty by the will of one man! Shall war come? Does Adolph Hitler dare touch the Polish frontier?

The *Paris-midi*[15] is sold out an hour after it is on the streets. We await *Paris-soir* with breathless eagerness as evening approaches.

The autobuses have disappeared and taxis rush by full of officers and soldiers going to their different barracks. Every other vehicle is piled high with bags and trunks; there is no possibility of finding an empty one. The atmosphere is electric as I drearily cross the Place de la Concorde on foot and see the tense faces of the crowds. It is half past six, the time they leave their offices for home. The newsstands are crowded.

I reach my apartment later than usual, as the Embassy had been filled all day with our nervous and frightened citizens, all being advised to leave Europe. The amount of work had kept us long after the usual time for departure.

I was filled with misgivings as I climbed three flights to my apartment. The electric lights had gone off, and there was no elevator.

September 2, 1939

Morning came after a sleepless night. No wonder it was sleepless. I must have had a feeling of apprehension during those wakeful moments, for the press gave out that at midnight Hitler entered Danzig,[16] bombing some of the Polish frontier cities. England and France have proclaimed a general mobilization. The Paris *Prefecture of Police* has repeated its orders for all those who have nothing urgent to keep them in Paris to leave the city. The police are wearing helmets and carrying their gas masks. The Embassy has given a mask to each member of the staff. I have instructed Mademoiselle to buy one as soon as possible. Mademoiselle is my Swiss governess. Her name is Marie Durussel. She was the governess of the children of a friend of mine, but now the children are grown, and Mademoiselle takes charge of my friend's large apartment in which I have a wing.

On entering my domicile this evening, my governess greeted me with the news that my friend, with her husband and children, were leaving in a few minutes for Spain. They were grouped in the salon waiting for a taxi to take them to the station. I had scarcely time to say goodbye when the taxi was announced—the last one apparently left in Paris. It took them to the station where they caught the last train leaving for the Spanish frontier. Mademoiselle and I are left alone. She has no place to go, and I have told her that she may remain with me, at least until we see what events will bring.

From the *Préfecture de Police* came orders for a general blackout of the city. Tonight, no glimmer of light may be seen from any window or opening. Black paper and dark curtains are everywhere. The notices *"ABRI"* are pasted on almost every other house, indicating the number of persons that could take refuge there during an air raid.

The newspapers state that the German air force had been able to go through the Polish anti-air defenses and that numbers of German planes have been brought down by the Poles. England and France are ready to keep their engagement to Poland. Italy remains neutral.

The elderly Rumanian gentleman in the apartment above mine has sent word to me through Mademoiselle that as he is the only man in the house, I should call on him at any moment of the day or night if necessary. It was very kind of him, and I sent up my thanks. As one can imagine, a word of such courtesy amid these seething events brings a feeling of security. Mademoiselle has indeed been God-sent for she is of untellable help. Her devotion to my friends and their children, whom she taught from tiny tots, assure me that I shall have the same loyalty and devotion. And so here we are together facing—what? Total disaster or a sudden peace? No one knows today—of the morrow we must take no thought.

The evening air is sultry and yet there is a suggestion in the atmosphere that the cool, crisp days often found in the beginning of September may soon be here. En route for home after a surcharged day, I turn right from the great Place de la Concorde and walk through the gardens of the Champs-Élysées, crossing the Avenue past the restaurant Ledoyen[17] where the waiters are arranging the tables for dinner on the terrace. I feel the crunch of a dead leaf under my foot. The leaves are already beginning to fall. Still verging toward the right, I reach the bridge of Alexandre III where the Seine[18] curves so beautifully. One cannot see the matchless towers of Notre-Dame[19] from Alexandre III. One must view them from the Pont de la Concorde[20] where in the distance they can be seen in their beauty, shimmering in the morning mist or at midday clear as crystal under a full sun, or again in the evening with the red or gold of the sunset blazing over them.

American Embassy Windows Covered in Black Paper

September 4, 1939

Dear D.

Your letter came this morning. I had waited for it a long time and re-read it several times. The change you are contemplating is an important one. It may lead you in this direction [to Paris] which would please me immensely.

The *École Militaire* subway station, a three-minute walk from my apartment, is a direct line to the [Place de la] Concorde. It is a very active corner, and the large café there is full almost twenty-four hours of the day. Toward the south lies the Military School of Paris, built during the reign of Louis XV (1752) by Gabriel.[21] Many of our own officers have studied there during the centuries, and many officers of the different nations have been taught in the famous war college. Today as I passed it walking along the Champ-de-Mars, I saw young French lads being trained and drilled for the army. They seemed so young, another generation preparing as their fathers did over twenty years ago for that other war. They are facing the same bitter strife. Will it be the same? Shall their sacrifice be in vain?—once again?

> Take up our quarrel with the foe:
> To you from failing hands we throw
> The torch; be yours to hold it high.
> If ye break faith with us who die
> We shall not sleep, though poppies grow
> In Flanders fields.[22]

The first thing I saw this morning as I reached my subway station was *L'Intransigeant*[23] blazing the headlines "France at War" and "France Declares War on Germany." I found a taxi, but the chauffeur hesitated saying that the few taxis that were left in Paris were now only for people who were being evacuated or for the military en route to the various stations with their bags and kits. He consented, however, to take me when I told him I was going to the American Embassy.

At the Embassy the building superintendent was directing the men who were placing black paper on all the windows. Again, the crowds of Americans, with the sole idea of reaching the United States by all means available, flooded the building. The news was indeed frightening, and instead of the usual cheerful attitude of our compatriots when they meet each other, there was silence. They were subdued and quiet.

Throughout the day there were fewer people on the streets. I met one elderly man who had evidently come from some distance. He seemed almost too tired to go on. He was muttering to himself. I heard him say as he looked at me, "If I stop walking, I shall fall; so, I keep going."

The press tonight announced the death sentence for anyone caught stealing from the closed and darkened apartment houses.

You have already read in your papers of 14,000 United States citizens on the list at the French Consulate General in New York who want to come to France as volunteers. It reminded me of those other days (1916–1917) when I, too, was pulling every wire to come to France. Shall we be able to stay away with a sentiment of that kind at the very beginning of hostilities in this year of 1939? I wonder....

I am writing this under a lamp covered with dark blue cloth. My governess has gone down on to the street to see if any light is coming from our windows. A light might be considered a signal to the enemy. The atmosphere is tense with talk everywhere of air raids and shelters. I hope that my strong faith will be strong enough to depend on Divine protection rather than on an *abri. Adieu....*

September 5, 1939

Today my letter goes to you, dear V.[24] You are anxious about me as I gathered from your letter. This morning as I read about the operations on the Maginot Line, I thought of my visit to you in Philadelphia when I last returned home. I remembered the film we saw showing the magnificent construction of the Line. I can hear again the voice of the announcer as the film ended saying, "The French have built this great defense of their country, for never again will they run the risk of having their fair land destroyed by the enemy."

Tracts that the British have let fall recently over Germany, calling on the people to resist the terrible aggression that is leading their country to disaster, may have some effect, but I doubt it. The Nazis believe so completely in their Führer who is, in my mind, leading them indeed to destruction.

For many centuries the village drums in the small villages of France have announced the wars. Today once more they are being heard in many parts of the country calling the people to battle.

SS *Athenia* (British),[25] carrying hundreds of passengers including many Americans, has been reported torpedoed by a German destroyer. How long can we remain neutral?

Orders from the French authorities came to the Embassy today that everyone must carry a gas mask and remain indoors after dark.

As I write this, I look out from my balcony toward the west. The sun has already set, and the afterglow is being dimmed by the oncoming night. The atmosphere is soft and warm. I pray God to keep this beautiful Paris for centuries to come—keep her in all her loveliness to satisfy the hearts and consciousness of other generations by her beauty, as it does mine tonight.

September 6, 1939

The French, Russian, and British members of the Embassy staff are being called to the defense of France.

American citizens are somewhat distraught after the torpedoing of the SS *Athenia*. They do not know whether to sail and chance the same thing happening to them or remain and take the risk of air raids or invasion. One woman who was in such a quandary laconically remarked, "Why doesn't Hitler get married and settle down?"

I am not familiar with air raids, and this morning at two o'clock I was startled by the sound of the siren. I threw on a dressing gown and went into what Mademoiselle and I call our personal abri. Our abri is a small square room between two large rooms where the cupboards set in the walls and are used for linen. It is quite dark and there my governess, who is only too willing to watch and follow my every move, and I install ourselves. The Rumanian gentleman in the apartment above knocked at the door to see if we were all right, and when he saw that we were not fully dressed, insisted that we dress quickly and have our coats, handbags, and identity cards ready as an explosion might come at any moment. I thought the idea of dressing a very good one. After the Rumanian left, I hurriedly put on my clothes then sat for three hours and ten minutes in total darkness waiting either for an explosion or the all-well signal.

September 7, 1939

Today at the Embassy the siren was heard at twelve o'clock and everyone filed down to the cellars carrying their masks. Any visitor in the building was obliged to do the same as the doors were immediately closed. There were very few persons outside of the members of the staff, as it was the luncheon hour and most of them had left. We remained two hours downstairs before the all-safe signal was heard. The danger signal was only for reconnoitering planes, which was not as exciting as it might have been.

It is a rest to walk back to my apartment after the rush of the day's activities. Subway trains and taxis are becoming scarcer each day. As a result, the subway trains are overcrowded, so I walk. The exercise is good, and, in a way, it takes the place of riding, for there are no horses to ride. They have all been requisitioned. My beautiful mare has gone from the stables at Rochefort-en-Yvelines in the Seine-et-Oise Department,[26] where I spent four years riding on weekends or on vacation. Dear Picardie!,[27] who took me galloping or trotting over the hills and countryside of that superb country. She, too, has gone. She must hate war as much as I do, but I was glad when I heard that she had been taken by some officers and will be well-cared for. A cavalry officer told me that in his headquarters, where men and horses were waiting to go to the front immediately after mobilization, there seemed one day to be much noise and confusion amongst the horses standing a short distance from where the men were gathered. One particular horse was stamping and neighing incessantly. A man crossed over to see what the cause of the commotion was and found that it was the horse he had groomed for many months in the stables of his employer. The animal knew instinctively that his master was near and called out to him in the only way it knew. The groom moved beyond speech could only repeat: "He is my horse, my own horse!" They were going into battle together—together they were facing danger and death. Their love would carry them through....

Officers and soldiers are everywhere. They fill the streets, giving the city a warlike aspect. It reminds me of my first sight of Paris in 1918 when that dream to come to France that had been with me all my youth suddenly came true. Do you remember? I talked and read and dreamed and lived France. Today in 1939 war again has invaded the country. I crossed the Concorde Bridge as I did that first time twenty-two years ago when the *poilus* crowded the city. Today again the French uniform is on the Place, the bridges, and the highways.

The red of the sunset was sweeping the Seine. It lighted the towers pointing upward, straight and true.

U.S. State Department *Daily Bulletin*: September 7, 1939

This morning the *Daily Bulletin*[28] placed on my desk had the following text:

> The Government of the United States appreciates the situation in which its officers of the Foreign Service may find themselves in belligerent territory because of the probability that this war will bring greater danger from the air than any preceding conflict. The Department confidently expects each officer of the American Government to remain at his post as long as it is possible in view of military operations, or until a local evacuation of civil servants. We realize the risks which may attend this devotion to duty in certain places but are confident in the patriotism and integrity of the American Foreign Service, its officers, and employees.

It is eight o'clock in the evening. My governess is drawing the curtains. In a few minutes I shall arrange on my chair by the bed my coat, gas mask, dress, shoes, handbag with passport, money, identity card, my electric lamp, and a candle—ready for the sound of a siren. Outside the agents of the *Défense Passive*[29] are sounding their whistles and calling *Lumière au premier!* ("Light on the first floor!"). Members of the *Défense Passive* have been recruited from the citizens of the quarter who, not fitted for army duty, do their work in the defense of the city.

The Poles flew over Berlin today and gave the Germans a taste of their own medicine. The Nazis, however, did much damage over Warsaw with their seventy planes. The Poles brought down a number of them while the British bombarded Kiel, destroying two German warships. Real fighting will begin soon no doubt unless the astrologers who think they know are right and "there will be no great world war." I do not seem to have any fear and shall sleep like a two-year-old unless the siren thinks otherwise—and so goodnight....

September 9, 1939

No siren last night and no German planes over Paris. Somewhere in France, however, a German plane was brought down by the French. The German pilot was a 16-year-old boy. I hear the tramp of soldiers' feet outside my window—French soldiers. They, too, are young, very young....

September 12, 1939

Two nights with no siren but last night, or rather this morning at four-thirty, it woke us up. It did not last long, and I am beginning to think that the French are

---

° *Poilu* is the name given to the French soldier of 1914–1918.

becoming more nervous; the German planes were not near the city. Anyway, I dressed quickly, gathered up the paraphernalia on the chair, and stepped into the "shelter" of my apartment for an hour until the all-safe signal was heard.

Orders came today to carry passports and identity cards at all times. Every foreigner (diplomatic corps excepted) must present himself at the *Commissariat* of his district and have his identity card inspected and stamped. All German nationals must report to the authorities; they are being placed in concentration camps.

Many people are "decorating" their windows with strips of paper. They look like slats and are said to be a protection for the panes of glass against blasting.

Paris-soir sent out the notice that Germans are deserting to the French. I wondered if the astrologer had really said something when he noted also in his book that Germany will collapse from the inside ending the Hitler regime.

It was warm, a touch of Indian summer, as I crossed the bridge with the sunset utterly beautiful. A woman close by where I was standing, watching the tense red on the water, turned to me and said with real emotion, "*Regardez, c'est beau, n'est ce pas?*" ('Look, it is beautiful, isn't it?'). I assented and a line in *Memoirs of My Dead Life* by George Moore came to me, "It is pleasant to notice everything in Paris."[30] One cannot help seeing the loveliness of the sunset over the Seine....

The shops are closing one by one in the Concorde section. I miss them—they seem like old, familiar friends: the flower stand where I often stopped for flowers, the printer's shop, and the old man, my *tapissier*, who covered my Louis XVI chairs with eighteenth century silk. They are all boarded up now—even my hat shop where red-haired Madame Annette made such pretty hats for me and who once asked me in broken English, "Mademoiselle, what it is to be a lousy American?" She had not the slightest idea what it meant. She had heard it, she told me, from an irate American who was protesting about some inconvenience saying, "You need not think that I am one of those lousy Americans." The shutters were drawn over her shop as I passed it today, and a silence pervades it.˙

In the subway I found a seat quite near two women who were weeping bitterly. From their conversation I learned that they had just seen their men off to the front.

The wounded are beginning to come in. Hospitals are preparing for them, and war organizations are working overtime on bandages and medicines. Tonight, the Director of French Information warned over the radio against deceptive reports that are being given out by the Germans who are proclaiming victory.

The British uniform is beginning to be seen on the streets. I saw two very smart-looking officers enter the Travellers Club[31] on the Champs-Élysées. The British are receiving a warm welcome from the French wherever they go. The French police are particularly responsive and quick in their salutes. One British car passing a red light

---

˙ Madame Annette was ill. She died a month later. She was a Jewess and was overwhelmed by fear of the persecution of the Jews by the Nazis. I saw her the day before she died.

was stopped by the traffic police. After apologies from the driver, the police let him go with only a slight reprimand in French (which the Englishman did not understand anyway) and called after him "beefsteak," the only word in English he knew!

Some members of the Embassy staff have been stopped by the police asking to see their identity papers. Now rumour has it that in all probability gas masks will not be needed as the Germans are not using nor will they use gas bombs. Certainly, the French will not begin that measure.

Steamships going to the United States are full and have been over full for a month, which is not very good news for the thousands of Americans trying to secure passage. The Embassy is still crowded. Recently there have appeared handsome young U.S. officers and attractive American girls offering their services, ready to serve in any capacity and at any post to which they may be assigned. Somehow, I feel that it will be a long war, and if we come into it, I shall be here with our men, as I was in 1917–1919.[32] Be here, did I say? In Paris with our men? I wonder....

September 14, 1939

Dear D.

Between the lines of your letter, I sensed a bit of anxiety about myself. You must not be anxious, however. I am not afraid of anything and really feel very safe. (There goes another police whistle from the street, signaling to someone to turn off his light.) I shall turn mine off. I shall write again soon. We have so much time at night. There is nothing else to do as we must remain indoors. And so to bed.

This is not a diary although almost every day I find something to talk to you about. It is somewhat of an effort in a few letters to give you a picture of life in Paris today and of France at war and under military control.

Returning home from the house of my friend Baronne de Ropp[33] where I dined tonight, I found the streets almost deserted. It was only eight-thirty but already the blackout was hanging heavily over the city. In tonight's press, the author of one paper said he did not see how it was possible for the present state of things to continue much longer. He said the Germans are poorer today than they were in 1914 and that he expected them to lay down their arms in the near future. I wondered if he really believed this or if it was said to give a bit of courage to the populace. One cannot tell—all seems confusion and contradiction.

Troops leaving for the front passed me as I went through the Champ-de-Mars. I wanted to throw flowers after them or raise a hand in benediction (the sign of good will of our American Indian). But there are no flowers. Every shop is closed. Even the flower stands and flower wagons have disappeared. There are so few people on the streets that one feels a close friendship with anyone who passes. Of course, the plainclothesmen and policemen are everywhere. One finds them on every corner, in groups in the middle of a block, in front of the subway stations, or standing around the government buildings, embassies, and banks.

The air is beginning to be crisp. The perfume of burning leaves pervades the parks and gardens. It breathes the oncoming autumn. The prognostications are for a cold winter with little probability of any heat in the apartments.

I am searching for another apartment. The lease is almost ended in this immense place I am living in. Besides, to face another winter with little or no heat is not a cheerful outlook. Members of the staff are moving into the Hôtel de Crillon and other hotels that will have central heating.

The Poles are fighting valiantly, surrounded as they are by the Germans on one side and the Soviets on the other.

An American citizen told me today that he is collecting money and organizing a group of American women for hospitals and welfare work. Everyone available will be needed. France is in great need.

The whistles of the police are more frequent tonight, warning people about their lights. I wonder why it is that so many cannot obey the laws and regulations! It seems so easy.

This morning at seven-thirty there was the sound of soldiers' feet tramping under my window. Going where? To what destiny? There is no one to throw flowers after them as they pass. Are they on their way to victory? God grant it be.

Letters from home full of affection, telling me of a warm welcome should I decide to return, which I shall not do, of course. The letters were not censored.

Marion came from Vichy today. She told me of life there and in the provinces: rich Egyptians, Syrians, and other Orientals splurging their wealth. Their luxurious automobiles are much in evidence. They are creating a bad impression and are being hooted on the streets. On the other hand the wounded are being brought from the front and are being cared for by the Red Cross and French civilians who are doing splendid work.

A letter from my brother from America states that we shall without doubt come into the war.

Some Germans came into my apartment house today. They were selling stockings and lingerie. One had a letter for me from a friend of mine. I wondered how they could be going about Paris apparently with no difficulty as all Germans that I have heard about are in concentration camps. My governess told them that I was not at home, which was a good thing; they may be friends of France and again they may be in the 5th column; technically they are enemies of this country.

I walked across the Seine on the Pont d'Iéna this evening. The air was clear and soft. A barge was winding its way up the river carrying coal that glistened under an autumn sun fast disappearing into the night. Beyond is the *Parc du Champ-de-Mars* (Field of the god of war), for today so appropriately named. The Eiffel Tower is strung with radio wires, and farther on are the *saucisses* (barrage balloons) with their wire network to entangle and trap enemy planes flying low, or at least force them to fly at a higher altitude. Shelters are dug in the ground, about fifty of them, all along the wide expanse of the Champ-de-Mars; they are waiting for their "guests" ....

Some Members of the Embassy Staff Are Dispersed

September 29, 1939

We were told yesterday that we should be ready to leave Paris, if necessary, within twelve hours. The air may become too thick with German planes. I wonder if they will really come in large numbers! All this is unanswerable today.

In the Tuileries there were clusters of falling leaves at my feet being swept by the early autumn winds. The winds are blowing fresher each day and the nights are cold. Young French soldiers pass me. I am probably becoming emotional because tears welled up at the sight of those young faces. Their uniforms made of rough material were worn and discolored. They were not smiling, and I felt an immense sadness at the human pathos of it all. Yet when some pretty girls passed, laughing and chatting, they did smile as they said, "Elles sont jolies, n'est ce pas?" (They are pretty, aren't they?). This was said to each other but obviously to attract the attention of the girls.

A German plane is reconnoitering. My lights must go out at once. My bag is lying on the bed ready for anything that might happen.

September is slipping away quite silently as if it does not want to attract any notice. The atmosphere is tense with expectancy, ready for the critical times that lie ahead. Everyone is geared for eventualities with courage and the *élan* of high purpose. Members of the Embassy staff have received their orders to leave for different posts: Bordeaux for some, Nantes for others, and for others the Château de Candé.[34] Some of us volunteered to remain in Paris. I was one of them. Paris will be safe or as dangerous as any other place, perhaps safer as every effort will be made to protect the city with its priceless works of art and its beauty. It is difficult to find gas masks. I have mine from our Government but I feel responsible for Mademoiselle who so far has been unable to find one.

The first tragedy of war came to me today. A German Jew was about to be taken by the police to be put in a concentration camp. A few minutes before they came for him, he tried suicide by taking an overdose of veronal. Instead of the concentration camp he was taken to a clinic and is not expected to live.

The Duchesse de la Rochefoucauld[35] spoke over the radio tonight to the women of France. In a dramatic address she appealed to them to give all the help possible to their men at the front. She said that she was one with them in the desperate sorrow they were experiencing, but that "in the sacred cause of justice, they must hold to their courage."

The siren roused us out of bed early this morning. It appeared that it came from a factory by mistake, which did not help much to relieve the shattered nerves of the population.

A number of Americans want to remain in France, but at the Embassy we are kept busy telling them to go. However, those who have the courage, nerve, poise, and health are needed and can do much good work. Some are afraid to sail as it is impossible to know whether at sea the ship will be attacked or not. With the mentality of the Nazis to cope with, anything is a risk.

Ambassador Biddle[36] arrived today with his staff. They are all at the Embassy and happy to be here. Their exit from Warsaw was an exciting and dangerous one. Everyone is safe, which is a feat indeed as they were bombed in the city and bombed en route; they were obliged to leave the train after they had left the city limits, remaining in the forest while planes were dropping bombs around them. They wondered which one would be hit first. The Ambassador who was responsible for the lives of his staff had a right to be proud and satisfied. It was grand work, Mr. Ambassador!

October 8, 1939

I found the gas mask for my governess at the American Legion.[37] I purchased a small one for myself as the one I have been carrying is too bulky and difficult to drag about. We are still under orders to have them with us continuously.

Mr. Lord[38] of Tuxedo Park called on me today bringing me messages from Mrs. Griswold Lorillard, a friend of many years whom I have not seen since 1933. He told me that he was accompanying Colonel S., who was recruiting 15,000 Americans (artillery) to join the French Army. When I pointed to instructions from the Department concerning the neutrality laws, that the Government did not look favorably on American citizens joining the fighting forces of a foreign army, he replied, "Oh, by the time we are organized, the neutrality laws will be changed."

October 10, 1939

Dear V.

I can understand your anxiety when you say that you feel as do most of our people that only a miracle can keep us out of war, that already the men are applying to be put on the list of reserves, and that the younger generation cannot wait to be called. It all sounds ominous, really incredible.

The French police look very smart in their helmets. They stand in groups before the different buildings and subway stations as though they were about to start on some crusade. Well, perhaps they are, sooner than they think. The British officers, too, in their well-cut uniforms are here in great numbers. There is no dressiness amongst the women: no veils, or flowers, or white gloves. The dressmakers are having their own troubles and are turning to other work. Many women are going into munitions factories and other activities for the war.

Mr. Daladier's address over the radio tonight was impressive. The Prime Minister is coming down with great severity on the food profiteers with a fine and prison sentence for shopkeepers found guilty. One citizen has already been sentenced. As a result, food is cheaper. President Roosevelt, too, addressed our nation. The President sees so much farther ahead than any of us.

Hitler, the press tells us, is now bidding for peace leaving in the wake of Poland's martyrdom broken promises to Europe and to his own country (German-Soviet agreement). Brutality, crime, inhumanity—can there be any peace when there is no peace?

H. R. Knickerbocker,[39] one of our foremost journalists, came to the Embassy this morning. I congratulated him on his illuminating article that appeared recently in the *Paris-soir* and the *New York Herald Tribune*, exposing the enormous sums of money placed in foreign countries by the Nazi chiefs: Goebbels, Göring, Himmler and others.[40] They will see to their own safety no matter what might happen to their people. Mr. Knickerbocker's articles are always excellent and interesting, notably his remarks on the work of the French Army at the front. A French woman quite recently asked one of her colonels what she could do for the army. He replied, "Knit, Madame, knit. The men at the front are cold. It is going to be a long, hard winter; woolen socks, sweaters, gloves, scarves are needed. And" he continued to the woman—or any woman who might be allowing time to elapse before regulating her bills for clothing, "Pay for that pretty hat you have on that pretty head; business must be carried on."

Gentlemen of the American Colony[41] in Paris have been requested by their friends, who are officers of the French Army commanding troops in the north, to send shoes for their men as the need is very great. Hundreds of pairs have been collected. Huntington Harter,[42] a well-known member of the Colony and a long resident of Paris, told me that the notes from the men were touching in their gratitude. He felt certain that every man who received shoes had written to the sender a letter of appreciation. It is hard to believe that such circumstances should really be; that is, there is unpreparedness to the extent that in icy weather the need of shoes should be so vital. After all, it is God's prerogative to care for His own. Can we doubt that He will fail? He is caring for them.

The trees are turning to brown and gold; soldiers *en permission* are coming from the front. I passed a café where a group was sitting. From their table came the singing of the rallying music of the "Madelon," that song of 1914–1918, which was and is so popular today.[43]

Tonight, when I arrived at my apartment house on the Avenue de la Bourdonnais, I found a line of people waiting in expectancy. In a few minutes I saw them bowing respectfully to a man of small stature who was just entering the building. It was Monsieur Beneš,[44] former President of Czechoslovakia. The Czech government is now in Paris; today Monsieur Beneš is inaugurating the Press section situated in the house I am occupying. I felt as though I were a part of history in the making.

M. Daladier spoke again over the radio. This time he spoke to the men in the trenches; to the men, women, and even to the children of the whole country, telling them that as Germany had violated treaties and international laws with a brutality and cruelty against humanity unheard of in the world's history, France was called to arms in defense of *La Patrie*, to protect the people and their homes against such aggression and violence as the Nazis leave in their path of what they call victory. It was a sincere address. The Prime Minister spoke it with deep feeling. "La Marseillaise" rang out triumphantly at the end. Shall he be able to gain and hold the faith of the nation? I wonder. One feels as though one were living in a world of intrigue where it is difficult to know what is true, who is true.

The rains have set in, and the days are dreary. Our hearts that once were carefree and gay are now heavy with foreboding. You say that you are receiving my letters. I do not know if they are being censored, but their delay is caused by the exigencies of the moment. It is impossible to count on the French post now as everything is so feverish. I am sorry that you have missed my feeble attempts to give you a picture of Paris during these momentous days. In spite of my optimism, I am unable to rid myself of the feeling that circumstances will oblige me to leave Paris eventually.

The food situation is normal so far. Word from the front is that no more food be sent. For the time being there is enough, particularly since the arrival of the British troops.

At the Vouillemont Hotel[45] on the rue Boissy d'Anglas, I saw again the French uniforms. My mind went back twenty-two years when I stayed there. As I stood in the lobby, I could not help but feel that the atmosphere is the same today as in those far-off days when we were making war to end all wars. So little has changed fundamentally in the hearts of human beings. I had been reading *Wickford Point* by John Marquand on the subject of change. He went home, as I did, after 1918 and found that the people had not changed. The last war tragedy seemed to have done very little for them, had left no mark. The author describes a conversation between two people in his book:

"What happened when you got back home?" Patricia asked.[46]

"That's the funny thing," I [Jim Calder] answered, "The most curious thing about it. Nothing happened. Nobody really seemed to understand that I'd been away. It just seemed to everyone that I had been around the corner. They just asked what I was doing—that was all."

Again, I am here in France, in Paris, but I am with many who do understand and love the French as we did in 1917, 1918. This has nothing whatever to do with our love and loyalty to those back home—they simply cannot understand.

October 20, 1939

In *Le Livre Jaune Français* that I have been delving into from time to time recently, I opened to page 24. I was enthralled by the brilliant report of M. François-Poncet,[47] the French Ambassador to Germany, written from Berlin to the *Ministère des Affaires Étrangères* in Paris, dated just one year ago: October 20, 1938. Mr. François-Poncet had been invited by Chancellor Hitler[48] to come as soon as possible to Berchtesgaden for an interview; the Chancellor had sent one of his personal planes to fetch the Ambassador. His description of the strange habitation of the Führer, hidden far up in the rocks, reads like a fairy tale:

> There was the hermitage perched at 1,900 meters on the top of a rocky crag. Through a winding route of about fifteen kilometers the path was cut through stone, ending at the entrance of a long subterranean passage sunk in the earth and closed by a double bronze door. At the end of the underground road was a large elevator whose walls were covered with copper plate. Vertical shafts of 110 meters were dug out of the rock and rose to the level of the Chancellor's abode. There in front of the visitor was a broad, massive construction comprising a gallery of Roman pillars in an immense circular room enclosed by glass windows, and at the farther end an enormous fireplace blazing with great logs.
>
> From every side through the bay windows, the look plunged as from a plane to an immense panorama of mountains. Below were the surrounding villages almost lost to view by a horizon of mountain ranges, peaks, prairies, and forests. Near the house itself, that seemed suspended in space, was an abrupt wall of rugged mountains.
>
> The whole scene, bathed in the subdued light of an autumn day, was grandiose, wild, and almost bewildering fantastic.
>
> Is it a dream? Is it the castle of Monsalvat where the knights of the Holy Grail lived? A Mount Athos sheltering the meditation of a cenobite? The palace of Antinea rising up in the heart of the Atlas Mountains? The fantasy of a millionaire, or only the den where thieves hide their treasure? Is it the work of a normal human being or that of a man tormented by a mania for greatness and domination, or only by fear? Perhaps, the author writes at the end of the weird picture, the psychology of Adolph Hitler may be determined by the fact that the slopes, the openings to the subterranean passages, and the approaches to the house are militarily controlled and protected by machine guns.[49]

I was tremendously impressed by this beautiful description and the conception of such a dwelling place. As one follows this leader of the German nation in the press or in action—as one country after another falls before his astounding will and his tremendous machine, that is the German Army—one wonders whether this evil thing that has come upon the world can possibly have any permanence; or whether it will someday crumble to pieces by the weight of its own malevolence. Shall something unforeseen such as a stronger power—the spiritual, God—arrest an unleashed course and obstruct any further advance?

Goodnight, I am tired. Evil and the thought of it is devastating, wearisome, devitalizing. That is tonight. With the dawn of another day will come the assurance that good is the only real power.

October 22, 1939

The gardens of the Tuileries are deserted. The war has driven many people to work with little time to walk leisurely through the historic paths. I took time, however, today to sit for a moment near a great tree. The leaves were in clusters at my feet, fallen from the trees that are void of their summer loveliness, now turning to russet color, yellow, and brown. Through them one can see the centuries' old statues that make up the beauty of the gardens. Quite near where I am musing stands Prometheus by Pradier, farther on is Alexander fighting the lion by Dieudonné, and there is Cassandra imploring Minerva. Farther still is a Bacchante that seems almost alive and very beautiful. Here one forgets the twentieth century with the autos and taxis swarming the immortal Place. Here one breathes the air of a forgotten age, an age when great ladies and cavaliers swept majestically through the paths. It is something indeed during days teaming with war to stop a while and drink in a bit of beauty and romance. I shall come again to the Tuileries for a rendezvous with Cassandra and the Bacchante....[50]

Last night in the rain we climbed one of the streets that leads up to Montmartre. With difficulty in the blackout, we found the small but excellent restaurant La Côtelette[51] famed for its famous cave. Our host, a secretary of the South African Legation in Paris, had recently been *en poste* in his country's consulate in Hamburg [Germany]. His stories of Nazi cruelty and brutality toward the Jews were almost unbelievable. He had been in charge of the visa section which was crowded continually with Jews making every effort to emigrate to South Africa. While the Legation was giving all aid and help possible to those unfortunate people to leave Germany, the Nazis were placing every obstacle in their paths. It breathed an immense pathos.

October 29, 1939

It is almost the last day of October. The days are moving so swiftly toward the end of this fateful year. The radio announced that in the United States the embargo on munitions and arms had been raised. No American ships may carry passengers to belligerent ports; Americans are forbidden to sail on belligerent ships. Another blow for Hitler and the Germans. The moral support that the announcement of this measure is giving to the British and French is incalculable. These instructions that you, perhaps, find quite normal, are of vital importance to us so near the theater of war. We grasp at every small and big event or word that reaches us in the way of help from our great, powerful country.

American Embassy Personnel in the French Army

November 1, 1939

Rain, rain, rain as October gives place to November. With this dreariness outside and perturbation inside, I go from a full day's work to an overflowing day of work in a daze. November came in rather insidiously trying to keep away the entrance of winter, for the atmosphere is softer and the intense cold seems far away.

The announcement from Washington of the neutrality laws was received here with mingled feelings: very few boats may come to Europe; no Americans may come at all. It made us seem quite isolated from the home touch. If we were not a large (and not too large to be sure) American family, we should not be cheerful at all.

Rain, rain, rain. The men at the front are deep in mud and water. Trainloads of woolens and other warm articles go to them every day. The one idea in the mind of every woman of France is to see that their men keep warm this winter. I am sending my first knitted scarf with socks, cigarettes, and gloves to the young French lad of the Embassy who was called to the army about a month ago. Word came that he is in a small village in the north where it is snowing and where the inhabitants are pro-Nazi, which does not augur well for the French soldiers who are there waiting for orders. Waiting…. A short time from now events will disclose their secret. We become impatient as we, too, are waiting. We are impatient at inaction as the Germans press on, coming nearer and nearer.

November 9, 1939

The attack on Hitler's life yesterday while he was addressing the old Nazi guard, or rather just after he had finished his address, reverberated like a bomb.[52] An infernal machine had been placed in the hall where he had been speaking. It went off ten minutes after he left; he seems to be protected by one of his strange spirits! We grasped at the incident with hope, hope that it was proof of growing discontent in Germany. But we seize at anything that might be a sign of relief in a ghastly crisis.

In the meantime, while optimism has its moments, pessimism is strong today with word that Holland and Belgium are strengthening their frontiers; or with travellers from those countries en route to the United States telling us that they believe the war with Germany will last fifteen years; after that it would begin again with Russia….

As if to offset this feeling of defeatism, an article appeared in the *Paris-soir* by M. Georges Duhamel[53] appealing to the public to keep up their courage, to expect and to wait for inevitable victory—that justice is stronger than injustice and that God is all powerful.

The police whistle outside my window is very sharp, ordering someone in the building to put out his light. It distracts me as I write and makes me realize that it is past midnight.

November 13, 1939

Two alerts were sounded last night and the night before. German planes were trying to pass the French frontier. The populace in their haste to dress and run down to the cellars left their lights burning and their blinds open, which resulted in much whistling by the police. As this did not seem to have great effect on a frightened public, tonight loud speakers have been started in different parts of Paris. Just under my window I hear the stentorian voice of the guardian of the peace repeating, "*Éteignez vos lumières, éteignez vos lumières.*" (Put out your lights.)

Practically all the Americans that I met today told me that they heard the sirens, but that it was too much trouble, especially too cold, to get up. They rolled over and went to sleep, something I quite understood for I did precisely the same thing. I have no doubt many of the French did not bother to go to their abris. I could not help but recall what was said of the American soldier in 1918: that at Château Thierry, Belleau Wood, and St. Mihiel, they went into battle as though they were going into a football game.

Last night the lights that are dimmed on the streets when there is no forecast of the coming of German planes were completely out. Paris was as black as a shroud.

I am looking for the illusive apartment. I tramped today through the rue du Bac, rue de Varenne, rue de Lille, and rue de Verneuil. All these small streets I trod, as I want to make my habitation on the Left Bank with its atmosphere of ancient Paris. It is an experience. One penetrates deep into the lives of those who have lived in their homes, many of which have not been occupied for years; some have been hastily vacated at the threat of war, others seem to have been totally forgotten, yet all have left traces of the personalities of their inhabitants. Some are lighthearted and gay, filled with poetic touches of romance and love; others are dark with undercurrents of sorrow and tragedy. On the old rue de Verneuil, dating back through many centuries, and which in its day had been a fashionable corner of the aristocratic quarter of Saint Germain, I climbed to the top floor of a building where I was told there was a vacant apartment. Apparently, it had not been occupied for years. Cobwebs were everywhere—in the air and on the ceilings; they crisscrossed the piano and were on the piano stool where I am sure some lady sat and sang to someone she loved. Is he dead now or has he left her for another? For in all the rooms there were traces of desertion, of memories that were past and gone down to dust and decay. I thought of *Vieilles maisons, vieux papiers*—those delightful volumes by G. Lenotre.[54]

In the prelude to Philip Lindsay's fascinating book *Hampton Court: A History*, the author writes: "Each house, your own, has its individual echo. You know when you open the door if the silence be friendly or sullen, you know by the crepuscular breathing of boards, by the sigh of the wind in the chimney…if you be welcome or hated. No house is ever empty."[55]

On the Quai [d'Orsay][56] was another dwelling—half eighteenth century, half modern. I was sure when I entered that the owner had had it fitted out for his mistress. The windows of the bedroom opened onto the Seine. "A great bed wide and low, 'like a battlefield,'" to quote George Moore in *Memoirs of My Dead Life*, was covered with pale rose satin; the whole décor was tan and rose.[57] As a finishing touch in a far off corner was a large lamp with a black satin lamp shade. Now it is deserted; the concierge told me that the owner had been called away to the war, and I wondered if they were very unhappy at the separation, or if love had died and the parting came as a solution, if not relief.

Another apartment I looked at was in the Place des Vosges. This apartment had been occupied by two elderly persons, a man and a woman. The concierge there told me that they had gone away on their long voyage quite together, I imagine, after a full life, too tired to go on and each one too lonely without the other to live in this turmoil of an oncoming war and related difficulties. And so I keep searching. One day I shall look up from my wanderings, and there in front of me will stand my home.

November 20, 1939

The neutrality laws of our country are, as one American expressed it, "a pain in the neck." Business men returning home are having bad times with restrictions on their passports and travel arrangements: which boats must they take, when might they secure passage on Allied[58] boats; how long will their passports be valid and if they will be valid long enough, or until they find a place on a ship, and so on.

The nights and days are becoming colder, and the rains are still with us along with mud and slush. What must it be like up there in the north where some of the French lads are often knee-deep in water.

In an excellent film last night, I saw and heard the great Paderewski.[59] It was a Chopin and Liszt concert. The famous pianist went through the program with the old assurance and perfection of touch and technique. There is no age indeed. The vast hall, somewhere in America, was crowded to the last seat of the highest gallery.

It is late. I was about to turn off the radio that had been giving out some war news when my attention was attracted by a British voice. I was expecting the usual British broadcast. Instead the voice, angry and insistent, was sending out insinuations, sneers, and diatribes against the British; the targets especially were Mr. Chamberlain and Mr. Churchill.[60] The shots were firing their fury concerning the "lies" of these two gentlemen. I waited to hear what particular "lies" Mr. Churchill and Mr. Chamberlain were guilty of, but the speaker was not specific. He had no real facts or logic or interest or truth in his statements. I failed altogether to discover what he really had against the British. Then I realized it was the voice of Lord Haw-Haw,[61] the British traitor speaking over the German radio from Hamburg. It was the first time that I had heard him. I sensed neither vitality nor life in the voice, but hatred, evil, and untruths—it was all negative; I suppose that in negation and evil there is neither life nor conviction.

Thou must be true thyself
If thou the truth wouldst teach.[62]

It was disconcerting indeed, if not sad, to hear a British subject, a traitor to his country, speaking from Germany. Indescribably bored and disgusted, I turned the needle and found the quiet, well-modulated voice of Mr. Anthony Eden.[63] It was a great contrast, not only the charm of the voice, but it was rich and true, and what he said held conviction. He spoke in excellent French although he made no effort to disguise his English accent, however slight it is. He spoke of the Maginot Line, more particularly of the British and French soldiers up in the north working together symbolizing, as it does, the union of the two nations.

I moved into my new apartment today on the rue de Varenne, recently vacated by a young French officer who had been mobilized. He felt that he did not wish to continue the lease as he could only occupy the apartment every few months and only for a few days. My balcony looks down into the gardens of the Hôtel Biron,[64] which is also the Rodin Museum (*Musée Rodin*), and perhaps the purest expression of Regency architecture in France. Occupied during its history by great families of France and at one time by the Russian Embassy, it is now the home of the work of the famous sculptor. The bells of the clock of the château are a special feature. Rarely have I heard the sound of bells so soft, rich, and beautiful. All this must have been an answer to my dreams. Now the interesting work of searching in antique shops for furniture has begun for me. I am passing wonderful moments deciding as I learn about furniture of France's different periods of her history.

November 22, 1939

Dear L.

This morning one of the thousands of refugees came to my office. I could not understand his language, but his baptismal certificate showed that he had a claim to United States citizenship. He was born in Newark, New Jersey, and was taken to Poland when he was a few months old where he had lived until a month ago. All this gathered from his certificate and from a gentleman nearby who acted as interpreter. The story? Just another of the many human beings rooted up from their homes and families that had faced death and destruction and unspeakable misery caused by Nazi greed, ambition, and lust for power. He had lived peacefully as a simple laborer in the little home he had built for himself and for his wife and child. One morning as usual he had gone out to work. In the evening, returning with a light heart, he had found the home in ruins—the result of a German bomb—his wife and child buried beneath. His one thought was to escape from the scene of the tragedy. With hordes of other refugees, he had crossed frontiers clinging to freight trains until he reached Paris. He is one refugee out of the millions but the first that had reached me with his story of misery and sorrow.

The siren went off at midnight. I dressed quickly and went to my salon to await events. Two hours I remained in darkness and silence praying, too, for the Protection that I knew I could always count on. When I heard the French anti-aircraft guns near my windows, I opened my Venetian blinds and looked out into the blackness. A brilliant moon that had been hidden by a cloud appeared, shining full at me; it blazed the château opposite that stood out in strong relief against the clear sky. Tonight, was just the night for a raid, I thought. I could have remained gazing out and up into space and at the château for hours, so beautiful it was, with the sound of the guns gradually fading away as the all-well signal was given. Instead, I went back to bed thinking that, after all, I am a part of the raid and of the beauty of a seventeenth century château illuminated by a moon at midnight. I am one with a universe of other human beings and their problems, one indeed with that flyer above me alone in a plane over a city of France at war, and one even with that Nazi in his plane whose orders are to destroy. There is this difference however: the real me is ordered to struggle against aggression and destruction. The power of the spirit is still strong as it has always been, held aloft over other restless tides of our lives. It has pierced the dark and has conquered. Had it not done so, all would be chaos.

November 23, 1939

Thanksgiving Day.[65] In the American churches the President's Proclamation was read. As I listened to it, I thought of those Pilgrim Fathers in our country's early history, telling their gratitude to a Supreme Being, not only for successful crops but for safety and protection. It seems a far cry from those relatively peaceful days to our turbulent era. Yet today there is so much for which to be grateful.

Up in the Montmartre with some of my compatriots, I celebrated the Day with the customary turkey and cranberry sauce and left at midnight just in time to catch the last subway train. It was very cold, but the station had a semblance of warmth as I entered it breathless from the dash down the steep hill to the road leading to the Church of the Trinité.[66] The church was black against the sky as the moon had almost disappeared. It had lost some of its brightness of last night when a German plane had tried to impress the French.

The château and gardens opposite my dwelling look very wintry, but the bells in the tower striking the hour are soft and musical, breathing of an age that is past. The Hôtel des Invalides[67] to the right of my building is spread along the avenue of the same name. In the tower overlooking the city above the building stands a young French soldier keeping a sleepless watch for signs of the enemy as the war clouds hover over his land. His slight form is outlined against the cold sunset. I raised my lorgnette of long-distance glasses to look at him. Instantly he put up his binoculars and stared over at me. I felt there was suspicion, even distrust in his attitude; he no doubt has his orders and must be alert to the smallest detail of any untoward incident. I felt very small indeed and crept into my apartment. I shall leave the French soldier to carry out his duty without my interruption and, too, it may be to his dreams.

A student and a lover of birds and fowl, of all our feathered friends, reported the birds in the north—in Alsace and Lorraine—are flying over to Switzerland where they are finding a home in a neutral country. They have chosen their destination. Herons, gulls, woodcock, wild duck, and others sense the approaching war and are following the refugees. If they stay, they shall have nothing to eat. They must be very sad.

American Passports Require a Thumbprint

November 27, 1939

The Embassy is more crowded than ever: American residents, wishing to remain, endeavor to prove that they have been residing in France for years and are engaged in relief work; businessmen try to prove that their affairs oblige them to go to belligerent countries. The neutrality laws are very strict. Many United States citizens are striking snags and are not able to obtain the necessary stamp on their passports to remain in France or to travel to other countries. A new ruling obliges all American passports to have a thumbprint. Naturally there was a reaction. Old Mr. B. considered himself to be a long resident of Paris and an almost historic figure of Paris life; he is impatient at the news and the different formalities with his voice rising higher and higher in protest against a possible insinuation that the government might consider him a mere tourist. Lady D., married to a British peer, also protested; she did not see why she could not have her title placed on her passport; and why should she submit to fingerprinting. The Marquise de B. insisted that she be waited on immediately. The modest and more humble citizens waited patiently, silently, with no complaint. There was also a mother wishing to return at once with her daughter to prevent the latter's marriage to a foreigner of whom she did not approve; the daughter, in no uncertain angry tones, insisting that she remain. All this is so true to life—to our little lives—all, too, in the face of the horrors, the bigness, the fierce misery, and disaster of war.

December 10, 1939

December is with us. The French press is again very pessimistic. The prediction from the High Command[68] tells the public to prepare for a long, hard war with the uncertainty of numerous air raids. Hitler was quoted as saying that he expects revolution in France. He will then walk calmly in and take the country with no resistance—that the Maginot Line will cease to exist. Is it the last stand of a cornered man who knows he is beaten and who still holds on from bravado? Or is it possible that what he says might have some semblance of truth?

The French police force and the *Garde Mobile* have been increased. They guard the streets, subway stations, and government buildings night and day watching with keen scrutiny the faces of the surging crowds. There are dozens of arrests every day; many are found with false papers or false passports; some are Nazi spies and persons of the 5th column including, unfortunately, some French who are caught in the net as well. Guns are over Paris. Sounds from the French anti-aircraft cannons tonight are heard, preventing ten German planes from crossing the frontier. War seems nearer and nearer. Will they indeed touch this beauty that is France and this matchless Paris?

Is the forecast of H. G. Wells[69] to be believed, and are we on the borderland of new worlds?

Embassy Overflows with Americans Who Want to Help Refugees

The Americans are showing great courage. They surge into the Embassy in large numbers with the one idea, which is to help; to care for the refugees that are now pouring in from Belgium, Holland, and Italy; to do anything that might be useful.

We walk through black streets with no fear. Never was Paris so safe, never so fully policed. American ambulance drivers, the American Field Service, are arriving from America and are being attached to the French Army in the face of the neutrality laws. Some are going east to Finland and the Balkans; others are remaining in France awaiting orders.

Many paintings from the Louvre Museum are being taken away for safe keeping. As I walked through the familiar galleries yesterday, I found many vacant places. I felt as though I had said goodbye to many of my friends.

December 17, 1939

Christmas is in the air with crowded shops. This year they are filled with articles for the soldiers. Packages are being sent to the front every day in great quantities.

The young Pole who had escaped from Poland after finding his home in ruins by a Nazi bomb, and his wife and child dead beneath it, of whom I wrote a few days ago, has failed in his attempt to prove his U.S. citizenship for entry into the United States. He is considered a Polish national and is attached to the Polish Division of the French Army.[70]

My windows are pasted all over with black paper, arranged in a design of connected parallelograms. All over Paris the windows show curious designs. They are interesting, too. The war brings out latent talent in design and art.

It is bitterly cold. The French sentinel on the tower of the Hôtel des Invalides walks back and forth on his pinnacle to keep warm. I take furtive glances at him as I write huddled up in a heavy cape. I should like to send him some hot coffee several times a day, but I am afraid. The military section of the Invalides or the French War Department might not look favorable on the idea, so I desist.

December 19, 1939

We have been watching the press and listening to the radio with exultant interest these days, following the course of His British Majesty's battle cruisers HMS *Ajax*, HMS *Exeter*, and HMS *Achilles* in pursuit of the *Admiral Graf Spee*.[71] The proud German battleship that had sunk ships of the British Merchant Marine one after the other had made its way along the South American coast followed by the British battle cruisers which, at the port of Montevideo, had stopped the course of the *Graf Spee*. The crew of the *Graf Spee*, young lads of fifteen to eighteen years of age who had seen practically no sea service, was transferred to German merchant ships waiting in the harbor. The captain had received instructions from the German chiefs in Berlin. After scuttling the *Admiral Graf Spee*, the captain shot himself the following night.°

The excitement in Paris was tremendous.

And that is England! If the Nazis are capable of thought more profound than that of their own superiority over other peoples of the world, they might well consider the incident. It is indeed a forecast of the possibilities of the British to defend their country. The Nazis might also reflect on that vital spirit of tenacity and deathless courage so deeply rooted in the soil of England and the British Commonwealth.

> This royal throne of kings,
> This scepter'd isle.
>
> ....
>
> This fortress built by Nature for herself
> Against infection and the hand of war
>
> ....
>
> .... This England
> (*King Richard II*: Act II, Scene I)[72]

December 25, 1939

Christmas is here. The day passes uneventfully. It is not so easy to make the effort in these troubled times to be cheerful. Everyone, however, is making an effort to put a bit of cheer into each other's life, to help each other on the way toward an uncertain, inscrutable future, and to light the path even if it might be a dim light for those who are travelling with us. We are responsible for those we meet. What right have we to be morose and depressed in our encounters with our fellowmen?

I had dinner last night at Le Relais de la Belle Aurore[73] (famed for its hors-d'œuvres) with H. Ex. Monsieur Liébert,[74] former French Minister to different countries. With oysters and *oursins* (sea urchins), shrimp, caviar, and the best sherry and Alsatian wine one could find, life seems not as tragic as when one is

---

° In Sir Winston Churchill's book *The Gathering Storm*, Book 1, the Prime Minister quotes the letter written by Captain Langsdorff, Captain of the *Graf Spee*, before his death: "I can now only prove by my death that the fighting services of the Third Reich are ready to die for the honour of the flag. I alone bear the responsibility for scuttling the pocket battleship *Admiral Graf Spee*. I am happy to pay with my life for any possible reflection on the honour of the flag. I shall face my fate with firm faith in the cause and the future of the nation and of my Fuehrer."

alone with one's thoughts. For in solitude one embroiders and enlarges on the smallest adverse incident.

The restaurant was crowded with French officers and soldiers on leave and civilians home for Christmas. There were the British, the Poles, and Czechs with their wives or mistresses, and there was real gayety in the room. One has few places to go after dinner as most of the night clubs are closed. It is too late for the theatre, and there is always the difficulty of finding one of the few taxis that have remained in the city.

Until today Paris has not been receiving any coffee for the past few weeks. The delay is caused by lack of adequate transportation. When it did arrive, the *Paris-soir* announced:

> Mons. Q.[75] announces a very important arrival of colonial coffee beginning next month. France! Your coffee did not *fous le camp*....

Writing here in my little room under my lamp with utter blackness outside, in the silence of my soul, there is no illumination; and the rain outside pattering against my window is in keeping with my mood. No illumination of ideas, no inspiration—all is drab. As sleep is overtaking me, I shall stop and go for a time in that blessed oblivion where if one does not dwell in another world of dreams, there remains nothing—just nothing.

December 31, 1939

Dear D.

The old year has run its course. Tonight, I am wondering what you are doing over there in your comfortable lives in your determination to remain apart from the chaos that is enveloping Europe. Shall isolationism with its limited vision win the day? Shall it hold and keep our country in its authoritative smugness as the world becomes smaller and smaller? The realization that the world is one human family is beginning to dawn on the world. It is a family whose members all have the same problems, the same underlying, vital, unquenchable hunger and thirst for liberty, justice, and love.

It is the eve of the New Year. The holiday always evokes something of anticipation—a looking forward—of happier times to come. The feeling is hidden deep down in every one of us and springs to life at the very mention of "New Year." Very few, I am sure, are tonight moralizing on this eventful epoch, as I am alone in my apartment, as the few night clubs that are open are full; and the restaurants have put specially prepared food before the men on leave. There is cheer and wine, song, and music in the life of Paris tonight.

January 1, 1940

King George VI's New Year's message to the Empire over the radio was impressive. His quotation from an unknown writer made a sensation. Journalists and editors searched the kingdom for the name of the author. King George said in his soft, halting voice:

> And I said to the man who stood at the gate of the year:
> "Give me a light that I may tread safely into the unknown."
> And he replied:
> "Go out into the darkness and put your hand into the Hand of God. That shall be to you better than light and safer than a known way."[76]

The snow over my château and the church opposite is like a painting; it covers the gardens like a white blanket and garbs the branches of the trees and bushes in party dress. Rue de Varenne is so narrow. I feel that if I put my hand out of my window, I could touch the church windows opposite, so near they seem.

> The air bites shrewdly; it is very cold. (*Hamlet*: Act I, Scene IV)[77]

January 15, 1940

I shuddered as I left my house and crossed the Concorde Bridge facing an icy blast. Half way across I saw a big mare, a workhorse, plodding along slowly. Beside her was a filly tied to her mother's tail by a long rope around her neck. It was dancing and prancing in the freezing morning air, loving every bit of it. I unhuddled myself and tried to feel as exhilarated as the youngster. I found how good and elating and inspiring it was.

The Finns are putting up a courageous resistance. Their military organization is excellent. May the Almighty be with them and their brave little country. Every woman I know is doing something for the war. Today a young girl in uniform said goodbye to me. She is an American and has volunteered as a nurse in the Ambulance Corps going to Finland.

The suffering of the Poles at the hands of both Russians and Nazis, and the tremendous losses of the Russians, all tell a tale of brutality and stupidity.

Up on the Avenue (Champs-Élysées) I found the German Messerschmitt Bf 109[78] brought down in Nancy by a French fighter. It had been placed in "shelter" and looked like a great wounded bird, or a prisoner that had been stood up for public reprobation. The propeller was twisted and the body full of bullet holes from French guns. Even the large black Iron Cross[79] had been pierced. It spoke eloquently of the courage of some French aviator, and also pointed to some of the courage of the German aviator who defended his plane in a losing battle. The plane was surprisingly small compared to the enormous ones in action.

The French soldiers on leave in Paris look very lonely; to many it is their first visit to the capital. They are treated royally and are given priority in any food line. The Algerian and Moroccan troops in their picturesque uniforms—full trousers, long red capes, and red caps—give color and interest as they walk leisurely through the city. They are here today and gone tomorrow, but no doubt they have their own particular way of seeing and knowing Paris.

War work is going on continually. Every day someone tells me that he or she is doing something for war relief. Refugee work is the most important, after the army of course; and the American Field Service, those "heroes without guns," is gaining rapidly. Many military hospitals are opening. The American Hospital at Neuilly[80] is now altogether military with a small section for civilians. The *Foyers du Soldat*° are functioning in many of the French towns where soldiers are billeted. The director of the Foyer of the small town of Val-de-Mercy told me that his club was undoubtedly God-sent to the soldiers. They have so little to do—they wait and wait. But now they have a cheerful library, radio, and writing rooms which fill the vacuity into which the men found themselves when called to the army.

It is bitterly cold tonight. Many houses have no heat but the French in some inexplicable way can become accustomed to heatless homes and unheated apartments in this freezing weather. Many live literally in their kitchens.

The cold is penetrating. I look out into the blackness from my balcony. The half-moon floods the château and gardens. Where the snow has fallen the whiteness glistens like a fur mantle trying to give the arid flower beds some warmth. The church on the right has an eerie aspect. One of its portals that had been swaying back and forth in the high east wind for hours is quiet. I thought of *Wuthering Heights* and the wildness of the old manor house.[81] What a night for a raid! Should there be one, should I hastily, fearfully dress and go down into the *abri*? Should I stand and watch the flash and flare of the guns and, with no fear, show my vaunted trust in that Protection that I turn to "like a compass to north"?

> So long Thy power hath blest me, sure it still will lead me on
> O'er moor and fen, o'er crag and torrent, till the night is gone.[82]

The French soldier on the tower of the Invalides is not there. I am glad he is not, for had he been, he would have been frozen where he stood, like one of Rodin's statues in the gardens below. I count on the French Air Force to see to it that no foreigner plane will drop bombs on this Paris. *La Batterie Triumphale*,[83] the cannons that surround the front gardens of the Hôtel des Invalides, point ominously to the north.

A new French law begins today. It forbids anyone to say anything derogatory about the Government or in any way lower the morale of a soldier or civilian by defeatist remarks. It is somewhat different in other countries. Those returning from Hungary bring the news that one is arrested if he is heard expressing his political opinion in any way, either for or against the Government. This is living dangerously.

What are those French officers doing with a Montparnasse beard? The mustache was the fashion in the last war. Shall it be the beard in this war?[84]

° A club for soldiers on leave or waiting for orders.

White Russian Friend and Personnel of the Embassy Staff

Our White Russian[85] friend of the Embassy personnel, Alexander Ignatieff, who had been called to the French Army, returned from his barracks for a day *en permission*. He told me how difficult life was in uniform as a soldier: that he was making the effort to find food from the common bowl savory and satisfying, drinking water that is not too clean, and being obliged to become accustomed to a filthy toilet. At first, he said it was almost unsupportable, but on the other hand, he explained, there is comradeship that is interesting. Some men returning from vacation with their families are glad to rejoin their posts. Life is so vastly different from the life he had led for years at the Embassy and in Paris. He wondered which indeed was reality. This war has gathered them all up in a heap; it has uprooted them like a strong early winter wind that lifts the leaves and whirls them far away from the places where they fell. There the leaves and the soldiers will rest awhile until another strong blast of wind or strong action of war lifts them again and sweeps them on: leaves, men, refugees—all of us who seem so permanently established in our abodes—flotsam and jetsam on this vast sea that is life. Our friend of the Embassy staff brought the war very close.

The rains brought ice and sleet. The biting cold continues. I slipped and fell on the ice, picked myself up and, clinging to a wall, reached a place of safety. There is much suffering amongst the soldiers, and work for warm garments increases. How long can they go on?

The young guardians of the peace are on duty twenty-four hours of the day. They do not seem to see the casual passerby, yet they are aware and know everyone that passes. They know where each person belongs in the quarter and the haunts he or she frequents. If a stranger appears, they are alert to duty. The traffic police at night are visible even in the blackness in their long white capes. They have a very smart air, so intriguing that one pretty girl stopped quite close to one to admire his cape and said: "Mr. Officer, your cape is so pretty. I should like to have one. Would you tell me in which tailor's establishment you bought it?"

February 3, 1940

January rushed through at a great pace. Here we are in February. To me February suggests spring is in the air and in the heart.

> The winter is past, the rain is over and gone. (The Song of Solomon 2:11)[86]

Mr. Churchill's address to the House of Commons[87] today was not reassuring regarding an early peace. His words came over the radio. He said that there was a probability of the British becoming very active, so active that Hitler might wonder when and where a blow would strike Germany.

I almost went to the air shelter tonight, not because I was afraid to remain above, but because it would have been interesting to see the women dressed in abri pajamas and painted and powdered for the occasion—the eternal feminine.

Our Russian friend came in to say goodbye to me today. He leaves for the front. He had tears in his eyes as he leaned down the European way and kissed my hand. Will he come back unhurt? It was not lack of courage that brought forth those tears. It was only the possibility of separation, an unending separation from those friends of the Embassy with whom he has been associated since he was a boy. He loves the Embassy and the Embassy members love him. But this is war! He had no money. We all collected a few thousand francs to give him, and I know because I know him, that much of it will go to those comrades in arms caught as he is in this tangled web.

Foreigners are leaving for the front: Russians, Poles, and Czechs. The French are leaving for the front—Americans, too. Peter A. told me today, after his recent arrival from the United States, that he was joining the French Foreign Legion.[88] He said that he had struggled for a long time to resist a driving urge to come to France and fight with those who were giving their lives for that quest, as old as man himself. They are fighting for that same indefinable, vital force called liberty, for justice, and for love. He had left a successful business in Chicago and in spite of himself or of anything he could do or say or that his friends could say, he could not remain away. It was with him in his sleep, he said, and in his waking moments. It meant separation from homeland and home. But he was not alone, that he knew. Over here families, wives, husbands, and children were being dispersed and scattered over the globe.

Today young America is enlisting; they are taking their choice: Finnish aviation, if they have decided on the air force, or British or French, or even Chinese.

Tonight, the press gave an interesting account of what the French War Ministry requires in the conduct of its officers and men. From the officers: honesty and justice in dealing with the men, affection, and understanding in their difficulties. They must look after the well-being of their men. From the subordinate: he salutes his superior officer, but the officer may, when the occasion warrants it, extend his hand to the soldier. From the enlisted men: absolute obedience is required; they have a right to demand an explanation in what they might feel is an unjust punishment and may demand that justice be done. The tutoiement (the familiar "thou" and "thee" used in families and amongst intimate friends) is forbidden between officers and men.

I wonder what the Nazi military regime would say to such humane and democratic military rules.

Two and a half million men are under arms in France.

Walter Lippmann's[89] article in the *Paris Herald Tribune* today concerning hindsight and foresight was illuminating. Deep down in my consciousness I know, and I have often stated, what he said so clearly, i.e., that a system like the Nazi regime based on inhumanity and an utter disregard of those ideals what man has fought for over thousands of years cannot last. Evil is always finite. The Spirit is everlasting; it is perpetual.

Hitler in unsurprising arrogance and vanity has given out that he is destined to make a better world—that the United States is decadent, and that only when he shall have our country under his domination (which of course he will have!), shall it be well-governed. He "will take care of the United States in my (his) good time. Yes," declares Hitler, "all that will be arranged, and it will be arranged by force and brutality for they are the best means for enforcing better government." So wrote (in substance) Hermann Rauschning,[90] President of the Senate of Danzig, in articles published recently in the French press. Already, however, the writing is on the wall as one wonders how the end of the Nazi regime will come. As I write this, the German armies are victorious on every side. The German machine has taken twenty years to prepare, and it is strong, very strong. Yet, the signs are there: indistinct, obscure perhaps, but they are there—two, three, or four more years of war; but when men's souls are stirred within them, there is a mightier force than machines, and it is a spiritual force stronger than any material power conceived by man....

February 8, 1940

I mentioned in one of my letters that we were sending packages of necessary articles to some of the French and other foreign lads of the Embassy who had been called to the Army. Today I received a letter from one of them. He is the son of a widowed mother. His father gave his life for France in 1917, and he had bequeathed his bravery as a soldier to his son now twenty-four years of age. The letter I quote in translation:

> Dear Mademoiselle:
>
> How can I ever thank you for your kindness to me. You are too good and have given me too much. I am so touched by it all. Everything you sent me is very useful; you have sent me magnificent gloves, so fine that I dare not wear them; and you have overwhelmed me with cigarettes, not forgetting the chocolate, the little crackers, sardines, soap, socks and even the matches. You have thought of everything. They are all kind thoughts that make our spirits so much stronger because without all this goodness we should not have the courage to fight the difficulties and unhappiness that none of us was prepared to bear.
>
> I remember, I shall never forget how much you love France and the French people, and besides, this is not the first time that you have proved it. You must have innumerable remembrances of the last war which should have been the last; and amongst the sad things you must often think of is this fact, that in free sacrifice freely given with so much courage and bravery, it all amounted to so little, and today we are back against the same point. But I believe that this time the words 'last time' will find its true significance.
>
> Again my grateful thanks, Miss Dilkes, for your kindness to me. I present to you my respectful homage.
>
> February 5, 1940
> (signed) Robert Lemoine
> French soldier

205th Regiment of Infantry
E.M. 1st Batallion
Sector Postale 35.

The author of the letter would not wish me to express any word in admiration. He is modest and would not understand, but he is one of the thousands of Frenchmen whose love of country and deep patriotism are holding France together during these tragic times.

It is late. I am somewhat in love with the blackness and solitude of the nights as I wander through them with my electric lamp. It is winter now and we need our lamps early in the evening, but when summer comes with its long days, I may miss this indefinable sense of mystery, of the possibility of meeting with the unexpected as I make my way in the dark toward home from a day of intense work.

In the children's shop on the rue Saint-Honoré, I found a game called "*Bombardement de la Ligne Siegfried*."[91] There was the wall erected with the guns, machine guns, and the little tin soldiers all ready in imitation of the big people. Even the children want to be in the war in some way.

As I turned to continue my way, I saw quite nearby an interested group following with admiring glances General Gouraud,[92] famed and loved by the French, hero of the First World War in which he lost an arm. He was one-time military governor of Paris and at another, commander of the Foreign Legion, and one of the most picturesque figures of military Paris today. At the time of one of the big parades when the French Army in all its glory marched down the Champs-Élysées, I found myself standing quite near the General. As the Foreign Legion that he loved so profoundly passed, I saw tears in his eyes as he raised his one arm in salute to his men of the Legion.

Meat is obtainable three days in the week. Most of it goes to the Army which is as it should be. All is for the Army: the French with their "*Foyers*" scattered over France, the women with their knitting, and the Americans with their vast sums of money, time, and energy. The American Field Service is continuing its recruitment both in France and the United States. Those unforgettable days of 1914–1918 come back to me, when I saw our men in the United States coming to France, good friends of mine from Philadelphia and from other cities. The real work of the Field Service has not yet begun to any great extent; there is suffering from colds or pneumonia or pleurisy as the cold weather is intensified, but they are not prevalent and occur only in isolated cases.

February 24, 1940

Happiness is indeed within us. We take our joys or our sorrows or our worries with us wherever we go. We think that we may escape by change of place and environment. But can we? For a time perhaps, but if the bitterness inside is not controlled and thrown out of consciousness, it eventually comes back often with renewed force.

Throwing myself into the present, living or trying to live "supremely present in the moment," I am anticipating better times, serving and helping. I forget the tension, the uncertainty, the suffering, and all this treachery that lays its heavy lid on my being. If I look about me, I find comradeship and a working together for humanity, this one family in which we are all being merged so rapidly. It is a fight against the evil of Hitlerism and communism to which we are called.

The siren went off again last night. German planes dropped tracts which said: "Frenchmen, have your coffins ready, for you shall soon need them." All this was as stupid as it was futile. A small German bullet from a German gun was handed to me. Inside was a piece of wood. It had been picked up at the frontier after a short scuffle between French and German troops. The Nazis must be lacking in steel to have manufactured it—or was it a ruse?

There go the French anti-aircraft guns again. It is only 8:30 p.m. I turn out my light and go on to my balcony. There is no moon, but there are millions of stars, yet too dark for a raid unless the Nazis take it into their heads to frighten us. It is a "phoney war"[93] after all. From the Hun's point of view, there is no harm in doing anything out of the ordinary such as disregarding the rules of law and order, a system they are practicing so thoroughly today. Looking out into the night, I feel as though I were living in another world. Is it really myself that is moving through all these strange events, or is it someone else who has surreptitiously entered my body and is playing a role for me? The person that I know as myself should be in a city in America, rolling bandages for the Red Cross to send overseas—there where I am comfortable and warm in a well-lighted city. I must indeed be wandering back into the past, back to those days twenty-three years ago in Philadelphia when I was dreaming, always dreaming of coming to France. I can almost hear my father's voice, stern and perhaps somewhat sad saying, "I shall not allow you to go to France. You must remain home and work for the war here." Yet I took the boat, and in mid ocean, with no light permitted, saw the shadow of a protecting United States destroyer that, despite German submarines, escorted us safely to the port of Bordeaux. That was twenty-three years ago and tonight—there go the French anti-aircraft guns again. Is this reality?

Little that I have read during this international crisis has impressed me more than *Le Livre Jaune Français* ("The French Yellow Book"). No story or play could be more exciting. For here is described page by page the whole drama of the oncoming war. Here is the scene of the chief gangster. Hitler and his satellites, breaking solemn pledges, are trying to organize a world as it suits them regardless of the rights and desires of other human beings. The time is March 1939. The scene is in the Chancery in Berlin. Two of the Czech chiefs have been requested by Hitler to come to Berlin as the tension between Germany and Czechoslovakia becomes aggravated. They arrive in Berlin and are received in the Chancery by the Führer, Göring, Ribbentrop, and Keppler.[94] The document to be signed lies on the long table: it tells of the irrevocable decision of the German Chancellor to occupy Prague within nine hours and to integrate Bohemia and Moravia[95] into the German Reich.[96] Hitler puts his signature on the document and walks out of the room. It is after midnight. A tragic scene then takes place between the Czech ministers and their German interlocutors.

The Czechs vigorously refuse to sign the document. One of the Germans forces the documents before them and thrusts a pen in their hands. They repeat that if they do not sign, half of Prague will be destroyed within two hours by German bombs—that hundreds of bombing planes are waiting for orders. The Czech Prime Minister becomes ill and is given medical injections to sustain him, and "with death in the soul" he places his signature on the fatal document. As they leave the building, they turn to the Germans. One of the Ministers says: "Our people will curse us, but we have saved our country.[97] We have preserved it from a horrible massacre."

Farther on in The French Yellow Book are the vivid descriptions leading to the fall of Poland and the mobilization of the French Army (September 1939), thus deciding the destiny of Europe.

The guns keep on as if to accentuate the gangster methods. I find it impossible to read with all the noise. I hope the French are letting them have it.

Last night at the Bouffes Parisiens Theater[98] I saw the play *Fascicule Noir* with Gaby Morlay, a story of espionage of the present war.[99] Again those memories of twenty-three years ago stirred my consciousness. It is October 1918. The place is New York with its teeming millions of people and its atmosphere of war; propaganda films showing German atrocities; of ships being sunk by British torpedoes, others by German submarines; all the time my boat SS *Rochambeau*[100] is waiting in the harbor to take me to France. Again, the theater. The play was *Three Faces East.*[101] My mind is already filled with dangerous adventure on the eve of my departure. I follow the play. With the click of heels, the German Secret Service salutes the heroine who accepts the mission to depart at once for Europe where she will contact the great German spy. He has orders to give the word for the sinking of the British fleet; and the excitement to find out that she is in British Intelligence and would save her countrymen. The bewilderment and secrecy as I embark the next day—all these vivid impressions of this great adventure of my youth have haunted me down through the years.

February 28, 1940

For a few days' vacation I went to Brittany, to Dinard, where my friend from New York, a resident of France for many years, lives in danger-threatening magnificence in her immense villa with its Italian gardens stretching down to the sea. Here I thought to find quiet and forgetfulness for a time and a respite from the noise and glare of anti-aircraft guns. The guns were rare, it is true, but there were the 5th columnists working overtime. There were the shelters, the groups of perturbed families of American officials, elderly British subjects, and many French; there was the French police insisting that the rules of the blackout be kept; there was, too, all the talk and conjecturing: will the armies meet here? Will the war be over before we shall be obliged to leave? Shall the Nazi arrogance and boastfulness be silenced by a shot aimed at Hitler's heart? There were optimism and pessimism all in one breath.

A very active American War Relief was functioning in Dinard, night and day, principally to help the families who lived in Brittany and who had men at the front. These families were in great need, and the men returning on leave were dissatisfied and unhappy to find their wives and children with insufficient food and clothing. Their morale was at low ebb, and the American organization was successfully working to build it up.

En route to Dinard I had finished the book *Hitler et Moi* by Otto Strasser.[102] I gave it to my hostess to read, but she said that she had had enough of Hitler. I have not reached that point, nor shall I until he is placed somewhere where he can do no more harm. In contrast I found Nicolay's *Abraham Lincoln* burnished my ideals as I followed the path of America's great Civil War president.[103]

March 1, 1940

The guns went off at 2:00 a.m. in greater number and with increasing persistence. I was up in an instant and heard the rushing of feet past my door as everyone in my apartment house seemed to dash down the steps, some descending two at a time, for the cave. I dressed quickly: gas mask, passport, identity card, money, fur coat; and I was ready to join the parade. Then I heard voices: *Dépêchez-vous* (hurry up). I turned away from the door, however, and in the blackness of my apartment groped my way to the salon where my governess was standing, nervous and bewildered, waiting to see my next move. I told her to go down with the others, but she wished to remain with me. There was an ominous silence in the house, and I thought we were the only ones in it. Outside the sound of the guns kept up an incessant volley. I put my fingers over my ears; the roar seemed to have no end. Would they never stop? Every moment I expected a crash. I wondered just what I should do should the building come tumbling down about me. No doubt I should not know at all what happened to me as I was being precipitated into another world, perhaps. I bowed my head as my soul in utter faith went up in prayer, deep, strong, humble. With that impulse all fear left me and I felt the Everlasting Arms encompassing me. The noise of the guns ceased. I fell asleep as the sun in the east broke through the night.

Vacation days persist. I have only a few more so I make the most of them. I sit on my balcony with the friendly sun overhead. I should go to town, but I wait and procrastinate. It is so good, so utterly good beneath the sun. My plant is dancing merrily in this early spring wind. Clouds in great masses are moving swiftly through.

The blue and the pure lines of the château opposite are serene and harmonious revealing a past.

Gone—glimmering through the dream of things that were…[104]

Early morning in Paris. Wandering down along the Seine and delving into the bookstalls, I found Verlaine's poems. They seemed to be there waiting for me. With it under my arm I walked under the clear morning sky.

Le ciel est, par-dessus le toit,
Si bleu, si calme![105]

I saw fishermen on the edge of the water stretching out their rods. There was a man on a bicycle followed by dozens of pigeons and sparrows. He had a basket in front of him attached to his handlebars and was throwing bird food to his feathered followers. They perched on his shoulders and pecked at his face—how they must love him, I thought; but what seemed more important was how he must love them. A seller of old clothes passed me calling "Marchand d'habits" almost to the music of the opera Louise.[106]

The newsstands have hung high the morning papers showing in large headlines the news that Mr. Sumner Welles[107] shall be in Berlin soon. The Germans are preparing and the French press has shown how they are doing so.

March 4, 1940

On his arrival in Paris, Mr. Welles was greeted with enthusiasm by the French, not so much as an official of our Government but as the best-dressed man in Europe with the exception of Mr. Anthony Eden. He left after a few days for London just as the news came that Finland[108] was in the process of negotiating a peace treaty with Russia. It filled the minds of the French with forebodings. The atmosphere was thick with pessimism.

Toward midnight, as I was about to turn in, there was a ring at the door. Every slight move counts these days and has a meaning that would pass unnoticed in normal times. Danger may be lurking at the other side of the door. The question comes: should I open it? My governess who is afraid of nothing and who, besides, is prodigiously curious, answered the question by cautiously turning the knob and peering through the aperture. I heard voices speaking in low tones and wondered if I should be called for help. It was nothing at all like that however. It was one of the staff of the Défense Passive warning that a streak of light could be seen through my Venetian blinds and should be dimmed. I breathed more freely. Far be it from me to give a Nazi pilot the slightest hint! My Defense man apologized for disturbing me, and of course my light was completely extinguished.

The advertisements urging the public to buy are sometimes amusing. In a shop selling ladies' handbags was a notice: Il faut être belle pour sa permission.

("You must be beautiful when he comes home on leave.") The prices of course are formidable.

We are indeed one with a universe where time means little, for the years stopped in their flight when I saw standing before me at my desk a familiar face that I had not seen since 1919. He was then in uniform as a young captain. Today he is in uniform as a colonel.[109] The boy I knew was brown-haired. Now the Colonel is grey, that is dark grey, but the eyes are the same, perhaps the body not so elastic. Once more he crosses my horizon. Had he come as so many others to finish the work begun in 1914–1918? He has joined the American Field Service and expects to be in France for the duration of the war. He has not yet received his orders and will remain in Paris until sent to one of the cities in the north destroyed by bombing where he will evacuate the wounded.

As I write to you, I am listening to the radio and hear the soldiers at the front singing war songs and French folk songs. M. Reynaud,[110] the Prime Minister, will be on the air in a few minutes. I shall listen just as you will listen 3,000 miles away. I shall be one with you and my own people. It will be an appeal to our country for help. We know, you and I, that if there is any possibility, the appeal shall not have been in vain. One moment—the Prime Minister is speaking.

Later. It was a moving address. Shall it be possible to send the help in time, so needed, so passionately desired, to this frightened, stricken, almost despairing country, so utterly unprepared for war?

Food is being rationed. I filled out my card: sugar, butter, soap, meat, vegetables. Central heating has been discontinued in order to conserve coal. Electricity is with us still. I shall order another electric heater. There are no complaints. This is war and there is a grim determination in the minds and hearts of everyone to win it so we can have peace, permanent peace, please God.

April 8, 1940

This evening Colonel Winslow of the American Field Service and I dined at Chez Elle,[111] one of the night clubs. Lucienne Boyer, looking very beautiful, sang love songs to the British officers. Colonel Winslow, dressed in his American uniform of the American Ambulance Service, and I missed nothing of the charm of the singer. She sang to each man individually. Her principal and greatest hit was, naturally, a song entitled "*Parlez-moi d'amour*" (Speak to me of love). Toward midnight (the curfew for night clubs) "La Marseillaise" and "God Save the King"[112] seemed to ring out with greater resolution, with deeper feeling.

Out into the black night we went on foot to my apartment. Not a sign of a taxi, so through the spacious Place [de la Concorde] we groped our way on foot; across the bridge, back of the Chambre des Députés,[113] past the Place du Palais-Bourbon, on to the rue de Bourgogne and into the historic rue de Varenne, no. 94.

April 15, 1940

Great activity in the war zone. England is leading splendidly. France is employing 100,000 women in the munitions factories. Unquiet in Holland, Belgium, Switzerland, Hungary, and Bulgaria as the German legions press nearer.

The Nazi menace! That threat so full of danger to the world. Before me is Hitler's address delivered on February 24, 1940, on the occasion of the anniversary of the Nazi Party. It was printed in *The New York Times*, dated February 25, 1940. I quote from it:

> These people who tell us what to do are those who possess half the world, and they cannot even solve their own problems.
>
> God Almighty has not created the world for the English to dominate.
>
> We Germans lay no claim to world domination.
>
> Already during the Great War Churchill was one of the great warmongers.
>
> One thing we know: Neither in a military nor in an economic way can Germany be defeated…we are able to say at this time, with utmost assurance, that militarily and economically, Germany today is invincible.[114]

Thus, he continues, expostulating against the Allies as "democratic idiots" and "old toothless men talking about the reconstruction of Europe, a reconstruction which has already happened without them…."

Spies, as I have said, are everywhere. Some of them are not very subtle. At the tea room Boissier[115] on the Avenue Victor-Hugo, known for its excellent pastries, I was having an animated conversation with a friend. The subject had nothing to do with politics, international questions, or the war. I recall we were discussing the possibility of life before birth and after death. My friend bowed to a lady who passed me. He said quite seriously to me, "It is someone whom I met and knew in the year 1270." I was somewhat perplexed and did not reply. However, quite near where we were seated, I noticed a woman ostensibly reading a paper. The lady's ears (and intermittently her eyes when they were not "reading" the paper) were fastened on us and our harmless and unusual conversation. I was sure that she had not seen a word in the paper she was holding, her interest in finding some "information" was too strong. Tonight *L'Intransigeant* warned the public of *pas de bavardages* ("no useless conversation").

May 10, 1940

The siren went off at 5:00 a.m. as a number of German planes soared above the city. I went to my balcony. The "rose-red dawn"[116] was breaking in the east. One plane flew so low that I could distinguish the Iron Cross. The anti-aircraft guns were sounding so loud that they, too, seemed nearby. I had been dreaming all night of sirens and guns and was not surprised when I was awakened by one. I dreamed that I was walking along the Champs-Élysées, looking down along the side of the curb through large excavations that were hidden from the public. There I saw young French soldiers in uniform, training for war, those who were too young to be called during the first days of mobilization. I was glad when the siren woke me. War news is serious enough when awake, but to have it trouble one's sleep is dispiriting.

On waking, I wondered what relation our dreams when asleep have to do with our waking hours. Then came the news, startling and tense! The Germans entered Holland, Belgium, and Luxembourg last night. Luxembourg, unable to put up any defense, was taken by the enemy with no difficulty. The Grand Duchess[117] had fled a short time before the Germans had crossed the frontier.

The atmosphere in Paris is dynamic. It is the start of the weekend of the feast of Pentecost, but the holiday, normally so gay and full of crowds leaving for the weekend, is forgotten. The Prime Minister speaks over the radio to the nation, ordering everyone to be at his post of duty. He urges every French man, woman and child to give all that he can for the defense of the country. His address was short but dramatic in its deep feeling and sincerity. The Government is at work as are the foreign embassies. There is the silence on the streets of forebodings and fear as the country trembles in the balance and as we wait.

Winston Churchill becomes Prime Minister of England replacing Mr. Chamberlain and his policy of appeasement.

The battle is on in the north. New regulations are given to the police: every agent must carry a gun and shoot enemy parachutists on sight. With the 5th columnists on their shores, the French are taking every precaution. All Germans must report to the police. They are sent to concentration camps, "and," as the report reads, "those with undetermined nationality." Many of them having claim to American nationality come to the Embassy in an effort to establish that claim.

The entrance to the subways and rail stations are surrounded by police and secret agents who search every face.

Requests for Visas to Enter the United States

May 13, 1940

News from the north: the Nazis attack the French at Sedan. The streets remain silent as I write except for the swiftly passing car of the *Défense Passive* to make sure that no one is out after the curfew. A few planes are hovering overhead.

The Embassy is full of Americans. Those with documents whose nationality as United States citizens is in doubt are desperately presenting their papers and sending frantic cables to the Department of State for approval and confirmation and for the establishment of their citizenship.

There are five hundred requests a day for visas from foreigners to enter the United States. Most of the requests come from Austrian and Belgian and German Jews. Anxiety at home reaches us as our people follow the European situation. The construction of fifty thousand planes a year to be sent abroad has begun by America. Talk of the certainty of a third term for President Roosevelt increases.

May 16, 1940

Tonight, as I write, I relive the startling events of the past week. It is the end of an era. It is the beginning of changes that will affect the whole world for generations to come. It could not be otherwise for it is a struggle, not only against men and munitions, but against the Nazis who are strong and merciless, filled with hatred and arrogance. The Nazis are condemning moral values that have existed for centuries. They are reevaluating the fundamental principles of life according to the dictate of their own limited intelligence of life. Or perhaps they are not even considering those principles: honor, faith, love, individual liberty, justice, truth—the civilization and culture that have guided our lives and the lives of all human beings for countless ages.

The chief of the American Ambulance Corps[118] announced the disappearance of one of the drivers. The driver came from California, volunteered with the Corps and is the first to be lost. Apparently, the ambulance, too, has disappeared. Is he a prisoner of the Germans? Was it an accident? Death? The radio announcer was so moved that his voice broke. He finished in a superb effort to give the few details he had been able to find.

Mr. Churchill in his first speech as Prime Minister to the House of Commons tells his own people and the people of France listening over the radio that he has "nothing to offer but blood, toil, tears, and sweat."[119]

I learned Holland surrendered to Germany. Holland had resisted but was betrayed by one of its own people and the 5th column; the unlocking of their canals, their great defense, was not sufficient. Queen Wilhelmina has left for England.

I wrote to Prince Albert de Ligne, former Belgian Ambassador to the United States and to Italy, now living in Brussels, assuring him of my sympathy for Belgium and the Belgian people, and of my deep loyalty to the nation to which I had the privilege of serving in the Belgian Embassy in Washington for many years. I told him of my pride, stronger than ever, as I wear my ribbon representing the decoration of the Croix de Chevalier de l'Ordre de Léopold II. I reiterated my gratitude to him, as it was he who procured this Order for me and presented it to me at the Embassy in Washington. I hope the letter reaches him in this confusion of events.

May 18, 1940

Out into the darkness our car sped tonight through the streets, on to the Gare de l'Est[120] where the refugees from the northern countries, principally Belgium, had arrived and were spread over the immense station. I had been requested to go to the station to help in the work that was being done for them.

They were there in thousands: men, women, children, dogs, cats, and birds; there were old men and women falling from exhaustion, having walked miles and miles from their homes fleeing the German Army, seeking shelter in a foreign country. Young men and girls were supporting the old people; babies and small children unconscious of danger were sitting wide-eyed and still or sleeping in corners against the station pillars, near their baggage, suit cases, small trunks—their all. Dogs that looked utterly miserable and bewildered, whom their masters and mistresses could not leave behind, were shivering from fear. In the silence, numbness, and misery of their condition, they were all waiting for destiny to show them the path to a new life.

My partner was in uniform. I had none and was given a Red Cross button showing that I was in the station to help. I found a tray of hot bouillon soup and some bread and made my way through the masses. They did not seem hungry. It was not physical hunger they felt. That stoop of the shoulders of the old and the saddened eyes of all of them expressed a mental hunger for understanding, sympathy, and kindness. We gave them what we could: we listened to their stories and silenced their fears to the best of our ability.

Soon they began to move in one dense mass toward the entrance of the station where the French public buses were waiting to gather them in and take them to the outskirts of the city where shelters were provided. Down through her history France has welcomed the homeless, and she is doing so again today....

Two boy scouts, having made a seat with their hands and intertwined fingers, were carrying a woman, who must have reached her one-hundredth year, toward where the buses were waiting.

There were distinguished and titled French men and women carrying trays; they were supporting on their arms the poor and the wretched. There were the police, too, keeping order; they were waiting for the soldiers coming from the front; and they were on the lookout for the Communists in the crowd who, with their subtle and poisonous propaganda, had been lowering the morale of the soldier or in other ways trying to block the cause of victory.

Towards midnight as the crowds of refugees thinned out in the station, I crossed over to another section where a canteen was arranged for the men coming from the front. They came in hundreds: wounded, bewildered, and ill. Their battalions had already given way; some of their officers had fled, and they did not know where to go or what to do. I stood near one and asked him how he had arrived at the station. He said, "There is no army, no commanding officer—they have gone. There we stood, the Germans a short distance away. We threw down our guns and ran; we caught a slow-moving freight train that brought us here."

"And where are you going?" I asked. "Have you your orders?"

"I don't know," he replied. "We have no orders. We must go to our homes and await orders. But, Madame, there will be no orders. The army is collapsing."

I turned away as I smiled a farewell. My heart was far from smiling.

There is work to do. I must help those poor soldiers with bandages on their heads through which the blood is oozing; and those with one arm or one leg; that one with a patch over an eye. There they are—over there sitting on benches—silent, unmoved, waiting to go on, somewhere, anywhere.

As my co-worker motioned to me, I helped her with a seriously wounded man. He could only hobble on one leg. With one arm around her neck, one around mine, we slowly turned toward her automobile and with the help of the chauffeur raised him to the seat. We returned for a few more, and eventually the car left for the American Military Hospital at Neuilly.

It was 3:00 a.m. I found a taxi fortunately that was going toward my quarter. As it left the station, I looked back and saw Mary Allez (Madame Jacques Allez, an American citizen),[121] my co-worker, still helping those stricken men into her luxurious car. Beyond was her secretary holding in her arms a little refugee baby that had been taken from a mother who was too tired. Other French volunteer workers were still in the station.

War and blood, tears and death—defeat! But with it all come elements of compassion, selflessness, sacrifice, and that priceless desire to uplift. Is it the result of our reaching up toward the Infinite? Or does it come down from the Infinite, expressing through us the undying realities of Love?

May 23, 1940

Today the Germans are at Amiens. The anguish of the French is indescribable. Hopelessness is depicted on the face of every passerby. And yet "La Marseillaise" is being played over the radio in cafés and restaurants continually.

General Weygand[122] is the man of the hour. "If France is ever in trouble," declared General Foch, "call Weygand." The great general was called from Syria where he was *en poste*.

Arras has been retaken by the French.

The French are in strong and swift pursuit of 5th columnists. While some of the Germans have not reported to the police, their lives are not worth much should they be located. On the Place de la Concorde tonight, two blond-haired lads in French uniforms were trying to explain to *l'agent de police* their failure to produce identity cards.

I had luncheon with Colonel Winslow of the Ambulance Corps today. He expects to leave for the front at once. However, he bet several hundred francs that he will not go. I telephoned his barracks late this evening to find out if he would dine at my apartment and the answer came: "all the boys went to the front a few hours ago." They departed with their twenty ambulances, saluted the Tomb of the Unknown Soldier at the Arc de Triomphe,[123] and then drove out toward the city limits and on to their destiny.

May 25, 1940

My Colonel has just returned from the front with his ambulance. His orders had read "Amiens." He told me that he had never seen desolation such as he saw as he drove toward the city that had been systematically bombed by the Nazis: homeless civilians, wounded civilians, and soldiers; confusion, habitations in ashes, chaos.

Entering the town of Amiens he and his comrade went directly to their objective, which was a hospital, or what once had been a hospital. There on the ground floor enormous space had been made for the wounded. A few doctors and nurses were carrying on courageously. The ambulance drivers gathered a few wounded, those who could stand the strain of the return trip to Paris, and then made their way to the outskirts of the city. Before they reached the city, the Colonel suggested to his companion that he wait there while he went back to the village to find cigarettes and some food since they had not eaten since they left Paris. They had expected to find a café or bistro open after they left Paris. Did they really expect to find anything in the devastation they drove through? In that shattering of a corner of France whose inhabitants had recently, so recently been living their peaceful lives? As the enemy came nearer to their homes, they had left and had joined the refugees from the north as the exodus continued its relentless urge pushing them toward the unknown.

The mud splashed on his boots and farther up on his uniform. He walked swiftly.

"Halt!" The command sounded unchallengeable. "Who are you?" asked a French soldier holding his gun menacingly, barring any move forward.

"I am an American citizen," replied the Colonel in perfect French.

"In that uniform?"

"But it is the American uniform of the American Ambulance Service," the Colonel persisted.

"I know the American uniform and that is not one." His voice had a touch of pride. "Are you a Belgian?"

"No, I am not a Belgian. I am an American, I told you." The Colonel was becoming irritated. His ambulance, his wounded, and his buddy were waiting. He had said only for a few minutes, and this had to happen.

"You speak Engl-e-esh?" The soldier knew some English words.

"Of course I speak English," said the Colonel in English. "Do you want to see my identity cards?"

"Every German these days has false identity cards," replied the soldier scornfully.

A small crowd began to gather. A few children, women, and presently an elderly man with a beard joined the group.

The soldier explained the situation to the man who was apparently a representative of the law. He was in fact the *Commissaire* of the village.

"We'll take him to the *Commissariat*. An overnight interrogation will clear up the matter," ordered the Commissaire.

The Colonel was in despair. A night in the village prison was something totally unexpected and could not have happened at a more inopportune time. One last effort toward freedom:

"Monsieur le Commissaire," he began. "I am an American citizen, the driver of an American ambulance, recently arrived in France from New York. I have volunteered to help France. I have on the uniform of the Ambulance Corps. My ambulance is waiting outside the village limits with my friend who is with me in this work."

"Your identity card and papers," demanded the Commissaire.

The Colonel opened his wallet which he took from the breast pocket of his uniform and searched amongst his papers. His identity papers were not there! The situation looked bleak indeed.

"I do not have my papers with me. They are with my comrade in the ambulance."

The crowd became larger and was becoming menacing.

"To the Commissariat!" a group of voices insisted.

There seemed nothing to do but move forward with the crowd toward the shattered building that still had a semblance of a seat of the law.

The soldier, who had once been with Americans and liked them, turned to the Commissaire. "Before we take him, Monsieur le Commissaire," he suggested, "let us see if he really has an ambulance."

The Colonel's love for France touched a lower star! The crowd assented, as did the Commissaire, and they turned toward the main road leading to the outskirts of the city.

The ambulance was waiting patiently, but his comrade was walking up and down in uncontrollable anxiety, not knowing whether to continue waiting for his friend or return to Paris.

"Where the devil have you been?" he began.

"For God's sake, Joe, give me my cards of identity. These people are taking me for a German spy!"

May 26, 1940

All last night the planes soared above. In the morning the birds in the gardens opposite were, at times, gathered in groups and again flying about in hopeless confusion not knowing which way to go. The Power that hovers over the sparrow's fall must have protected them for, as I watch, they turned in body and flew south. They knew where safety lay.

Americans with no official business or those not occupied in war relief were again urged by the U.S. Government to leave France and return to the United States. It is unfortunate indeed, for how can that old man sitting near me go? He tries to explain that he has lived here since the Great War of 1914–1918 when he came over with the American Army. He married a French girl and has been happy, but now his home in America calls him. Tears of homesickness are in his eyes because today home seems to be the only safe spot on earth in the midst of a reeling world. His wife refuses to leave.

And how can that elderly spinster leave? Where shall she go in America with its teeming millions of people and every member of her family gone? Or that rich American with all his life in France having severed every connection with his homeland?

"What shall I do?" they ask me. "What should you do if you were in my place?" There is no answer; I cannot reply. It is an individual problem to be sure. Concentration camps have an agonizing continuity.

May 28, 1940

Paris is included in the war zone as of today. Orders are given to foreigners to have all circulation cards dated June 1.

Rain, rain. The elements are keeping time with the rhythm of events. There are admonitions in the byways and highways: "Silence, silence. The enemy is watching and listening to you." They are written on posters hung in the subway stations, on newsstands, and on the walls of the city.

All foreigners and French citizens as well are ordered to show an identity card[124] when requested by the police. A young girl born in Germany, living in France since a few years after her birth, is about to be taken to a concentration camp but commits suicide instead. She left word before dying that her heart was French with her French-born parents and that the accident of her birth was her sole relation to Germany.

King Léopold III[125] of Belgium surrenders to the Germans. Belgium had fought valiantly calling for French and British aid. Is the surrender a betrayal of the Allies, or is it loyalty to and protection of the Belgian army? Time only will judge. The Belgian Minister in Paris with the group of Belgians in France is carrying on. They are mobilizing 300,000 troops to continue fighting with the Allies. It has been suggested that I forego wearing my Belgian decoration until there is more light on the situation.

May 30, 1940

Memorial Day. No holiday for us. The day is being observed by ceremonies at the Suresnes American Cemetery and Memorial[126] and at the American churches. In no other year perhaps since 1918 has the feeling of this great day been more profound for Americans.

"If ye break faith with us who die…"[127]

June 2, 1940

A battle is being fought on the plains of Flanders.[128] Flanders Fields, that echo of a quarter of a century past when the blood of the French soldier was soaked with the soil to keep it France forever. Tonight—

In Flanders fields the poppies weep[129]
    Between the crosses where we sleep
    Nor rise at dawn; and overhead
    Winged argosies bring back the dread
    Of war to us in our dark keep.

So speak the Dead. If we could leap
    Into the fray we would march deep
    In mighty ranks across our bed
    In Flanders fields.

Once more take up our torch to reap
    A final victory and sweep
    The foe from ground where we have bled.
    You dare not fail the trusting dead
    In Flanders fields!°

The battle on the plains of Flanders ends as the British, after five days of magnificent operations, withdrew 300,000 British, French, and Belgian soldiers to the French port of Dunkirk. Mr. Churchill, Prime Minister of England, called it a "miracle of deliverance." These men were ferried across the Channel by every available boat. British subjects offered their luxurious yachts in the emergency. As one writer described it: "while a rear guard impeded the German advance, men crowded the beach waiting their turn at embarkation. The port itself was in flames."

More men in the United States are volunteering for the Ambulance Service and Field Service. Amongst them is Robert Montgomery,[130] the film star, whose photograph is in all the French papers. Fifteen men are sailing from New York today. Toward the middle and end of this month, when the universities and colleges close, there will be many more. Again, the spirit of adventure and of high ideals still lives in the heart of young America. It appears century after century.

One of the Belgian ministers spoke over the radio from Limoges where the Belgian government in France is represented.[131] He was so affected that his voice faltered in its intensity. He finished with "We shall fight for the independence and liberty of Belgium." Cheers resounded through the radio. Belgian soldiers, who have escaped from the German advance, are joining French units. "*Vive la Belgique!*" The spirit of their great King Albert I is with them, he who

Never dreamed, though right were worsted,[132]
    Wrong would triumph,
    Held we fall to rise,
    Are baffled to fight better,
    Sleep to wake.*

°   "Flanders, 1940" by D. Maitland Bushby, Humboldt, Arizona, May 1940.
*   Robert Browning as quoted in *King Albert's Book*, 1914.

Seen in passing: A French officer, insignia Colonel, stepping aside to allow a wounded French soldier to pass—*Noblesse oblige.*[133] Does the superior officer feel an infinite respect for his subordinates, many of them simple, unlettered men who are fighting with that renowned French bravery that has made their country great and who, today, are bearing much of the brunt of battle? He smiled as he returned the salute of the soldier. American citizens are rushing to Bordeaux today to take the SS *Washington,* which arrives from Genoa tomorrow; 1,000 will be on their way home.[134]

Bombs over Paris

June 3, 1940

Incendiary bombs fell over Paris today as the siren sounded. The Citroën factory was badly damaged.[135] They fell, too, around the Invalides section where I have my home. Danger is hovering around us, but there is danger everywhere—death everywhere. Danger? There is a Power stronger than any danger. Death? But there is no death, only a change, a crossing over into a vast unknown country where another adventure awaits the traveller; where we find ourselves liberated; where we find Truth and the continuity of life.

I waited until the firing ceased toward midday and started for the Embassy. I passed the beautiful Ministry for Foreign Affairs where in 1939 an enthusiastic crowd loudly acclaimed the Majesties (king and queen) of England. There was peace in those days when King George VI[136] and his Queen were driving along the streets of Paris down the Champs-Élysées. There was war in the air, but no war. The hope and prayer of Frenchmen and women and children was to remain in peace, to go about the daily routine of life in the city, the country, and the mountains. The farmer wanted to tend his fields, feed his cattle, smoke his pipe at night, and watch over the ever-changing miracle of the French sunset. That was a year ago. Today the country is at war and those farms are unattended; some of the villages are in flames. Priceless treasures of architecture and art have gone down to dust and destruction. Part of the French Army goes on fighting, knowing that it is useless. Those grey hordes are advancing, always advancing, cannot be stopped. It is too late to stop them.

Tonight, the search lights in the sky are in full force, playing about, crossing each other, separating and again returning to meet. I stood and watched them from my balcony. They are beautiful as they search for danger with the threat of catastrophe and death.

Even in the background of night, I could see the shadow of the château standing erect, like an old oak, and reflecting the spirit and genius of this land of France.

June 4, 1940

Last night's targets were munitions factories. They also shattered private dwellings. One thousand Nazi bombs over Paris left in its wake some 900 wounded women and children, invalids, and old people.

Camions coming from the front, riddled with bullets, camouflaged, and covered with mud. They rolled past my dwelling this morning following the broad boulevard of the Invalides. One drove directly under my balcony on the rue de Varenne. It seemed very much alone. I watched it disappear. It had come from death and blood, from great, deep waters....

Over the radio the Prime Minister is speaking to the nation, calling for renewed faith in the Allied armies, for more concentrated service. He does not speak in vain—for France is thrilling for action, in hope.

The British continue the struggle. The ringing words of the Prime Minister of Great Britain in the House of Commons thrilled the world: "...we shall fight on the beaches, we shall fight on the landing grounds, we shall fight in the fields and in the streets, we shall fight in the hills; we shall never surrender."[137]

June 8, 1940

The radio announces victory in the north. I hear the military music of the Moroccan Cavalry,[138] a regiment of the French Foreign Legion. Are they as optimistic as all that? Or is it a last effort to raise a tottering morale? Do the French recall today those words of Napoléon that battles are won by exhausted armies?[139] Anyway, they fight on with that eternal hope, with that reaching out for liberty so deeply rooted in the human consciousness as old as man.

"*Accrochons nous au sol de France*," ordered General Weygand to his army yesterday.[140] "*Quels que soient nos angoisses personnelles et nos douleurs intimes, accrochons nous à notre devoir, à notre tâche quotidienne–accrochons nous avec une fureur sacrée au poste ou le destin nous à places sans pensées de recul.*"[°]

June 9, 1940

The atmosphere of the city and the spirit of the Parisians seemed lighter today. The cafés on the Champs-Élysées were in action. The tables were filled with soldiers and officers and many civilians. I sat with the Colonel of the American Ambulance Service for an *apéritif* on one of the terraces of the Avenue. We watched the crowds who walked with a gayer step. The news vendors' voices were not so heavy with the forebodings of a few days ago. On the Alexandre III Bridge, as well as on some of the other bridges, were interspersed broken down camions and big wagons, placed there to stop enemy advance or to slow down enemy transport entering the city.

The Colonel spoke of his work and his orders for evacuation in the different villages. There the families for generations have lived and died, married, and borne

---

Translation: "Let us cling to the soil of France…Whatever are our personal anguish and our intimate sorrows, let us cling to our duty, to our daily task—let us hold with a sacred passion to the post where Destiny has placed us without any thoughts of retreating."

their children, laughed, and wept. They do not want to leave. The authorities however order their evacuation. If they persist in remaining, they risk death by bombing or being ravaged by the Nazi troops. Many who have left already are on the road. They have no homes. The road is jammed with tanks and troops, machine guns, automobiles, and camions. Human beings like ants on a hill swarm the roads. Above are the plains sounding like the beating of wings. The refugees are not individuals; they are a mass of humanity plodding on and on. There is no fear, even no despair, in fact no feeling at all—only a dullness, a numbness of mind and body and soul. "If the Germans arrive at the gates of Paris tomorrow or the next day or the next," said the Colonel, "I shall leave at once for Bordeaux where I shall wait for the next boat for the United States. If you do not see me again, you will know what has happened."

June 10, 1940

War in France is accentuated. Life today is thrown into the whirlpool of a world circle.

All night an air battle raged overhead. The hearts of the French are filled with desolation. There is little hope left.

Italy declares war on France and Great Britain.

In the large enclosure of the entrance to the Hôtel des Invalides where camions had been herded, there was much activity as the camions all left abruptly for the south. The Ministers of the Government were leaving in automobiles and in every available taxi. Every kind of vehicle was loaded with government officials, employees, and some civilians; they were heaped with mattresses, furniture, and sandbags (the latter were brought along as a shelter from falling bombs); the radio is silent; official documents are being burned. In front of the different American banks, wagons and camions are being filled with their documents and material that cannot be left behind.

Nearer and nearer to Paris comes the German Army as the British and French put up a heroic resistance. The exodus has begun from Paris and nearby cities and villages. It is a beginning of that tragic, bewildering trail toward the south. The intense heat adds to the fear and anguish.

Will Paris Be Declared an Open City?

I walked through the streets void of vehicle traffic toward the Embassy. The sale of morning papers has been stopped and the newsstands are closed. The shop are closing one by one. French soldiers whose units had scattered in the north a wandering about the city like ships without a rudder; with their packs and helme masks and personal effects on their backs, they are crawling slowly under th heavy loads beneath the blistering sun. It is forbidden to telephone, although ruling does not apply to the government buildings, or to commercial houses

private persons who give their names with the number requested. Some camions appear filled with troops being rushed toward the outskirts of Paris to defend the city should it not be declared an "open city."[141]

The Embassy was crowded as I entered. Our compatriots, frantic with fear, were making a brave effort to be calm. I was pushing my way through the dense mass along the corridor when suddenly I felt my arm held. I turned and standing against a pillar was a man, an American, whom I had seen frequently in the building for official services. His face was white, and as he slumped against the pillar almost to the ground, I took his arm and said:

"Courage, Mr. X., you must show courage. What is the matter, tell me."

"If I am here when the Germans arrive, I shall be shot at once. I have been informed that my name is on their list. I do not know what to do or which way to turn. You must tell me what to do."

For a moment I was at a loss.

"Come with me," I said.

We went to the next floor where I found the chief of my section and told him about the matter, asking him what could be done.

"You should start at once," he wisely suggested, "and walk to Bordeaux where you will undoubtedly be able to find a boat for the United States, or make your way to the French-Spanish frontier."

Mr. X. thanked us and with the swiftness of the proverbial eagle, he was off. He was not alone. Many others, for various reasons, found it wiser to be away from Paris should the Germans arrive. The 5th column had worked well for long months, perhaps for many years with the Germans.

No doubt it is love and spirit that really binds people together. I am one with these people, with this France, in love and spirit. Their tragic problem is mine. Their hopelessness, no, that is not mine, nor is a sense of defeat. If France should fall, it shall be to rise again. Thus, it is a sense of rising that is mine. Someone once said, "Out of defeat comes the secret of victory."[142] I have lived so long with these people; I have seen them in victory and I shall do so again. Today I cling to triumph....

When I awoke, I thought it was still night. A thick fog enveloped the city. It was a *faux brouillard* ("false fog") however. It may have been a curtain of smoke that had been spread over the city to hide it from the enemy. It seemed so futile. In their desperate efforts to stem the inevitable, it was like the Chinese beating great bronze gongs[143] in small villages to frighten away the giant dog of heaven, who they believe tries to devour the moon.˚ Or it may have been spread by the Germans to hide their operations.

˚ From Chinese Folklore as related in *Thunder out of China* by Theodore White and Annalee Jacoby.

June 11, 1940

Practically all the shops are closed. My governess told me that it was difficult to find anything to eat. Shutters are closed. At night the blackout continues. I am writing with a feeble light that is kept dim by the black cloth around my lamp. I hear the steps of the members of the *Défense Passive* walking up and down in front of the building. I shall not risk the slightest glimmer of light from my window.

The radio has this moment announced that new units are being sent to the front and new divisions with the hope that the enemy might be pushed back. President Reynaud appeals to President Roosevelt for immediate aid. It is two in the morning. I must find some forgetfulness in sleep before the day breaks....

U.S. State Department Notice: June 12, 1940

June 12, 1940

Yesterday morning at sea the SS *Washington* was stopped by a German submarine and was given ten minutes to be evacuated. The ship was carrying 1,500 United States citizens and was flying the U.S. flag. It was allowed to go on its way after a fifteen-minute discussion. Were the Germans seeking the illegal transport of arms? Were they trying to impress our Government by their power and prestige in their arrogance of victory?

I tried today to find my old haunts for luncheon. All are closed. In a small *bistro* I ate a sandwich and bread and drank some coffee. Returning to the Embassy, I found the following notice on my desk:

> All members of the staff should carry with them at all times adequate papers of identification (passports and identity cards). Domestic servants of staff members will be provided with certificates of identification.
>
> Except for emergency reasons, such as protection of American citizens and American property, members of the staff, until further notice, will not be on the streets after dark...Any member of the staff who finds it necessary to go about the city in the evening must be accompanied by another member of the staff.

The day is beautiful, one of those rare days of Paris in spring—all sun and warmth and clear, blue sky. The Germans come nearer and nearer. They are now 100 kilometers from the outskirts of the city.

Somewhere I read: "France is always saved in the eleventh hour by a miracle."[144] Are they the words of some great Frenchman, or a proverb, or an old law? Someone is speaking over the radio; the voice is calling on that great soldier and saint of France, Joan of Arc, with a prayer for help.[145] There is still hope. I hear another say, "I shall not believe they will come until I see them on the streets of Paris." With a sigh I remark, "If only every Frenchman and woman—everyone—would feel like that, they would not come."

The railroad stations are crowded with distraught people carrying heavy baggage. The police are ordered to remain at their posts or hand in their resignations. The populaces remaining in Paris feel that they are being abandoned by their own people....

The different roads leading out from the city are so jammed that in instances it has been impossible for an official or official messenger (with a legitimate reason for trying to get through) to make any headway. Along the roads are misery, hopelessness, fear, hunger, suffering from the intense heat, and bewilderment. Where to go, where can they find shelter? The homes in villages and cities lying toward the south that heretofore have given bountifully of their hospitality are already overcrowded. Those who are homeless clog up the roads and for hours are unable to move.

June 13, 1940

It has come—the great catastrophe. Tonight, the Germans are at the entrance to the city. Word came from the German Command that Paris would be declared an "open city," but that should there be any hostility on the part of the French, Paris would be bombed. There is calmness in the atmosphere. As I write, there is no sound except the eighteenth-century bell in the tower of the château opposite that tolls out its sympathy on this wounded France, stricken and sad. But listen! The voice of the Prime Minister calls—orders over the radio—"*France, debout!*" ('France, stand up!')

A Nazi spy dressed as a nun was caught in Passy by the French police....

I received a notice to be placed on the door leading into my apartment showing that it is the property of an American citizen.

Camions from the front are returning covered with branches of trees and painted in camouflage.

More refugees from Belgium and the north of France are pouring into the city. Other refugees returning to Paris from the exodus were finding their homes again, as it was impossible for them to proceed on the jammed highways.

The Nazis are bombarding the roads and machine gunning the old, the sick, women, and children. My White Russian friends who had gone with the exodus became separated—mother, father, and son. The son drove the automobile. Quite unexpectedly they were obliged to walk countless miles; it left her feet bleeding and blistered. At a pause on the road, the French soldiers procured some straw and with some water bathed her feet, after which she was able to continue until the unit dispersed. One of the soldiers brought her into Paris. The family was reunited after several weeks, strangely enough, but the experience left them with memories whose scars will remain with them always.

Help and sympathy are continually shown. I saw a member of the Garde Mobile aid an old woman too tired to lift her heavy bag, and I saw a French soldier take a baby from the arms of a young mother whose back was bent from fatigue, hunger, and loneliness. Love and sympathy are still here. Do the Nazis know anything about that? Do they care to know? They know more about conquering through cruelty and tyranny.

I picked up a leaflet that had dropped from a German plane. On it was written: *"Petites Françaises, nous danserons avec vous le 14 juillet"* ('Little French ladies, we shall dance with you on the 14th of July'). The 14th of July is the French national holiday, the day when patriotism is deeper in the hearts of the French than at any other time of the year. The leaflets were thrown away in scorn.

It was late when I left my office. There was much to be done. As I reached the lobby of the Embassy building, I was told that I would not be allowed to leave, that I must remain all night. It could not be divined what might be the attitude of the Germans who are expected to enter Paris tomorrow morning. I appealed to one of the chiefs and told him I was not afraid, that my governess was waiting for me in my apartment, although the building itself was deserted. It was nearing 8:00 p.m. The electricity had been turned off throughout the city. I left by the side entrance, and as I turned from the rue Boissy d'Anglas into the Place de la Concorde, there was a fine drizzle of rain. The Place was deserted. I crossed straight through the center. Half way through I met a man in a wheel chair; he was one of the wounded of the First World War. Beside him walked his wife.

"Where have you come from?" I asked.

"From the Seine-et-Oise," he replied. "We have walked miles and miles trying to pass through the roads overcrowded with people, machine guns, Germans, and the French Army.

"You must be tired," I ventured. "Where are you going?"

"We don't know," he said, "but we shall go on. Any place is better than to be here with them."

I said "good night" and waved a good luck. I walked away with a feeling of futility. What could I do for them? What kind of help could I give them in a world that seemed to be tumbling into an abyss?

I hurried past the Chambre des Députés, up the little rue de Bourgogne. Every shutter and blind of every house on the completely empty street had been drawn. What was in back of those sealed habitations? What thoughts? Was it abject fear, or, had fear, worry, and uncertainty plunged the occupants into a blessed sleep that for a time brought forgetfulness?

The bells of Notre-Dame toll slowly. They toll their grief....

France Has Fallen

June 14, 1940

I woke this morning to a troubled world. Never, it seemed, was a June morning in Paris more beautiful. I left my apartment early and went on foot to the Embassy.

As I walked toward the Chambre des Députés, the first thing that caught my attention was the sight of a German traffic officer teaching the French traffic agent how to direct the traffic. Above the building the swastika[146] was flying triumphantly. The German Army has entered Paris. They had marched past the Arc de Triomphe at 5:00 a.m. I turned away for my heart was heavy. On the Concorde Bridge, lined up along the sides, were the German motorcycles. Farther on, filling the immense Place, was a unit of the German Army with green uniforms, motorcycles, and machine guns. In a daze I went through the lines, reached the Embassy and blessed the Stars and Stripes flying valiantly from the building. Across the street over the Hôtel de Crillon[147] was the swastika—again the swastika! I climbed to my office, reached my desk, and burst into tears.

Here was defeat and the humiliation of a great nation. The Nazis—victorious, triumphant—were the conquerors of a proud people. France has fallen[148] to the enemy....

CHAPTER 2

June 15, 1940–December 31, 1940

Serving with the American Embassy
in Paris during the Occupation

June 15, 1940

The heavy tension of yesterday is gone. The waiting, the unyielding waiting, is over. Suspense can be so inflexible....

There is music in Paris. The national anthem of Germany is interspersed with German military music on the glorious Place de la Concorde. German planes are flying over the city, descending and rising, descending again and landing in the Place as an admiring crowd looks on. The admirers are naturally the Germans. The French, too, are there but there is scorn and resentment on the faces of the French as I watch them crowded together with German officers and soldiers. German tanks and camions roll heavily along the Avenue des Champs-Élysées coming from the Triumphal Arch. Soldiers in smart new uniforms carrying highly polished guns and fur trimmed knapsacks parade through the streets. The defeated nation's populace is obliged to witness this show of strength, power, and luxury.

It is a fine "show" indeed. Isn't that what it is? France is occupied by the enemy....

I did not believe that they would enter Paris until the last ray of hope had faded. I was so sure a miracle would happen. A miracle did occur; it lay in the courageous fight of French troops against stupendous odds as units kept on fighting until it was impossible to continue without their being annihilated. Some were indeed annihilated.

The tense waiting is over. It has opened the gates to a fermenting uncertainty.

A warm June sun pervades the city. Clouds are swiftly making their way through the upper spaces as the blue sky emerges intermittently. It is a beautiful day for the enemy....

Last night Dr. Thierry de Martel,[1] the eminent French surgeon and great patriot, loved by the French and many non-French friends, shot himself to death as the German Army reached the outposts of Paris. The few written words that he left revealed the secret of his tragic act; he could not go on, he could not live....

And Hitler danced his "jig of joy," as Mr. Churchill expressed it, when the news reached him that Paris was occupied by his troops.

The Nazis fill the streets. They buy up, and often take without buying, antique furniture, *objets d'art*, oriental rugs, food paintings, etc.

Curfew is at 10:00 p.m.

It is forbidden to listen to the news over the radio other than German news. The press gave out that anyone possessing a radio will be punished by a fine and imprisonment. The French listen, however, and when the British broadcast is able to come through, the news is informative and helpful.

Gradually the streets are filling with those returning from the roads. Many who had remained in their closed homes have emerged to see and feel what the city under a foreign command is like.

June 16, 1940

One by one the shops are opening. The panic of the exodus seems to have spent itself. What else can they do? Life must go on….

Loud speakers are placed in different sections of the city giving out German orders. It is almost ten o'clock in the evening, and the voice from the Invalides, quite near my habitation, is telling the people to be off the streets before the hour sounds. Although the French do not care to be told what to do by anyone, especially by the enemy of their country, they obey orders because if they do not in this instance—if they are found outside of their dwellings after the appointed hour—they are politely helped into an automobile and taken to their homes.

The blackout continues. Until quite recently there was a baker living in a section of Paris not far from where I live who is no more. Last night he was awakened by a loud pounding at his door below, which was the entrance to his shop. He and his wife had their apartment above. He descended to open the door, fearful and cautious.

"Who is it?" he asked.

"Police," was the gruff answer—naturally the Nazi police. Had they come to take him away? He knew this had happened to others. What order had he failed to obey? What had he done? He opened the portal. Two Nazi soldiers stood before him.

Éteignez vos lumières (put out your lights) was all they said in French with a strong German accent.

The baker said nothing. He closed the door as they departed, went to his room and to bed, never to rise again. He died from a heart attack during the night, brought on solely by fear.

As polite as the Nazis were told to be to the Parisians—indeed as they are—they do not hesitate to encourage, even to spread, propaganda of fear throughout the city. Their motorcycles, driven through the streets with limitless speed, brush the passersby or stop abruptly to warn a forgetful or defiant pedestrian to cross the road between the lines indicated. Other pompous incidents continually occur. Nazi planes descend as low as the roofs of the houses and fly past at a lightening pace. All this is done to frighten the inhabitants and to show them that they, the Nazis, are the masters.

June 17, 1940

The newspapers are reappearing and are controlled by the occupying authorities: *Le Matin*,[2] *Les Nouveaux Temps*,[3] *Les Dernières nouvelles de Paris*.[4] However well-written is the latest news of Paris in the general press, no one believes a word from any of them.

Bunau-Varilla, owner of *Le Matin*, visited the German High Command when the Nazis entered Paris and offered his services and the services of his paper to the Germans. Stéphane Lauzanne,[5] also of *Le Matin*, refused to remain with the staff. He left at once. *La Victoire*[6] also came to light. I have it before me. It consists of one page displaying on the first column in big headlines an article entitled: "The Truth to the Parisians." The article begins (in free translation): "Sad days have arrived for you Parisians, our brothers, for Paris is occupied by the Germans." On the last column of the page another article is headed:

> The Duties of Parisians.
>
> Parisians, my brothers and sisters, we must now consider ourselves prisoners. What are your duties toward the guests that war has obliged us to have with us? First of all, there is a correction, a politeness which you must not fail to change; you must stop, even amongst yourselves, calling them '*Boches*.' It is an insult to them, or they take it as such. Call them 'Fritz' as our soldiers call them. It shows, too, an absence of any hatred of the Nazis.

This paper lasted a few days only—no one would read it.

There is no excitement of war because one does not hear any news. We do not know whether the British are winning or losing. At times the British broadcast makes an effort to come through, but it is invariably stopped by the German authorities.

Large quantities of food bought by the Nazis are sent to Germany.

The French farmers have not yet returned to their farms although the women have been carrying on to some extent. The men have not yet been completely demobilized; the food becomes scarcer, and the food lines become longer and longer....

What does that Nazi soldier mean by pushing himself up to the head of the food line, demanding to be waited on at once? The French in line are silent, not a word of the angry complaint that is written on their faces. They dare not voice their sentiments. The conquerors have all the rights.

A German plane descends toward my window as I write. It almost touches my balcony. They have free access through this Paris, this "Earthly Paradise,"[7] and the pilots make the most of it. Do they really think they will remain indefinitely?

The government of France is taken over by Maréchal Pétain,[8] replacing Prime Minister Paul Reynaud. The Maréchal requests an armistice with the Germans to the consternation of the French. What about North Africa where the Free French[9] were to continue the battle, and where the government would administer, and where help from the Allies would reach them? France is asking the conquerors for an armistice?!

June 22, 1940

The Armistice was signed today at Compiègne,[10] which is where in 1918 another Armistice was signed. That was twenty-two years ago. It seems like yesterday. Included in the terms of the Armistice [of 1940] is the partition of France. The Germans are to have the north, the Italians the south. Hitler had consulted with Mussolini[11] on the subject. Also, in the terms the following appears: all German prisoners to be liberated at once; French prisoners to be freed when peace is signed.

Below I hear the tramp, tramp of soldiers' boots, heavy with war. It brings a feeling of anguish that hovers over the dark city like some evil thing....

This Paris is not theirs; their presence here is an anomaly, a discordant note in the rhythm of life, like a discord in music where the principle of harmony has been violated.

I turn on the radio and hear only the harsh guttural sound of a Nazi voice. I cannot understand it. Besides I don't like it. Something seems to clutch at my side as I listen. It must be because I do not like the Nazis in Paris....

I turn on another station and listen. This time I am entranced by the singing. It is a baritone, a German voice, rich and clear, singing a German love song. I wonder at the contrast: Nazi Germany with its arrogance, cruelty, harshness—like their sometimes harsh language; on the other hand, a love of music evidenced by a baritone voice singing almost to perfection. Are there two Germanys?

Some Italians passed me today as I was entering my apartment house on the rue de Varenne. They were going toward their Embassy about a hundred meters away. Today their flag is flying over the building. They are one with the conquerors. The Italians had entered the war against the Allies on June 10. This is Mussolini's Italy. Somehow the Italians do not seem altogether in sympathy with their co-partners in the war. There were bitter tears amongst thousands of Italians when the Duce and his Fascists "stabbed France in the back."[12]

French prisoners of war under guard are moving toward the Invalides; they look tired, indifferent, too. The German guard is impersonal. His face, as I saw it in passing, is impassive and unmoved. I wondered what he could be thinking of, or if he was thinking at all....

On the Champs-Élysées, quite near the Triumphal Arch,[13] an old French woman, apparently penniless, was surrounded by an angry crowd. She had put out her hand to beg some money from a German officer. He gave it to her, but the infuriated crowd hooted her....

Two French *agents de police* are shot for "insulting" a Nazi officer. I can imagine the lacerating provocation because it is still there. It shows itself at times in just one more galling incident, which afterwards bursts into flame.

The British are bombarding Venice and Genoa with long-range guns. Italy is feeling the war. Today the Italians took Nice.

I had almost reached my dwelling when at a bend on the street a little old trembling woman (she might have reached her 90th year) crept up to me and, pointing to the German soldier keeping guard on the corner, his gun by his side, whispered fearfully, "Madame, tell me, is that one of the Boches?"

I leaned down and also whispered, "Yes, you are right. It is one of them." She walked away muttering, "Yes, I thought as much. Oh, la, la!"

This life in Paris under an alien power is like a picture puzzle. One cannot find the parts that should go together, or one cannot find any picture to make. Everything is chaotic down here where human beings are striving, puzzled, distracted, and unhappy. I live this common life with them. It is only when I am alone trying to reach the mountain top of Spirit that I find reality, harmony, and peace above the chaos. There I can see more clearly and think more clearly. There I catch gleams of light in the darkness; they come in flashes as intermittent expressions of courage, sacrifice, and love. Suddenly the light escapes me, and I find myself in the valley again where I try not to see greed, hatred, selfishness, cruelty, and the continual grasping that shrivels the soul and contracts the consciousness. In that valley one is blinded to the expanding, broadening influence of giving of love, which is after all the secret of life....

June 23, 1940

Hitler came to Paris early in the morning visiting the Opéra, the Eiffel Tower, and Napoléon's tomb.[14] It was all held in great secrecy. He entered no restaurants for his time was short. Was there a hidden fear that he might pay for victory with his life? Members of his entourage remained: Göring, Goebbels and Himmler. There was much saluting with "Heil Hitler" here and "Heil Hitler" there....[15]

The Résistance[16] has begun and is taking on vast proportions.

General de Gaulle[17] in London is organizing his army, that network of the Résistance for the continuation of the war. With his Cross of Lorraine,[18] he is the symbol of every Frenchman. From the far-flung Colonies of the French Republic,[19] the Governors and Chiefs arrive in London to offer their services to the General. One five-starred general tore one of his stars from his uniform before presenting himself to General Charles de Gaulle whose uniform bears four stars....

If the French are unable to continue the battle above ground, they will take the fighting underground. Their fierce courage and their passionate defiance persist. Their disregard for danger in their struggle for liberty lives on. They know that if the Germans win in the whole of Europe, life will be even more tragic for them than it is today. Every day the Nazis and the Nazi chiefs show a mercilessness, a brutality, a persecution of the peoples of the already conquered countries unheard of in the history of our civilization. Shall France escape? Already the news comes from the south of France of Jewish children torn from the arms of their mothers who will never see them again and of wives and husbands separated and lost to each other forever.

One by one the French—men, women, and even children instructed for action—leave for work and join the network in the Résistance, carried on a wave of deep faith in France, in themselves, and in the cause of liberty.

The signing of the Armistice sent thousands more Frenchmen underground. They leave their wives and children, their friends, their relatives, and their occupations—all that has made life dear to them—to enter that secret life where they are fully aware of the dangers that await them. There in that vast solitude they risk torture, imprisonment, and deportation. Their individual lives are unimportant before the greater life of France imprisoned today. They dream because they know that one day France will be free and will be their own land again. They think of the others, their comrades in arms. Here they are one, a great army united in the struggle....

They say goodbye to their wives wondering if they will let them go, asking themselves if their women will hold them back by the strong chains of their love. Almost invariably the women assent through their tears. "It is for France," say these brave women of France.

Notices are put up throughout Paris and in the suburban villages reminding the population that the city is under German military command. It counsels them to be prudent and intelligent. Prudence means coolness and self-possession. How can one be consistent in this virtue with the enemy at one's elbow?

There was the concierge walking on the narrow street that attaches itself to my street who found herself beside an Italian. *"Sale macaroni"* (Dirty Italian), she expostulated. The Italian pushed her, and she fell to the ground. A crowd gathered and with it the French police. The latter took her off to the police station of the quarter where she was subject only to a reprimand: "Remember we are at war. The enemy is in Paris. Be careful because the next time...." The next time she may be obliged to deal with the conquerors. The French guardians of the peace know their own people and all the tension and the fear, the provocation, bitterness, and resentfulness—all those sentiments that stir in their consciousness today. To the Italian not one word was said. He went free because he is one of the victors.

In the United States there is the cry of war. On Boston Common 500,000 of our people are shouting for America's entry into the war.

Russia has entered Esthonia[20] and Lithuania. Spain has sent a high Spanish decoration on to von Ribbentrop....

Today the German Command has assured the population in Paris of the normal functioning of gas, electricity, the subway, street cleaning, and food. There will be order under German authority.

The streets are still almost deserted except for the German soldiers who are stationed at almost every corner of the principal streets. The Germans wear green uniforms. Khaki uniforms are worn by the Belgian prisoners of war put to work on the camions.

A woman passed me today crying bitterly. A few moments ago she had left the Invalides where she had been a guardian for fifteen years. A section of the German Army is now in command there. She was found allowing French prisoners to escape from the cellars of the vast building where they had been placed and where they had no food for days. To see her own people starving, tortured at the hands of the Nazis, was too much for her to bear.

But this is war, Madame, a bitter, tragic and uncompromising war. The Nazis are not solicitous of your soldiers' hunger or of the suffering of their prisoners of war. They do not care for international treaties, particularly for the pact to which they gave their signature concerning the treatment of prisoners of war....

The Nazis are quite sure that the French will be cordial to them. I passed two young mademoiselles on the rue Royale this morning. Walking quite near them was a German soldier trying to attract their attention. The scorn on the faces of the girls as they turned to look at the soldier, taking him in from his heavy boots up to the green cap on top of his blond head, was enough to make him retreat and cease his pursuit while the mademoiselles were soon lost to sight.

What do these "privileged" beings of a so-called "super race"[21] expect? Their Führer has had them educated and trained according to his dream of the superiority of his people. He did not reckon on the French, however.

The French women refuse to sit next to a Nazi in the subway. They rise at once if one sits next to them. The Nazi officer and soldier in Paris today have been especially chosen for their training on conduct in the French capital. They open subway doors for women and old people; the women pass by, heads up, with never a word of acknowledgement. As a German in uniform comes toward them on the street, they at once turn and look in the opposite direction.

The Nazis are indeed courteous and "correct." A Nazi officer informed a French officer that he and his comrades were instructed before leaving Germany to show the utmost courtesy in Paris. The French officer replied, "When I was commanding my troops in 1918 in occupied Germany, such instructions for us were not necessary."

The German soldiers are simple, slow mentally, with little education. They often show kindness and politeness, and they mean well as a rule. They believe, as they have been taught, in the superiority of the German people. They have a fanatical faith in their Führer. Are they to be blamed? Are a few to be condemned with all Nazis? The winds of destiny have swept them from their simple firesides in isolated farms or perhaps some distant village of their native land into this dream of Paris. They are bewildered at rebuff and scorn.

And yet, I almost hear the words that I read some years ago written by one of their own people: "They will cheat you yet...they will crush you under their heel as conquerors...they will cringe and cry at your feet when conquered."[22]

We speak in whispers. All is secrecy or silent. Spies are everywhere. I have instructed my governess to inform me if the Nazis attempt to enter my apartment. I should not like to have a Dictaphone secreted in some corner of my salon or have my furniture molested in search of documents. As there are no documents or letters of any importance in my dwelling, the enemy's work would be futile. I am a citizen of the United States, and my country is not at war with Germany. But the country that I am living in is governed by a ruthless, tyrannical enemy. There is little that will stop them.

There is German music again over the radio. Hitler must have exacted the best, for the voices are utterly beautiful as well as the music. English folksongs and Scottish melodies are on the air as well, coming through Luxembourg. The announcers are British and German. French music is not heard at all.

A French soldier is now speaking on the radio. He is a prisoner of war and is saying how well-treated he is by his Nazi guards. He is saying that all France should rise up and protest against further bloodshed. As he speaks, his voice trembles. He continues with difficulty; it is obvious he does not believe what he is saying. Is there a Nazi gun nearby forcing him to go on? His words are not spontaneous, that is quite clear. Now there is a sob. I can bear no more and turn off the radio. I turn on the radio again, and this time a German voice is telling news of the political and international situation. But what can he tell me that I can believe and that I want so desperately to know?

United States Ambassador and Staff Away on Retreat

June 24, 1940

Tonight, as the warm sun sets, bathing the Invalides in the glow, from my balcony I look toward where the young French soldier held watch for the enemy before the enemy came. He has disappeared. The enemy came in. This young French sentinel had not kept his guard strong enough. The enemy is within his portals. I see France the beautiful, but there is suffering within your gates; there is humiliation and betrayal and defeat. You are torn and wounded. The blood of your brave men inundates your land. The enemy flies her victorious planes over your loveliness tonight. Despair haunts your quiet valleys, your streams, and fairy woods. Your cities and towns are invaded by a strange people. But I see you struggle to your feet. There is rapture in this cup of bitterness. "God…, the Compassionating, the Compassionate" is with you, with your high spirit that ever lives.[23]

The news? Everyone asks everyone else. It penetrates our waiting senses as with difficulty and only intermittently it reaches us: Berlin and Essen [Germany] bombarded. The peace terms are too severe and should not have been accepted. American citizens returning to Paris were bombarded on the highroads; they had tried to reach the Spanish border through days without food, days hunting for a place to sleep, barely escaping death, and being blown to pieces by falling bombs.

Candé in the Department of Indre-et-Loire,[24] where the United States Ambassador and his staff have gone temporarily, was about to be bombed by the Nazis but was saved by the discovery of one of the Germans in command that it was American property. The French government is still in Bordeaux. American journalists hover around the government buildings eager for comments.

Paris-soir reappeared tonight after *La Victoire* failed from lack of readers. The Germans are not very subtle. If they wish their controlled press to be a success with the French, they should see to it that it has a less German tinge. *Le Matin*, too, is Nazi-controlled. *Le Figaro*[25] has disappeared completely—it will have nothing of Nazi news disguised as French....

More shops are opening. More French are returning and more children, too, as the schools begin again.

The French government under Maréchal Pétain is administering the country's affairs from the city of Bordeaux. Maréchal Pétain is consulting with the Nazis. Is the hero of Verdun and a Marshall of France playing a double game? Is he fulfilling his mission by helping his people obtain better terms by using his great influence with the occupying power?

There is trouble in Biarritz where thousands of people are gathered waiting for permits to cross the border into Spain. They have little to eat. Many possessing great wealth are offering large sums to those who might be useful in helping them leave France. Luxurious automobiles are being given away or sold for 1,000, 2,000, or 4,000 francs° and little more in payment for the priceless documents that will permit them to cross the barrier to safety. The Jews are amongst the greatest number. (Many who did not succeed in escaping from Paris have been placed in concentration camps under conditions of untold privation; many have been sent to Poland.) Hitler's fierce hatred of this race has forced them to flee.

The Embassy Goes to Market for Food

June 27, 1940

Sleep has been fitful for many for the last two nights. I have been awakened by cries of distress that seemed to be coming from the Invalides. I gave the matter little attention at first because so many strange sights and sounds come to us in our confused state of nerves. Does the war impress me too feverishly? Am I becoming a victim of these tragic events like so many others? I waited to see, before enquiring, if my imagination was playing tricks on me. I waited for two nights. Again, last night came that rumbling sound of voices in pain. Today I spoke to a Frenchman in authority. The sounds were all too true, he informed me. The Nazis have placed their

---

° The exchange rate today is 45 francs to $1.00.

French war prisoners in the caves of the Invalides where they were being tortured. The French and International Red Cross are working on the matter. Eventually I heard no further cries of distress coming from the building.

The Embassy goes to market every day; the Diplomatic Corps receives food cards from the German authorities. Early each morning the section of the Embassy staff in charge of providing us with food for our needs drives to Les Halles,[26] the central markets of Paris. They fill their trucks with the necessary amount of food to keep our physical strength and our morale for the great amount of daily work there is to do. Our "market" is arranged in the basement of the Embassy building. We stand in line, as is the fashion now, and buy our food. It is amusing and a new phase of life in France at war.

It is 9:30 p.m. Time to go to bed. It is really 7:30 p.m. I have not been to bed at 7:30 p.m. since I was a child.

Madame de Ropp[27] dined with me tonight. She lives in the Champerret district of Paris. She told me that in the large apartment house she occupies she is the only *locataire* in the whole building. Even the concierge has flown. The big door at the entrance remains open day and night. My friend lives on the seventh floor with no elevator functioning. She has no fear, but I suggested that she speak to the police and have someone remain in the building or at least have a guard to watch it. The regulations concerning apartments are very strict: anyone found entering a vacant apartment to steal is punished with imprisonment. A lady returning from Angoulême, where she had gone in the exodus, found her apartment in Paris wide open; every piece of furniture had been taken....

My young concierge did not leave Paris to follow the refugees. This was due to the excellent counsel of my governess who, when she saw the girl climbing onto her bicycle the day the Germans entered Paris, asked her where she was going. The concierge replied that she was leaving, that she was too frightened to remain. Mademoiselle, my governess, told her not to leave as she would not be safer on the road with thousands of persons who were prevented from proceeding on their way from lack of gasoline, illness, starvation, and homelessness. The Nazis were bombing automobiles, women, and children. The girl was convinced and remained in Paris.

June 28, 1940

My pretty bag bought in Monte Carlo in 1935 to carry my bathing outfit is now being used to carry potatoes, butter, milk, eggs, and vegetables. In that time years ago, many years it seems, the search for amusement and good times was the high note in life. Times have changed indeed since I whiled away luxurious, leisurely vacations on the Riviera. Shall those times ever come back? Is another civilization about to be born? One wonders what form it will take....

Statues of famous French generals that have been placed in different parks and places throughout and around Paris are being taken from their pedestals by the Nazis. Some are removed, and some are blasted where they stand in military glory honored by the French. Are the Nazis afraid of that spirit of courage in the French, of that heritage of her great patriots and generals of the past? The statue of General Mangin[28] of the Great War placed in the Place Vauban[29] facing Napoléon's tomb is no more there. It has disappeared.°

Along my path when I leave my house in the morning, I see pasted on the wall of the Boulevard des Invalides the poster of a German soldier. He is smiling and holding a child in his arms. Around him are gathered children with their mothers, looking up at the soldier with confidence. Underneath is written *Population abandonée, avez confiance dans le soldat Allemand.* ("Abandoned population, have confidence in the German soldier.") Splendid propaganda! But shall it really lessen the hatred in the hearts of the French for the enemy? Shall they ever forget those little ones taken by force from their mothers by Nazi orders to German soldiers? Can the French forget the exodus and the sight of women and children machine-gunned to make way for the triumphant Nazis? Or those bombs falling from Nazi planes on people fleeing the oppression in other countries as well as their own?

Yet even the picture of a German soldier protecting a French child is a light of love in the blackness of Nazi cruelty....

Yesterday I had tea at the hospitable home of Mademoiselle Adrienne Monnier,[30] the well-known French writer, whose attitude is kind yet at the same time discerning and just. She said to me, "The Germans are hearing much from the different peoples whose countries they have invaded. After they have finished with their *naiveté* in thinking they are a superior race, they will see that France, Poland, Belgium, Austria, Holland, Czechoslovakia, England, and the United States have national instincts and feelings; and that these nationals, too, have a right to live in their own way."

The Germans are carrying on their good work of "courtesy" and of trying to be "correct." One tall, blond German officer, his face slashed by the time-honored effects of wars and duels, today opened the door for a French lady as she descended the step of the subway train. The Germans hope to be successful in their efforts to impress the French not only by their politeness but by kindness and helpfulness. Unfortunately for them, as news reaches the French of the tyrannical hand the Nazis use over their newly gained countries in Middle and Western Europe, confidence in any kindness quite naturally vanishes.

° As I passed the pedestal on which the statue had been placed, I saw written on it: *Ici s'élevait la statue du Général Mangin détruite par Hitler le 18 juin, 1940.* ("Here the statue of General Mangin was raised, destroyed by Hitler June 18, 1940.")

Having the Nazis in Paris is like having a person in one's home who has had an education of a lower order and who, in an effort to be like one and to act according to one's training, exaggerates every move.

June 30, 1940

Military music is heard coming from the Invalides. It is the salute being given to a high ranking French officer who has gone on his long journey. He has finished the war. I hear the *Réveille*.[31] The French are honoring a soldier of France....

The American Embassy Copes

July 4, 1940

This is our great day. Preparations were almost finished for our gala at a hotel on the rue du Faubourg Saint-Honoré where many guests are United States citizens. There are also many German guests there. The Management seemed to think that the feelings of the Nazis might be "hurt" should the United States Day of Independence be celebrated, and our party was therefore cancelled. The Management is right. Today we are the guests, not of France, but of the Nazis.

July 5, 1940

The Musée Rodin, which is in the château opposite my dwelling, is being aired and sunned. Pieces of sculpture of the great master are being cleaned for the reopening of the museum tomorrow.

Headlines in the press reveal our [U.S.] Ambassador has gone to Vichy where the French government will have its administration. The German press gave out that the Vichy Government with Maréchal Pétain as Prime Minister is the only French government now recognized by other countries.

De C. is an American citizen. He has recently arrived in Paris with a fellow citizen from Saint-Jean-de-Luz. He was stopped at a point on the border of France where the Nazis had decided to discontinue their triumphant march through France and which is the line of demarcation of the occupied zone. The occupied zone begins at the Swiss border going west to the Indre-et-Loire Department almost to Tours. It then takes its course straight down along the western border through Dordogne and Landes to the Basses-Pyrénées, touching the Spanish border.

De C. was informed by the German guard that he should not be allowed to proceed to Paris. He then appealed to the Kommandantur and explained that he and his friend were Americans. It was urgent for them to reach Paris as soon as possible and requested a *laissez-passer*.

"Oh, yes," said the officer in charge of the Kommandantur. "Your Ambassador hates us. He is paid by the French. That we know very well."

"That may be," replied de C. "That is not my affair. I should like to remind you, however, that my country is not at war with Germany."

He received the laissez-passer much against the will of the Nazi officer who did not even reply. Nor did he consent to shake hands with our Americans as they thanked him.

All Americans in Dinard in Brittany who own automobiles are ordered by the Germans to leave Brittany. The German authorities informed the inhabitants that a battle against England would shortly begin along the coast, and that if they remained, they would be in danger.

American women in France recently engaged in war work are proceeding to Lisbon[32] from where they will sail for America. There is little for them to do, or that they will be allowed to do by the occupying power. The sense of failure and of further difficulties for United States citizens are increasing. The last members of the Field Service are leaving as well. Times are becoming critical for us.

In Fontainebleau, about one and a half's day drive from Paris, two estates belonging to Americans but which are in the names of their French wives have been commandeered by the Germans. The family of one man with his guests and servants, about twenty-five persons, were obliged to leave late in the evening. They found sleeping quarters in the stables of the house the night the Germans moved into the main building of their home. They came to Paris the next day. Here fortunately the American had an apartment.

July 6, 1940

I am learning many things. I see many things that I might not have seen had life been different for me, things that in the past I have been oblivious of. Hovering around me always is a feeling of apprehension. It is above me and beneath me. I cannot explain it. I have had a relatively placid, ordered life for years. I take the details of daily conveniences quite naturally. If a window pane is broken in my apartment, I at once have a new one put in. If my carpet wears out, there is more in the shops. If my plumbing goes wrong, the plumber is just around the corner. Suddenly life has changed; war invades my heretofore harmonious existence, and I realize how much these details were part of the routine of the days. It was like the air I breathe, never thinking about air or about breathing it. They are always with me, and I expect them to be with me indefinitely. Today it is different, however. My arm chair needs mending, but there is no one to do the work. The basin in my bathroom leaks, but there is no plumber. I wish to move furniture to the cellar, but there is no one to call on. Those who did such work for me in the past have not returned from their flight and their fears. Mass mesmerism of fear has gripped them like a vise and sent them into the hell of the exodus.

The British have ordered planes and munitions from the United States and Canada. The shipment will be greater than any previous one. Britain is sure of its increasing strength and ability to go on to victory. Does Hitler know what lies before him? Did he know about that indomitable spirit of Britain when he decided to throw his forces against it?

There are times when the pent-up feelings of the inflammable French personality blaze into action or at other times into vituperation. Turning the corner of the rue de Constantine leading into the rue de Grenelle at the angle of the Boulevard des Invalides, I heard a woman's voice shrieking invectives against the Germans. Her own people, too, came in for some of it: *pourriture* (rottenness), *canaille* (scoundrels), *crétins* (idiots) she called out against persons, anyone, people in general. A policeman called to her, "*Taisez vous* (keep quiet). You are making straight for prison." She went on, however, until the menacing arm of the law touched hers. She then realized that the situation had become *serieux* for her and moved slowly away. And who could blame her completely—certainly not the young *agent de police* who doubtless felt as she did, but being disciplined and with more control, refrained from voicing his sentiments.

We are all a confraternity. Each one is a part of the happenings involving the others. We are all of one mind; nothing is thought by one, but another somewhere, sometime catches the same strain.

The French policeman raised his shoulders as he was in all respects a true Frenchman. He turned to greet a colleague who came towards him to replace him on duty. "*Eh bien, mon vieux,*" he said mockingly as the other left. "*Il faut te coucher ce soir à dix heures.*" (Well, old man. You must go to bed tonight at ten o'clock.)

July 7, 1940

Tonight, the hour for the curfew will be at eleven o'clock.

Our purses and budgets are benefiting during these days, for we are not buying any new clothes. The French are dressing very simply, and we Americans are too busy to go about to parties and galas, too tired in fact at night. One has not the heart for much dressing and festivities. The wives and families of the Nazi chiefs are doing all that. They go to Maggy Rouff[33] and the few other big dressmaking houses that have remained open. During September and October of 1939, when most of the shops were open, there was a military note in the fashions. A dress had *épaulettes* on the shoulders and a hat suggested a helmet. Now there is no particular note, and few women are wearing hats. I long for a uniform and hinted at the idea to one of the chiefs of the Embassy. "What a lot of trouble I should have if I did not order the right color and material, something that would suit everyone," he retorted. "All the women of the staff would be at me with guns. I shall let well enough alone."

A group of German soldiers are passing. They are singing and trying to express Hitler's "strength through joy" program. Every day they walk quickly and in groups through the city. One can hear them at a distance early in the morning or in the afternoon. Their voices are well-trained, and they sing in perfect rhythm. But there is no melody, indeed no joy in their voices or on their solemn, expressionless faces. If they wish joy to enter into one's consciousness, they must be free in thought....

France is to become part of a totalitarian State—so Hitler announces. Is Maréchal Pétain to be named the *Gauleiter?*

Thumbs down for the British. The French are up in arms against them, or at least that is what the Nazi controlled press is giving out. The Nazis have made much of the British–French naval battle at Oran and Mers-el-Kébir[34] in North Africa last Wednesday. The British blasted the ships of the French Navy who had opened fire, and who had refused to surrender. The Nazis had posters put up throughout Paris concerning the event. One pasted on the walls of the Chambre des Députés had written on it: "Remember, and never forget, Mers-el-Kébir." The Nazis are doing everything in their power to create friction between the French and British. Every tactic is used to separate them. They know so well of that unity wherein there is strength. Other posters show cartoons of Mr. Churchill as an ogre trying to hold France within the grasp of England, and England as the real great "enemy" of France....

Today I went to church. The lesson was quite appropriate: "Love your enemies." As I listened, I thought perhaps it might be better to send thoughts of kindness to those green uniformed Nazi soldiers as I pass them instead of thoughts of bitterness and resentment. How can life be truly lived unless love destroys all semblance of hate?

July 8, 1940

A letter reached me today from America. It was dated May 26. There are few post offices functioning today in northern France to distribute letters coming in on transatlantic boats arriving at Le Havre and Cherbourg. In the south near the Pyrénées, someone I know is frantically waiting for a letter from me giving news of a relative in the United States; in Spain, Helene is worried about her daughter and awaits a letter from me telling her all is well. The bombed bridges do not help, and the train routes are barred. Some persons carry letters secreted on their clothes or in a hidden place in a valise as they cross the line of demarcation between the zones. The Germans search every passenger for written material very carefully.

There is very little gasoline to be had for private owners of automobiles. Americans, doing everything to leave, are prevented from doing so by lack of gasoline and oil. This adds to their difficulties. For if America comes into the war, it means concentration camps for those who have been unable to leave the country.

There is no place in Europe today for the self-centered and weak. It is only for those who have a mind to work and to help. It is for those who have courage and who can stand hardship in any form. And they are needed; they are greatly needed.

Incidents in these troubled times occur every day. Around the corner from my house there is a beautiful eighteenth-century house belonging to a rich Jew and his family. As I passed it today, I found written on the main door: *Mort aux Juifs* (Death to the Jews).

Orders come from the Germans that anyone who has a safe deposit box in any bank must open it in front of a German officer or soldier who will be on guard.

Thousands of American pilots are volunteering in the Canadian Army with rumours growing that the United States will soon be in the war.

The British Royal Air Force threatens to bomb Nazi troops if the Nazis carry out their intention to parade along the Champs-Élysées on July 14, the French national holiday. And why not? Do the Nazis think they are powerful enough with their material machines, however numerous they may be, to crush every vestige of feeling with the French, particularly their love of country, their patriotism? The 14th of July is France. Can machine guns submerge the spirit?

The Germans have their parade every day. Down the Champs-Élysées they march from the Triumphal Arch where they assemble precisely at midday; this they have done since the day after they entered Paris. The troops are headed by an officer on a beautiful white horse that keeps perfect time with the music of the military band, and that is the admiration of the populace—the horse, not the officer.

July 9, 1940

The American Export Lines[35] office is running boats from Lisbon to New York every week, thus enabling many Americans and refugees to leave Portugal where some have been waiting for months to leave for the United States.

The sun is warm over my balcony, and my flowers are a riot of color. The red begonias resemble Christmas bells about to ring out like carillons in some belfry. The petunias are like ballet dancers with their skirts spread out, and the geraniums look dressed for a gala. I like the white petunias best, so frail they are. Their yellow faces are enshrined in large white hats that flap in the summer breeze hiding their eyes. The large green leaves of the golden and red nasturtiums lean far over the balcony boxes....

I turn from my balcony and my flowers and hear over the radio that 60,000 French prisoners of war are somewhere in France in relative misery. They have little to eat, and at night they have straw to sleep on.

Mr. A. told me today that in his home in the country where Nazi soldiers are billeted,[36] beautiful objets d'art have been mutilated; silk curtains have been stained with black shoe polish, and priceless rugs torn and destroyed. Is this all done deliberately, or are some soldiers totally devoid of any sense of beauty and of the work of men's hands, delicate workmanship, and symmetry that does so much to ennoble life?

French Employee of the American Embassy Is Questioned

July 10, 1940

Further Nazi regulations:

For a German officer killed in Paris, fifty French will pay with their lives.

For a German captain, twenty Frenchmen will die.

For a German soldier, fifteen Frenchmen will be shot.

For a member of the Gestapo,[37] thirty policemen will pay the penalty of death.

Such are the orders under Nazi rule that are appearing in the press.

Efforts of the Nazis to have a dictatorship rule in the Chambre and in the Senate are being made.[38] Maréchal Pétain is to be the Dictator. He is at present the French Chief of State.

Looking up from her desk in the Embassy, a young French employee was surprised to see a plainclothes man seated in front of her. She wondered what business he might have in the Embassy....

"Madame," he began. "You are for or against the present regime in France?"

"Monsieur," she replied. "I am a French citizen. Beyond that there is nothing further to say." Could any diplomat trained in the tactics of his profession have answered with keener discernment?

Paris has always been a "holiday" to me, even in work, as it has been for many millions through the centuries. It has become my daily life. The Nazis, too, are making it a holiday for themselves. The heavy clod of German boots instead of the light tread of the French are heard, and they bring with them an atmosphere of "that curious dread of life which steals through the twilight."[39] They are gay at times and their voices ring out in triumph. Last night in one of the night clubs they drank too much champagne.

"Yesterday," shouted one, "Holland, then Belgium, today France, soon England, tomorrow the world; the world will be ours!"

Have they forgotten that somewhere in the United States of America there are sentinels waiting and watching? The tired old American woman, waiting in line for hours on the Spanish border for her permit to enter Spain, believes in those sentinels....

"I want to go into Spain at once," she shouted to her lawyer near her. "What is the matter with the United States government that it cannot stop all this? Why should America be afraid of Spain or Germany or any country?" Why indeed?

Mico, whom I met on the Boulevard de la Madeleine, almost pushed me into the Café Viel[40] for an apéritif and a talk. Mico is an attractive young Guatemalan and heir to an old Spanish title that he refuses to use. He is also the nephew of a native-born citizen of the United States who has been a friend of mine for many years. Mico has not been in Paris for many months. We talked of life in the city before the great *débâcle*[41]—how wonderful it was then, how we dreamed of the future, and how we were suddenly pushed into the feverish present.

In front of us on the terrace of the café were German officers clicking their heels and giving the Nazi salute to each other every second. They were big and blond. Emerging from their personalities is always that air of *moi, c'est moi* (I, it is I) and "we are conquering the world." But it is like a big bubble surrounding them. I thought how easily bubbles burst....

Mico had recently left his country home some distance from Paris. The German soldiers who had seen action in war are billeted near his house. They had been sent there to recuperate for further duty. "The French soldier is lucky," one said to Mico. "For him it is over. Not for us, however; we must keep on and on. To what? Where is it leading us?" He turned away with a gesture of despair.

Mico was awakened one night by the tramp of soldiers' feet. When he opened his gate, he found four Germans carrying the body of a comrade who had been found dead near the railroad track. They asked the direction to the nearest cemetery. They were directed first to the Commissariat where they were informed that they should get in touch with the Kommandantur in the next village. "*Un de plus disparu—un de moins,*" (One more gone—one less) said the French guard, happily in an undertone and not understood by the Germans. Incidents of dead Germans occur every night in Paris and in the country. They recall the orders given in Holland by Dutch secret organizations and the underground whereby a different Hollander is sent on duty each night to find a German officer or soldier and, after killing him, to throw his body into the canal. Flaming passions boil over in the fiery tempest of war; the "conquerors of the world" must pay.

The Germans are giving gasoline to those on the road, the refugees who are unable to proceed without it. They are helping the old and the infirm who are too feeble to walk, taking them in their cars to their destination. We are indeed a confraternity, bound together in love however violent is the work of evil....

In England the words "if we win" are forbidden. "When we win" is the order. That is England with that great, unconquerable spirit that is hers.

In a French paper this evening one headline states that "this is a French newspaper, published and edited by the French." Opposite, another headline reads that German women and children in French concentration camps are being brutally treated by the French. It takes a wide stretch of the imagination to believe that the paper is wholly French if they accuse their own people of brutality....

July 12, 1940

People on the roads in the exodus are dying from filth and malnutrition. It took my Guatemalan friend four days to come from Rennes to Paris by car. It took me four hours by train returning from Dinard and changing at Rennes. En route he said women, carrying the bodies of relatives who had passed on from fear and starvation, were searching for a place for burial.

Passing the French prisoners of war in their enclosure, too small to hold so many, the prisoners called out to Mico for bread: "Bread, bring us bread." He gave them the little he had and went on his way bewildered, beaten down by the immensity of human suffering.

The Nazis insolently say they will parade on July 14.[42] They have ordered the schools to see to it that all the children will be on the Champs-Élysées to witness it.

The days are epoch making. But this phase of life of not knowing what is going on outside the country is difficult indeed. Perhaps one of the secrets of German success so far is their ability to keep their plan of action and projects in the dark.

The bells in the tower of the church opposite my habitation have tolled ten o'clock. The clock in that château, the *Musée Rodin*, had kept its former French time for some days, but when threatened by the German order that any clock in Paris not showing German time would be taken down, they changed the clock according to the command. The confusion throughout occupied France concerning the time of day is immense. In one city the trains are scheduled on the French hour (one hour later than the German hour); church bells ring on German time. The mayor of one town decided to return to French time, but his idea did not reach all the inhabitants of his village at the same time; thus, the postman, the milkman, church bells, trains, and schools start and end at different times!

The safe deposit boxes in the different banks have been opened following the German order; the Germans took pieces of gold and unmounted precious stones. They left any other articles in the boxes.

July 13, 1940

German music is heard this morning. It is German military music coming from the Invalides. "*Deutschland über Alles*,"[43] the German national anthem, is being played as I listen, solemnly and beautifully. The German bands are located in different parks throughout Paris. Today the concerts are being given to celebrate the French national holiday tomorrow. They make little impression on the French, however, who close their ears to this music of the Nazis; they hear instead machine guns killing their women and children as they travel over roads filled with escaping refugees....

Rumours of the orderly entry of German troops into Paris are reaching the French who have left. They are learning that no one has been killed in the capital, that the shops are opening, that food can be had although in limited quantities, and that their homes await them. Those who still live are returning to their habitations. The Germans are lending their aid; if the roads are not cleared, there will be epidemics of diseases. There is the stench of filth, even of dead bodies. When found, these dead bodies are buried at once. Many persons hold on to the remains of relatives until the Germans force them to surrender their dead for burial.

England is worrying the Nazis very much these days by bombing German towns. The German people wonder why Göring, Chief of the German Air Force, cannot do something about it.

American and French war relief workers are concentrating on help for French prisoners of war. American doctors, nurses, and the Red Cross are united in doing splendid work for the wounded.

The Deux Magots,[44] the well-known café on the Left Bank where painters, artists and writers of all nations have gathered day and night throughout the centuries, has been closed to the Germans by an order of the German authorities. This café has been the center for the intellectuals, where freedom of thought and the expression of liberal ideas have been and are debated and studied and put forth. The Nazis fear, perhaps, that there might be incidents in this time-honored café. Freedom of thought and the expression of liberal ideas are not looked upon favorably in Nazi Germany and Hitler's army....

Today a German officer, not knowing the recent ruling, entered the café and asked for some beer. It was refused by the waiter. The officer called the manager who shook his head. My friend who related the incident did not speak of the probable desolation of the young German. No doubt the officer felt deeply that the familiar meeting ground of student days, of happier times in Paris, was closed to him.

The women of the Gestapo are arriving in Paris. Their bearing is as arrogant as their men. They watch and listen and denounce. So far, however, the French often speak relatively freely with no untoward consequences. Can this last? If the French become too critical and outspoken regarding the Occupation and occupying authorities, they may meet with unfortunate consequences.

July 14, 1940

There is silence in the Capital today on the great national holiday, Bastille Day, as it is sometimes called. The Germans did not parade on the Champs-Élysées, and there was no dancing in the streets. The leaflets thrown from German planes two months ago bearing the words *Petites Parisiennes, nous danserons avec vous the 14 juillet* (Little Paris ladies, we shall dance with you on July 14) have no meaning.

The British were successful in preventing the parade. Today the swastika flies over the Eiffel Tower, the Chambre des Députés, the Ministry of Marine, and other French government buildings. It waves triumphantly in the July wind. But there is no celebration. Paris on her national holiday is silent.

The rent for my apartment will be due tomorrow for the third trimester. The manager of my building left Paris with the other thousands of refugees. There is no one to give the money to. The concierge wrote to the head office of the company for instructions, but the administrators, too, were wandering somewhere in France. All delays in the payment of the rent for apartments are in order. A manager of one apartment wrote that the majority of apartments in Paris are without janitors. Many tenants are without work and are unable to pay the rent at all. Employees of the big apartment houses have not returned from the country places where they fled to their friends' homes. Another manager replied to a tenant who had written to him concerning the matter, by writing the word "paid" on the bill. All is fair in war it seems. However, in many cases there has been a moratorium, and the settlements will be taken care of after the war.

There are no laundresses and I need clean sheets. The laundresses, too, are on the road. Mademoiselle helped out in this, washing and ironing the sheets as well as possible in my small apartment. Luckily, I have some soap.

Embassy Certifies American Interests

At the Harrison Dulles Apartment at 40 Avenue Foch, I pasted a notice on the door indicating that it is the property of an American citizen. The Nazis are commandeering many beautiful apartments in and around Paris, particularly in the sixteenth district where a number of wealthy persons live. The concierge of 40 Avenue Foch told me that the Germans had already been to the house, but when they were informed of the citizenship of the owner of the Dulles Apartment, they did not go up. The notices on the doors of our citizens are written in French, German, and English; they are issued by the Embassy, signed by the secretary in charge of American interests, and bear the red seal of our government.[45]

In the country the Germans do not always take the trouble to confirm the nationality or proprietors of homes and estates. Mr. X. came to my office today in distress. The Nazis had entered his house in the Seine-et-Marne Department while he was absent and appropriated 25,000 francs worth of livestock and used his furniture that is practically all destroyed. He told me he would relate the illegal actions of the Nazis when he returned this week to America. He felt that liberty and personal freedom are being lost under their rule which might reach our country, and that, to his mind, death is preferable. He is not the only American who has this thought. However, Nazi rule shall not reach America, he may be sure.

German wounded soldiers are being brought to Paris. They are taken care of at the Hôpital de la Pitié.[46] Their morale seems very low indeed. A nurse at the hospital told me one man was weeping. When she asked him if he was suffering very much, he replied that he was not, but he had just heard that his wife and child had been killed by the British bombing. The British in an effort to destroy munitions factories in Germany had unavoidably let fall a bomb on the small house quite near a factory. This is unfortunate for the Nazis. Battles cannot be won, nor countries conquered, by the falling morale of an army.

Tonight, the greatest man in Europe is on the radio. Mr. Churchill spoke over the BBC. He, with his indomitable courage, warned that the war would go on through 1941–1942; that if the Nazis think it will be over before that time, they are deceiving themselves and trying to deceive the world. The war will go on until the Nazis are defeated.

July 16, 1940

Turning to the French broadcast that is, of course, controlled by the Germans, I hear in French that it was a mistake for the French to welcome so many Jews in France for so many years; that they are all spies, and that the Nazis had been using them as spies in this country for many years.

In the subway tonight members of a Nazi musical band entered. They were young men. It seemed inconceivable that back of the frank, simple, smiling exterior, the spirit of Nazi principles of inhumanity and brutality should be impregnated. With his back turned to the young Germans was a man, perhaps fifty years of age, a Jew, with his head bowed. Was it sorrow and pain that had touched him? Was it because he feared that if he turned and looked up he would have insults and mockery thrown at him? The Nazis do not hesitate to humiliate and abjure the Jew in public.

July 17, 1940

At times one feels old, very old. Within a few months, years seem to have gone by. Shall one's youth, the carefree feeling of youth, no matter what is the age, ever return? It was not so long ago, however, when France was gay, spontaneous, and enthusiastic. Is it all ended? Today there is no spontaneity in her spirit. She has faced disaster and defeat....

It is 1:00 a.m. Sleep leaves me. I live over in my mind the tragic tale I heard yesterday, an incident that took place in one of the French prison camps. It was nearing the time for lunch. Red wine so much enjoyed by the French is waiting in barrels together with hundreds of loaves of bread banked along the side of the camp. A Nazi guard, an officer, irritated by the sight of it and with little control over his unfortunate character, turned the barrels over, letting the wine flow on the ground. He then picked up the bread and threw a number of loaves at the heads of the prisoners. Investigation brought a denial of the incident by the officer. His subordinate, a young German soldier, in whose soul burned a sense of justice that was stronger than any Nazi training or military discipline, shouted, "He lies! I saw him do it!" Drawing his gun, the officer shot the soldier through the heart. The officer was hanged immediately.

"Cowardice and cruelty," writes Romain Rolland, "amongst mankind do not prevent me from loving humanity. I know the power of the spirit. I see from history how its lightening flashed on blacker skies than cloud the heavens today."[47]

Strained Relations

July 18, 1940

The policeman who is on duty watching the food line in my shopping district—to see that the rules are obeyed—said to me as I stopped a moment near a long line waiting to buy milk, "C'est curieux (it is curious) that today women prefer being old. There was a time not long ago when no lady would admit to being older than perhaps 50; certainly not to 70." I was a bit puzzled then remembered that because of the scarcity of milk, only children and old people over sixty-five years may purchase it. The policeman is a very observing young man.

Today a much painted French woman with bright, too bright, gold hair left her apartment on the other wing of my apartment house. She had been living here since 1939. A French naturalized citizen of German origin and, as it was told to me, one of the well-paid spies who received many persons in her hospitable dwelling. She deemed it wiser, however, to leave France precipitately, which she did today crossing the frontier into Spain. Had she worked for her country of origin or for her adopted country, or both?

George Douglas was a Scotsman before he became an American citizen. For years he has been known and liked by members of the Embassy staff. He has amused us by his tales, which were told with a strong Scottish accent. He is a brave type (a good soul), and besides he sells us excellent products such as jam, biscuits, and *porto*. George lost an eye in an accident and now has a black patch over one eyelid. He came in to see me today and told me that while he was placing his products in a truck, a Nazi officer stopped him and told him that he wanted all his food; that if he, George, would go to the Kommandantur, he would be paid. The officer in charge of the Kommandantur paid him at once but gave him German marks. When George protested saying that he wanted to be paid with French francs, the officer replied in English, "So you are one of those impudent Americans, aren't you? You will take what I give you and nothing else." Well, we are not at war with Germany, not yet. Shall we be soon?

The Germans are becoming nervous as the RAF continues letting bombs fall on their cities. The French are experiencing it, too. Le Bourget,[48] the French airport taken over by the German military authorities, was badly bombed by the British yesterday. There was not a word of complaint from the French. There is a growing faith in the British amongst them. The French feel that the British are their friends, fighting for them. All Hitler's and Goebbels' propaganda in an effort to separate the British and French is unsuccessful. Even the announcement that "the British will fight to the last Frenchman" has fallen on ears that will not hear.

Some of the new laws in occupied France are very German: only a Frenchman born of a French father may hold a position in the government. Wives of officials and employees of the government may not hold positions. Women must remain home and have children. Everyone is to be put to work. Those who leave their work or their business for no adequate reason shall not be permitted to return.

"You are an intelligent and courageous woman," a Nazi officer said to Madame X., a French friend of mine who is working in refugee and Red Cross organizations, "but in Germany we have no use for intelligent and courageous women!"

These are some of the ideas of the "new Europe" that are being born according to the projects of Nazi Germany, propounded by them with an irrepressible air of domination accentuated by the blinding dazzlement of victory. Hitler no doubt on "his lonely peaks of power" is thinking it all out and planning it.[49] Carrying out his projects is quite another matter....

July 19, 1940

"This struggle," said the Führer in his speech over the radio "will result in the annihilation of either Germany or England."[50] Does he think for a moment that it would be England?

The [U.S.] President is elected the Democratic Party nominee for the Presidency at the Democratic Party Convention in Chicago.[51]

"To make America strong," announced the chairman, "every American must give of his talents and treasure in accordance with his ability and his country's needs. We must have democracy of sacrifice as well as democracy of opportunity."

There are hours of waiting for exit permits along with hours of standing in line at the different points on the line of demarcation separating occupied France from the unoccupied region. When the old cannot stand the strain, when they faint from exhaustion, they are carried away to be replaced by others who may or may not succumb in the same way. Others who have waited all day are often told to return the next day, and the waiting begins again....

July 24, 1940

British broadcast informed its listeners last night that eighty German planes attempted to land in England. German troops are nearing the British coast. German pilots protest when ordered to face the Royal Air Force. Is certainty of victory merging into fear? Hitler seems sure enough. In his victory over France speech, he said Providence has been with "all of us" and will continue to be. So all must be well with him, with his machine, and with his military tactics.

Germany has made a peace offer to Great Britain, which was refused. British children are being shipped to Canada and the United States. Old people in England are being sent far into the countryside. England is alert and every British subject is prepared for defense.

America is preparing to send thousands of troops to England.

The rain falls in torrents. It rages over the gardens opposite my home and tears through my balcony of flowers. Are the elements and the chaotic thoughts of the masses of people related in some way? Does the violence of war, of destruction, of fear and despair bring storms, winds, and deluges on our planet?

The new regulations in occupied France require a German exit permit to everyone leaving the country. The confusion is immense. The French authorities had not informed their representatives on the frontiers in time, and at Hendaye[52] at the

American Asks for Help with Imprisoned British Husband

August 8, 1940

All British subjects are being placed in the French prison of Fresnes;[56] men past sixty-five are taken as well as those of fifteen years of age. They are tried after an investigation concerning their sentiments and activities against the Nazis. The majority of British women in Paris are being placed in concentration camps in different small cities in France. One man, the elderly husband of an American citizen, was ill and weak in bed when the police came for him. He was forced to leave at once with time only to put a pair of trousers over his pajamas and to put on a coat and bedroom slippers. His wife said that, as a writer, he had written for years against the Nazis and the Hitler regime. She does not hope that he will survive the rigors of the prison. She has no money and comes to the Embassy to get in touch with her people in the United States to find some help.

The Nazis attacked Britain's airfields and air fighter production sites.

Word has reached Paris that a German general has committed suicide. Not every German is happy under the regime of the supermen. I have no doubt that when the story of World War II is written, the truth of Germany's real patriots will be known, those who knew that the Führer was leading their country to certain destruction.

Perusing the *Failure of a Mission* by Sir Nevile Henderson,[57] British ambassador in Berlin during the fateful days of Munich, I stopped at his graphic description[58] of the memorable night of March 11, 1938, when the Germans entered Austria. The scene was like a drama of the theater. There was the large reception given by Göring at Haus der Flieger,[59] to be followed by the performance of a ballet of the State Opera Company. The British ambassador arrived at the reception that was supercharged with dynamic tenseness. At ten o'clock Field Marshal Göring had not yet come, being detained by an unexpected meeting of the Cabinet with Herr Hitler. Every one of the 2,000 guests was discussing the Schuschnigg[60] and Seyss-Inquart[61] radio messages. The orchestra tuned their instruments in this environment, heavy with impending catastrophe. The secretary of the British Embassy rushed into the large hall with a telegram for the British ambassador with every eye on His Excellency as he read the message. Field Marshal Göring entered the hall as the ballet began.

"Every diplomatist and a great number of the Germans themselves," Sir Nevile writes, "were conscious of the tragedy of music and dance, at a moment when all that had been left in 1919 of the old Austrian and Hapsburg Empire[62] was crashing to final extinction."

As the British ambassador shook hands coldly with Göring, the latter a moment later tore a sheet from a program and writing on it: "As soon as the music is over, I should like to talk to you, and will explain everything to you," and handed it to me across the American Ambassador's wife.

Sir Nevile goes on to say that in that explanation "the only point that mattered was that German troops and airplanes were already crossing the [Austrian] frontier" while the music was playing to a German ballet.

Tragic moments they were for Austria. They were dazed and apprehensive, not only concerning the events of two years ago, but what of the future? What would that future hold for them after the German coup d'état? Austria in 1938—France today—1940.

I have gone back two years, lost in Sir Nevile's book. Today in Paris at the Hôtel Lutetia[63] the Gestapo has its offices. At the Hôtel Majestic there is another German administration. The building at 72 Avenue Foch houses the Gestapo headquarters. Another section occupies the Hôtel Meurice,[64] another the Hôtel Matignon.[65] The Austrian cannons of 1870 have been removed from the Hôtel des Invalides.[66]

The French, who feel crushed, defeated, vanquished by an organized military nation, go through the days strong of spirit. They know that the night is black but that another day will dawn for them. Their spiritual superiority penetrates the crisis. They know that in their country's history they have passed through times more bitter than that which holds them prisoners today; they know that the last card has not been played. They hope on. The French genius lives on. One sees it in the faces of agents de police on duty and in the eyes of the military police watching the expressions of those who pass him. In their trained perception and keen insight, with their flair for searching and finding activities of the enemy, nothing escapes them. Nothing must escape them in their immediate vicinity. These are dangerous days....

Yes, one speaks in whispers. I speak in whispers when I give orders to my governess and when she gives me the news that filters in from the outside world by way of the marketplace where those in the food line listen. News is heard in the parks where women take their knitting as they listen and speak in whispers, if they speak at all, while children play during these summer days. News comes again from the concierges who obtain information from unknown sources, which is sometimes very valuable for the French.

A second peace offer has been made by Germany to the British. The British have refused it. What kind of a "peace offer" are the Nazis capable of making that the British Commonwealth would accept?

In France sixteen English girls have been arrested and placed in concentration camps. Other British subjects, men between twenty years of age and sixty, are also arrested.

At the German battlefront thirty German soldiers are shot for refusing to obey orders and remain at their posts.

In Paris and northern France, the remaining refugees slowly are making their way back to their homes. They tell of help from young German soldiers en route. They speak of the enemy to their country with gratitude; the maimed, the injured, and the weak are taken by the Germans in their cars to their destinations; their wounds are bound by the medicine and the hands of the enemy. If we look close enough, deep enough, we find the good that exists in every human being. It shows itself in crises of human suffering. Today the help comes from the enemy, as well as the French, who is experiencing the torment in their own lives. They hear of the deaths of their own people in the daily and nightly bombardment of their cities. They, too, hope that their people may have a hand stretched out to them in love, that their pain may be softened by the kindness of another.

August 10, 1940

Inspiration escapes me. I try to find it, that mysterious, illusive, vitally important something termed "inspiration." I stretch out my whole being in an effort to seize it, but it alludes me. For the fraction of a second I feel its breath as it brushes past; again it slips from my consciousness, a *vision fugitif* (fleeting vision).

A great writer of France once said that when inspiration has fled from him, he stops all work and thought; he listens to a Beethoven symphony; he then returns to his writing with renewed force.

I discontinue my efforts. I take a long pause, a repose. Beethoven is out of the question today; there are no orchestras in Paris.

Inspiration may have come as I crossed the Rond-Point[67] des Champs-Élysées and followed the spacious Avenue as night was beginning to fall; it may have touched me with its magic wand as I entered the Place Clémenceau and looked up at the face of the "Tiger."[°] The great man[68] seemed alive at that moment with the élan of his whole body toward the *Étoile*. There he stands in uniform as though watching over his beloved country of France. Would that he were here today! And yet today's problems are not his. No doubt he is following greater missions than were his when he made his voice so grandly heard in those other tumultuous days in France. Today is another epoch: other resolutions face a world of uncertainty. I left *Monsieur le Premier ministre* to his dreams and went on my way.

The new moon was flooding the river as I turned to the bridge. The night was beginning to be dotted with the oncoming stars, and the blue heavens were darkening.

Qu'il était bleu, le ciel, et grand, l'espoir![69]
("It was blue, the sky, and great, hope!")

Verlaine's lines come to me in hope. Yes, in hope. I close my eyes a moment and hear the rumours of peace. Peace, it is being said, will be signed by August 25th: all the occupied part of France is to be kept by Germany; all Jews are to leave France; no money will be demanded of the French. Ah, no–there is no hope here....

Italian planes are flying high over the city.

[°] Georges Clémenceau. Statesman, Prime Minister of France, Minister of War, hero of the Great War when he negotiated the surrender of Germany.

German soldiers are tramping the streets of Paris. They march, march, always they march. One sees them in the Bois de Boulogne,[70] on the Grands Boulevards,[71] on the bridges and the Esplanade of the Invalides, on the Place de la Concorde....

At dinner last night I was the guest of Peggy de Nemours[72] and her husband in Le Cabaret,[73] the restaurant on the Avenue Victor-Emmanuel III.[74] There were a number of German officers and a few French civilians. Peggy and I were the only Americans. The Duke of Nemours is a nephew of the late King Albert of Belgium and a cousin of the present king.° The Duke and Duchess have recently returned from Brussels and were told that in reply to General Weygand's question why his Majesty's armies ceded to Germany, the King's answer was, "I was told there was a French Army; there is no French Army. I am a king before I am a soldier...I cannot continue."[75]

All over Paris the food lines are long. The waiting lasts for hours in an effort to obtain the simple substances for daily living. Some go away only to return and stand for longer hours, as the line grows longer.

"There is not enough food," declares a Frenchwoman along the line. "I think we should have more."

The laughter of the Nazi guard is heard. "You would get more if you deserved more," he replies. Who can tell who is or who is not deserving? The Nazis are presumptuous. One wonders how so, or they, too, shall be standing in line waiting for food.

My friend (nationality not given) was asked by a German officer to be his guest at dinner. "You are very courteous," said the lady, "but I should not be able to be with you or to be seen with you in uniform." He assured her that if she would give him the pleasure of being with him, he promised not to cause her any embarrassment. The lady chose the restaurant Chez Francis on the Place de l'Alma overlooking the Seine. When she arrived, there was no German in uniform. Her host could not be found. Instead, an attractive man in civilian clothes greeted her. It was the German officer who had bought a complete civilian outfit, wearing it instead of the uniform, so as "not to cause her any embarrassment."

The Spanish frontier is closed. No mail may pass. Fortunately, our diplomatic couriers have free passage which means that we may contact our people by letter at home.

Last night British bombs fell on a German military section near Pontoise, very near Paris.

These "raging contemporary times,"[76] this "turbulent Germany that gives us all no rest." Where are they leading us? Where are they leading Germany? Shall they lead the latter to revolution, or is this wishful thinking? A wounded German soldier holding a paper in his trembling hand shook it at his trained nurse in one

---

° King Léopold III.

of the hospitals and cried in broken French "*Berlin est comme ça*" (Berlin is like this). Does he doubt the invincibility of his country? Is Berlin trembling to its fall? The war is not going so well for them. Rumours of anarchy come over the British broadcast. Attempts to fly German planes over England yesterday ended in disaster for the Luftwaffe. The Royal Air Force is making superhuman efforts. If starvation faces the French, it is equally true of Germany, as the bombing of the German cities continues.

As a change from the German scene, I took up my book *Stalin: Czar of All the Russias* by Eugene Lyons.[77] It is interesting to try to find the secret of Stalin's amazing power, and I read Lyons' version on the subject with interest. What effect shall that power have on the world after the war? The author states, in substance, Stalin knew that he could not compete with the scintillating minds of the fathers of the revolution, such minds as that of Lenin, Trotsky, and Radek.[78] Stalin was on a lower level than these minds mentally and morally. He "must wait for the inevitable day when the whole revolution would sag down to that level."[79] As I read, it seemed that the German picture was child's play compared with the Russia of Lyons' thought. Or is it that with the author's "superb sense of drama," he has made today's tempestuous events in Russia seem more vital and realistic than the present perilous days in Europe? One lives these events in Moscow, Leningrad,[80] and in the isolated outposts of the Siberian desert[81] with the author.

I left Russia as a squadron of German soldiers rushed past under my balcony. With their noisy presence I was awakened from the horrors of Stalin's Russia that had entranced me. I returned to Paris.

The German soldiers look tired and worn out with the war. For them it has gone on for three years. Many of them have not seen their families. Their "leaves" are being spent in camps. No doubt there is the fear in the minds of the Nazi chiefs that should the soldiers go back to their country and to their people, they would not want to return to their posts. Force, threats, and punishment do not make good soldiers....

Americans speaking English on the street were taken to the nearest commissariat for questioning. They were allowed to leave, however, after they had produced satisfactory proof that they were citizens of the United States and not British subjects. Some of our compatriots did not have their identity cards with them and were kept by the police for hours.

At night while French, Americans, and other non-belligerent nationals are obliged to return to their homes by 11:00 o'clock, which is the beginning of the blackout, the Nazis are commencing their gay times. Cafés are open and, if other than Germans are seen on the streets or in the cafés, a member of the Gestapo fires blank cartridges at them to fill them with fear. Fear, always fear! It is fear they are counting on. They have been counting on fear for twenty years to climb the now tottering ladder of victory....

The Chambre des Députés is decorated today with red velvet carpets. There are draperies on the tribune in the large hall. The swastika, too, is there, and the doors of the building are thrown open to welcome anyone who wishes to enter. The populace is allowed to enter because the Führer will speak on the radio from Berlin today.

U.S. Embassy Issues Warnings for Americans to Leave Europe

August 13, 1940

News comes through that the Albanians are rising against the Italians.

The American Red Cross is receiving supplies by shiploads from the United States for French babies and old people.

Le Bourget is in flames from British bombing.

German soldiers are continually saluting Nazi officers who do not even see them. Even when the officers' backs are turned, the soldiers keep on saluting. The French police are not so active now in giving the military salute to the Nazis, as they were in the first days of the Occupation. Some of them do not even touch their caps when a Nazi officer passes.

The Embassy is still crowded. Americans from Dinard are nervously waiting for their exit permits. They feel sure that it is only a question of time when we shall be in the war.

Ledoyen restaurant, nestled amongst the trees back of the Avenue des Champs-Élysées, looked almost deserted as I passed the front terrace. There I had promised to meet my host, Edward Huffer,[82] Assistant Military Attaché in the Paris Embassy during the First World War and now retired and living in France. I was to see him at the entrance to the restaurant at the rear of the building. As he had not yet arrived, I asked for his table indicating the terrace. The *maître d'hôtel* told me that, most unfortunately, every table on the terrace was taken. Besides, he explained, it was damp outside and much more pleasant inside. I was somewhat puzzled at this, and when Edward appeared, I told him that it was nicer on the terrace on this warm, late summer evening, and there seemed to be a number of vacant tables there. Could anything be arranged with the maître d'hôtel who seemed reluctant to give us a table there? Nazi officers were beginning to arrive as the maître d'hôtel rather unwillingly ushered us to the terrace. Was there a feeling with the management that the conquerors would object to Americans dining so near to them? Did the management fear an incident, a clash perhaps?

We were four in our party including Edward's sister and his brother-in-law, a high ranking French officer recently returned from camp where he had been a prisoner of war for many months. His wife, originally a citizen of the United States, had been working in one of the military hospitals near Paris where a number of German soldiers and officers were interned for medical care. One German officer, as told to me by Madame, awoke suddenly from a coma, and finding himself in a hospital, cried, "Where am I? Is it over? Is the war over? I am so tired. I want to go back to Germany."

We were talking in low tones at our table, in English, commenting on the war at times or on the general topics of today. My host told me that our Embassy had said to him that if a third warning comes for Americans to leave Europe, he must go at once as it would mean war. The [American] Embassy, he stated, has already given two warnings.

August 14, 1940

Edward Huffer telephoned me today and asked if I had read *Le Matin*. I told him I had not seen the paper. He said that there was an article in it stating that Americans apparently think it quite smart to speak English in "loud tones" in the restaurants where Nazi officers are gathered; this insolence on the part of the United States and its citizens is only too obvious. The "supermen" must have things their way! I felt quite sure that the article referred to our delightful evening on the terrace of the Ledoyen restaurant.

Today the Bois de Boulogne was forbidden to the public. A German sentry was shot to death by an unknown person last night. Three persons suspected of the crime received the death sentence.

August 18, 1940

Last night the moon hung over the gardens opposite my window. It was shining over England, too, as a big air offensive was raging. I hold my breath and await the news. I cannot contact the British broadcast on my radio, and the French news is so distorted that it is useless to listen in.

Later the news from another radio said that 2,500 German planes flying toward the coast of England were met by 2,000 British planes; that more German planes than British planes were brought down. It was to the contrary over the German-controlled French radio. I prefer to believe the British broadcast.

French lads from the Italian front returning to their barracks around Paris had a difficult time in the Menton sector in the south and a short distance from the French–Italian frontier.[83] They faced the Italians with no munitions, high up on a cliff where they were located. They defended themselves by throwing huge stones down on the enemy below. Their unit had been dispersed, there was no command, and it had become everyone for himself.

Passing the Avenue de Breteuil this evening, a French boy selling the evening papers was calling, "*Achetez les journaux des mensonges—Achetez ces journaux des mensonges*" (Buy these lying newspapers). His face was quite serious as he sold his papers to the amused passersby who wanted to help him. And perhaps they might also have wanted to see the lies....

In contrast, there are others who cross our paths on whose faces tragedy is written. One sees it in a glance; one knows it by a few words. Today I bought some flowers from a lady who said to me, "Madame, I must sell my flowers to keep from starving. I am very unhappy, so unhappy. My husband fell in the first days of the war. We were settled in our home, comfortable and happy together, and now…." She could not continue and turned her face away to hide her misery. I gave her some money and took the flowers. It seemed so little. Perhaps the sympathy that I felt and tried to show, the understanding, too, may have lightened the heavy load.

The Hôtel Majestic on the Avenue Kléber near the Triumphal Arch holds the German exit permit office. Crowds stand in line while others bring their cots and beds to spend the night with the hope of being first in the morning to obtain the precious paper that will enable them to pass through the line of demarcation of occupied France to freedom. Freedom is the great cry of the day! "If I ever get out of Paris," exclaimed my American friend, "and find myself in touch with the outside world, it will be long before I shall return. This being a prisoner in France where I have lived so free and for so long is terrible."

American Embassy is a Bulwark against the Nazis

August 19, 1940

Somaliland is taken by the Italians. These are dark days for the Allies. It cannot, it must not be for long—please, God….

Those who will write the history of France under the iron heel of the conqueror will not perhaps relate the small details of this extraordinary life we are leading in Paris.[84] Incidents that before October 1939 were too insignificant to mention, even in a letter, have taken on new meaning. I think today of my hairdresser who has been arranging my hair for five years. His shop is near the Place Victor Hugo. This afternoon when I kept my appointment, there was an unusual silence; no conversation relating to the war or politics mingles with the sound of the clipping of hair and the splashing of water in a shampoo. We had gay times in the shop before these grim days came upon us. Now the Gestapo, as I have said, is everywhere. The wife or daughter or relative of a Gestapo agent may be in the next cabin having a permanent wave or seated on the chair next to yours. The *coiffeur* shops have become amongst the most informative (to the Nazis) listening posts in Paris. Monsieur (my hairdresser) and his wife cling to me as an American and friend. They ask me each time I come if the Embassy staff will remain in the city. They enquire anxiously if I think we may leave. To them the American Embassy is a bulwark against the Nazis. They feel that we, their friends, are with them and in a way protecting them; that the United States will never forsake them in their trouble. I assure them that we have no intention of leaving Paris and that we shall not indeed abandon them.

August 20, 1940

The BBC radioed Mr. Churchill's speech giving us added confidence.[85] The Nazi broadcast was hesitant and less confident.

Rauchen verboten (Smoking forbidden). It is a strange twist of the times to find the German language written on signs in Paris subways and trains. The sight of German orders in German in this land of Louis XIV and Napoléon is misplacement.

The Nazis are still pillaging French homes. Americans, too, are complaining of "mistakes" being made in the ransacking of their homes. The German exit permit office, as an example, near the *Étoile* recently moved to another building. They remained there until the authorities found they had requisitioned a building belonging to a United States citizen who had been absent for some time. He returned yesterday to find it occupied by the Germans who immediately vacated the premises with many apologies.

In Dinard German soldiers came to the beautiful villa of Adelaide Spofford of New York and a long resident of France, requesting two rooms for their officers. Adelaide, not perturbed at all, received the men and in English told them coolly that it would be necessary for them to look elsewhere for quarters for their officers as she preferred living in her home quite alone and undisturbed by the enemies of France. When they learned of her nationality, they withdrew. Adelaide wonders what will become of her villa in Dinard if we come into the war.

The steamship lines are working courageously in their desire to have space to send the great number of Americans waiting to embark to America. The U.S. Lines is using every available cabin and extra rooms on their ships. Mattresses are even placed on the decks and in cabins large enough to hold more than the usual number of two, three, or four persons.

"The speed limit for automobiles does not exist for the Nazis but only for those of other nationalities." So said Mrs. Lyne who was stopped by a traffic officer while driving at a lively pace along one of the broad avenues.

The news comes in intermittently. While England is fighting for her life and the life of the world, America watches, watches. Often there is a long silence with no news, no word of how the battle over England is going except in the French, albeit German-controlled, papers shouting German victory.

Ambassador Defines the Fighting Line of the War

August 24, 1940

My mind turns tonight over 3,000 miles of ocean and land to my own country, to America, "the greatest adventure in human freedom that the earth has known," Ambassador William C. Bullitt declared. "In our land the spectacle of a once free France now bowed and bound is awaking our people to the Nazi menace."

Ambassador Bullitt's address in Independence Hall in Philadelphia reached us today, parts of which I quote:[86]

> Fellow citizens of my country, men and women, Americans…. America is in danger. It is my conviction, drawn from my own experience and from the information in the hands of our government in Washington that the United States is in as great a peril today as France a year ago. And I believe that unless we act now, decisively, to meet the threat, we shall be too late.
>
> …. Do not imagine that the French citizen was less intelligent or cared less about his country than the American citizen. The honest French patriot did his best, but he just could not see through the smoke screens of bribery propaganda, lies and threats which the dictators spread in his country. For every Frenchman who acted as the conscious agent of a foreign dictator, there were thousands who, with good intentions and high patriotism, unwittingly played the dictators' game. How many Americans today are playing the dictators' games without knowing it?
>
> What stands between the Americas and the unleashed dictatorships? The British Fleet and the courage of the British people.
>
> France had learned that the lie, the solemn pledge, given and broken, had become Germany's normal weapon of international affairs. Yet today there are Americans who argue that we should believe the dictators when they say that they have no intention of extending their conquests to the Western Hemisphere and certainly not to the United States. France believed. Where now is France?
>
> …. And you may be sure that if the Nazis have an opportunity to turn it [the powerful German Army] against us, it will be as strong or stronger than it is today and will be used in the most unexpected manner. I cannot tell you where and when the attack will come, any more than the French General Staff could have told you that the German attack would be made at Sedan on the 13th of May; but I am certain that if Great Britain is defeated, the attack will come and that all the strength of this nation will be needed…
>
> The fighting line of the war for the enslavement of the human spirit is nearing our shores. For every American 'there is no discharge in that war.' An American is a free man, or he is nothing. Our fate and the fate of our children depend on what each one of us does—now.

So spoke our Ambassador. He has lived amongst the French a great part of his life. He knows the French people and loves them. He is also a great American and loves America as we all do. What he said was so clearly what we need to hear to be awakened from our sleep of complaisance and comfort and easy living. How could he do otherwise having been with France during the tragic days leading to her fall and her overwhelming defeat? He can do no less than send the word of warning throughout the vast spaces of our own great country.

It shall not be, it could not possibly be, that the Ambassador's splendid efforts to alert America to action should be lost….

August 30, 1940

British leaflets are being thrown from Royal Air Force planes; they scatter in the parks and on the streets; they are picked up surreptitiously and read with wistful hope: "Patience, patience," the Parisians read. "We shall soon be with you." I found one and leaned against the long wall of the Boulevard des Invalides to peruse it further. There was nothing more, however, but as I was about to walk away, I found that I had been leaning against a poster portraying a criminal-looking British officer with his arms folded and his gaze fastened scornfully on a poor Frenchman with his wife and children around him. Underneath were the words in French: "See what the English have done to us!"

No German propaganda today, however, is strong enough to have the French believe that the British are their enemies.

The times are heavy with tragedy: Countess Trotti, an American citizen well-known in the American Colony, died today; Mr. R. was obliged to take his wife to an asylum; Lloyd Hartshorne, another United States citizen, also passed on. These are only three that I have noted. There are many others who succumb to the difficulties of the times in which the physical and moral torments are increasing, incited by harrowing uncertainties and fear. Paris of today is not a happy ground for ill and dying or for those with frayed nerves and unquiet minds. It is for the brave of heart, the courageous, and the strong in will and in health. The times, so full of danger, must be lived by the "sword of the Spirit," with love and an inner calm.[87] It is not possible otherwise.

The press is agitated and weighty with disaster as news comes from the battle aimed at England: mounds of dead Germans stretched out on the English Channel coast of England, mown down by a desperate British defense. There are dead Germans standing erect, knee deep in the water with their heavy boots counterbalancing the weight of their bodies. This story was related to me by an eye witness. Has Hitler lost his mind?

Maréchal Pétain is protesting, so one reads in the French press, that in the United States the opinion exists that France is not free and independent. He admits, however, that the country is bound by the terms of the Armistice. One wonders what is the Maréchal's definition of "freedom."

Efforts are being made by the Nazi masters to bring back *la vie de Bohème* of Montmartre and Montparnasse, that unique life in France that belongs to her history. Life in Montmartre and Montparnasse is part of the being of the French, of the French genius. It is in the blood and body of the nation. It is France. Does Germany really believe in the possibility of their being a part of it? *La vie de Bohème* is silent now. It will wake to new life in Montmartre and Montparnasse when France shall come into her own again, and not until then.

Today on page one of a Paris press newspaper is printed: "Infamous bombing of Berlin by the British." On page three there is the notice of "a successful bombing of Bristol (in England) by German planes." "Infamous" and "successful" are words describing a point of view.

From the American press:

> The royal children of Norway and Sweden have arrived in New York to remain until after the war.
> Conscription bill has passed the Senate.
> Appropriation of five billion dollars for the Army and Navy.

> Registration of all aliens in the United States ordered.
>
> Everyone who has reached his or her fourteenth year must be finger-printed.
>
> The Dies Commission[88] is working day and night seizing books, magazines, and propaganda of the Communists and of the German–American Bund Committee.

At the Embassy I learned that Robert D. Murphy,° our Chargé d'Affaires in Paris and beloved by every member of the staff and the American Colony, is preparing to leave us. He has been called to the Department of State for another assignment.[89] We shall miss him. We shall miss the understanding and sympathetic help that he never failed to give us when he was our personnel officer. He was a brilliant diplomat and one of the finest officers in the United States Foreign Service. Shall he return? We dare not hope so for we feel sure that his path will take him upwards and onwards toward a larger sphere of work in world events. Our need today is greater than ever before—for leadership and the splendid qualities that are found in such men as Robert Murphy.[90] God speed him and give him happiness and success! In the words of the poet, Rudyard Kipling,[91] his is the ability to "Walk with Kings—nor lose the common touch."*

High prelates of the churches in America and England are strong in hope. We read of the confidence of these men rich in faith, fanning the embers of fervent trust into flame.

"France cannot die," is the cry. "Christianity shall live. To wait for victory must be the aim of everyone." Monsieur Reynaud in France has sent over the radio a plea for the prayers of the people for victory. Can a profoundly sincere petition to the All-Father[92] remain unheard?

Private automobiles are not allowed on the streets of Paris. Gasoline must be used for the war, for planes and tanks. As a result, the *cocher* (coachman) has appeared. He sits on his high seat and drives his horse and carriage resurrected from the past. Private *coupés* with light stepping horses and a coachman and footman in smart uniforms are seen. One's memory races back to the gay nineties. It is a breath from the past to hear the trot of the horses' hoofs on the asphalt. It is amusing to see the luxurious air of the flunkeys in front, the calmness and dignity of the owners inside. Dignity and calmness are adapted more to the coach-and-four (or two-and-one) of the times at the turn of the century than to the fast going vehicles of our volcanic era. It breathes of an age that has gone forever, like a dream lost in unreality.

The *voiturette*, a two-seated car run by electricity, is making its appearance as is the "one-man power taxi."[93]

° Hon. Robert D. Murphy, hero of the Allies landing in North Africa, former Ambassador to Japan and Belgium; now Deputy Under Secretary of State (appointed 1954).

* From Kipling's poem "If."

Four million refugees are now in unoccupied France: Belgians, Czechs, Americans, English, South Americans, White Russians, Poles, and other nationals. In the different groups and faculties of medicine, education, music, agriculture, and the legal courts, the percentage of foreigners is very high. A high percentage includes Jews. They all must leave. This is another chapter in the persecution of these unfortunate people. The aim of the new regime is to make it one hundred percent French.

Will the United States Enter the War?

August 31, 1940

Today is one of those late August days that envelops one in all its perfection before the crisp winds of September fall. Insistent rumours are everywhere that the United States is on the verge of entering the war. Americans in large numbers come to the Embassy requesting information. No one knows. Our instructions are to continue warning all United States citizens to leave the country and return to America.

In the German-controlled French press I read a German–Russian military pact was signed "that will forever guarantee the friendship of the two nations." There was also criticism of British hypocrisy.

Strains of Viennese waltzes float on the night air as I write. They send forth a breath of beauty and blot out the ugliness of the so-called hypocrisy of anti-Semitism, of

> Envy and calumny and hate and pain
> And that unrest which men miscall delight.[94]

Would that music might go on! It fades off, however, into the distance, and one is found again in the tangled web of the present.

September is with us. The days are rushing on. We cannot stop them. We would not if we could. For a dim light has arisen on the horizon. It is seen in the new offensive against England. England bends deep in the storm, like the branches of a great tree in a strong wind. She rights herself every time with her unconquerable spirit. This glimmer of light is seen on the streets of Paris and in the marketplace where the long lines of people wait for food and where it is heard: "Yes, the Americans are coming to help us." It is seen in the tracts printed by *La Légion Étrangère Française en France* (French Foreign Legion in France) sent down by the Royal Air Force. I have a tract before me. It reads (French translated roughly into English):

> Frenchmen–Frenchwomen:
> Let us have confidence in England, in the untiring struggle the Royal Air Force (RAF) is engaged in every day. They are bombing German cities…. Today the German population is learning the cost of the horrors of war and of air bombing.
> An eye for an eye, a tooth for a tooth is the principle reflected by Hitler and his followers.

Those who have known the cowardly bombardment on the highways of France: Rennes, Étaples, Orléans, Issoudun, Sully-sur-Loire will applaud the British air raids.

Paris overflowing with German troops is not a free city. Paris will be bombed by the RAF as well as other French districts where German troops are concentrated.

.... Avoid being around barracks and camps where German troops are located because at any time, they are liable to RAF bombing.

.... Avoid taking the trains of German military and munition convoys that are ploughing through the railroads of the occupied zone; any moment the roads may be blown up or bombed.

.... English parachutists are arriving every day in France. Do not put obstacles in their way. You profit by every blow aimed at Hitler; each loss for Hitler is a victory for you.

.... Do not forget that the Paris newspapers are German newspapers.

Every garage in Paris is guarded by a German soldier. Gasoline must be carefully watched. It is a precious fluid today. Today I stood by a German soldier on guard at one filling station. He was standing without moving a muscle. Every time an officer passed in an automobile, the gun on the right shoulder came down in front for a moment or until the car passed, then it was shifted to the left shoulder, and the soldier took up his motionless and impassive stand again. He was like a marionette, as if someone above him had pulled the strings supporting his joints and the movement of his gun....

The BBC announced over the radio today that every Nazi plane carries a member of the Gestapo to see that the pilot does his duty. This was denied by the German French press.

September 1, 1940

Sunday. Even in these days of war, Sunday means rest and quiet. I went off to the Embassy later in the day to finish some work. The day was radiantly beautiful. The air was soft. I reached the bridge and stopped a moment to look down into the Seine whose deep waters were rolling, rolling, carried on by a strong undercurrent.

Roule, roule ton flot—indolent, morne Seine[95]

The brooding plaint of Verlaine had its reflection in the faces of German soldiers passing me. They, too, were peering deep down into the waters. Of what were they thinking? Where has the joy of those first triumphant days of last June gone? They seem apprehensive as they walk along silently and mournfully; the singing, too, has stopped, as well as the quickened stride of youth and joy that were theirs in the first flush of victory.

September 3, 1940

Letters from my people in the United States show the trend of America towards anything but neutrality. They all refuse to employ German servants.

I rub my eyes and see myself in my U.S. home twenty-three years ago with Gustav, our new found German butler, waiting on our table. Gustav, as it appeared later and, of course, quite unknown to us, was a German agent. He came into our service as a "refugee" and anti-German, before we entered the war of 1914–1918. There was consternation amongst the guests at a dinner party at home one night when I told them of his nationality. One guest rose and said, "I cannot remain while he is in the house." I quieted him with the promise that he should not be here after dinner. It seemed incredible that with the face of a simple lad, blond hair and pink cheeks, he should be a spy. But of course, that is the way some spies should be. Gustav left immediately after he served the coffee and liqueurs. I have never seen him since. Life was full of dangers for such persons, for German refugees, in America in those days. Certainly, it was for spies.

I hurry back from my youth and return to France 1940. I continue my story of today. Feeling against the Nazis, my family writes again, is becoming stronger every day.

The United States government trades fifty destroyers to Britain for rights on naval bases[96] in Bermuda,[97] Trinidad, Jamaica, Saint Lucia, Newfoundland, and British Guiana.[98]

From my brother in South America comes news that 5th columnists are becoming so numerous that United States citizens are wearing small American flags to show their nationality and the fact that they are not pro-Nazi....[99]

September 4, 1940

From the Pont Neuf Bridge I watched private yachts moving through the brisk waters toward the north. Their ornamentations glistened in the bright sun. However, the yachts are not so bright as they had been in the past; nor were they moving on their former luxurious ways. Today they have been requisitioned and turned into barges carrying munitions, coal, and other products for the war effort. They are doing their part as bravely as the rest of us try to do ours. No doubt they are not regretting too much the heydays of other times.

September 5, 1940

"You are going to blind me with your lamp, Madame!"

I was returning from a small dinner party groping my way in the blackout. It was nearing eleven o'clock, time for everyone to be under cover. I had arrived a short distance from my street, which turns in from the Boulevard des Invalides when I heard myself addressed. I could not see anyone in the blackness, but I knew it was one of the Garde Mobile, a section of the French *Gendarmerie*, who is stationed in every quarter of the city to keep watch on the people in order to detect any untoward event or incident that might occur. They know the passersby of their quarter, not personally perhaps, but they recognize the familiar step or silhouette of those who live around them. This guard apparently knew something of me for, after I had apologized for almost "blinding" him with my electric lamp, he asked, "Have you stopped work?" (He, of course, spoke in French.)

"Oh, no," I replied. "I have been dining with friends; work stops after seven o'clock."

"But you are a foreigner! Are you British?" My Anglo-Saxon accent betrayed me.

"No," I answered, "I am an American. Would you like to see my papers, my card of identity?" He was still only a shadow in the darkness. I had a glimpse of a man's outline under the few stars that were shining above.

"Ah, non, Madame," he said quickly. "I did not stop you for that." He then began a tirade against the Nazis; how they were entering apartments, stealing valuable furniture and objets d'art, and often destroying them.

I listened to it all but my only remark from time to time was "yes" or "it is too bad." Even though I was sure that he was a loyal Frenchman, it was wise to be careful; there had been a large 5th column, unfortunately, which still exists. As he finished and paused a moment, I said, "Now I must reach my apartment before eleven o'clock as I should not like to be taken to the poste (police station)."

"But the police station is not too bad," he replied. "The benches are hard perhaps. You would, of course, be more comfortable in your apartment."

"Yes, *Monsieur*," I said, "but I should really not be happy in the poste polishing boots until five in the morning." Orders had been given by the Nazis that any woman taken up after the blackout hour and driven to the district police station was obliged to clean the boots of the men.

When I heard his reply to that, there vanished from my mind any suspicion I might have had as to his loyalty to his country. I could almost see him draw himself up in the darkness as he said with great dignity, "Ah, Madame, a Nazi might ask a lady to do such a thing, but never a Frenchman."

As I moved away, I said, "*Bonsoir, Monsieur.* What you said is very true—never a Frenchman."

British agents are in our midst. The British Intelligence Service knows no fear. They have minds filled with infinite resources that keep the Nazis guessing every moment in their efforts to track down the members of the British *contre-espionnage*.

In her château in the north, the lovely *châtelaine* opened the heavy doors herself. Before her stood a presentable looking officer in German uniform. He courteously asked the lady, in impeccable French, if she would be so good as to let him have a room for the night. The lady was not partial to the Nazis. Coldly she told him to enter. (She did not care to have any trouble with the occupying power.) Her old servant showed him to a room.

In the morning the officer could not be found. He apparently had left quite early. The room was in perfect order with no trace of his personal belongings, which spoke eloquently and satisfyingly to his hostess of his decision not to return. No personal belongings, but a card of thanks lay on the table to which was attached one red rose. On it was written, "Madame, please accept my thanks for your kind hospitality to a member of the Royal Air Force."

Madame's son is with General de Gaulle in England....

Another tale, with its immense possibilities of danger, comes to me with a feeling of the admiration I have for brave men. It was late, quite dark, and the rain that had sent everyone indoors added to the desolation of the little village of X. The most important restaurant seemed to be the only building open. An officer entered, brushing the rain from his German uniform. He stood at attention for a second, clicked his heels, and gave the Nazi salute to the surprised, elderly restaurant keeper seated at his desk.

"Heil Hitler," the owner of the restaurant heard.

"*Monsieur,*" said the visitor in French with the suggestion of a German accent. "I have seen and tasted your excellent cakes. I should like to buy one for the officer in charge of my Kommandantur in the village a short distance away. The *capitaine* of my Kommandantur likes chocolate cake, and yours are delicious. I shall stop by for it myself in the morning—shall we say about eleven o'clock?"

The pleased restaurant keeper assented, and the officer paid the price asked, clicked his heels once again, and opened the door. He closed it again, however, to prevent the rain from entering and said, "*Monsieur,* should I not be able to return in the morning for the cake—one never knows what to expect these days—would you send it to the capitaine of my Kommandantur with this card?" He presented a sealed envelope, bowed, saluted again and departed.

The chief of the Kommandantur was undoubtedly pleased the next day to see a large chocolate cake on his table with an envelope addressed to him. He tore it open and found a blank card except for a small water color of the flag and wings of the Royal Air Force painted in the left-hand corner.

September 7, 1940

Further rumors of the Government of France returning to Paris appear. There is much confusion regarding the news. When the Germans entered France, the government went to Bordeaux. Eventually they had headquarters in Vichy. We wait patiently for further word, hoping that they will indeed come back to the Capital. Another rumour is that they will be installed in Versailles. It does not seem possible for them to return to Paris while the Germans are in authority in the city. And the deadlock continues.

Guns over Paris. The British bombed Charenton-le-Pont outside of the Paris district last night. They will continue where German military and munitions sections are located.

Silks from Lyon in large quantities are being sent to Germany. They have been requisitioned, and the manufacturers in Lyon are paid either in francs or in exchange products.

September 9, 1940

The air was fresh and crisp in the morning, but later the rain came, giving the city a doleful aspect such as we have not had for many weeks. It heralded the hard winter that is predicted with unheated apartments and no hot water. The shops are advertising heavy stockings. Nylons seem to be out of the question.

The delays and uncertainties of exit permits are discouraging to the waiting Americans. They came to the Embassy this morning having passed sleepless nights. If war is declared between the United States and France today, no American will be permitted to leave France. The tension increases as visions of concentration camps rise on the horizon.

Fishermen and fisherwomen along the edges of the Seine try to catch something for the day's meal, as food becomes ever scarcer. The children, brought by their parents, play in the sand while the elders toil with their lines. Above, on the quays, the bookstalls are crowded. The crowds are drawn no doubt by the gay prints and engravings as well as by the books that they buy to take back to their unheated rooms and apartments. Their books are friends that bring a bit of warmth to the unfriendly cold of their dwellings....

September 10, 1940

Summer passes on toward autumn. Again, the smell of burning leaves and again the ever changing colors from green to red, to gold, to brown. Memory turns to my own land, and I am lost in that maze of vivid, tense tones of autumn colors such as those in France never reach. The leaves that spread out at my feet in brilliant shades, like oriental rugs, stay only for a moment. They are blown by the wind, whirling above me in circles, swept right and left, backwards and forwards.

Camions rumbling past, camouflaged and warlike, bring me back to France at war. Nazi soldiers crowded in wagons, their guns beside them or in front of them, seem not to see the splendid curve of the river or the sweep of the broad avenues. They stare vacantly on a world that seems to have stopped completely for them as their trucks carry them north toward the thunder of bombs, guns, blood, and death. The news from their country reaches them. They know that their homes and their people are in danger. Will the war never cease?

No British subject—man, woman, or child—is allowed to leave France. No French citizen is allowed to leave France.

American Embassy Is Asked to Intervene

September 11, 1940

A child, thirteen years of age perhaps, is selling roses at the foot of the Church of the Madeleine.[100] Her eyes pleaded with every passerby to buy her roses. It was what she had to give: roses. She had nothing more. She smiled when I took her flowers. Roses and a smile—she seemed very rich.

At my desk today was a letter from Berlin, Germany. "I am writing this," it said, "to urge you to have an American consul prove that I am an American only and that I have no other citizenship. I miss you more than I can tell you. Please act speedily for I am very tired."

So wrote a young United States citizen to his parents in America. The boy had come from America with his father and mother and was caught in the times so "out of joint." Apparently, he was left in Germany to continue his studies while his parents returned to their home in the United States. The lad was taken prisoner by the Germans. Why? The Embassy is making every effort to find out. The last words of his letter were significant. Is he ill? Unhappy, certainly. He must be too tired to reach his people in the bitterness and loneliness of separation while he is in trouble.

September 14, 1940

A northeast storm is lashing its fury over the city. The rain and wind together held me back, trying to prevent me from reaching the Embassy. I arrived at the bridge with difficulty and looked down where the waters were swirling underneath. They were fierce and angry. I turned away and looked up toward the towers of Notre-Dame. They rose above the mist and the storm. I could feel their quiet and strength. I thought of the French at the dawn of their history turning to their churches for sanctuary, fleeing before the enemy.

The rain ceased later in the day. I walked over to the Tuileries passing the site where the beautiful sculpture of a great woman, Edith Cavell,[101] once was. She was honored by almost all the countries of Western Europe and America. The sculpture was placed here after the First World War. Only the pedestal remains and some flowers recently placed there. Hitler ordered her statue be removed. Had it annoyed the Nazis too bitterly? Had the sacrifice of one who had given her life to suffering humanity offended their sensibilities?

A camion driven by a German soldier sped swiftly past me as I left the gardens. It had come from the war front and was riddled with bullets.

I am writing with shutters closed and curtains drawn. The authorities are becoming stricter concerning the blackout. Besides, they are continually alert about either photographing or writing or taking notes of any kind. A woman told me that on one night when her lights were too bright, or even not sufficiently concealed, she heard a loud knock at her door. Upon opening it, she was greeted by a Nazi officer brandishing a revolver who told her that the next time her lights were not covered, he would shoot the light right through her window.

The exit permits are coming through; Americans are leaving for the border. One man said goodbye to me and told me that he was glad to go, as Paris will not be the same for the next fifty years. He spoke of the Paris that he had lived in for over forty years. Who knows what the France of the future will be? It will be different, changes are certain. Progress is a law of life....

September 16, 1940

It is four o'clock in the morning. "Sleep that knits up the ravell'd sleave of care"[102] evades me. The rain is the only sound on the still street.

Posters, depicting the "evils and cruelties" of the British towards the French that were placed on the walls and buildings by the German authorities, are being torn down at night. The poster "Do Not Forget Oran,"[103] which showed a drowning Frenchman holding a torn Tricolor[104] aloft above the waters, disappeared a short time after it was put up in a village outside of Paris. The French, braced by the news giving them gleams of light, are rising in courage.

September 20, 1940

A camion carrying former French prisoners of war stopped a moment on the Champs-Élysées to await the traffic signal to proceed. Some of the men were wounded while all were emaciated from hunger and illness. They were immediately surrounded by sympathetic persons who stretched friendly hands out to them. The wounded did not even try to conceal their emotion; they were free and were going home.

Conscription in America becomes a law. Registration of men between 21 and 35 is due October 15.[105] For us in Paris, life is becoming more dismal.

"When are you coming into the war?" a Nazi officer asked one of our compatriots today. There was no reply. Did he really expect any?

The British bombed German military objectives outside of Paris last night.

September 22, 1940

Today is a grey Sunday. The strollers seemed more listless, sadder, and perhaps more than usual as I walked along near them. The Germans are doing much to make the city gayer, however. There are motor races along the Seine with large crowds watching from the bridges and along the edge of the river. And yet, the morale of the French seems to have reached a standstill.

I missed the luncheon party given by a friend that included a few German officers. I wondered what conversation might be possible between guests with ideas directly opposed to each other. The result showed that it was indeed little possible. The exchange of reflections and observations ended in a series of insults and heated remarks.

And yet, strangely enough, it is not always so. At one *soirée* an American began his remarks in French when a German guest protested and asked him why he did not speak in his own language. The American replied, "Your Foreign Minister, von Ribbentrop, refused to speak English to our President's representative in Berlin, and I concluded that you and your people did not wish to speak our language."

"You do not judge every German by that idiot, I hope," was his reply. "And," he continued, "the sooner that imbecile is fired from our Government, the better it will be for Germany." As the American fully agreed with this observation, there was harmony after that between the different nationals. This one gala ended smoothly.

The Nazis are inciting the French to arm and fight with them against England. Rumours are insistent that there will be revolution in France, that secret meetings, notably in Auteuil,[106] take place every night. Sentiment is rising higher each day as some of the French come out openly in favor of a German-controlled government; others proclaim vehemently against it.

September 27, 1940

The persecution of the Jews which began moderately a few months ago has become more aggressive and more malevolent.

Every Jew is obliged to register at the *Commissariat* of his district. No Jew may remain in the medical faculty; no Jewish lawyer is allowed to practice in France. Trades people of the Jewish race must display a notice on their shops or factories with the sign: *Jüdisches Geschäft* ("Jewish Enterprise").[107] Jews who find it possible are fleeing the city or hiding in the homes of friends who are risking their lives to protect them.

Arrests of the French are made every day. The Parisians who find it difficult to restrain their words and feelings are continually getting into trouble with the police. They resent the amount of food that is daily carried away in great quantities by the Nazis while they are obliged to spend weary hours waiting for a small quantity of butter or milk or potatoes, often to find at the end of waiting in a long line that everything has been sold out. How long can it last? Seemingly they are submitting to defeat, but those undercurrents of fierce pain, at times "sick with hate," stir restlessly, unceasingly....

Japan has joined the Axis powers.[108] The pact pledging them to fight if the other two countries [Germany and Italy] are attacked was signed in Berlin.

October 5, 1940

As feeling in America against the pact becomes strong, the alliance is assailed in the press. Speaking before the Senate, Senator [Claude] Pepper[109] said, "There has never been a time in the history of this nation when another nation could level such a challenge to the courage of our people without the assurance that it would be flung back into their scowling faces with the aroused spirit of a strong and brave people. This time is no exception." He continued, "It behooves us to redouble our efforts at defense and preparation so that...our strength would be twofold and threefold, more than it would have been had this challenge not been leveled from those insidious and iniquitous sources...."

October 6, 1940

Crossing the Esplanade of the Invalides in front of the Hôtel, the few cannons that are left in the gardens dating from the seventeenth and eighteenth centuries were the object of conjecture by a woman who was talking so vehemently against the occupying power that a French policeman warned her, "You had better keep quiet," he said. "We are all obliged to keep quiet; we are only *fainéants* (ne'er-do-wells) ....

Marshal Göring was reported killed.[110] The swastika at the Hôtel Meurice, where he has his headquarters when he comes to Paris and where the offices of the German Air Force, the Luftwaffe, are located, was at half-mast. This is the second or third time that his death has been announced by the Nazis. Is it a farce? Is there a reason for the Hitler government to send forth this news from time to time? Is it useful for the war effort?

October 10, 1940

Riots broke out in Les Halles. A German officer was killed by a French patriot who subsequently shot himself to death. Several women jumped on a German soldier and threw him to the ground; he had orders to carry food away and was attacked while putting the food into his truck.

There is some confirmation of the deaths of Göring, Himmler, and Brauchitsch[111] while at a festive gathering in a château in the north of France that was bombed by the British and completely demolished. Can it be true? There is always a doubt in any information the Nazis give out.

At the cinema last night there was an ominous silence when the newsreel portrayed the "splendid" work of the Nazi bombing of England. Another picture, showing the "dastardly" bombing of women and children by the British, brought forth a subdued hissing, which was not entirely silent. This was due to an article that appeared in last night's paper stating that if the audiences in the different film houses did not refrain from hissing the Nazis and applauding the British, as they have been doing, every cinema house would be closed. At one spectacle recently, when British "cruelty" was depicted by a Nazi film, a woman in the audience shouted, "*Ce n'est pas vrai!*" (It isn't true!). This was followed by "*Vive l'Angleterre!*" (Long live England!).

The day was dying slowly. I had an appointment on Avenue George V near the *Étoile*. I was late. If I hurried, I just might make it. Down into the subway of the Concorde I raced, almost sliding in my haste, with ticket ready as I reached the ticket agent. There I was stopped by the closing gate as the incoming train arrived, discharging a flood of passengers. They started up the steps marked *sortie* ("exit") when they were met by a young Nazi soldier coming down the wrong way, of course. I was first in line waiting for the next train. The ticket agent was about to open the gate when he saw the soldier.

"Go up and come down the other way," he cried, pointing to the long line in back of me coming down the steps. There was no reply from the soldier who continued to descend. "Go back there," again called my ticket agent directly in front of me. Still no reply. "I told you to go back," he said.

The soldier stood for a moment, not knowing quite what to do. Obviously, he had no intention of receding from his stand. He then shook a threatening finger at the agent and in broken French informed the Frenchman that if he did not let him pass, he would live to regret it.

The French ticket agent, quite unperturbed at this, called to him, "I know all about that. You think that you can do anything you want in this country because you are the victors. This is one place where you will obey orders. I know you: when your officers give a command, you are on your knees." The ticket agent clasped his hands as if in prayer, mockingly imitating a supposed plain soldier receiving orders from his superior. "And away from them you think you can do anything you want—now go!" He waved him back and the soldier angrily turned up the steps. I said, "Bravo!" to the agent. He replied, "They are all alike, all like that. I am not afraid of them. I know them!" The French who were in the long line in back of me were not saying a word. They would normally have hissed, protested, or execrated anyone trying to go ahead of others contrary to the regulations. But this is war; they prefer not to have trouble with the occupying power.

The French are becoming more courageous; doubtless it is because they are now less fearful of the future. Every poster in Paris that is anti-British is being torn down during the night. "*À bas Hitler! Vive l'Angleterre! Vive de Gaulle!*" are written on the vacant spaces.

Over the radio last night, the chief of the *Anciens Combattants* ("War Veterans") appealed to the French to prepare themselves for orders that would soon come from England. Later the British broadcast began, "Frenchmen, Frenchwomen...." The announcer stopped suddenly. The communication was cut. Not succeeding in their broadcast, the British threw tracts today from planes announcing that within a few months the Allied flags would be in every city in France.

I strolled along the Avenue des Champs-Élysées watching the crowds trying to make a Sunday-like holiday. I lingered before the Petit Palais where there was a long line waiting to enter the building. There the "secrets" of the Freemasons "uncovered" by the Nazis were shown by various documents.[112]

Nazi Sympathizer Questions Why the Embassy Is Busy

October 11, 1940

Today's *Le Petit Parisien*[113] newspaper stated:

> Forty-six milliards appropriation for reorganization of work and improvement in the status of the unemployed.
> Pensions for retired workers.
> Work to begin at Saint-Malo (small city in Brittany) concerning betterment of fishing industry.
> Racecourse at Auteuil to open.

The newspaper showed two photographs of mannequins in smart dresses.

Maréchal Pétain spoke over the radio telling the French to have courage and patience; they are passing through a bad time but that it would not last. Coffee, meat, sugar, potatoes, and other products are soon coming in great quantities. All this is indeed bewildering. Is everything to be normal so soon? Normal?

Today my path led to the Trocadéro.[114] I had accepted an invitation to tea at the beautiful home of a compatriot whose wife is French. I had often dined there and looked forward to being under my friends' hospitable roof again.

When I entered, the salon was crowded. Perhaps forty guests were standing about. Some were playing bridge at a table in a far corner while others, sitting in large armchairs, were talking in low tones. Even in private gatherings it was wise not to voice an opinion too openly. One gentleman, whom I had met quite often in the hours and who had always led the conversation by talking more than anyone else, I noticed was not saying a word today. I was pondering somewhat about the matter when from across the room a French woman, whom I knew, married to a German national, called to me and said, "I was just thinking about you. I want to talk to you. I shall join you in a moment."

I had not seen the lady for some time. She had only recently arrived in Paris to remain a few days, coming from Berlin where she was domiciled. She came over to where I was sitting, balancing her teacup as she sat down on the arm of my big, comfortable chair. "I hear that you are very busy at the Embassy," she began.

"Yes," I replied. "Very busy indeed."

"But why?" she repeated. "Why is it so urgent that they leave?"

"Don't you think it wise for foreigners to be in their own homes, in their own countries, during these troubled, confused times in Europe?" I asked. "Certainly, it is wise for Americans to return to the United States."

Suddenly her answer to my question made me feel that I might be in a dangerous corner. She said, "Can't you understand, you Americans, that everything will be quite normal very soon? Norway is normal and Belgium, too. France will follow."

For a tenth of a second I wondered if she really believed what she was saying. Did she really think that Norway, Belgium, Holland, and France, fallen in defeat, would remain fallen?

The words of an old Northumberland[115] song came to me.

> I'll lay me down and bleed a-while,
>   And then I'll rise and fight again.[116]

Her face was quite serious. I gave her a scornful look, rose from my chair, and did not reply. Either she had been sent to obtain information from someone whom she knew, someone who was attached to the American Embassy in Paris, or she was trying it on her own hoping to learn and perhaps report. Like the often-voluble French gentleman referred to above who today was silent, I remained so until I said goodbye to my hostess and left the house.

Today German troops occupy Rumania.[117]

October 14, 1940

Numbers 1 and 2 of *Pantagruel*[118] of October 1940 came to me today. *Pantagruel*, the clandestine information sheet, is being diffused in occupied France. Its name was taken from one of the great works of Rabelais[119] and is one of its principal characters. The editor was at one time a defender of Germany. His Alsatian origin gives him a clearer insight into the German character than he might have if his ancestors' nationality had been different.

I have translated a few paragraphs. It explains that it is indeed an informative sheet, not a vain struggle against the occupying authority. Its main object is the spread of news from England by radio, of which too many people are deprived.

No. 1. *Pantagruel*
While the attitude of our enemies is correct and often courteous, Frenchmen, understand this: that although there are many Germans who are cordial to France, the theory "*Deutschland über Alles*" is that everything must be crushed, if necessary, for the glory of Germany.

Dakar.[120]

It is most unfortunate that in Dakar there are many Frenchman working for Nazi and Italian interests….The British Fleet came exclusively—and this fact must be insisted on—as a convoy for French vessels…and was bombarded with no discrimination by the coastal batteries and the Richelieu….Dakar is an important strategic point that the Axis [powers] want to control….

The Nazis and their satellites have more reason to be anxious than you suppose….

The object of *Pantagruel* is neither hatred nor revolt against the Nazis; it is simply to uphold our millenarian right to think for ourselves.

News from America.

About one hundred and twenty-five planes reach England from America every week…. The number will be doubled very soon. Packard factories are manufacturing for the R.A.F. 6,000 motors for airplanes of the Rolls-Royce type.[121]

The possibilities of resistance together with the high morale of Great Britain are cause for great optimism.

Do not read this sheet in public. Do not mention it to the Germans nor to their friends.

Circulate this paper as much as possible prudently without the name of the sender. Do not be lax or indifferent. France is not conquered!

Frenchmen, you who are the spiritual heirs of those who are humbly giving their lives for the grandeur of the French cause... you who courageously laugh at the sufferings the destiny of *La Patrie* impose on you, rally in spirit to General de Gaulle who alone is upholding the French tradition of heroism; respect the given word before the whole world. Sustained by the English whose resolution and unshakable tenacity are legendary, you will win!

End No. 1—extracts from *Pantagruel*

No. 2. *Pantagruel*
The chances of victory for England are great and increase each day. We understand those who may doubt it, but we dishonor those who do not wish it….

The soul of Germany: the German sensibilities have produced a beautiful literature.... It is very rich in visions of romantic myths, of supernatural beings...that give it an exaltation and mysticism, far from Hitler and his ideas....

But there is a lack of logic, of lucidity, of clairvoyance, which is surprising in such a great people as the German, whose intelligence is inferior to no other.... This lack of logic is shown in their notices as to 'who started the war.'...For instance, (according to the Germans) the French and English have not responded to the wishes of Germany and have revolted against her laws. In other words, Germany is all right, and we are all wrong!

Imagine the reply of a criminal in a court of law such as, 'Sir, I decline all responsibility in the murder. I warned that if the victim resisted, I should kill him; he resisted, so he alone is responsible for the murder!'

The Germans show a lively taste for the cannon that they prefer to butter, which does not prevent them from sending our butter to Germany where purchasers are easily found....

End No. 2—Extracts from *Pantagruel*

American Embassy Is Taking Care of British Interests

October 15, 1940

All night long the sound of German planes overhead disturbs my sleep; they are waiting and watching. When shall the turning point come? It must come. At times it seems near, so near; at other times it seems lost in an impenetrable future....

Red leaves are at my feet as I reached the Seine. Autumn is again with us, yet the day was like spring. A man, walking along the side of the bridge, passed me. He was poorly clad. In his eyes, it seemed, was desperation. He was young, not more than twenty-five. My spirit went out to him as I wondered what tragedy was his. I wanted to do something, to say something, but I felt as confused as he seemed to be. And so I passed on without a word. I was conscious of him long after he left and of his hopelessness in his face, in his whole body. Tonight his eyes haunt me.

There is a three-hundred-francs fine for a French policeman who does not salute a German officer. Some of the agents prefer to pay the fine.

There is a large fine for anyone caught listening to the British broadcast. However, at four o'clock this morning someone in the apartment above was listening in. I shall try my own radio at 4:00 a.m. tomorrow to see if I shall be able to hear from the outside world.

The Embassy was busy today principally in an effort to help our British friends. (We are taking care of British interests.) Some had not registered as they should have done; others were making an attempt to cross the border into freedom *en fraude* (secretly, illegally). There seems to be a way of doing this as the number increases every day for those who have been successful in this venture.

Canadians must register with the Nazi authorities. I hope my dear Dr. Barton is still in Paris. I am almost afraid to telephone to find out.

Hurry, my Americans! Hurry home! You may not have much time. Events are moving swiftly. Dangerous moments are often upon us before we even have time to think....

October 17, 1940

Between sixteen million and sixteen million five hundred thousand men in the United States registered for military service. The President's noble address to the country was simple, clear, and convincing. Volunteers were below and above the age limit. Former Secretary of the Treasury McAdoo,[122] who appeared in Washington to register, gave his age as 76 and his consent to do whatever he could and to go wherever he was sent. Registration of the "sick, invalids, and semi-invalids" was noted; special arrangements are being made in hospitals and war welfare organizations to meet these courageous demands.

The reaction in the United States, in the press everywhere, regarding the response of American youth to the draft registration was with that same spirit of those great men in our history who pledged their lives, their fortunes, and their sacred honor to our new, young country;[123] it was as *The Washington Star*[124] stated "an acceptance of the challenge flung down to western democracy by the dictators."

The Philadelphia Record[125] wrote, "The unflinching answer of American youth to registration for the draft is a great tribute to the unity of our country....This nation's young men threw back into the teeth of the Axis spokesman their sneering statement that democracies are soft. From all parts of the country came reports, not of men trying to avoid registration, but of men reporting before the offices were open, of men reporting who were too young or too old, of men undergoing operations to make themselves fit for service, of men gladly accepting a duty not only of registration but the chance of giving a year of their lives to this country.... President Roosevelt had confidence in the American people. Yesterday shows that his confidence was justified."

"Yesterday was a serious moment in the lives of men who filed in millions past the service registration desks," we read in the *New York Herald Tribune*.[126] "It was a serious moment in the history of the United States, and a very great one. Rank on rank, a million an hour, they trooped by for the great 'muster' of American manhood, without disturbance or confusion, without shirking or recalcitrance, in the spirit, as the President well said, of the pioneer militia in which every man kept a rifle and every man knew that the time might come when he would have to use it....This demonstration of the immense latent vitality and power of democracy in action will not soon be forgotten anywhere. None of these men knows where the road which yesterday he took up may end for any one of them.... Their response yesterday was magnificent and because of it the whole nation today has a greater knowledge than before of its strength and of its value in this dangerous world."

October 18, 1940

The excitement in Paris was great today as British planes flew over the city, making a formation of the letters R.A.F. It was a sign of salvation that seemed nearby. There were tears and laughter and prayers of gratitude all at the same time swelling up from the hearts of the French as they looked up at those young pilots bringing the strong light of hope in the darkness. They were young pilots, some of whom were their own countrymen....

October 22, 1940

Nazi plainclothesmen are entering apartments passing themselves off as radio experts enquiring if the owners are satisfied with their radios and if they find the news from London clear enough. Naturally everyone is on alert....

Rushing home from a dinner party, I found the streets deserted. It was only ten o'clock, but the blackness had an air of hidden danger. My haste was noticed by the military police as I turned into the wide, desolate, deserted Boulevard des Invalides and made toward my street, rue de Varenne, keeping close to the high wall as if for protection. The police were on the opposite side. As I came nearer, one crossed over coming toward me. He must have felt my relief and my feeling of safety at his presence, for he walked a few steps beside me and left quite silently but not before I said, "*Bonsoir, Monsieur l'Agent, et grand merci.*" (Good night, Mr. Policeman, and many thanks.) I was glad when I reached home. Some months ago, I wrote in this journal that Paris was the safest city in the world. Today it is a different story; the scene had changed. Stories of civilians disappearing never to be heard of again are prevalent; German soldiers are killed every night; Nazi patrols do not hesitate to turn their guns on those whom they find on the streets after eleven o'clock sounds.

A wet passport was given in at the Embassy today. It had been taken from a dead body found in the Seine. It belonged to a United States citizen of Swiss origin. Was it suicide? Foul play? Who knows?

The Spanish border is again closed. No Spanish visas are being issued. I talked with the Spanish Consul General[127] over the telephone today concerning the necessity for United States citizens to leave France urgently. He was most courteous and suggested that the [U.S.] Consulate General cable Madrid. Undoubtedly the matter will be considered favorably.

American Embassy and Passport Issues

October 23, 1940

Gold and brown leaves are falling from the trees in the garden of the château across the way; gold and green leaves are falling from the trees along the Champs-Élysées; they are under feet on the terrace of the Embassy as I pass through the stately courtyard with expectancy in the early morning, wondering what change in the war phase will greet me.

What did greet me today was the beauty of lovely Princess de X., a United States citizen from New York, ostensibly an ambulance driver, but deep in protective work for British aviators parachuted into France. She came in for a passport service, also to obtain information as to what help the Embassy might give her for her British aviators. There was nothing that could be done by the Embassy; this same request had come to us a score of times by letter and telephone for those working in the Résistance and for others in civilian lives who were risking much in the cause. The Embassy might not be able to help them, but hundreds like her were engaged in this same patriotic work. She eventually contacted some of them.

It is very interesting to feel the pulse of Paris, the pulse of the French spirit, changing as it does and as it has done so many times since 1938: Munich and the glad tidings of peace followed by a tension and half peace; 1939 that ushered in the mobilization of the French accompanied by the sureness of victory; the tragic days leading up to May and June of this year; the convulsive hours of defeat as the conquerors entered the beautiful city. Following these events was the curious sensation of the Occupation, with the feeling of tolerance by the French for the Nazis during the first awestruck days after their arrival. The Nazis might have had tolerance turn into liking. It has, on the contrary, turned against them and has left a burning hatred. The elaborate propaganda, that is the posters and notices the Nazis placed throughout Paris and the French villages in an effort to create dissension between the British and French, has been a boomerang, striking the Nazis with full force. The home of the French today is in England.

For the sorrow, the suffering in the minds of the French is mingled with an optimism and confidence that is carrying them on. They are facing a hard winter, but the presence, although secret, of the British in their midst assuages their anguish and puts courage into their spirit.

A young French lad outside my window is singing "It's a Long, Long Way to Tipperary."[128] He, too, has caught the spirit of a new hope. I hope there is no Nazi near him as he sings the British war song.

One of the terms for peace is that France will declare war on England.

For a long time, rumours have been circulated that Göring, or Goebbels, or Himmler has been killed by the English. There is a funny side to many rumours. The moment someone announces that one or the other of the Nazi chiefs has passed on to his reward, there is someone who at once replies: "Not at all, he was in the Café de la Paix[129] (or the Ritz[130] or another restaurant) last night. Most probably they are all safe and well."

Curfew is now at midnight. The population is allowed on the streets until then, unless the siren sounds.

Americans Want Visas to Cross into Spain

The Spanish frontier is still closed. The Embassy is streaming with Americans with the one idea of visas to cross into Spain and be on their way home.

Notices were given out by the Nazi chiefs that the fashions for women's clothes would now originate in Berlin. In spite of this the Nazis in Paris do not hesitate to see the collections of the big dressmaking establishments, nor do the German women wait for Berlin's last word in fashion's art. They buy their dresses from Maggy Rouff, Lanvin,[131] and others that have remained open. It is a bit difficult to picture Berlin, Germany, as the seat of this famous art of the French. Do the Nazis really believe that their limited taste in women's clothes compared with the French could take place of this century-old skill?

The same thing might be said of the celebrated *L'Illustration*,[132] the most beautiful of all the illustrated French magazines and perhaps the oldest in France. Today I found a copy of the first German-controlled edition that had appeared (in August): there was a faint effort to keep it French, but the bad taste in some respects, the utter lack of that delicate beauty of color and design, the interesting reading that filled it before the Occupation, had all gone and the savor was typically Nazi.

I stopped in front of the Ministry of Marine building[133] on the Place de la Concorde today where a large crowd had gathered. It was the midday hour when there is the change of German guards at the entrance. The expression on the faces of the French, many of them young *midinettes* off for their luncheon, was amusing. They stood open-mouthed (not believing it could be true) at the solemn-faced German soldiers goose-stepping down toward the curb as the others goose-stepped up from the curb to the entrance and took their places as guards. I heard a voice at my side whisper, "*Eh bien*, Madame, have you come to see the Punch and Judy Show[134] with us?" It was one of the policemen that I recognized as being frequently on guard at the Embassy.

Emile Heidsieck[135] told me today that a large quantity of his own champagne had been stolen and that seven million bottles of champagne of the Charles Heidsieck[136] establishment had been requisitioned by the Nazis. The incident was radioed last night over the British broadcast lines.

Rumours afloat that President Roosevelt has been approached by mediators for peace. Others say that negotiation for peace is being carried on between Germany and England and that the war will be over by Christmas. These [rumours] could only come from the Axis Powers—a victory is not won so easily over the spirit of men in their fierce determination to fight for liberty.

The Nazis are attempting to recruit for employment in Bordeaux. They are looking to hire from amongst the French. The work consists in taking boots from the dead Germans in the Gironde [Estuary]; the bodies had floated down from the north. The Nazi authorities did not dare give the work to German soldiers for obvious reasons....

Mrs. Edward Curley, a British subject who is married to a United States citizen, was refused permission to leave the country by the German Command.

The French are still staunch in their faith in England as their hope of victory and salvation; yet Mr. Churchill, speaking over the radio, held out little change in the war before 1942. They will and they must hold on grimly until the tide turns.

November 2, 1940

The American Red Cross is liquidating its affairs and leaves soon for the United States.

La Toussaint[137] (All Saints' Day) passed uneventfully. Yet, it was observed by the French who took time off from their daily work to roam their city.

"We are all impressionists today," wrote George Moore. "We are eager to note down what we feel and see."[138] Am I an impressionist with an impetus to write in these pages details in the march of events that come to me each day, even as I am now writing far into the night? All is silent; there is no sound but the light step of the French police. It is a contrast to the sound of the heavy German boot that reaches me. How expressive boots are! The boots of the German soldiers have a heaviness, darkness, thickness, significant of dullness, brutishness about them. These Nazi soldiers cannot conceive of the importance of their boots in this lightsome, heretofore gay atmosphere of the French. Boots: war, rain, clouds, mud, bombs, prison, brutality, fear, blackness, evil, hate; they make an impressionist painting.

But I find another picture, another side to all this negation. Nazi boots evoked the one above. I search for the colors and designs of reality, for real substance: a night of stars lighting a path of a war sentinel that he might "walk abroad in the darkness without stumbling";[139] a soldier at the front, perhaps a German soldier; it might be any national of any country, risking his life for a wounded comrade. There we have love in the painting, universal love, sacrifice, loyalty. Or, again, someone giving his life for love of country; his so-called enemies are doing the same for their country; here is patriotism; millions giving their lives for liberty, that treasure of untold value the price of which, someone has said, is eternal vigilance. This is my real painting; the rest is a mirage, a counterfeit, a dream, and unreality; only the good is true.

November 3, 1940

We pause for a moment and wait in eager expectation for the results of the election in our country. Tomorrow the country goes to the poles.

November 4, 1940

"Willkie is gaining."

"The President is losing."

"Who knows? A war is on. These are dangerous days; there should be no change now."

"The President must stand by. He must remain at the helm."

"But Mr. Willkie[140] is so fitted for the presidency—so...."

November 6, 1940

It is over.[141] We know now that the President [Roosevelt] is still with us—thank God. He again has the confidence of the nation. May he steer the ship of state into still waters. Shall he be able to while the turbulent Nazis "make our world one of immense unrest?"

November 7, 1940

Report at the Embassy from another American that yesterday he had been taken to the Commissariat for speaking English. On the street he felt a hand on his shoulder, saw a revolver at his side, and heard a voice say, "*Marchez.*"

"March where?" he replied in English, much surprised. His card of identity made the matter clear. He, of course, had been taken for a British subject; we Americans do speak English after all.

Embassy Personnel Help French Citizens

November 8, 1940

It feels like late autumn. It is cold in wartime Paris with her heatless apartments. I lie in bed watching some dull embers still in my open fireplace. Last night I watched a flame fall asleep as a few bright embers bade me a good night and sank into the ashes. I postpone getting up to dress in my unfriendly room where there is no joy. There were other days, other mornings, when I could scarcely dress quickly enough to be on the street, going down the stairs two at a time in my haste to feel a morning in Paris. There was joy in those days at the turn of a corner: the sound of the *marchand d'habits* ("clothes vendor") ringing his bell and calling his wares and the trot of the white horse of the milkman after he had delivered his milk and is on his way home.

Now there is the sound of the wind through my shutters; there is a cold sun peering through my window trying to find my open fireplace so that, as Proust wrote, "to warm itself before the fire."[142] The wind blows my curtains away from my casement; through the parting of the curtains from time to time I see a few gold-green leaves on my balcony blown from the trees in the château gardens. The church bell is sounding eight o'clock. I jump quickly away from my soft eiderdown for there is work to do....

The press tells us that soap may be had at the shops. When one goes with all speed to fetch it, there is a sign on the closed door: "*pas de savon*" (no soap). Is it a trick? Or are the efforts to place soap on the market unsuccessful? One is suspicious of everything, yet hopeful at the same time. I distribute some soap furnished by the Embassy to French friends in my quarter: the concierge, the butcher, and the milk and butter man.

The Nazis wonder why the Danes do not like them. Why wonder? If you steal my possessions, I am not inclined to love you much. The Danes have no poultry, barley, or wheat. These commodities have gone to Germany.

November 9, 1940

Mrs. A. told me at my cocktail party today that her permission to leave France has been refused by the occupying power. As a British subject, though married to an American, she has no alternative but to remain or take the risk of crossing the frontier en fraude as many are doing. She is afraid to chance that. Her husband risks going to a concentration camp should we come into the war. I thought over every possibility I could gather in my brain to help her. When she told me her British father had built railroads in a South American country and that she had been presented at the Court of St. James's[143] by the Ambassador of that country in gratitude for her father's work, I suggested that she go to the Embassy of the South American country and request a passport in order to leave France. Her eyes brightened with new hope. It did not take her long to do this, and within a day she was across the border and on her way with her husband to New York. Isn't there always a way out?

November 11, 1940

Today is Armistice Day (1914–18 war).[144] Any celebration has been forbidden by the Nazis. The French are bitter indeed. The circumvention of the law, however, did not prevent a crowd of students from marching on the Champs-Élysées to lay a wreath on the Tomb of the Unknown Soldier. It was the first time an open resistance against the occupying power was shown. The students were met by the French and Nazi police with machine guns. Many were killed, more were wounded, and some students were crowded into camions and taken away to a destination unknown. Their parents were frantic; one mother enquired in almost every police station in Paris in her efforts to find her son. The Gestapo would not deliver its secret. The German Military Commandant ordered all universities in Paris closed.

Today my path led to a reception given by the Turkish Consul General in Paris. It was an interesting gathering with a number of the Diplomatic Corps: many French, a scattering of Americans, and a few of the military and of the Navy. There was a notable absence of Nazis.

Standing near our host, I heard someone ask him what Turkey's attitude was in world affairs today.[145] He quickly replied, "The contrary to what you read in the German-controlled French press." The Turks have no love for the Nazis. Nor did they have for the Germans in the last war when, as the Turkish Ambassador in Washington told me in 1925, "We were drawn into this war against our will and against the will of every Turk."

Before leaving the reception, I crossed the room to say goodbye and a word of sympathy to a French lady whom I had met for the first time and to whom I had spoken of my love for France. "Madame," she said, "I am happy to shake hands with America." There is always this spring of hope toward our country.

November 12, 1940

The New York Times arrived from home today. The war in Europe is the most important news in the United States today. There was a trend of doubt in the paper as to which country should win the battle over England. How could there be a doubt?

In Paris, feeling against the Nazis increases each day. In the central markets of Les Halles, seventeen persons were killed in a riot; the populace is protesting the requisitioning of several tons of food by the Germans. This sentiment seemed to penetrate the whole city. In the subway an awkward German soldier jostled against a woman who turned on him, shrieking in French and voicing her resentment and bitterness toward the occupying power. The young soldier, who did not understand a word but sensed the hatred in her tone, was so frightened that he walked to the farther end of the car and left at the first station.

And yet, the Germans at times bitterly speak their agitation toward the Nazi regime quite openly; they know that it is leading to the downfall of their country.

November 13, 1940

A large portrait of Hitler, draped with the colors and medal of the Iron Cross,[146] is prominent in one of the bookstores on the rue de Rivoli. Two guns are spread out before the portrait and two large vases of chrysanthemums complete the picture.[147]

The students' riots on November 11 had their repercussions: universities are closed as well as the lycées° and faculties. Students must return to their homes. Many are joining the Résistance; many go to unoccupied France.

The population is so casual about the sound of the siren after the Germans gave out the false alarms that the air battle over France and the alert last night made little stir. It seemed quite over my roof. I went to my balcony. The stars were out, millions of them. Against the background of night and stars, the battle raged. Up there were danger and possible death. I wondered if I were becoming accustomed to air raids and danger because, looking upward, I felt a thrill such as I had in my childhood on a night of the Fourth of July when fireworks were active. I almost expected to see the skyrockets rise from the ground, open up in the heavens in myriad colors, and fall slowly, grandly into the void. War, death, beauty, darkness, and light are all in one breath. It was over in a moment....

November 16, 1940

The swastika flies over the public buildings. A barge winding its way along the Seine toward the Cathédrale of Notre-Dame was flying the same insignia this morning.

° Lycées—High schools.

I entered the Embassy market to find a large pig lying on the floor waiting for its purchaser to take it away. On its head someone had painted the swastika.

November 19, 1940

A British plane was brought down by the Germans last night; the pilot, a Frenchman, was killed.

Guns, sabers, revolvers, helmets, salutes, patrols, planes above us, and camions on the streets: they are symbols of war and hate, and they surround us continually. Every step we take we meet this war. It is above us, before us, and behind us; it surrounds us. We speak in low voices and look to the right and left before speaking, or we do not speak at all.

I met Diana FitzHerbert[148] at La Crémaillière[149] for luncheon. The restaurant was full of German soldiers.

"What news?" was her first question.

"Lots of it," I replied. "But I shall not tell you any of it here." One Nazi hearing us speak in English changed his table and took another near ours. No doubt he hoped to learn something....

A Jewish woman ordered to place the sign "Jewish Enterprise" on the door of her shop refused to do so saying, "You may shoot me at once if you care to, but I shall not put that sign on my shop." The German agent told her that she was not obliged to do so and left. I am afraid the story did not end there....

Food is becoming scarcer each day; bread is becoming darker; there is no butter, eggs, or milk on the French market.

There is news from America. Every citizen is working at something for national defense. The Gallup Poll[150] in late June after the fall of France showed a leaning toward Germany as the victor in the war; today it has turned toward England.

In France, eighteen students who had been cleared in the Armistice Day riots at the Arc de Triomphe were shot today for carrying arms. They had carried out a deliberate plan of manifestation: with a photograph of General de Gaulle they marched through the streets shouting "*Vive de Gaulle!*" Their professors had locked them in the *lycée* to prevent them from parading, but they escaped and stepped up their activities.

Two English women, openly distributing British tracts and BBC programs they had written up, are to be tried as spies....

November 28, 1940

Rising from my warm bed in what seems to be night, and trying to believe it is morning, may be interesting in wartime, but it is anything but comfortable.

It is indeed dark at 7:30 a.m. as I close the apartment door. I reach the river as the night becomes almost light with a cold sun trying to force its way through. And there she is, the Seine, this human Seine; she has a responsive note as I greet her and watch her beauty swirling in tiny eddies under the bridge.

This year the annual reunion of coiffeurs will not take place. Designers of hairdos must go to Berlin for inspiration and reunions; the styles must all come from Berlin, so the Nazis have decreed....

There was recently a woman having her hair arranged at her coiffeur in Paris. She was speaking in French to her coiffeur and wished to tell her impressions of the occupying power apparently to anyone who would listen. She did not know that the adjoining section was given over to gentlemen who, as she did, wished to improve their appearance; nor, alas, did she know that a Nazi officer was seated there. The officer, before leaving, whispered something to the lady's coiffeur; it was an order to keep her there until he should return. He came back within ten minutes with a Gestapo agent who ordered the hairdresser to shave his client's head.

November 29, 1940

He seemed somewhat impatient and was standing in his German uniform at the perfume counter waiting for the saleslady to ask him what he wished, so my French friend related to me. My friend was buying some Houbigant,[151] if I recall the mark. I know she likes Houbigant because it reminds her of days long ago in Monte Carlo when Houbigant's *Quelques Fleurs* breathed its perfume on her great romance....

She turned to the saleslady with, "Do wait on the gentleman. He seems pressed for time, and I am in no hurry."

The man looked at her and almost laughingly said, "Thank you, but I am not really as hurried as you think."

While the saleslady was searching for a perfume that she felt might please the officer, he leaned toward my friend and whispered, "Be patient. Hold on until we come. It will not be long ... and tell the French that England will not fail them."

With these words he quickly disappeared, lost in the crowds as he made his way toward the entrance of the immense department store. He was a British Intelligence Officer wearing a German uniform.

December 1, 1940

The year is drawing to its close; this vital, epoch-making year, weighty with events, will soon be over as its course streams into history.

Looking backwards the scenes tug at the heart. In June France fell and alone was invaded by an alien power. It is alien in culture, alien in a meaning of moral values, and alien in intellect. Today in December the occupying power is administrating the affairs of France by their own conceptions: the Gestapo watching the inhabitants in their homes, offices, on the byways; screaming planes above; on the streets, the heavy tread of soldiers' feet; Nazi uniforms, tanks, camions; intermittent, clandestine news from England; French news (so-called) giving only information the Nazi authorities wish the populace to read whether it be true or false, or even no news at all; unheated houses; difficulties in transportation with the absence of taxis and buses; scarcity of food, clothes, wood, coal, of the normal functioning of the post; black nights....

Those hidden embers of the Résistance in faraway places reach and inflame the cities and villages as riots and protests against injustices continue pitilessly, relentlessly.

France is silent today. She works on in silence and waits....

The Embassy and Citizenship Issues

December 4, 1940

The British are damaging railroads and the trains transporting German munitions and soldiers. They are bombing the hangars belonging to the Luftwaffe, and they touch the Bois de Boulogne where some of the Luftwaffe officers have installed themselves in luxurious requisitioned apartments. The Nazis feel it is wiser to find other quarters not quite beautiful, perhaps, but safer....

In Holland the sign "Jewish Enterprise" has been taken away from the shops. The populace was buying from these shops while the "Aryans"[152] (whatever Hitler understands by that) protested against their lack of clients. In France the signs remain.

In the Paris subway, notices inform the public that the seats are reserved for the Nazis; four, however, remain for the French.

Today all British women and children were taken up for internment in concentration camps. The police went down from house to house gathering them into wagons, which took them to the railway stations: Gare Saint-Lazare and Gare de l'Est (Saint-Lazare Station and the East Station) and onto a destination unknown, but known to be a long distance from Paris. One woman of eighty years with a serious illness was taken. Diana (Lady Diana FitzHerbert) telephoned me from the Hôtel Le Bristol[153] Paris, where she is staying, to say that the police had come for her.[154] They gave her twenty minutes to be ready. One thoughtful policeman told her to be sure to take some woolen clothes with her, as where she was going, it would be very cold. Diana is British but claims United States citizenship by her birth in America where her parents were staying when she was born. An American passport had been issued to her, but as her French identity card showed British nationality, the occupying authorities would not release her. I told her to send her passport and documents showing her United States citizenship to me, as the Embassy would investigate the matter.

In the prisons in Paris where the British men are interned, there were distressing moments as the men listened for the names of their women, relatives, and friends who had heretofore visited them. Today no names are being called as the women, too, are suffering the same fate as the men. British clergymen from the British Embassy Church,[155] nuns, members of other churches, too, are being taken. Some are being sent to Germany, others to Besançon and Vittel [in France].

Pictures in the movie houses showing the bombing of Berlin by the Royal Air Force are applauded with enthusiasm by the audiences. This has so annoyed the Nazis that when the newsreels are shown, the house is brilliantly lighted; the Gestapo in the building is thus able to spot those who applaud. The Gestapo took this measure after the threat to close the movie houses (should applause for the British continue) had no effect. Besides, the Germans, too, enjoy the movies. I saw a number of the French walk out when the German news began on the screen.

There are rumors of revolt in Italy; the men refuse to be remobilized to fight with the Nazis.

December 8, 1940

A child is playing in the gardens of the Luxembourg [Hotel]. I sat near the Medici Fountain for a moment, beautiful with its Doric columns, its faun, and young huntress. I was musing (the gardens in Paris seem to be made to muse in) far away from these tempestuous days. Here the great men of France in sculpture look out on the gardens: Verlaine is here along with Chopin, Sainte-Beuve, Boucher, and Watteau—men who lived in the seventeenth, eighteenth and nineteenth centuries and who gave luster to the country's brilliant history.[156]

The child is throwing a ball. It is caught by a young officer in German uniform who brings it back to the young child.

"*Merci, sale Boche*" (Thank you, dirty German), I heard her lisp to my consternation.

"Someone has told you to say that, little girl?" he quietly asked her. She looked at him and repeated, "*Merci, sale Boche.*"

The officer stooped toward her and said, "Fortunately for you, you are not in Czechoslovakia as you say that." He passed on his way. The incident ended my musing and brought me suddenly back to the present, to France imprisoned by the enemy….

December 10, 1940

Peggy de Nemours arriving from Biarritz told me that all was not rose-colored there. She and her husband had been asked to occupy the beautiful home of Mr. Frederick Prince, who is now in New York. Before the Duke and Duchess took the house, the Nazis had already been living there. The Nazis left in their wake ruined furniture and marred parquet floors. A Van Dyck[157] painting had been thrust in an out-of-the-way place, and other valuable pieces had been damaged. Nazi *kultur*[158] perhaps does not appreciate Van Dyck's paintings. The de Nemours had not been in the villa long before a pompous, monocled Nazi officer came to see them requesting several rooms for his men. He insisted on entering, pushing past the footman; he came face to face with the Duchess. The latter, as I have said, is an American citizen. In straight-forward but unmistakable terms she told the officer that not only could he not have the rooms in the house, but that she did not wish him to enter the house at all; that it was already occupied by her husband and herself and that they did not desire any other occupants. The officer startled at the vehemence with which the lady spoke, clicked his heels, saluted, and departed.

December 13, 1940

Pierre Laval[159] is sent away from the Government of Vichy by Maréchal Pétain.

The Duke and Duchess of Nemours are now in Paris; they found their apartment uninhabited and are making arrangements to remain for some time. They had been here but a few days when one night the Duke found that he had remained from his home after the time limit of the blackout. Time had run on too quickly, and His Royal Highness had completely forgotten that there was such a thing as the curfew. He was walking quickly.

"*Monsieur*, you seem to be in a hurry. Where are you going?" It was the voice of the law. A policeman was beside him.

"Mr. Policeman," he said. "I am simply taking a walk, a fast walk."

"So I see," replied the agent. "At this hour? It is long after the hour when people should be off the street. Your identification papers, please," he said coldly.

The Duke produced his French passport on which was inscribed "Charles Philippe, Prince d'Orléans, Duc de Nemours."[160]

The policeman having scrutinized the document, looked suspiciously at the owner and said, "Is this correct? Is it true that you are a Prince d'Orléans?"

"Yes, *Monsieur*, it is quite true."

"Well, *Monsieur le Prince*," said the policeman, "walk any place you wish, at any time you wish. We need men like you in France today."

Not all the policemen in Paris are Royalists, however....

Diana FitzHerbert will be released from the concentration camp in Besançon at once. The Nazis have decided that "an error was made"; they have acknowledged her United States citizenship. She leaves for New York within a few days.

December 15, 1940

The night in December was bitterly cold with a light snow covering the ground when the ashes of the Duc de Reichstadt,[161] brought from Vienna, were placed in the Invalides near the tomb of Napoléon, his father. As the press stated, it was a thoughtful act on the part of Hitler toward the French. The French were not at all impressed by the great "generosity" of the Nazi Führer.

December 16, 1940

An inhabitant from Dinard, while walking along the Champs-Élysées, stopped abruptly in front of a British subject whom she had known for many years and, to her amazement, found him in a German uniform. She stared and was about to speak when the man suddenly put his finger on his lips and left without saying a word. She looked after him, but he was soon lost in the crowds. These interesting and important incidents of war in France, with members of the British Intelligence in our midst, occur frequently. How vibrant with hope they are!

Rumors again come to the populace that the Pétain government will soon be in Versailles. The Maréchal, however, is averse to the idea; he refuses to leave the unoccupied zone. Is the report a trick of Pierre Laval to isolate Pétain and take over the government himself? When the Maréchal ejected Laval from the government, he told him that he had no confidence in him. He felt Laval was selling the country to the Nazis....

The cold is intense. At dinner last night every guest kept on his or her coat. While electricity is almost normal, the electric stoves dispersed through the different rooms give little heat. At another dinner party I attended recently, the guests were given woolen shawls or blankets to cover the knees.

Vegetables and fruits are not to be had at any price. A few potatoes have appeared on the market as well as the much ridiculed and non-nourishing rutabaga. Meat is expensive and rare, except horse meat if one cares to eat it. I ordered some sausage in one small restaurant. After one mouthful it was put aside with grave suspicion. Later I was warned never to touch "sausage" today in France. What it might consist of one does not know: dogs, cats, any animal may have its part in the making of what is called "sausage." Today there is little, if any, inspection or control of food.

Conversation in Paris that once upon a time had dress as its preponderant topic amongst the women, now gives place to food and the effort to keep warm. A neighbor of mine is raising rabbits in her cellar; another has chickens in a room of her apartment. Every space in gardens in Paris is now used for growing vegetables instead of flowers. In the shops where once delicious French cakes, chocolate éclairs, vanilla cream, etc. were to be had in abundance, now they are replaced by other sweet dishes made of dark flour, sugar, a kind of chocolate, with dates or nuts. It is disheartening. Still, it is indeed courageous of the shopkeepers who are making such valiant efforts to satisfy the need for sweets.

The gold-winged horses on the Alexandre III Bridge were silhouetted against storm clouds as I passed late today, wending my way homeward. The torrential rain has spent itself. From the back of the clouds, the peculiar light of a sunset was trying to force its way through the grey. It gave a singular illumination to the city as the day died and left me with a sense of impotence. In the vastness of the heavens the great masses of clouds seemed to hang over the city, ready to drop down and crush everything in its path, including our little lives as well. The feeling no doubt comes from this destructive war: bombs and black clouds, a melancholy, a confused mass of heavy thoughts in one's consciousness as the dark days move on....

The light became brighter as I left the bridge. It came through the clouds, or perhaps the clouds were held back by the taut strings of light that scintillated in back of them. I thought that beyond and above the vicissitudes, the tragedies, even the sometime dullness of our lives, there is that mount of inspiration, of light, where we may rest for a while before continuing our journey. There we find peace and truth, always, always there....

All British decorations are forbidden to be worn.

The new posters that hung on the walls of the Chambre des Députés showing France crucified by the English (naturally) have been torn down.

Mrs. Oldenburg, a United States citizen, widow of the late Danish Minister in Paris, after a short conversation on the street with one of her compatriots, was followed for several paces by a member of the Gestapo. He stopped her and asked why she was speaking English in public in Paris. She replied, "As I am a citizen of the United States, as have been my ancestors for generations, it is quite natural that I should speak my native language anywhere...."

Seated before my open fireplace, I am warm in front. My fur coat prevents my back from being stiff with cold. The atmosphere is glacial. I bought a sweater today with the same idea in mind, that is to keep warm. The saleslady told me that it was among the last in the shop. "When they are sold," she explained, "there will be no more." Shoes as well have disappeared. As there is no leather, I am unable to order any.

German Questions American about Embassy Operations

An American known to the Embassy staff was followed by a German in civilian clothes, a secret service member, no doubt. He asked him to tell him about the Embassy: what the work consisted of, how much the members of the staff were paid; finally, were there any spies in the building? The American coldly replied that he knew nothing about the Embassy....

Lights out as usual at midnight. There is a fine of two hundred francs for anyone who has not extinguished his light except for the occupying power. They may race around in Paris in their cars with bright headlights. Their offices, the different Ministries, the Chambre des Députés, and the Invalides are all illuminated....

In the early morning when it is still dark outside, I leave for the Embassy. As I near the Seine, I find the river rubbing her sleepy eyes, not yet awake, dreaming under her dark coverlet of night. One stumbles against someone else in the blackness, but there is good humor in these daily happenings....

December 22, 1940

A restaurant where I often had luncheon before the German Occupation, which was once filled with French officers and soldiers, now is frequented by Germans in uniform. Some young French students came in today and hung their bicycle pumps as usual on the wall in raillery at the Germans whose daggers were hanging beside the pumps. The German regulation is that their daggers must be taken off when they enter a restaurant. Indeed, the French have not lost their *esprit* (wit or sense of ridiculous). It was seen again when the *Faculté des Lettres*[162] of the University of Paris reopened a few days ago. The students had a piece of macaroni fastened to the lapel of their coats in mourning for Italy. (The Italians were driven out of Egypt on December 12 by the British.[163]) Again when Martini,[164] the French singer, appeared on the stage of one of the night clubs, after his song he raised his right hand apparently giving the Nazi salute to the applause of the Nazis. Martini waited until the noise subsided, kept his hand raised and said, "The French are bored, fed up, up to there!" Grand applause from the French and bewilderment on the part of the Germans who did not understand....

December 23, 1940

Ambassador and Mrs. Leahy[165] sailed today from Norfolk [Virginia] aboard the USS *Tuscaloosa* for Lisbon, en route to Vichy....

December 25, 1940

Christmas Day. Music and midnight Mass in the churches were forbidden by Hitler.

My path took me toward the Cathédrale of Notre-Dame this morning. It was bitterly cold. The sun was making every effort to warm the city, but I wrapped my fur coat tightly around me and went into the building to see my armored knight on his horse in the thirteenth century-stained-glass window near the north transept. He was on his way to the Crusades in those far-off days. I wondered if it had been the Christmas season when he started on his journey. Outside the church the gargoyles looked down leeringly on this desolate, defeated France. The gargoyles had not prevented my knight from beginning his mission in that fight for freedom the Crusades were engaged in. Again, the liberty to set free the Christ spirit from the spirit of the unbeliever.

The flower market under the shadow of the Cathédrale towers was almost void of flowers; the plants were there but were too heavy to carry. I found some roses. My day is full with dinner preparations, and my table is complete for my Christmas dinner table, which will be white for a white Christmas. There will be red roses, red ribbon, and candles for festivities to cheer a few of our fellow citizens far from home and to cheer a few French in this troubled land.

We Do Not Know the Future

December 31, 1940

A dreary rain covers the city. Are the elements in tune with the dying year as its light flickers out over wartime France? The "Explosive forties" have run their course.

Assistant Secretary of State Long's[166] message to the Foreign Service touched each one of us profoundly. It was "an individual and personal message because it is directed to every member of the Service whatever rank, be he or she a Chief of Mission or the most junior member of the clerical staff on U.S. Foreign Service..."

> To the members of the Foreign Service wherever they may be:
>
> We do not know the future...Times of crisis make for great opportunities. Difficult times prove the man or the woman as no amount of easy living can possibly do and consequently, the times through which you are now living and doing your part prove the value to the United States of the service of which you have so ably, so effectively and so unselfishly formed a part. We in the Department are proud of every one of you—we have no doubts that you will completely measure up in the future as you have done in the past to whatever demands may be made upon you, and we send you our heartfelt congratulations upon a spirit which refuses to complain or quit when the going gets tough and which surmounts physical discomfort and dangers of separation from loved ones or whatever else may confront them for the glory of the service and the welfare of the United States....
>
> ....to all of you our best wishes for the coming year....

A cable from Robert Murphy in Dakar, North Africa, reached the Embassy yesterday. Dakar—Free France!

I do not know what was in the cable—that is not my affair. Important? Most probably. For me, word coming from a representative of our country in a part of France that is free, bringing a message to this enslaved land, has untold significance. As the tragic days of 1940 pass into history, as 1941 dawns on a bewildered world, we have thus the inspiration to look upward and onward with love and new hope.

End 1940

CHAPTER 3

January 1, 1941–June 3, 1941

The American Embassy in Paris Relocates to Vichy

January 1, 1941

There were no festivities last night to usher in the somber days of the year that lies ahead. Private parties at home were quiet as the French and Americans made an effort to bring cheer into their own lives and into the lives of so many bending under burdens that seemed too heavy for them to carry. The Nazis were making the most of the coming in of 1941 and were loud and riotous in the night clubs and restaurants. I woke feeling a wearisome in the atmosphere, a dull hope, or it might have been no hope at all.

The snow grated under my feet as I left the apartment of Mrs. Freeman late this evening. On the little rue Barbet-de-Jouy where she lives, all was silent. It had been snowing all day and a white mantle covered the city; no one was on the streets. To be at home in the struggle to keep warm was the aim of the population. The château opposite was like a Christmas card. It, too, was covered with snow, and the light from the windows might have been candles lighting a Christmas tree inside. Tonight, there are no Christmas trees....

Is there nothing that can lift up my spirit, or that can lift up the spirit of those out in the dark to a plane where hope is? Not tonight, but tomorrow it will shine; the evil hour is fleeting, ephemeral, the light of faith lives on. We wait and turn to God....

> That even the weariest river
> Winds somewhere safe to sea.[1]

January 2, 1941

President Roosevelt's address that came to the Embassy by radio bulletin and which, in spite of every effort of the Nazis to prevent it from reaching the French, filtered through to them and pierced the darkness. Is the entry of the United States in the war so near? The address unnerved the Americans in France; however, they do not know what to do. Some are too ill to take the trip to America; others are too poor. Should they remain and hazard the harrowing probability of a concentration camp? Should those who are ill risk death on a voyage that in these days would be precarious even to those who are strong?

January 3, 1941

No food in the market today. My governess told me that there is no food line as there is no food. The expensive restaurants are filled with the Nazis; in the smaller ones and *bistrots* the French find cheaper and simpler meals. Food and restaurants—where to go, what are the prices? These are the only topics of conversation. The ration tickets issued by the Nazis give more than one can possibly eat, even should one be able to procure the food. These tickets are given to the Diplomatic Corps, and we in turn pass them on to our French friends and, of course, to our compatriots not attached to the Embassy. The Nazis seem to have the capacity of eating a great quantity of food. They have a kind of appreciation of the French cooking but, as a French friend of mine remarked, "We cannot forgive the Germans for eating oysters with red wine." An unforgivable sin in the French mind is to serve the wrong wine.

My shoemaker informed my governess that the next time my shoes needed mending, it would be necessary to take them to the police station where the agent in charge would decide whether they really needed new leather. Leather is scarce, and what they have today will soon give out.

From the British radio: success and important British victories in Libya[2]....

January 8, 1941

Down in Vichy, Admiral Leahy has arrived as the new American Ambassador to the Vichy government. He will present his credentials to Maréchal Pétain.

The French cling to the predictions from the *clairvoyants*. Today the prediction of Sainte Odile[3] came to my notice. It was a letter foretelling present events by this same Saint who lived centuries ago: that a second Joan of Arc would appear to lead the Allies to victory, that the war would end in 1942 with the defeat of the Germans, and that Paris would be free. In the concentration camp where the British are interned, a fortune teller had told Diana FitzHerbert that she would soon be free and that the war would end in 1942.

January 9, 1941

There are rumors that Hitler is putting pressure on Spain to allow German troops to pass through the country; that the British are bombarding the French coast.

From the *Paris-soir* (German-controlled): not one British subject believes in victory; failure of preparation being the cause of defeat....

Notices on the walls of buildings in Paris read: "*Vive Pétain*" and "Let me alone with your talk of the de Gaullists, the British, the lies."

January 10, 1941

Today I went to escape from all this tragedy. I want to leave the war to others. Why should I bother about it? It does not belong to me. It is not my war....

I almost ran to the rue de Verneuil to visit again the apartment I had seen in 1939 when I had searched for my own; I was being drawn to it again; it seemed so familiar as though I had been there long ago, had lived in it, had indeed known the people in it; I wanted to be sure that it was not only a dream. I wondered if the people had come back, or if the dust was still thick on the furniture because no one had come back; if the pictures loosening in their frames were still crooked against the walls; if the cobwebs still stretched from the ceiling down to the piano; or if, indeed, the restless spirit of the owner who had passed on to the Beyond, was still hovering around his dwelling seeking what? whom?

I was never to know the answers to these questions; I found an answer, however, in the impulse to wander into the past. I left rue de Verneuil and the apartment undisturbed as there was no response to my knocking or ringing from the concierge.

I turned to the rue de Lille that is quite nearby. Here I went backwards across the years, twenty-three to be exact, to that other war when I first came to France. Rushing past the concierge, I climbed the four flights and entered the tiny apartment that I had lived in for so long. There was the open fireplace; the embers were there, too, as quiet as they were in that time long ago when I sat before it trying to keep warm waiting for him....

Quite near was the small room where every bit of space seemed taken up with an object of antique art; next to it the bedroom, and beyond was the kitchen where I prepared a simple meal for him when he came for dinner. Romance was stretched out through the rooms as though it had never left. Love had been there; it must have stayed. I closed my eyes; love was a living thing in those past years. Where had it flown? Where does love wing its flight when it seems over and gone?

I ran down the broad stairs. There were tears in my heart; love had left its scar.

I crossed the spacious courtyard. The snow was falling in large flakes. Out on the street the concierge, the same concierge, older and grey, was shoveling the snow making a path for the tenants. She gave me a glance and turned away. Had the years changed me so much? All the memories of my life in rue de Lille rushed past. They disappeared, however, as I ran and ran. Even the nostalgia they had left in their wake vanished. I held one memory close, however—the one that had left a scar....

In the blackout I could not remember if I was living in 1919 or 1941. Time is an illusion....

A group of German soldiers passed. That brought me back into the present. German boots were not heard on a Paris street in 1919. Paris belonged to France in those days....

I am late. I must hurry on to my rue de Varenne, my dwelling. I must follow on with my people, my Allies, in this—my war. It makes me one with the great heart of the world. This is my war.

Names of Embassy Staff Given to German Authorities

January 11, 1941

The names of everyone on the Embassy staff were given to the German authorities a short time ago. The occupying power must take count of friends and enemies alike.

The clandestine tracts from the Résistance come to us more frequently as the Gestapo becomes stronger and crueler. The Musée de l'Homme[4] at the Trocadéro is one of the centers of the underground. It is a glorious, courageous group of men and women, and it is in direct contact with England. The pamphlets issued by the different groups[5] are diffused throughout France from such groups as "*Résistance*," "*Le Coq Enchaîné*," "*Libération Sud*," etc. The members of some of the groups are charged with the sabotage of transportation lines and munitions factories, attacks on isolated German soldiers, and the cutting of lines of communication. The reprisals by the Nazis go on, but instead of stopping these patriots of the underground, the resistance groups continue their work with ever greater activity.

Every day Frenchmen are taken by the Nazis: sent to camps, to Germany, to prison; some are shot or denounced sometimes by their own people. God forgive them.

January 16, 1941

From the bridge I watched the ice floating swiftly down the Seine. My fingers were almost frozen, and the icy wind attacked my ears. Leaning over the parapet quite near me was a Frenchman with only one arm; no overcoat covered the thin body; his suit was worn and of light material; tragedy and misery were in his eyes. Indeed, this is my war. There is no escape; so little one can do in the immensity of it....

In *Le Matin* yesterday appeared an article describing a Franco-American incident,[6] scarcely amicable, which took place in Vichy. In a gathering of French and Americans to celebrate the Eve of the New Year, a Frenchman of the Vichy government protested that the gramophone was playing the British national anthem. Outside the building where the Frenchman and one of the American guests, who had resented the Frenchman's remarks, discussed the matter somewhat forcibly; the former was given to understand that the gramophone had been playing one of America's anthems, which has the same music as that of the British "God Save the King." Unfortunately the German-controlled *Le Matin* made no mention of this, but suggested that the American be requested to leave France to "exercise his talent of a boxer somewhere else."

It is 10:00 p.m. Not a sound is on the streets. The blackness outside is thick. It is not as safe in Paris as it was a year ago. Incidents occur every day of handbags being taken from women after dark, of assaults on passersby. One does not express any opinion concerning the present regime; those who have done so have suddenly disappeared leaving no trace. When an investigation begins by the family of the vanished person through the police, the Nazi authorities, naturally, are unable to find him or her....

The press continues to reiterate the intention of the Nazis to feed the Paris population. Germany is sending 400,000 tons of potatoes, 100,000 tons of meat, etc. to France they say. So far it has not arrived. Nazi promises!

Reading Mademoiselle's household budget, I find for the week the following items for food: bread, barley (to mix with what is called coffee), onions, cheese (with no taste, a kind of Swiss cheese), apples, watered milk, lemons, ham, turnips, oranges, carrots and rutabaga. One day there was some butter. This is what we had for a week. It is excellent for reducing one's weight. A friend asked me what I did to have become more slender.

It is time to write and read during these winter evenings by my fire, when all is dark outside, making it difficult to roam about even with an electric lamp. I take up my *Middle Ages in France*.[7] There is a similarity in those far-off days and in Paris of the present time: dark streets, narrow streets, women with hoods as the snow falls in great flakes. There are few vehicles; at times none can be seen at all. Over in the Latin Quarter today I met Sylvia Beach,[8] the attractive owner of her library "Shakespeare and Company." Afterwards I wandered through the small byways leading to houses built in the tenth, eleventh, and twelfth centuries. Beneath the snow there was the aspect of the villages of that dawn of French history, the beginning of French culture that has never been equaled....

I leave the French Middle Ages and return to the dynamics of today of this twentieth century full of explosives from the English Channel down to Africa. There are days when one does not know whether a bomb will land some place near; or whether tomorrow will bring forth enough food for us to carry on; or whether an ultimatum or a simple invasion of another country will send us into different parts of the globe or even to our own land in defense of our liberties; or whether a member of the Gestapo will knock at our door some morning and take us up for questioning for something we are ignorant of, or make some grave accusation.

Embassy work goes on with increased tension. Crowds still remain to be repatriated; foreign refugees from other countries are still seeking visas to travel to the United States. There are American wives who must leave, separated from French husbands who cannot leave but who want their women to reach safety. There are sons separated from parents who want their children away from the danger of being sent to Germany or imprisoned. There are rich women leaving all the beautiful things they have collected during the years to return home.

January 23, 1941

The British took Tobruk yesterday.[9] There was uplift of morale and in the atmosphere, as the voice over the radio rang out this splendid victory. It gave us new hope. Even those French who distrusted the British caught the glimmer of a light of liberation for their country. Twenty-five thousand Italians were taken prisoners by the British.

The German soldiers refuse to remain in their barracks around and in Paris. They know that the British bombs are merciless, as merciless as the Nazis have been and are, with this exception: the British make every effort not to kill women and children. As a result of this bombing, the Nazis are requisitioning more hotels. They give the residents already there twelve hours to vacate.

It is warmer during these days; there is a lull, so to speak, in the intense cold of last week. One can almost smell the spring. One cannot, however, be too optimistic. There is much cold ahead before the buds begin to show their first green in the gardens.

Some Embassy Staff Members Reassigned to Vichy

January 28, 1941

Some members of the Embassy staff have their orders to proceed to Vichy. Our radio bulletin chief was one. We shall be without news from the States. The Naval Attaché's section of the Embassy leaves at once for Vichy; other members of the Embassy staff depart. As a group we are becoming smaller. Shall we remain until victory comes? Shall we be forced to leave?

German music over the radio was exceptionally beautiful. There were nostalgic love songs sung by a baritone of rare perfection. It was followed by French music in a lighter vein. The French prefer gay music today; the country has enough sadness. A voice sang "*Chaque chose à sa place*"[10]

> *Chaque chose à sa place*
> *Les vaches dans le pré*
> *Le chat sur le toit*
> *Les oiseaux dans leurs nids*
> *Et vous, Madame, dans mon lit…*
> *Mais, oui!*

> Everything in its place
> Cows in the meadow
> The cat on the roof
> Birds in their nests
> And you, Madam, in my bed…
> But, yes!

Edward Rothschild's beautiful Château de Ferrières-en-Brie[11] in the Seine-et-Marne Department has been taken by the government for the services of the youth of the country.

Le Matin published in big headlines this evening "Great Britain reaches the end of its strength. American aid arrives too late." As we have already arrived and have been with England for many months by sending munitions, planes, etc., the Nazi-controlled French press is juggling with the truth as usual.

January 29, 1941

Rumour persists that Maréchal Pétain is working toward closer contact with England; that war will be over this summer.

There was a feeling of optimism by the news; it was felt in the shops, on the streets. True or not, the rumour is grasped at by hearts that are reaching for peace, for freedom from this intolerable present. The man who sold me a battery for my electric lamp had listened to his radio and, hearing that I was an American, expanded his talks in criticism of the Nazis and of the great hope that the rumours were true. "*C'est vrai, n'est-ce pas?*" (It is true, isn't it?), he asked me. For some reason he seemed to think that I had accurate inside information on these matters.

Even the market gave out more cheer as food appeared: rice, cauliflower, and *yaourt*; and *pas cher du tout* (not dear at all), said Mademoiselle, whose one idea is economy.

January 30, 1941

The cocktail party today was gay enough and crowded enough. But today in Paris, which is occupied by the enemy, cocktail parties are dangerous. All went well as I held an animated conversation with a Frenchman whom I had known for many years. "Yes, he is going to organize everything well," called an exultant voice from across the room. "He will reorganize Europe; all will be different and a better world to live in after the Führer completes his work and develops his ideas. How wonderful he is! How well he knows!" The Frenchman who was lauding Hitler was standing next to a beautiful young blond woman. I asked the man next to me who she was. He told me that she was the daughter of the Chief of the Gestapo....

The Gestapo! My host is Hungarian; my hostess is an American from New York. They had dared to ask me under the same roof as the Nazis! They know my feelings on the matter....

The Nazis! It is not altogether for what they do, but it is for what they are, the measure of their inmost being: cruelty, inhumanity, pride, arrogance, hatred, ugliness. Because of their blindness to beauty, we hold them in dishonor.

Our actions are the result of what we are, that which is our being, our essence, our soul. The Christian philosophy teaches forgiveness of one's enemies, for it is "not for the sake of the enemy," writes Oscar Wilde, "but for one's own sake."[12] It is for the betterment of our being.

I left the cocktail party with Paul R. of our Embassy. Out on La Place de la Muette[13] we groped our way in the semi-darkness. A young German soldier, who had been drinking too much of his country's very good beer, jostled against us....

In the restaurant Marius[14] on the rue de Bourgogne there were few people. It had always been crowded; the copious menu was known to show excellent food, and the cuisine was one of the best in Paris. Tonight meat and vegetables were crossed off; no cheese, no dessert except fruit which, with a kind of soup, and an omelet, we had dinner. With the coffee being nationalized, which means undrinkable, we took none.

February 2, 1941

Optimism and hope endured only for a day. The feeling of apprehension returned. In the restlessness at night, in the silence before dawn, one hears the sobbing of France....

The French, while longing and watching each day for the defeat of Germany, at times are afraid that in the end Germany will win. What can they do? Countless persons are mesmerized by the propaganda and the news of the victorious enemy. It reaches us coming from the Russian front where the Nazis seem to be triumphantly reaching their objectives and aims. This mesmerism of fear is an individual as well as collective menace; it is an evil in our private lives that struts about like a Goliath with a long sword, a helmet of brass, and a coat of mail. "But there was no sword in the hand of David."[15] His power was born of God.

Snow was falling and covering the château and gardens opposite my balcony when I awoke as the sun came through the clouds. It vanished, however, but again there was the promise of spring.

Arrests by the Gestapo continue; the victims are increasing in number each day. Last night toward early morning three long police whistles sounded on the street coming from the alarm box on the corner quite near my apartment; then silence for ten minutes followed by gun reports. Overhead German planes flew above the city, above the activities below. The press gave out no news concerning it, but the rumours and whisperings grew that the underground had started an uprising.

The press states "the greatest air raid that has ever been known in the history of man begins soon." It is the great German offensive in the air over England. The Nazis shout their victories. "German submarine warfare is on its way. Every Atlantic transport ship will be attacked!" Does that mean United States transport as well? If it does, it means war with our country. Hitler brags, or is he too drunk with victory to think?

February 4, 1941

Before me is one of the many predictions of future events of the war that are found in the press or in leaflets disseminated amongst the populace. They give a light of hope although their accuracy is to be contested:

February 20, 1941   Occupation of Tripoli by the Allies
March 13, 1941   Attempt to land in Plymouth by the Germans. The Germans are thrown back into the sea. African troops under the orders of General Weygand contacting British Army and under British Army orders.

April 20, 1941 New attempt to land at Glasgow by German troops
May 7, 1941 America enters the war
May 27, 1941 Landing of American troops at Bordeaux, of the British at Boulogne and Calais
January 21, 1942 Peace is signed

Hope indeed springs eternal....

Through the Door to the American Embassy in Paris

February 5, 1941

The notable, the famous, and some not so notable pass through the door to the American Embassy in Paris. Spies are around us; we are careful.

Madame Dubonnet (Jean Nash)[16] swathed in a mink coat entered the Embassy for her travel documents for America as she was accustomed to do.

The Jewish rabbi, too, came in, he who a few months back was caught entering a foreign country in an attempt to smuggle cocaine hidden in his prayer book! A naturalized American citizen, he came to the Embassy wearing a long, dirty soutane; an unkempt beard covered his chest; he spoke with a strong Jewish accent.[17]

Then came Mr. X., one of the "confidence men" who had, with the much-played "rosary game," swindled the simple and too credulous American tourists out of their money, their jewels, and American Express Travellers Cheques.[18]

Two lovely young things entered the passport office to have their papers in order for return to America. They were not enthusiastic about leaving Paris. They had lived here for some years; had been seen about in expensive restaurants and night clubs, on the Riviera, at Deauville and Le Touquet,[19] any resort where gentlemen were willing to pay their fantastic prices. They were hatless and simply dressed at our government building today, while at Maxim's[20] where I saw them yesterday, their castor [hat] and mink coats might have been made by Revillon[21] and the smart hats by Reboux or Valois.[22] They are courteous and simple and very, very clever; it is wise for them to leave Paris. One of them greeted me with a kiss and told me that she was contemplating marriage. I hope she makes it....

The Queen Consort of England[23] is sending packages of food, *médecines*, and clothing to British subjects in concentration camps.

Monsieur L., *Préfet de Police*, has been arrested with thirty-five members of his staff.

February 8, 1941

Over in the Saint-Germain-des-Prés district I stopped at the Deux Magots café where I had the *café national* and a biscuit. Facing me was the Church of Saint-Germain-des-Prés (Saint Germain of the Fields), the ancient abbey built in the sixth century, and older than almost any other church in Paris. It stands there, the survival of a past age in its superb Roman-Gothic architecture, having withstood invasions, wars, and revolutions. They have left their scars but have never extinguished that inner flame, that expression of spirit one feels in the great cathedrals and churches of France of the Middle Ages.

There are few students in the café of the Deux Magots today, this renowned meeting ground for intellectuals of every nation. It seemed so desolate that one wonders if it will return to its former fame and activities when this nightmare of war and government of France by a foreign power is finished. I gave fifty grams from my German ticket for my tart; five for *matières grasses* (fats, butter).[24]

In the packed house where a German film was being shown today, the newsreel pictured a Nazi plane bombing a British cruiser. Suddenly the house became brilliantly lighted. A policeman stationed along the aisles of the movie house scrutinized the members of the audience to note criticism and remarks against the Nazis. The punishment for any subversive observations was arrest and the closing down of the movie house.

February 10, 1941

"We shall not weaken or tire. Neither the sudden shock of battle nor the long-drawn trials of vigilance and exertion will wear us down."[25] Mr. Churchill's voice was strong and resolute over the radio as we listened in on the BBC.

Paris-soir in big headlines informed us that "eight months after M. Reynaud sent his anguished cry to the United States, Churchill is sending his." How desperately the Nazis want it to be so! There is indeed anguish in the heart of the Prime Minister of England. He can but give his people "blood, sweat and toil." He tells them however in his magnificent courage "there will be no compromise." Does Hitler hear as he flaunts his words to his satellites who still believe in him?

There are rumours that numbers of French police have been shot by the Nazis; that numbers have sailed for England; that they are being replaced by the Gestapo.

Living as we do in this atmosphere of danger continually, we ask ourselves, as someone asked of me today, "Can it be possible that at home they are reading newspapers that give facts and events of the war, talking openly, leading normal lives?" One does not seek to escape or to be relieved from this immense opportunity for service in the great cause and in our daily work. There is hate, defeatism, and suspicion that we meet at every step of the way. If we are not vigilant, we, too, turn toward fear and loss of faith, which are useless weapons of defense.

February 12, 1941

My young French friend, who recently escaped from a military prison in Germany after killing the sentry, taking the sentry's gun, and succeeding in crossing the border, told me that there were Germans of kindly feelings who hate the present regime in their country. Of course there are! He said that when the German guard in his section of the prison said goodbye to him, the German guard remarked, "I am ordered to take a medical examination. It will be the end, for there are no mutilated Germans in Nazi Germany. I shall never see you again." Man's inhumanity to man....

White narcissus blossoms fill my room. Their fragrance penetrates the apartment. Their message penetrates my consciousness. It is a vague message but very real.

At Rumplemeyer's[26] today I had luncheon with Jean. He was still in mourning for his wife who had committed suicide the day he left her for mobilization in the French Army in 1939. They were very much in love; she could not go on without him. His black tie and black armband were eloquent of his deep sense of loneliness. We were talking in low tones when we suddenly became aware of the waitress waiting for our order. At her side was a man, ostensibly the manager of the restaurant. It was the first time I had seen the "manager" accompany the waitress in. Was he another Gestapo agent? If so, he must have been disappointed as he listened to our conversation....

Rumour—the American Embassy is Leaving Paris

February 14, 1941

Vladimir gave us excellent Russian food last night at his small and delightful apartment on the rue de Chateaubriand. Baron Vladimir de Stukenberg is of British and Russian descent. He is a friend of the de Nemours whom he invited along with two White Russians and me. He had in some mysterious way found enough food to feed more than six persons which, with some vodka and red wine, made the party gay with the war far away until the conversation turned toward the war and the probable time for the war to end and which side would be the victor. Some were for Britain; others were sure of a German victory. Suddenly from across the table, Peggy de Nemours leaned toward me and, in her rather high voice with its suggestion of her Virginian birth, said, "Marie-Louise (that is my name), I hear that you are all leaving the Embassy—in fact leaving Paris very soon."

"Really?" I questioned. "You seem to know something that I, a member of the Embassy staff, do not. We are not leaving Paris. The Embassy will remain. We are here to stay."

"But, yes," she persisted. "Within a few months the whole U.S. Diplomatic Corps is leaving the occupied countries. You will travel in private, luxurious trains toward the Spanish border, then on to Lisbon. From there I do not know where you will go."

One of the war bombs might have burst quite near me as Peggy continued her story. The Duchess talks a great deal; however, it is always interesting, and I dismissed the idea. With a shrug I said, "You are mistaken, I am sure."

Leave Paris? France? Abandon our friends in their difficulties and misery? It is unthinkable....

I came to my apartment alone although Vladimir wanted to see me home. If he had, he should not have been able to catch the last subway train, which would have left him in danger of being on the street in the blackout and of being taken to the police station to remain until the next morning at five o'clock.

Walking up the rue de Bourgogne in the dark with my electric light guiding my path, I recalled Peggy's words about our departure from France. Could Peggy be right? How did she know? Where had she heard something so important that we of the Embassy were ignorant of?

Can it be true? There is too much to do. Some of our Americans are still here. And what of our French friends, those who count on us so hopefully, so trustingly. Shall we leave them utterly alone?

February 16, 1941

Rain, wind and cold in the early morning hours. Tonight it began again. I can hear the tap, tap on my window as I write. On the radio there is an Italian program; someone is playing Toselli's *Serenade*.[27] I turned back in memory to 1918 when I first saw France, when I played and loved and danced, when every day was an adventure and every night a dream. The Armistice of 1918 had given new life to the world....

The sound of the storm outside brought me back to the present.

A German announcer came on the air a few minutes ago. There was a loud applause as the news of German victories was shouted over the radio. Is all this going on forever? I brush my arm across my eyes to efface the thought. Where has my courage gone? What right have I to a moment's, one moment's feeling of defeat? I must be very, very tired....

February 21, 1941

There was the other side of the picture as the British broadcast gave the news. Ten thousand German troops nearing the coast of Dover in an effort to invade England were burned to death as oil was poured on the waters. The Nazis, it was affirmed, were using poison gas.

The enemy was too sure of victory. What did they expect? Weak, futile resistance? Or no resistance from that indomitable, unbending spirit of England? There is nothing weak about the British during these perilous days for their country.

At the Foucher[28] chocolate and candy shop, I tried to find some chocolate for my cocktail party tomorrow. There is none in the shop. An old man at the entrance, poorly clad, peering in at the almost empty windows said to me, "If you have nothing else to eat, eat salt."

There are soup kitchens, however, around Paris, and there are Red Cross restaurants. Other inexpensive restaurants are valiantly carrying on. Yet the misery goes on. There is not enough for everyone....

To order a suit, I must have a card which is obtained at the *Mairie*, which is the police precinct of each city district. To have a card, I must allow an inspector to come to my apartment, look into my wardrobe and decide whether in his opinion I actually need a new suit!

Persecution of the Jews continues. At Maxim's restaurant, which is controlled by the Germans, there is a sign on the door of the *lavabo*: "Reserved for Aryans."

At the entrance of the subway, a German officer opened the door for me. As I waited inside for Mademoiselle X., a Jewess attached to our Embassy whom I was to meet here, I noted that the German officer had made no motion to give her the same courtesy....

A French lady was asked by a German whom she knows why the French disliked the Germans so much. She replied, "Oh?' He continued, "Yes, in the subway when they find themselves next to a German officer or soldier, they at once move away to another section of the car." She again replied "Oh?" She said nothing more. He must still be puzzled, or can he guess why?

Mussolini asked General Franco[29] of Spain, so a story goes, for naval bases near the Spanish coast. "But what good will naval bases do you, Duce?" asked the Spanish Chief of State. "The British are taking your bases in Africa and in the Mediterranean countries and will undoubtedly take the ones you are asking for now. So what could you do?"

March 2, 1941

March opened like a lion with high winds and cold. A brilliant sun, however, shone over the city later in the day.

While some of the population goes to the races[30] toward the Bois in motor scooters and other curious improvised vehicles, I climbed into a carriage drawn by a horse and driven by the auburn-haired lady in red coat and tan breeches known throughout Paris. It was like a novel. Up the Champs-Élysées the driver was greeted by almost every traffic policeman on the way; some gave the "go" signal with an exaggerated stiffness of the arm as though it were a fast motor car passing. Men, women, and children were all for her; some applauded her, clapping their hands in cheer. Coco, the name of her five-year-old brown horse and the gentlest animal that ever was, was given sugar incessantly by the passersby.

Over in Africa war is going on. England is fighting for her life. British bombs are falling on Berlin, on Italy, on France. The sounds of battle reach us in Paris. The British broadcast, muffled by the Nazis, tells us that the German Army is facing defeat. Even a pro-German White Russian, whom I know and who told me recently that it was useless for the Allies to keep on against the tremendous strength of an unconquerable Germany, said today that he believes in an Allied victory....

The Bill for aid to England passed our Senate by a large majority.[31]

Norwegian Islands, whose food had been requisitioned by the Nazis leaving the inhabitants practically no food, were visited by British and Norwegian planes that dropped food down to them.

March 3, 1941

In the Tuileries Gardens the first indications of returning spring brought new life to heavy hearts. Fountains were playing under a resplendent sun, children were sailing their boats in the basins or throwing their balls; the budding of tiny green leaves were seen on bare branches of trees; lovers were walking arm in arm. It all brought to the surface a joy that is in the consciousness of all human beings. This joy is my rightful gift; at times it is latent, held down by a heaviness too great for a surge to surface....

The great dome of the Invalides was black, outlined against the night of the stars, as I neared it. I thought it looked swollen in the blackness, as though it were about to burst, correlated to the tension of the times in which we live. Are the times so big with events that soon they will explode into a climax?

Trouble was brewing at the Solférino subway;[32] women were protesting their husbands being kept prisoners. The French policeman was trying to reason with them and to keep the Gestapo from any knowledge of the affair. Their voices grew louder, and their words became vituperative. The policeman shook one woman who kicked him. He promptly retaliated by giving her a blow on the cheek with the palm of his hand. She was so surprised that she stopped speaking and quickly disappeared. The others followed and there was peace.

March 16, 1941

The French-German press is full of blistering words against the British because of the *blocus* [blockade], which is preventing food from the United States from being distributed to "starving French children." The British are preventing food from reaching the Nazis who, instead of giving it to "starving French children," either send it to Germany or keep it themselves in France. A compatriot told me today that he was giving up his work of distributing food coming from America and returning to the States. The food, he said, reached the Nazis and no one else....

March 20, 1941

There is no further talk of the German invasion of England. The conquering Nazis were so sure. The French are reacting jubilantly as the word "*Victoire*," or the letter "V" is being written everywhere in chalk on the buildings and walls. "*Victoire*" was chalked on my apartment house. As I entered it, the concierge was washing the writing away upon instructions from the police. The light is coming through; fleeting and evanescent, it shines toward liberty....

April 11, 1941

I tried to reach Vladimir's apartment on the rue de Chateaubriand but could not find it in the dark. The concierge had disappeared, having been called by the Gestapo to answer questions concerning the whereabouts of her son who had escaped from a German prison. She denied knowing anything about him although they suspected her of hiding him. If it were so, she risked being shot immediately. Her son had gone with the Résistance we learned later; he had left no word with his mother, as he knew it would be dangerous for her.

The Résistance grows. More and more French lads go out to that dangerous existence—that vast network leading from General de Gaulle's headquarters in London.[33] They give up family and friends, their homes, all they have. If they are caught, they will be tortured or shot and often both. But they keep on, fearlessly, secretly, bearing false names, false cards; they are alone, intensely, cruelly alone....

I crossed in front of the Sainte-Clotilde Basilica[34] in the dark. There was a brilliant moon. The spires of the church looked like sentinels keeping watch. Around the corner I turned into rue de Varenne and my home....

Embassy Staff Receives Privileged Treatment in the Marketplace

April 12, 1941

Mademoiselle, my governess, is having a lively time with the German ration cards. At first, she was afraid to show them to "*Monsieur Bœuf*," the butcher, or to the delicatessen shop, or to the milk, butter, and egg store; she thought she might be taken for a pro-German. When the shopkeepers knew that she was employed by a member of the staff of the American Embassy, she suddenly became an important person in the neighborhood. However, I was requested to sign my name at all the shops and to show my card of identity.

Big Ben rings out in the night from London over the radio. The news is serious. German troops are victorious in Libya. This, after the British gains. French morale will be low tomorrow. It affects us all. British determination to go on to final victory and the destruction of the Axis powers is accentuated. Nothing daunts these intrepid subjects of the British Empire who are commanded by a superb leader, their Prime Minister.

Mrs. G., a naturalized United States citizen of French origin, came into our building with all her French blood racing at high pressure. Young, beautiful, and intelligent, she had been accused by the Germans of being a spy. It was eventually proved that she was not. "Yes," she almost shouted through the echoing walls of the Embassy, "I am selling the whole d... business and returning to America." One of them who is the Kommandantur had said, "*Ma belle petite espionne*" (My beautiful little spy), and when I [Mrs. G.] replied, "*Mon sale Boche*," (My dirty German), I was free at once!

April 21, 1941

Miss Neeser of New York came to us for news of her brother, Robert,° who had not been heard of for several months. He was last known to have taken a train for Vichy,

---

° Robert Neeser has lived in France for years, highly respected by the French and the American Colony. He has left no trace. He has never been heard of since his disappearance.

but since then no word. The Embassy is investigating.[35] What could be the reason for a tragedy of this kind? We are continually in danger, and no one is immune. We can put our trust in no material help today as capable as it may be. So far we are alone. We must look to God....

Gun shots at four in the morning heard below on my street. Is the Résistance at work again? Those relentless, defiant, brave men of the underground....

May 1, 1941

The French Labor Day passes uneventfully. The Communists had no demonstrations. The air is warm although it is a grey day, drab and dull. It is a holiday, however. The *promeneurs* (the strollers) move about listlessly and silently. But they are pensive. Where are they going? Where is the whirl of events leading them and their country? They do not know. They only know that England is trying to stimulate them to stand firm in trust, to inflame their hearts to know that victory is theirs, if they will only believe in it. But they only hear the triumphant echoes of Nazi victories resounding from North Africa. What are they to believe indeed? It takes an illuminated faith to know that evil cannot triumph unless men, individually and collectively, accept defeat.

Tonight, over the radio the French from London are calling on all workers of France to stand together as one united people in the struggle for liberty. Here is confidence; here is a spirit of resolution. The reason for the silence on the streets on this first day of May, everywhere amongst the population, is clear. They had been urged by London to show no demonstrations today. The speaker told them tonight that the French in England were proud of them for their stand in abstaining from activities, hostile or otherwise. There were no lilies-of-the-valley on the streets nor flowers in the *kiosques* (flower stands on the streets). Everything was vacant and silent.

On my balcony the begonias and petunias were giving out their color and fragrance....

May 11, 1941

The first buses appeared on the highways today.

News from the women's concentration camps came from a British subject, a woman of 65 years of age who had recently been released. Every night she was obliged to stand in a line of hundreds to use the lavatory outside the building; that the beds were so close together, they were obliged to leave by the foot of the bed as there was no room between beds to stand; that rooms which ordinarily hold a few persons were packed with double the number; to wash they were obliged to fetch the water outside the rooms along the corridor, bring the bucket to the bed, lift the mattress and let the bucket of water stand on the slats while they had their daily sponge. This English woman, who had been accustomed to every comfort in her home, said that she had been in the camp only four months, but that it was the longest four months of her life; she would remember it until the day of her death, so horrible it was....

The United States Chargé d'Affaires[36] left Paris on May 7th for Lisbon en route for the United States.

One hundred and sixty French and German prisoners at the French prison in Fresnes have been shot: some of the French were held as hostages while others were caught in the Résistance by the Nazis; the Germans had been interned for desertion or attempted revolt.

Staggering news over the radio that Rudolf Hess, Nazi Deputy Führer and Hitler's right-hand man, had taken a plane and had landed in Scotland. Was it a trick of Hitler's to send him as a spy? On a peace mission? Had Hess lost his mind? Was it fear of the Gestapo that had decided him to escape? The speculations are numerous. Hess was at once imprisoned by the British. The radio stated that the English and United States, even the French press, were full of the incident.[37]

Lost dogs wander through the streets, whining for their masters who were obliged to leave them behind as they took the long, dangerous path of the exodus; or who had forgotten them in their feverish haste; or who had left them with friends until their return. The friends, however, have not been able to find food for these unhappy wandering animals. If they are caught by the police, they are put in the pound where, if they are still alive after the war, their masters may find them again. Not only our four-footed friends are suffering, but the pigeons, the sparrows, and other birds are dying for lack of food. At night I hear the weird cry of the pigeons, hungry and desolate.

Embassy Gathers Staff Names, Telephone Numbers, and Addresses

The names of the Embassy staff, telephone numbers, and addresses were taken by the administrative section yesterday. It was a further intimation of the probability of the United States entering the war and of our leaving France. The uncertainty amongst the remaining Americans is growing. I am stopped on the street by our compatriots who ask me frantically what they should do.

"I must talk to you," cried a voice near me today on the Place de la Madeleine. It was someone whom to my knowledge I had never seen but who knew me as being at the Embassy. She took my arm and led me into the entrance to one of the buildings....

"You must tell me," she said. "Are we coming into the war? All my possessions, everything I own in life, is in France, in Paris. If I go, it is possible that I shall lose it all; if I stay, I face a concentration camp. You have heard what that means. What shall I do?" She was indeed distraught. What could I tell her? What advice might be useful? Would she take it?

I closed my eyes for a moment and saw the beds close together in the concentration camp, so close that the occupant was obliged to leave it by the foot; I saw the hundreds standing in line for hours to fetch water for washing....

"Madame," I said. "I cannot tell you what you should do with your life. You ask me what I should do under your circumstances. I can only answer that from what I have heard and from the tales I have listened to from those unfortunate English women who have experienced life in a concentration camp. I feel that the loss of all my possessions would be worth it if it meant avoiding such a life." She made no reply, and I left her not knowing whether what I had said had helped in any way.

Queen Wilhelmina of Holland spoke to her people over the British broadcast from England tonight.[38] A great woman indeed! Her voice, clear and determined, counseled her people to stand strong until victory comes; her gratitude to Great Britain and her faith in her country were profound, and her words were filled with deep feeling.

The sounds of triumph were almost deafening as I turned on the radio in the small hours of the morning; the King of Abyssinia was entering his country—the first nation that had fallen under the power of the Axis Powers to be liberated![39] The national anthem was sung as their flag rose over the palace....

A faint light of hope, dim but ever shining, takes on an added brilliance....

May 12, 1941

"Our industries, the tremendous steel industry of the United States and our other industries," said Alistair Cooke[40] over the radio, "are larger than that of Europe, Asia, and Africa together." With a "goodnight" in a tone that left no doubt in any mind which country he wished to impress, he left the air.

Today is the day to honor the canonization of Joan of Arc. The population was told that they must have no demonstration. However, they gathered in a great crowd at the *Place des Pyramides*[41] in front of the golden statue where the *Pucelle* [Joan of Arc], astride her horse, holds her banner triumphantly above the assembled masses. The spirit of battle and victory of those far distant days in the history of France seemed to emanate from the youthful figure as the people, who must have felt it, unrestrainedly and fearlessly shouted, "*Vive l'Angleterre, Vive la France—à bas les Boches.*" The press noted that the women were louder than the men in their acclamations....

Rumours spread that the clandestine newspaper *Combat*[42] will soon be distributed; also, that de Brinon,[43] appointed representative of occupied France to the German High Command, has been threatened by the Free French if he continues his policy of collaboration with the Nazis.

May 15, 1941

Le Matin (German-controlled) explained the recent radio broadcasts of the Rudolf Hess affair.[44] Rudolf Hess flew to Scotland feeling that he might arrange a peace or compromise between England and Germany—so *Le Matin* explains. The newspaper continues, "His humanitarian sentiments are particularly acute." Knowing the great military power of Germany, Hess was afraid the English people would be completely annihilated in the next phase of the struggle. From papers Hess left (it was pointed out), he felt that England would not continue the war were it not for Mr. Churchill and his clique, who were intimidating the mind of the public. "They alone," wrote Hess in his notes, "are preventing peace in the world. The consequences will be terrible for people living in the British Isles."

The article states that as it seemed useless to Hess to discuss the matter with Mr. Churchill—that he did not wish to speak to the Prime Minister in any way. He decided that the Duke of Hamilton,[45] whom he had met at the Olympics of 1936, would be the one man in England whom he might persuade to arrange a "peace of compromise." The article stated that Hess expected to return to Germany within two days.

The surprised British imprisoned Hess immediately. How little Rudolf Hess knew the British! Compromise? The British will consider peace after there will be a surrender of the Nazis unconditionally. The Germans must be coming more nervous than is thought. Another peace offer is made to England!

May 18, 1941

To inaugurate National Fair-Trade Week, Secretary of State Cordell Hull said: "Threats to induce this country to refrain from all real efforts at self-defense until Hitler gets control of the high seas of the world ... this is the favorite method to induce many countries to refrain at efforts at self-defense until Hitler is ready to seize them."[46] The Secretary's words were the answer to the German Grand Admiral Raeder threatening our convoy plans.[47]

May 21, 1941

The SS *Robin Moor* (U.S. Merchant Marine)[48] was sunk by a German submarine off Brazil.

Soap is one of the luxuries of life. Its scarcity becomes more accentuated every day. Our *Carte de Ravitaillement* (supply card)[49] does not give us enough tickets for soap. A list of those who may have a larger quantity was printed in the press: those with occupations that accumulate dirt, dentists, surgeons, sanitary places, persons with special illnesses, and those with whom German soldiers are billeted. (The French ask if Germans are dirtier than most people.)

Spring days in Paris. In the Élysée gardens the first small daisies and purple clover appeared. The chestnut trees are almost in full bloom. The lilac branches are bending under the weight of their own heavy blooms. There is fragrance, light, and beauty around us....

More Embassy Staff Members Move to Vichy

May 22, 1941

Ascension Day![50] "Ascension Day," a speaker over the BBC began, "is ascension after great tribulation!" Was he thinking of his country's ascension soaring upward through tragedy, untold tribulation and pain?

The news that the Embassy is closing reached us like a thunderbolt. Part of the staff will move to Vichy. It is fraught too heavily with impending war in our country to leave us untroubled.

May 28, 1941

Why are waiting and uneventful days in our lives more difficult to endure than any action might be? This year, 1941, opened in shadow, in gloom, and moved on toward a despairing blackness. A "somber winter" someone called it. There was no light, no illumination to show us that there was a way out. A cruel enemy seemed to be always triumphant. Its victories were shouted to the world. The British held fast to the ship as great waves passed over her. Yet during those dark hours her strength and faith reached France. The Free French with General de Gaulle in England inspired their people in France to action, as the Résistance, unstopped, incessantly harassed the enemy. The light was still dim, however. In all these relatively inactive months, there was suspense, uncertainty, and contemplation; with many, unfortunately, there was an infinite trust.

Psychologically, spiritually, perhaps this period had its meaning. It was a preparation, a wandering in a wilderness of doubt and loneliness but which led to a vestibule of great events to come.

Activities seems about to begin....

President Roosevelt's address to the nation and to the world was broadcast early this morning. The British said that the United States from Canada to Florida, from the east coast to the far west, or, in other words, our country was aflame with anticipation. Our President said, "But those people—spiritually unconquered: Austrians, Czechs, Poles, Norwegians, Dutch, Belgians, Frenchmen, Greeks, Southern Slavs—yes, even those Italians and Germans who themselves have been enslaved—will prove a powerful force in the final disruption of the Nazi system."[51] He issued a proclamation that "an unlimited national emergency exists."

May 31, 1941

So much has happened at sea. Last week the British cruiser, the HMS *Hood*, is sunk by the German battleship *Bismarck*.[52] The German-controlled French press made the most of it and of the splendid German victory when 1,300 British officers and men went down. It was not long before, to the amazement of the world, word came from the British radio that the whole British Navy was following the *Bismarck*. They sank her within a few days; two thousand officers and men were lost. A British spokesperson noted that as one German officer was being carried into port on a stretcher, the officer exclaimed, "Do not think we are fighting for Hitler. We are fighting for the Fatherland."[53]

The British advance in Africa.

The great oil fields in Iraq are in the hands of the Allies.[54]

Our Ambassador in Vichy, Admiral Leahy, is vilified in the Paris press as he travels to Marseille to receive shipment of food and *médecines* for starving France.

German Authorities Order All Staff to Leave the American Embassy

June 3, 1941

Orders came from the German authorities that every French national and every foreigner must leave the Embassy.[55]

CHAPTER 4

June 4, 1941–July 20, 1941

The American Embassy Facility in Paris Becomes a Consulate

June 4, 1941

The Embassy is no more an Embassy.[1] Today in the Ambassador's reception room we gathered to receive our orders.

Fifteen Americans of the Embassy staff (three women and twelve men) will remain in Paris to carry on the work of the Consulate General of the United States of America. The sign "Consulate General of the United States" is placed on the side entrance of the Embassy on the rue Boissy d'Anglas. The main entrance to the Embassy is closed. Laurence W. Taylor,[2] American Consul, is in charge.

Mr. Taylor spoke to those of us who will remain in Paris in a gathering in the reception hall, urging us to give our best to the work ahead. I was one of the fifteen Americans to remain in Paris. He counseled us to refrain from any observations outside the Embassy; that strict silence on the confidential matters we should be entrusted with must be absolute; that our small group was selected to carry on the traditions of the United States Foreign Service; and that we must not fail in any way. When later on I thanked him, he said, "It is a great adventure we are facing; I hope you will be happy. We do not know for how long it will be."

Sitting before my fire tonight, I watched the bright flames quickly turn to embers. I close my eyes and memory goes back to those first days eight years ago when the Embassy building was new, scarcely finished in fact, when I began my new life in it. There were two hundred and fifty members of the staff. It is over now. Something else is ahead. The uncertainty might be unnerving were it not for the fact that fifteen members of our country's Foreign Service are ordered to carry on its tradition and that "Neither snow, nor rain, nor heat, nor gloom of night"[3] shall swerve us from completing our task. There may be danger ahead. These are perilous days. We cannot do otherwise than be ready for them....

June 5, 1941

Miss Marie-Louise Dilkes:
This will inform you that the telegraphic instruction from the Department dated June 3, 1941, has designated you to remain in Paris.
E.A.P.

My orders are definite.

June 8, 1941

Sunday. The holidays blend in with the ordinary days. There is no festal hour.

The French cling to any news that might hold a ray of hope. Today word goes about that the government is returning to Paris, that the occupying power will leave the city. Leave? The Nazis leave, now? The conqueror yielding?

Yesterday there was the rumour that General de Gaulle and his troops were in Syria; the day before we heard that the United States cannot keep out of the war and that soon the American troops will be on the streets of Paris.

The bread becomes blacker. At times it is not edible. *Biscottes* are better, so I resort to them.

Camembert cheese today is so different from the renowned French camembert before the war that one scarcely recognizes it. One eats it all, however, as there is not much else. There is no scraping of the outside of the cheese; food is too rare to lose any of it....

Madame de Seguin, a widow living in Nice with her two grown sons, has found some potatoes for her boys; for her the skins are sufficient to keep her from total hunger. The Nazis had promised more food after the Armistice, "but there is less," complained one shopkeeper.

The radio announced the death of Kaiser Wilhelm[4] at Doorn, Holland. It evoked other days, another war, another German aggression....

In the subway a Frenchman losing all control took a German officer by the shoulders and shook him and said, "We have had enough of you. When will you leave our country, never to return?" The surprised Nazi moved away but said nothing.

An automobile driven by a Nazi officer ran over and killed a Frenchman. A French bystander (perhaps a secret police) immediately killed the driver. The matter was hushed up.

The Embassy corridors are dark and silent. Only the ground floor shows signs of activity. Other floors and other sections of the building are under lock and key. Up on the first floor where I went in search of some papers needed in my work, there was no sound but the echo of my footsteps—there where the tread of hundreds of feet were heard, and the sound of gay voices rang out day after day....

June 23, 1941

The news rings out over the radio. It passes from one mouth to another as it filters through: yesterday Hitler attacked Russia. Ignoring the non-aggression pact made with Russia in 1939, with no declaration of war, Hitler suddenly sends his divisions toward the East.[5] The French, at first bewildered at this turn of the wheel, slowly begin to realize that it may mean a turn for the better for the Allies.

Dorothy Thompson,[6] the noted United States journalist, triumphantly and jubilantly proclaimed, "Everything I have predicted so far concerning international events has come true." In a BBC address she said, "I did not think that Hitler would at this moment attack Russia. I did not think he was so stupid." Her words reached us in Paris.

It is the beginning of the end of Nazism, the downfall of Germany.

New Orders for the American Consulate in Paris

June 27, 1941

Events in our personnel lives are rushing through the days with rapidity not known since the end of the tumultuous 30's.

From our representative in Berlin by telegram June 25 comes the following to the American Consul, Paris:

> I have been directed by the Department to instruct you as follows:
>
> 1) All officers and permanent employees are directed to leave your post in order to be out of Germany or occupied territories before July 15[7] and to proceed to Lisbon[8] for further orders. You should proceed by the most direct route possible before that date allowing yourself sufficient time to comply with these instructions....
>
> 2) Arrangements are being made for the despatch of American passenger vessel from New York to Lisbon carrying German and Italian Consular personnel and will bring American personnel from Lisbon on the return voyage....

June 29, 1941

Preparations are beginning immediately. We had hoped to the last moment that we would remain in Paris until the war ended. It is all over now; we are leaving France....

Five thousand Russians throughout occupied France have been arrested. Elderly General Goleweski of our Embassy for many years has been taken. Alexander Ignatieff, also attached to our Embassy for many years, loved and respected by everyone on the staff, left for Marseille before he was taken. He has gone and will cross the frontier en fraude to join our Consulate in Marseille. We are awaiting word that he crossed over into unoccupied France safely, but we do not know yet.

July 3, 1941

Maxim's was crowded last night as our party of eight sat down to our reserved table. I had been invited by an American with three other United States citizens and three French.

I was much surprised on entering the restaurant to find a long table in the middle of the large room where twenty German officers in civilian dress were seated. At another large table were the Italians. It was a gay party; champagne flowed freely, and the seven-course dinner included the finest cuisine in Paris. At the left of our table along the *banquette*, Pierre Laval was dining alone; on our right, Madame Lanvin of the famous and perhaps oldest dressmakers' establishments in France was dining.

The orchestra seemed to be endeavoring to please these guests who had invaded their country, or was it a *force majeure*?[9] I tried to hear the beautiful strains of a Strauss[10] waltz, but in vain. I wondered why beautiful music is played so often to those who do not listen....

We left toward midnight. I was glad when it was over. I seemed not to have realized, before accepting my hostess's invitation, that while food would flow in abundance at Maxim's, my French friends were searching for enough food simply to keep alive. All is confusion. Much is contradictory in this tangled skein of world events and in this Occupation of France by a ruthless foe.

I did not return to Maxim's; I shall not return until it once more belongs to France....

Consulate in Paris Prepares to Leave Occupied France

July 4, 1941

Our great national holiday passed in preparation for our exit from occupied France, which is set for July 19th. I am celebrating it in spirit. I look up to that Power that governs the universe and pray that as our entry into war moves nearer, our nation will be protected, and as our men and women go into battle, it will be without destructive hate....

Word came that Alex Ignatieff was taken by the Vichy government police at the frontier. The prison was at a distance from where he was arrested. He was obliged to find someone to pay his transportation to prison, but no one wished to do so. It was therefore somewhat ironic that Alex paid for his own travel expense to prison. However, when he arrived, and when the inspectors realized that he had fought in the French Army before the fall of France, and that he had been attached to the American Embassy for so many years, he was free to go on his way and proceeded to Marseille.

July 14, 1941

The French national holiday was quite different. Whether it is because there is sentiment in the heart of everyone that the Nazis are at the beginning of their fall from power, or whether it is this glimmer of optimism that gives courage to the populace, we cannot know. There is dancing tonight on the streets of Paris, and the crowds stroll up the Champs-Élysées and into the cafés. There are no fireworks, however. The cinemas are closed, and the police are entrusted to see that order is kept. A few persons who had the courage to wear the blue, white, and red cockade of the French had them torn from their shoulders. A young French girl with the colors of her country draped around her was taken up by the police. Blue, white, and red flowers were taken from a French woman who was carrying them home.

"V" for victory was written on many of the buildings. I was mixing with the crowds and moved over toward the Rond-Point des Champs-Élysées. I stood on the outside of a group surrounding a man being taken off by the police who kept shouting, "*Vive de Gaulle—vive la France!*"

July 15, 1941

Not finding any leather shoes in the shops, I bought a pair of wooden shoes.[11] If I had searched throughout the country for a souvenir of France at war, there could not have been one more in keeping with French art and these stirring times than these beautifully made shoes. The soles and sides are of solid wood with a cut of exquisite design; the upper parts and straps are of woven straw. Besides, they are amazingly comfortable....

July 18, 1941

Special trains from Berlin carrying the United States Diplomatic Corps from Germany, Italy, Holland, and Belgium went through Paris tonight and passed on to the Spanish frontier at Hendaye.

Tomorrow we leave; we count the hours, the moments. Tonight, I left the Embassy overwhelmed by depression. French friends met me on the way home. They are sad and apprehensive; their friends, the Americans, are leaving. They feel desperately alone, deserted as it seems to them by their protectors. I could only urge them to wait, to hold on, and to bide their time. "We shall return to you without fail," I said....

Consulate in Paris is no More

I awoke after a sleepless night. Nothing seems real. I am leaving France. My bags are ready. I look over longingly at the château and at my flowers on my balcony. Shall I ever see them again? They have been such friends....

The car belonging to Mr. Whitcomb,[12] the well-known U.S. journalist, took me to the Austerlitz station where our special train was waiting. En route I thought of the dinner party five months ago when Peggy de Nemours told me that the Diplomatic Corps would leave France on special trains. I did not believe her; I could not....

Mademoiselle, my governess, reached the Quai [Austerlitz] a few moments before the train was ready to leave. "Dear Mademoiselle, I am so grateful for your kindness, your loyalty and devotion; nothing was too much trouble for you. You will take care of the balcony, the flowers, and the apartment until I return?" Shall I return?

The French members of the Embassy, the journalists, photographers, and others were at the station to see us off. The young French girls were carrying baskets of flowers from which they took carnations, lilies-of-the-valley, etc. and, with tears in their eyes, handed them to us as we leaned from the windows. The journalists were taking notes and the photographers were flashing their cameras as the train moved slowly away....

CHAPTER 5

July 20, 1941–December 26, 1941

The American Consulate Leaves Paris

July 20, 1941

The ride was dusty beyond all count. The intense heat obliged us to keep the windows open, and the dirt poured in covering our clothes, faces, hair, and valises.

At Hendaye this morning we were ordered to go into Biarritz as the German authorities would not allow us to cross the frontier.[1] The Hôtel Carlton had been requisitioned, and with private rooms and baths, we felt most luxurious.

July 21, 1941

At 10:30 a.m. we left Biarritz for Hendaye to cross into Spain. Again we could not cross the border, and we returned to Biarritz. The Nazis had orders from Berlin to prevent our advance. Again, we spent the night in the Hôtel Carlton.

July 22, 1941

This morning we were across the border and into Spain. We wondered at this sudden decision. We learned President Roosevelt had called the captain of the USS *West Point* bringing German and Italian Consuls from America. The cable instructed that if we were not across the border within twelve hours, the captain was to return to New York where, in the United States, the Germans and Italians would be interned for the duration of the war.

July 24, 1941

Lisbon with its brilliant lights, its great quantities of food, its free press, and its heat impressed us greatly. Spies were everywhere; espionage and counter espionage were at work.[2] After the empty counters in department stores and shops in Paris, we were dazzled by the abundance of clothes, silver, jewels, books, materials, and food.

Lisbon has a rich background of early Moorish history and architecture; its reconstruction from the 1755 Lisbon earthquake that destroyed the whole city, and its South American (Brazil) and Indian (East Indian) coloring make it unique and different from any other large European city.[3] I climbed the seven hills of the city. From a tenth-century Moorish castle I saw the panorama of the city with the clear waters of the Tagus River beyond, glistening in an ever-brilliant sun. I went down to the old Moorish quarter where brown, naked children run about on the dirt roads of the small alleys and passageways. I sat at tables on the Avenida [da Liberdade][4] underneath the stars and wandered into old churches and buildings of old magnificence. At Estoril, I joined the crowds of refugees and summer vacationers on the beaches....[5]

Orders to Return to Unoccupied France

August 11, 1941

My orders were given to me at the Lisbon station. I was to return to Lyon, France, which was of course unoccupied (or practically) by the Germans, to await further orders.[6] The American Consulate General in Lisbon immediately applied for a visa for my entry into France. Most of the other members of the U.S. Foreign Service boarded the USS *West Point* for its return voyage to the United States from where many will be sent to North Africa, South America, and other countries, or remain in Washington at the Department of State.

Rumours were incessant that the Germans would eventually occupy the whole of France. The Portuguese press announced the triumphant progress of the German Army into the Ukraine....[7]

August 31, 1941

The train was overcrowded as it left Lisbon on the twenty-eighth, carrying thousands of restless travellers. What activities during these eventful times were taking them through the countries of the world?

In Madrid[8] food was scarce. The roads were dusty, and all the ancient splendor of the city seemed lost in this epoch of war that appears to be destroying everything of beauty in every country....

We reached Portbou, the Spanish frontier [with France] at midnight. Fifteen pieces of our luggage were taken from the train and placed on the platform of the station for inspection by the Spanish custom authorities. The declaration of all the money in our possession came under the same rule of inspection. Two United States diplomatic couriers were with us helping us in every way. With our diplomatic status we had no trouble.

Within an hour we reached Cerbère, the French frontier [with Spain], where again the inspection took place. I offered some chocolate to the French woman who marked my valises, but she refused it, saying it was not allowed. A chief inspector was quite near, and it was obvious the lady was afraid he might think she was accepting a bribe.

"Mr. Inspector," I said to him, "may I give Madame some chocolate?" He nodded an assent, knowing no doubt that my intention was to give her not a bribe but this small gift. Chocolate cannot be found in France today.

September 3, 1941

I am once again breathing the atmosphere of this France that I love. We are on our way not to Paris but to Lyon and Vichy. For how long? How long shall it be before I move on again? This war disturbs the routine of one's life....

Swarming crowds were at every station getting on and off the train. The corridors of the train were lined with suitcases. People were sitting on them as the coaches were too full to hold all the travellers. In what seemed to be a hermetically sealed coach I occupied, it was impossible to sleep with no air or with air that was not fresh. I went out into the corridor and sat down on my valises. My thoughts were racing through my surcharged brain almost as fast as the train rumbling at fast speed through the night. I thought of the French, so carefree, so effervescent, caught in this web of government by a cruel master. Their country was cut in two. Somewhere brother was fighting against brother: Vichy French and Free French.

I had a French paper in my hand, one that I had picked up at Cerbère. It told of the increase in crimes of the Nazis against the French in Paris. There were reprisals, of course, as the Résistance was becoming more active. German officers were found shot in the subway stations. The bodies of German soldiers were picked up dead or dying on the streets of Paris after dark or in isolated places throughout the occupied zone. The hatred of the French towards their captors was increasing at the same time. Where is it leading them, captor and captive? Hatred, revenge, reprisals, torture, death....

How can I love my enemy under such appalling circumstances? But, I thought, when shall I ever learn that hatred is not, cannot be, a solution to the problem of evil? When shall the universal education begin, and the teaching that only in love is liberation found? Fortunately, this spirit of love is found in individuals. Were it not so, there would be complete chaos. I thought that only by love can the nations be guided intelligently. World problems are becoming too great for human minds to solve. "Nothing can bring you peace," writes Ralph Waldo Emerson, "but the triumph of principles."[9] Nothing can bring love to me but the love I bear; I must love, and I must spread my love....

"Lyon!" I was awakened from a half sleep, one from my thoughts. The rumbling of the train had come to a stop. It was seven o'clock. From my window, as the train slowly entered the station, I saw a grey, dismal sky. There was a feeling of rain in the air.

There was nothing to fear I thought concerning a room as we, my traveling companion also of the Foreign Service and I, had sent a telegram from Lisbon to the Carlton Hôtel[10] in Lyon requesting them to reserve two single rooms. One of the few taxis at the station took us to the hotel. Our sense of security regarding rooms was quickly dispelled. The management said that he had never received our telegram and that there were no rooms available.

To find a room therefore was a problem indeed. Hotel after hotel refused to give us a room. In the lobby of the Grand Hotel where we had breakfast, we sat until nine o'clock when the American Consulate would open.

We learned the Hôtel Carlton is the headquarters of Nazi officers. Is this unoccupied France? The Nazi reins are not as taut in this so-called unoccupied zone as they are in Paris, but they are here. The Gestapo, spies, collaborators, secret service men, and people of all nationalities are gathered in this dismal, cheerless, gloomy city of Lyon.

September 12, 1941

Lyon is an old city of France and the birthplace of great Frenchmen and beautiful women: Philibert Delorme (the architect who designed the Tuileries), Coysevox the sculptor, Maréchal Suchet, Madame Récamier, Chenavard the painter of French history, and Meissonier the great painter.[11] Its great silk industry dating from the 10th century and its university make Lyon the third largest, and an important, city of France.

Lyon lies between two beautiful rivers, the Rhône and the Saône, surrounded by lovely hills and suburbs. Rarely have I seen such a luxuriance of trees and foliage. Built in 43 B.C. under Roman domination, the city was subsequently governed by the Burgundians and later the Counts of Provence. It was ruled by the German emperor in the 11th century. It was the scene of religious wars when the Huguenots destroyed part of the city (1562) and of the execution of [the Marquis of] Cinq-Mars (1642) on the Place des Terreaux. In the 1789 French Revolution, Lyon resisted the [National] Convention after a siege of six months. The Revolutionary Tribune condemned 1,800 citizens of Lyon to death.[12]

Today the city is again passing through tragic days in its history. There are two million more persons in Lyon than stay in or even visit it in peacetime. It is filled with refugees and government employees attached to the administration in Vichy, which is only a thirty minute trip by plane from Lyon. In a way Lyon takes the place of Paris as a business center. It is somber, ugly, dirty, and ill-kept. La Place Bellecour,[13] said to be one of the most beautiful places in Europe, is today arid, dusty, and desolate looking. My hotel is on the Place. We were successful in finding rooms here only after the Prefecture at the request of the American Consul requisitioned them; otherwise, we should be still hunting.

Every day more persons cross the line of demarcation of the occupied and unoccupied zones. Every day there are arrests of those who have attempted to come through illegally as the German authorities will give no further general exit permits. The Gestapo continually watches the populace in this supposedly free part of France.

No one dares to carry a letter across the marked line. No letters are allowed through; postcards may be posted.

The Germans, losing ground in Russia, are beginning the path that is leading toward their downfall....

In Paris the Nazis have placed machine guns on many of the buildings. They are on the Place de la Concorde, on the roof of the Chambre des Députés, and on the Hôtel de Crillon. Do they fear a general uprising?

The American Consulate in Lyon, France

September 26, 1941

And so I take up life in Lyon.[14] In its greyness and drabness it is not conducive to inspiration. I make an effort to be more cheerful than I feel. However, the Consulate with our official family of United States citizens gives me something to hold on to. I work with people of my civilization, my countrymen. There is Mr. [Marshall M.] Vance, our Consul-General and chief; there is Dale Maher, Consul, with his delightful sense of humor; and Benji, Dale's big, dignified boxer: Prince Benjamin Lichtenstein of Hungary. He is now "Mr." Lichtenstein, as, belonging to an American, he has been naturalized and is not allowed to carry the title. As time went on, Dale lost weight; and we learned that he was keeping any meat or other food he ordered at a restaurant for Benji, while he ate very little. There is Clark Husted whom we call "Charley," Vice-Consul, who had been educated at the University of Heidelberg that had left him with happy memories of Germany and the Germans; he was not at all happy with the French and counted the days when he would be sent to another country. There was also Lee Randall, Vice-Consul, young and very good looking; and Alice Soelberg, my nice traveling companion who is making every effort to join our staff in Vichy. The French members of the Consular staff have been in our government service for many years. They are helpful and are interested in this new contingent that has descended on them in their work.[15]

The restaurants are overcrowded. For any meal a table must be reserved. People are continually being turned away on Saturdays and Sundays. The American members of the staff of our Consulate meet every day at a restaurant called "Marie's"[16] where the food is good and where there is enough, although less than in ordinary times when Lyon was noted through France for the best cuisine in the country.

September 26, 1941

The mosquitoes in Lyon were numerous due to the lack of an adequate sewerage system. I was obliged to ask the hotel for netting for my bed. As for the sewerage system, one would think that with the great wealth of the Lyonnaise people this would be changed; one passes a beautiful house or apartment where the bad smell strikes one as far out as the street.

September 28, 1941

The Lyon Fair opened today.[17] Maréchal Pétain arrived at the station early in the morning to be present at the ceremony of this great event that has been held each year for the past twenty-five years.

Tonight, I watched the parade of soldiers and cavalry marching to the music of two bands in honor of the Maréchal. There were several companies of young lads, some with no uniforms; others were in complete military dress, all carrying torches.

Their faces were serious, and they seemed proud to be parading before the Maréchal. Crowds lined the sidewalks watching them. Rumour was about that there were difficulties recruiting any great number of French soldiers for an army under the Vichy government. Most of the men had gone with the Résistance; others had been deported by the Nazis to Germany; others were hiding. I stopped with the crowd on the edge of La Place Bellecour and waited to see the Maréchal pass. I did not wait long. With a great effort the band announced his coming. He rode swiftly by in his automobile to the applause of only a few. Then a silence followed; indifference was the attitude of that straggling crowd. Here was a great French General, a Maréchal of France, the hero of Verdun[18] in the First World War, now Chief of State, who at one time had the applause and acclamations of multitudes of his countrymen. Today he passes through a city of France greeted by a few reluctant hurrahs....

What did the Maréchal think, I wondered? How did he feel? Was it true, as a Frenchman remarked, that he is now too old, his sensibilities are too dulled to realize the infelicitous change in incidents of this kind? I turned away, lost myself in the crowds, from what might have been a day of victory for the Maréchal.

I set off to explore the historic part of Lyon. The *funiculaire* took me to the Church of the Notre-Dame de Fourvière high up on the ruins of the ancient Roman forum built by Trajan. The interior, except for the mosaics, is not especially beautiful. Down underneath the basilica, however, are the old walls of Roman architecture sublime in their simplicity. Outside on the terrace I looked below where 10th, 11th, and 12th century houses are still standing. I wanted to enter those habitations where people of another age had lived and loved, were born, and had died. I raced down the steep ascent, ignoring the funiculaire, and reached the narrow streets of cobblestones and earth. The little Rue Saint-Jean has the same aspect, I am sure, that it had in those far-off times. Only the facades of some of the buildings had changed. Modern small cafés and food shops have replaced heavy doors and iron gates. I opened one great mediaeval door and entered. There I found a spiral stairway that had not been touched by the hand of man since it was built in the 12th century, or even before. The thick walls, the balconies built above interior courtyards, and the lights slanting from small windows across the corridors gave an atmosphere of that magnificent past of France of the Middle Ages. I could not believe it—it was entrancing.[19]

Quite near the evening bells of the Cathédrale of Saint-Jean-Baptiste de Lyon were calling the people to prayer as I went out again on to the street. I looked up at the towers. The gargoyles were bending over, laughing at the chaos, the turmoil of this stricken France. Night was coming quickly, hiding the remnants of the cold sunset that was fast disappearing. Had I indeed lived for a few moments in those centuries? Life was simple then; people lived by a simple faith. It was at a time when chivalry taught them to fear God, serve the King, protect the weak, speak the truth, never turn away from a friend, and shun unfairness, meanness, or deceit. There was then a habit of direct thought, a training of the intellect. It was the birth of that culture of France that has never been equaled by any other country in any other age....[20]

It is autumn now in Lyon. The leaves are only beginning to fall from the trees heavy with branches. I shall return to rue Saint-Jean some day in winter, and watch the snow fall in great flakes on the earthen road, and once again hear the bells of the church resounding as if through another age. And I will look to see its people plodding silently along toward the edifice to join their brothers in prayer.

October 5, 1941

Notices through the city of Lyon plastered on the walls read, "They count their crimes enveloped in the folds of our flag."

Word from Paris reaches us: Hitler announces that Russia is defeated.[21] Is the Führer dreaming? Are his "spirits" leading him astray?

The Résistance grows.[22] Hundreds of French lads join the underground.

At the movies today a picture was shown of the Maréchal passing through Marseille and Toulouse where the applause was clamorous. On the other hand, during a drive for the benefit of the Boy Scouts, when a portrait of the Maréchal was being auctioned off by a speaker who told of the splendid work Pétain was doing for the country, there was indifferent silence. Only when the speaker shouted, "We need no foreigner to help us in our efforts at reestablishment. We can do it ourselves without help from outside. France will rise again. France is eternal!" The applause was loud and long.

Travel to Vichy on Official Business

October 12, 1941

I flew to Vichy yesterday. Thirty minutes in a plane brought me to the famous spa, now the seat of the French government.

I made my application for permission to travel to the authorities and presented a letter from the American Consul. It requested that I, a citizen of the United States and attached to the Consulate of the United States at Lyon, France, be allowed to go to the American Embassy at Vichy on business; that facilities to enable me to do so would be appreciated. The document is signed by the Consul and bears the red seal of the Consulate. At the ticket office I was requested to sign a paper stating that I was traveling to Vichy on official business; that I would not divulge the route the plane would take; that I would not talk about the present political situation.[23]

Vichy was quiet as I drove from the airport into the town. It was quiet and calm on the surface. There was nothing to tell me that underneath conspiracies, plots, and counterplots are going on: Hitler's "new order" in Europe is being planned; fears by some that France may fight England; fears by others that France is about to make an accord with Germany. There was nothing to show that Hitler is losing faith in France as echoes of another kind of collaboration, Franco-American, is at work in the defense of North Africa; this defense is silently, secretly being prepared.

Official dinners and luncheons and others that are not official have their place in the life of Vichy. Mrs. Louis Biddle[24] gave a dinner recently for the Maréchal whom she has known for many years. The Maréchal received her at dinner a week later.

A splendid sun flooded the town of Vichy as I took off for my return to Lyon. A happy memory was with me: that of the immense kindness of Penelope Royall[25] of the Embassy staff who loaded me with food and in many ways eased the situation of scarcity of provisions in Lyon. So scarce were they that I appealed to my family in America. My sister, Mrs. John [Virginia] Harrison, in Philadelphia was immediate in her response and sent a large box of food products to me. I shall always be grateful to her....

October 14, 1941

When I landed in Lyon, I was welcomed by rain and fog which made the city look gloomy indeed. As a relief I turned to music. Last night in the Salle Rameau,[26] Casadesus played to a crowded house.[27] It was a beautiful program performed with his superb execution and deep feeling.

Notices on the billboards referring to victories of the Allies in North Africa have been torn from the walls of buildings. The radio announces Allied successes on the Russian front and the retreat of the German Army at several points. The feeling here is becoming stronger for an Allied victory.

At a movie recently an American speaker, after the world news, shouted to the Italians, "Come to my country. There you are free to eat spaghetti and macaroni." And to the Germans, "In America you are free to drink your beer and eat switzer cheese. Come and see for yourselves." "The Star-Spangled Banner" was played followed by long and overwhelming applause. As I left the theater with the crowd, I heard a voice near me say (in English), "Well, I'll be d...!" To think that today someone on the screen in a movie in France is permitted to voice such sentiments is beyond belief.

Support for U.S. Foreign Service in France from America

October 24, 1941

At my hairdresser's shop I must bring my own soap and hairpins; soap is non-existent in Lyon. Mine comes from Paris where such articles were sent to our commissary for the Embassy staff from America.

The newspapers, *Gazette de Lausanne*[28] and *Tribune de Genève*,[29] from Switzerland reach us here giving us details of world news, which includes activities in North America and on the Russian front. It looks worse every day for the Axis Powers....

There is news from "Ivan the Terrible"[30] on the radio coming from Russia via the British broadcast. Imitating the throaty voice of Hitler, the speaker called out, "So long as I am the German leader, I will lead you from victory to victory—to the final catastrophe. I will lead the Army to the last German."

From one of the French generals,[31] as quoted in *Time Magazine*, "I have no confidence in the generosity of our conqueror. I not only hope but expect a British victory. Moreover, I share this opinion with the majority of my fellow citizens whether in the free zone or occupied zone." The general was the appointed delegate to the German Army of Occupation. He did not like the job and was removed. He was subsequently thrown into jail by Darlan.[32]

Operas, concerts, and theatres have started the winter season. They lift one's morale; they give cheer to the somber days of this interminable year of 1941. I often wonder if it will go on forever, if I shall remain in the city of Lyon for the remainder of my official life. Over the week I attend the opera and theaters; over the weekend it is difficult to leave the city on Saturday and Sunday because of the scarcity of trains that are overcrowded. And, too, there is the impossibility of finding rooms. I must await the spring days to go to Grenoble, Avignon, Grasse, and Nice.[33]

November 9, 1941

The cold is penetrating. In my hotel room the long French windows will not close. The cold winds enter. When I awake, I take a seemingly long trip, walking very quickly into my bathroom where the hot water warms me, and then back again into bed before making the great effort to dress in the icy room....

A prison inspector said French prisoners are low in spirits. They feel that they are forgotten. The defeat of their country touched them very deeply. On the other hand, the British soldier is convinced of victory; his spirit is high....

A German colonel was shot in Nantes a few weeks ago. Fifty hostages were arrested by the conquerors and shot.[34] The sleepless, desperate work of the French underground brings bitter, cruel reprisals by the Nazis.

Lyon is filling up with more Nazis. The German Armistice Commission, the German Consulate with fifty employees, the German Red Cross, and other German organizations are being installed.[35] A French Military Mission[36] has arrived today at my hotel.

In Paris notices are placed on the doors of the French hospitals and on the building of the Faculté de Médecine stating that volunteers amongst the physicians are requested to go to Germany to care for the wounded of the German Army as well as the civilians. The notice stated further that if they would not accept, they would be requisitioned. My informer said that, as far as he knew, there was no response to this appeal.

The intense British bombing of the Ruhr[37] and other districts is so great that the electricity has been destroyed. The Nazis have told the French Government they must send supplies to Germany. Are all the supplies of the vaunted well-provisioned German military machine disappearing?

Life Principle

November 10, 1941

"Life is in ourselves and," writes Dostoevsky, "not in the external."[38]

Tonight, I feel very much alone. My traveling companion, who has had her room in the same hotel I am occupying since our arrival, has received her orders to go to the U.S. Embassy in Vichy. I am glad for her as she has wanted this for many weeks. As for me, I must cling to this Life Principle within me, which is in every man, and which will lead me on as I await the direction of destiny. I am swaying on the branches of events; I am on a journey in the midst of war....

November 16, 1941

The Maréchal's portrait is in every shop in Lyon. It hangs high in every restaurant, in every café. Hitler, who believes thus in the need of worshipping an idol, sees with his eyes of a German. Will Germany ever understand the soul of the French?

Tonight over the radio Germany calls for a million men from Italy to help her on the Russian front. They will do her no good. She is destroying herself; hatred bears within itself the seeds of its own destruction.

Food is becoming scarcer and poorer in quality. The result is that diseases are prevalent. There are 4,000 cases of a skin disease in Paris; 400 to 600 cases of the skin disease enter the hospitals of Lyon. Undernourishment causes the skin disease; depression and contagion cause the various other illnesses.

I had luncheon with Maître Marcel de Gallaix[39] and his colleague Maître T. They are lawyers in a rising young law firm in Paris. The former is married to an American friend of mine,[40] and I have known them for many years. His colleague has brought his young daughter, twenty years of age, into Lyon for a change of scene; she has just left a concentration camp where she was incarcerated for sticking her tongue out at a German officer.

November 29, 1941

Over the radio: Retreat of the German Army from Rostov.[41] Russian successes are stopping the German advance. "Let us resist until death—not one step back," cry the Russians. "We must be and shall be victorious."

The Allies and the Axis powers are fighting for mastery in North Africa....

December 4, 1941

Quite near to this hotel where I am staying is a movie house, one of the most important in Lyon. I have been puzzled lately when passing it to find crowds lined along the street waiting to see the picture. Recently, however, the crowds have disappeared and only a few moviegoers have entered the building. Deciding to see for myself, I passed through the doors into the darkness of the hall. The picture was entitled *Marie Stuart*[42] and was the story of that beautiful, unfortunate Queen of Scotland when Elizabeth reigned over England. There were few people watching the picture. The scenery of those days in cold, gloomy Scotland was admirably portrayed. It was soon brought to my consciousness, however, that it was a Nazi film given in the French language. The story, instead of depicting the true facts of that unhappy life of Marie Stuart, was a caricature of the different personalities: the Queen herself, Lord Darnley, and Lord Bothwell. It portrayed the British women as prostitutes—even the Queen did not escape. It showed Englishmen as weaklings, tricksters, and mountebanks. It ceased to be interesting before very long and I left quickly. The French were indeed not fooled by the picture; it was considered a complete failure financially, for soon no one went in to see it, and it was soon changed.

December 5, 1941

American and Japanese negotiations are going on, so we learned by the radio. We are sitting on an inflammable mountain. Is Japan plotting a war with our country? Why? But some of her representatives in Washington and in Spain are professing friendship for us....

Pearl Harbor

December 7, 1941

It must have been late this evening that I heard the news. Turning on the radio there was a not too clear announcement about Pearl Harbor, our naval base in the Hawaiian Islands. I soon understood that it had been attacked by the Japanese fleet with no warning; it was a brutal, dastardly assault.

It is late, after midnight. I must wait hours before I may go down to the Consulate to join my people and be with them in this overwhelming catastrophe.

America attacked! My own people, hundreds of them sent to a sudden death. I am unable to sleep. Will morning never come?

December 8, 1941

I reached the Consulate earlier than usual. I forget everything except that the United States has been attacked. France has held and still holds my love and loyalty, but it has taken second place in my thoughts. This onslaught against my country of birth seemed almost to be aimed at me, at a part of me that is America. I am America. It is my being and that which makes me who I am, steeped as I am in the very soil of our land, in its traditions and in its history. Now it is in danger....

The United States and Britain declare the existence of a state of war with Germany....

Congress declares war on Japan....[43]

December 11, 1941

Germany and Italy declare war on the United States.[44] The radio was silent after this announcement. I was waiting for more news when a knock at my door changed the trend of my thought. Opening it, I came face to face with the French Inspector of Police: "*Carte d'Identité, s'il vous plaît.*" The order was curt. I asked him to wait a moment; I threw on a dressing gown, found the card, and at the door showed it to him. It shows, naturally, that I am a citizen of the United States and attached to the American Consulate in Lyon. The inspector obviously had not expected to be handed a diplomatic document. He read the printing on my card: "Government of the United States," he said almost to himself. His "*tiens!*" (which means—hello! look at this!) was eloquent, for he gave me a special salute and left. He was looking for someone of questionable activities, I was certain. Indeed, the city is full of such; the police are on the alert, and there is the desperate effort on the part of the hunted to hide and escape.

The United States declares war on Germany and Italy. Echoes of the impact of the news in the United States filter in. Our nation is united in a tremendous war effort. Our magnificent strength as a people and our inexhaustible supplies of materials, munitions, and industries are being mustered into action. The spirit of our faith is being held aloft.

We of the Foreign Service are carrying on abroad.[45] What different or even greater work shall be ours? What will be its nature? Where shall it have its place?

The time is becoming short for preparation. Meanwhile United States passports are being stamped for travel to the United States by any route available for those Americans who still must leave France. Telephone messages are continually coming in to the Consulate with enquiries for instructions. Americans being arrested attempting to cross from the occupied to the unoccupied zone without permits seek help from the Consulate....

An American journalist coming from Paris told me that French morale rose higher as America entered the war. Outside of the government in Vichy, every French man, woman, and child was behind the United States.

December 12, 1941

Japan occupies the island of Guam....[46]

A few days ago, in response to Japan's attack on the United States, Mr. Churchill said over the radio, "When we think of the insane ambition and insatiable appetite, which have caused this vast, melancholy extension of the war, we can only feel that Hitler's madness has infected the Japanese minds...In the past we had a light which flickered, in the present we have a light which flames, and in the future there will be a light which will shine calm and resplendent over all the land and all the sea!"[47] The great Prime Minister of England lifts us up to victory....

December 13, 1941

From Paris the news reaches us of the reprisals of the Nazi authorities following the shooting of a Nazi officer in Paris at the end of last week. The Résistance is using desperate methods. The French were given until December 8 to find the culprit and to denounce him. To the glory of the patriots of France, not one citizen spoke. As a reprisal, the blackout began at 5:30 p.m. No one in the city was prepared for it; no one had arranged his life to meet the situation. Those living in the country left their offices or work at 4:30 p.m. to reach overcrowded subways. Schools were opened for only a half day: for the girls in the morning, for the boys in the early afternoon. Every shop in Paris closed suddenly at 5:00 p.m. At 6:00 p.m. a silence spread over the city. But not one French man, woman, or child opened his mouth concerning the culprit of the shooting of a Nazi officer....

Britain is successful in Libya: the British held off the siege of Tobruk,[48] the radio reported. The German General Rommel[49] retreats....

Dramatic Exit from Paris

December 17, 1941

Russell Porter, the well-known American lawyer in Paris, risked the dangerous crossing of the marked zone without a permit and appeared at the Consulate today. I had luncheon with him; he told me of his dramatic exit from Paris.[50] After Pearl Harbor he felt that it would be wise to leave occupied France. He left his apartment in Paris at night, motored almost to the zone of demarcation, then walked for miles and miles through the night. He reached a house in the wilderness through which he was walking. Seeing a light, he knocked at the door not knowing whether a German or Frenchman would open it for him. The days are dangerous and the nights hide unexpected occurrences on one's path. The risk, however, must be taken....

A young boy about 15 years of age at the door looked at him enquiringly. "I am an American citizen," said Mr. Porter. "I am on my way to Lyon but have lost the right road. Would you indicate the path to the highway?"

The lad beamed! This was no German, Porter decided. The boy asked him in, but our compatriot wished to be on his way. It was not yet dark, and the young French lad led him through byways and narrow lanes until at the highway he indicated the signal showing the way to Lyon. Mr. Porter wished to give the boy some money, but he refused it....

"*Merci!*" he said. "But, *Monsieur*, I am happy to have been of aid to an American. If some day you remember, would you send me a postcard from the United States showing that during the war I had helped an American to escape from the Nazis? I should keep it always as a souvenir of this meeting."

Many other Americans coming into Lyon have had similar experiences. They come through continually; other nationals arrive. The city becomes more crowded as the times under the watchful eye of the Nazis, if not under their complete control, grow tenser.

Many Jews already in the city are forced out of the hotels; in Lyon there is a lack of food, a lack of rooms, or no place to spend the night. There is sadness and fear and loneliness. Nerves are unstrung by the bitter experiences so many have passed through. The Consulate is doing everything to help financially and otherwise; we, personally, give what we can to these unfortunate people....

It is cold and the rain beats against my window as I write. All is still in the hotel, but underneath the quiet surface one knows that stirring, tragic events take place continually. This atmosphere of apprehension surged through me so vividly that I was obliged to go out on to the street. I wandered to a movie—any movie to force my mind away from the moment.

I cannot sleep. I take up my Bible lying on my table and find the story of Elijah who fled in his discouragement from his own work. Life had become too difficult for him to bear, so he had taken refuge under the juniper tree. Up on the mountain where wind, earthquake, and fire passed before him, he heard the still, small voice of the Spirit....[51]

I tightened my armour after that and went to sleep.

December 18, 1941

Orders came this morning for me to proceed to Vichy as soon as possible....

Assignment to U.S. Legation in Bern, Switzerland

December 22, 1941

Orders changed. I must be ready within twenty-four hours to travel to Switzerland to our Legation in Bern.[52]

This keeping one step ahead of Hitler is trying the nerves of everyone. It would attack my optimism were it not for the prospect of this sudden change. I begin a new life....

December 23, 1941

My departure is delayed until the 26th.

A notice at the desk of my hotel announces that every Jew in the building must leave before the end of the month.

The radio announces the occupation of the Wake Islands in the Pacific by the Japanese, which is a victory for the Japanese, so far....[53]

December 25, 1941

Christmas bells ring for "peace on earth." There is no peace today; there is little joy....

But there is a light ahead! For me it becomes brighter as I turn toward Switzerland to take up the struggle there: for France, for England, for my own land, and for free peoples throughout the world.

For France, too, the light is there as this long, tragic year of 1941 draws to a close, and 1942 opens in expectancy of a change in the march of events. In North Africa the Allies go on from strength to strength....

December 26, 1941

The news that the victorious Japanese have taken Hong Kong[54] reached me as the automobile in which I traveled with Clark Husted,[55] one of our vice-consuls also assigned to the Legation in Bern, moved slowly away from Lyon, France.

This beautiful France that I love! I may not remain with her in her sorrow, and today I am not permitted to walk with her in her own land; but where I am going, I shall be working with her. And after the dark shadows shall have left, I shall return. For neither German nor Nazi nor any enemy or any evil thing can destroy that undying spirit of France. Could it speak, it might say in the words of a great writer:[56]

> Nature, whose sweet rains fall on unjust and just alike, will have clefts in the rocks where I may hide, and secret valleys in whose silence I may weep undisturbed. She will hang the night with stars so that I may walk abroad in the darkness without stumbling, and send the wind over my footprints so that none may track me to my hurt: she will cleanse me in great waters, and with bitter herbs make me whole.°

° *De Profundis.* Oscar Wilde.

January 1, 1942–October 11, 1944

Serving with the U.S. Legation in Switzerland[1]

Bern, Switzerland
January 1942

The long, gloomy year of 1941 finally came to an end. It was a year filled with anticipation, forebodings, and pessimism as well as optimism, of waiting for events to take their course. It was filled with the hope that the end of horrors, deportations, tortures, and the killing of hostages would come with the dawn of a New Year and peace. It was the coldest year in France for the past seventy years according to the records. If the temperature was frigid, as indeed it was, the hearts of the French were in keeping with it.

As we take up life[2] in this neutral country of Switzerland,[3] we are surrounded by the enemy: Germany and Austria on the north and east, Italy in the south, and France bordering it on the west. We wait and work and look forward to the day when we shall return to the France that we love so well.

The light grows brighter as the swiftly changing scenes point, however slowly and with however great and numerous setbacks that try to bind us, to the real issue—to victory.

As the New Year dawns, the battle for North Africa between the Allies and the Axis powers becomes more active and takes on more extensive proportions.

The Swiss press that until recently has been somewhat pro-Axis, such as the *Gazette de Lausanne*, the *Tribune de Lausanne*, the *Journal de Genève*, and the *Tribune de Genève*[4] is now almost 100 percent pro-Anglo-Saxon. The latter paper has a fear of communism. *La Suisse*[5] is anti-Anglo-Saxon with a clever Axis propaganda; *Le Courrier*[6] is pro-Allies.

Of the German printed papers, *Die Nation*[7] is pro-Allies; *Das Vaterland*[8] (Catholic) is also pro-Allies, while the *Neue Zürcher Zeitung*[9] makes an effort to remain neutral.

We avidly read the press. From the headquarters of International Command[10] in London, by radio we are kept *en rapport* with events in the Pacific and France. We watch our maps and follow the German victories and losses, the Russian victories and losses on the Eastern Front, and the operations of our armies and navy in the Pacific.

February 1942

Singapore falls,[11] which is a defeat for the British. Mr. Churchill speaks over the radio in a sad and strained voice. He is unshaken in his determination and in the determination of the British people to fight with increasing strength.

Although food is plentiful in Switzerland, a number of products are rationed: meat, milk, butter, cheese, and chocolate.

A War for the Survival of the United States

During these historic days for us on the staff of the United States Legation in Bern, from time to time we receive written instructions from our able minister, Mr. Leland Harrison.[12] He warns us:

> Remember that the present is a war for the survival of the United States and the continuance of our political ideals and concepts, our institutions, our way of life.
>
> Each of us individually has an important part in this war. We are fighting for America.
>
> Let us guide ourselves accordingly.
>
> This is war.
>
> The slightest detail of our procedure may be of great usefulness to the enemy.
>
> He is always desirous of learning the intimate details of our personal lives. An enemy agent wants to know where we live, how much money we spend, how much money we earn, and whether we are in debt....
>
> Nail a Nazi lie when you hear it. Trace it.
>
> ....
>
> We will win.
>
> We are confident; we accept temporary news or reverses with equanimity; we take success in our stride and move steadily, quietly but inexorably forward, [which is] the surest, deadliest weapon against the faltering morale of our enemies....

The war goes on. It seems outside, away from us in a way, in neutral Switzerland. In France we were in contact with our own people; England and the news seemed nearer. However, by radio and press we are able to follow our own armies in the Pacific, the Philippines, and Australia. We hear the news of our splendid American pilots, of their courage, their simplicity, their victories and defeats. At the end of February we read about the pilot who was given a decoration for bravery after he had recently cabled headquarters in Washington: "Sighted sub—Sank same."[13] For him, trained and disciplined to obey orders, he was merely proceeding with the daily routine.

British planes over Switzerland last night gave us a sleepless time. The Swiss anti-aircraft guns were not quick enough, or did it only seem that way? The Germans certainly cannot stop them. The British fly through this small country in ten minutes going 400 miles an hour.

March 1942

The Italian papers are still pompous in their sureness of victory. I quote from the *Il Giornale d'Italia*[14] (translation from *Gazette de Lausanne* March 20, 1942):

> The French [who] are not content to have been beaten by arms are climbing toward a total political defeat....They do not consider themselves yet out of the conflict nor reconciled with Germany and Italy, and still hope for the defeat of the Axis. This is confirmed by the challenging attitude they assume the moment the semblance of failure appears for the Axis in North Africa or on the Soviet front.
>
> The French continue to wish for victory for England and the United States, which they are ready to support by all their available means, with many phrases of protestation more or less sincere, of the fierce and contemptible British bombardments that destroy their houses and kill their laborers, without any evident reason.
>
> This state of the French soul is perfectly well-known to and strictly watched by Germany and Italy....

April 1942

Bern in April. Spring comes again. The purplish pink quince trees are blossoming in their beauty, and the cherry blossoms are luxuriant and colorful in their display in the surrounding gardens.

Clouds and light play over the peaks of the Bernese Oberland,[15] still covered with snow and ever changing with every mood. At night over the mountains the little Swiss châlets are lighted one by one like candles on an altar.

There is a little calm and strength in those bewildering heights, a vastness that makes our little lives, our petty ambitions, our destructive wars, our discontent, and our selfishness vanish as in a mist.

Arcades, cafés, all these thirteenth and fourteenth-century structures and homes, and the fountains and their statues are scenes such as I had seen in pictures in my childhood before I ever came to Europe. In their quaintness and exotic coloring, they seem to have been placed there for my special interest and amusement but would soon vanish into unreality. They do not seem real, that is they do not seem part of the common day. In contrast, in France I am one with the country as I drive through it; I am one with every street in Paris, every bridge, every view. It is part of me....

Spies Are Everywhere

Summer 1942

Pierre Laval, who has returned to power as Prime Minister with the Vichy government,[16] urges the French to go to Germany to help win the war against the "enemy," as the radio tells us. The response of the French is an increase in the Résistance and the clandestine press.

We live in an atmosphere teeming with intrigue of spies and 5th columnists. Two young Swiss university students recently were executed as spies working for a "foreign power," accused of being corrupted by the "foreign power." As one Swiss remarked to me, "We are not accustomed to executing people in our country. Every day it is a question of giving away military secrets followed by penalties, typically death and life imprisonment. These boys are only twenty-five or twenty-six years old, even younger."

Five hundred thousand men are reported to be in the French Résistance.

With Germany developing all fronts, the news of a second front of the Allies becomes stronger.

"British and American forces stationed in Great Britain," writes the Neuchâtel *L'Express*,[17] August 5, 1942, "are animated by an offensive spirit as seen in the numerous *manœuvres* of landing" (in North Africa).

The end of this month finds little headway being made toward victory. The Russians are holding on, and we are fighting our way in the Pacific through victories and defeats.

I motored to Lugano and Locarno in Italian Switzerland for a vacation. I forgot for a moment the war-torn fronts, the catastrophes, and the news of the incessant trend of blood and death that reaches us every day.

I found Lugano[18] to be like a lovely woman who has lived and loved throughout the years. She played for high stakes in her casino when she was young and beautiful—when she had rulers of empires, diplomats, and reigning sovereigns at her feet. Now, perhaps a bit tired, she is still a hostess to the great and important and to thousands of tourists and holiday makers. The tourists do not come during these war years in such numbers, and the hotels are only half-full. The war, this injurious war, has victimized beauteous, neutral Switzerland, and she must wait with the belligerent countries for the Allied victory before her thousands of guests will again visit her.

Locarno, too, is a great lady.[19] She has had a distinguished past and has been a proud hostess. She has received statesmen and officials, and her landscape has been the scene of international treaties and conferences. There is an élégance about Locarno as she lies with languor and stateliness along the beautiful Lago Maggiore; she, too, waits for the war to end so that she may again receive her visitors.

Our diplomatic section in Bern, lying outside the central part of the city and across the bridge that separates it from the business district, is singularly interesting in these war years. For here, friends and enemies elbow each other on trams and in the public gardens, on the streets, or in the shops. There is no salutation between the Allies and the Axis powers. Recently on the tram going into town stood a big German quite near us on the platform. Last night a party of Japanese attached to their legation was celebrating at the same restaurant where one group of Anglo-Saxons was dining; their table was placed quite near our own. The Italians, too, are much in evidence; they sell their products in the city: laces, leather goods from Florence, and shoes from Rome. One of the buildings belonging to the Italian Legation is next to one of the châlets our government took over to house our numerous staff, and the one in which my work is done. I see them at the windows, young and gay, and I often wonder of the destiny that has thrown them in with the Nazis; they seem so apart in character and spirit.

American Embassy in Vichy Faces Uncertain Times[20]

November 1942

November was ushered in with snow and cold and events. American and British troops with the fleets arrive off the coast of Africa. Algiers has surrendered to the Allies.[21]

Swiss troops are moving towards the Italian frontier. The Swiss obviously are nervous.

Vichy France and the United States sever diplomatic relations as the Germans take over all of France.[22] In November the Embassy of the United States in Vichy was interned by the German government in Lourdes.[23]

The French fleet at Toulon is scuttled with the loss of nearly all the crews of more than sixty cruisers; two submarines escape.[24]

Christmas came and went and was much like another day but for the delightful reception our minister, Mr. Leland Harrison, gave to the staff.

Admiral Darlan is assassinated in Africa.[25]

The *Maquis*[26] becomes organized and is a meaningful participant in the Résistance movement. Hundreds of young Frenchmen are taking to the mountains to escape deportation; they do not want to work in Germany or work with German organizations. They leave their families and their homes in groups or alone. Patriots of France, they refuse to become slaves of the enemy. With no army, they join a clandestine legion in the fight to free their country.

The Start of a New Year: 1943

The year 1942 passed quickly and 1943 was upon us before we realized that it had actually come. The end of the war is predicted this year by the Allied generals.... How immense, how intense is the prayer in every heart for peace.

The Swiss press related the great fear of the Nazis as the Allies land in North Africa.

Our Radio Bulletin quoted the *Los Angeles Times*[27] of January 25, "The two British raids on Berlin[28] are admitted from German sources to have done considerable material damage.... Coming at a time when Nazi backsets in Russia were reluctantly being conceded by the Nazi propagandists, they must have been profoundly discouraging. For two thousand days they (Nazis) have been bullies who could not take it when the going got rough, and on whom decent treatment was wasted because they construed it as a sign of weakness...."

And from *The New York Times* of February 1 (1943):

"There was drama at the Nazis' celebration of the tenth anniversary[29] of their rule....But it was drama in reverse....There was drama in the absence of Hitler himself, who did not dare to face his people, his party....There was above all supreme drama in the British bombs falling from the skies in the midst of the festivities—bombs which interrupted the show, terrified the listeners and provided a fitting handwriting on the walls of the Nazi citadel....The German people are told to suffer and sacrifice more than ever on the ground that Russia is now using up its last reserves. They are not told that behind the Russian armies stands the American arsenal as well. Instead, the Nazi leaders attempt to paint in glaring colors the Bolshevist menace facing Europe in case of a Russian victory...."

Our Embassy, now in Lourdes, leaves for Baden-Baden, Germany. (They will be interned for the duration of the war.)

German General von Paulus, and what is left of his army, surrendered to Russia at Stalingrad.[30] The Swiss press recounts the slow awakening of the German people to the danger they are in.

British and American aviators downed with their planes in enemy countries, or having parachuted from them, escape to Switzerland. They arrive in Bern every day to report to their Legation. Their stories, teeming with interest and danger, are many and varied.

Our Military Attaché, General Legge,[31] related to me the time he went to the army hospital to visit a young wounded aviator. The aviator had fallen in Germany and was barely able to walk to the frontier to safety. Our General asked him how he had escaped. The man seemed embarrassed; he hesitated and did not reply. After a few kind words from his commanding officer, he said, "Well, you see, Sir, it was either him or me. I'm sorry, Sir, awful sorry, but I had to kill him—the German who was following me with his pointed gun. I turned quickly and, I'm sorry, Sir, but I had to kill him...." A tale of war and death, told in all simplicity by a plain lad who had never learned in all its fullness the brutalities and exigencies of a desperate war.... He was "sorry."

Throughout the year we followed our lads in pride and sorrow in the Pacific: from Guadalcanal in the Solomon Islands[32] to Tarawa in the Gilbert Islands...[33]

In July Sicily is taken by the Allies.[34]

Mussolini resigns as Badoglio takes over power.

In September the Italian peninsula is invaded at Reggio Calabria by the British and Canadian armies.[35]

In September the Nazis evacuate Sardinia.[36] General Giraud enters Corsica.[37]

November sees the bombing of Berlin; it was the greatest of the war by the Royal Air Force. There are now unmistakable signs that they have gone beyond the handwriting on the wall....

The Dawn of a New Year: 1944

Again the New Year. It dawned with hope. Far from war operations, we were avid for news as day by day victory was blazoned over the radio or in the press from one mouth to another....

The Allies pass through Rome taking the city on June 4.[38]

The Allies land on Normandy beaches, France, June 6.[39]

The Allies take Caen in August, as the Russians cross into Germany.[40]

The U.S. Army advances toward Paris coming through Chartres.

August. The French Army enters Paris as the German General von Choltitz[41] surrenders to General Leclerc[42] at Gare Montparnasse.

The Wehrmacht continues to leave the country. The confusion in France is beyond all count. Each man is for himself. No general law exists. Later, groups headed by patriots enter the *Préfecture de Police* and the public buildings as the swastika is torn down and the Tricolor is hoisted high above the city.

The insurrection of the French in Paris and throughout the country takes on great proportions.

The French General Kœnig becomes Military Governor of Paris.[43] We listened hour after hour to the radio; we heard the bells of Notre-Dame and the churches tolling triumphantly; we heard the cheers and "La Marseillaise" sung with voices echoing victoriously:[44]

> *Aux armes, citoyens!*
> *Marchons, marchons...*
>
> To arms, citizens
> Let's march, let's march...

We heard the journalists who were following the victorious armies. "I have been kissed," shouted one American, "by every woman in Paris: beautiful ones and ugly ones, old and young, fat and thin...."

American Embassy in Paris Is Reestablished

At the end of August the telegram from the Department of State in Washington, which we had waited for three years, reached the Legation in Bern.[45] Urgently needed in the American Embassy in Paris, it said in substance.[46] There were ten or twelve names in it. My own was included.[47]

Six weeks passed before we were able to travel in France.[48] There was no way, no means of transport from the French-Swiss frontier through the country to Paris. Railroads and bridges were destroyed. Motor roads were almost impassable; they were obstructed and demolished by the bombing or the sabotage of the French Résistance.[49]

We appealed to the Army.[50] After negotiations between the Department of State and the War Department,[51] we took the train from Bern[52] to the Swiss frontier[53] where the automobiles of General Patch's army met us.[54] The sight of the Tricolor, of the French uniform, of the Customs officer, and of the French soldier on guard on the soil of France moved us deeply. We, who had seen this land fallen in defeat, humiliated and crushed, were privileged to be among the first to enter it victorious and free.

"France, my country," writes a patriot, "you will be reborn, more alive and younger, always new with a countenance, no doubt more serious; but, little by little, the scars and suffering of the past will be obliterated."

"One and regenerated, France will lead on to her destiny!"

On October 11, 1944,[55] we swept triumphantly through France in the cars of General Patch's valiant 7th United States Army,[56] over broken roads and deep excavations, past countless buildings completely destroyed and beautiful forests turned into arid wastes, on to Paris, to our Embassy.[57]

I have come to the end of my journey. I am going home.[58] Home? Can you go back home? Can you go back "to romantic love,[59] back to…dreams of glory and of fame,…to singing just for singing's sake,…back home to the ivory tower, back home to places in the country,…away from all the strife and conflict of the world,… back home to someone who can help you, save you, ease the burden for you, back home to the old forms and systems of things which once seemed everlasting but which are changing all the time—back home to the escapes of Time and Memory"?[°]

Only as I seek my home in love, in hope, and in an unwavering faith in the Principle of all harmony can I find it—can I find that freedom of the soul which is the only freedom for me….
Paris, 1955

[°] *You Can't Go Home Again.* Thomas Wolfe.

Endnotes

The notes are designed to provide insight into what it was like to work for the American Embassy in Paris and live in Paris during the time leading up to and including the involvement of France and the United States in World War II. The reader will come to understand life in Europe, especially France, and experience the events through the eyes of Marie-Louise Dilkes (MLD), who served as receptionist for the American Embassy in Paris during these fateful dark years. The reader will travel with her as she flees Paris and occupied France to American consulates in Portugal and unoccupied France, ending up in the Bern, Switzerland legation before receiving orders to return to Paris to help reestablish the American Embassy in Paris. References are made to declassified documents researched at the National Archives in College Park, Maryland (NACP). The notes include anecdotal information on the background of the people she knew or who played a role in the unfolding of these events. They give detail of the history, art, literature, religion, and newspapers that impacted her life. Winston Churchill wrote in the *Hinge of Fate*: "Memories of the war may be vivid and true, but should never be trusted without verification, especially where the sequence of events is concerned."

Preface

1   In 1917 Marie-Louise Dilkes was sent by the Emergency Aid (of Pennsylvania) to France to work in support of our country's involvement in World War I. One of her overseas responsibilities was to coordinate receiving the supplies and comforts from the Emergency Aid for the Pennsylvania men engaged in the war effort. The Emergency Aid organization continues to function today. See Emergency Aid of Penna. Foundation, Inc., "A Small Sampling of 100 Years of the Emergency Aid."

2   MLD was appointed secretary to the American Soldiers' and Sailors' Club, which was established in 1917 as the receiving arm for the supplies sent by the Emergency Aid (of Pennsylvania). Funding was provided by Rodman Wanamaker. See "Phila. Emergency Aid Girl Goes to France," *Philadelphia Inquirer*, September 18, 1918.

3   Marie-Louise Dilkes was working for the American Soldiers' and Sailors' Club in Paris at the same time Charles Edward Dilkes, her brother, was serving in WWI with the U.S. AEF in the Army of Occupation in Montabaur and Wirges, Germany. He was granted an R&R leave in April 1919, upon which he went to Paris to visit his sister, Marie-Louise. She gave him her American Soldiers' and Sailors' Club calling card. He related the time he spent with her

in his WWI book. See Dilkes, Charles Edward, *Remembering World War One: An Engineer's Diary of the War.* 130–133.

4   Dean Beekman, who would recommend MLD for her appointment as the receptionist for the American Embassy in Paris, was awarded the French Legion of Honor in 1924 (see Green, *Other Americans in Paris*, 240 and made a commander of the Legion of Honor in Paris in 1947 (see "Dean Frederick Beekman Dies," *The New York Times*, March 23, 1964).

5   Colonel Thomas Bentley Mott (1865–1952), also known as Col. T. Bentley Mott or Col. T. B. Mott, was a Lieutenant Colonel in the U.S. Army. He was the liaison officer between U.S. General John Pershing and French General Ferdinand Foch, Supreme Commander of the Allied Forces, in WWI. Mott delivered messages between the two leaders: Pershing told Foch he wanted an unconditional surrender; Foch told Pershing the Armistice to end hostilities would take place at 11:00 a.m. EST on November 11. (Pershing, *My Experiences in the World War* (368, 388). Mott was a military attaché serving with embassies in Paris (1900–1904; 1909–1913; 1919–1930), St. Petersburg (1904–1905), and the Philippines (1914). MLD worked for Col. Mott from 1919–1921 when he was assigned as Military Attaché to the American Embassy in Paris. He would be a reference for MLD on her Application for Appointment as receptionist for the American Embassy in Paris. Dilkes Family Collection.

6   Baron Emile-Ernest de Cartier de Marchienne (1871–1946) was a Belgian diplomat who served in Washington, D.C., as the Extraordinary Envoy and Plenipotentiary Minister for Belgium in the United States from 1917–1919 and then as the Belgian Ambassador to the U.S. from 1920–1927. (See Testelmans, Eddy. "de Cartier de Marchienne, Baron Emile-Ernest.") Marie-Louise Dilkes was his personal secretary. He would be a reference for MLD on her Application for Appointment as receptionist for the American Embassy in Paris. Dilkes Family Collection.

7   Prince Albert de Ligne (1874–1957) was the Belgian Ambassador to the United States from 1927–1931. Marie-Louise Dilkes was his personal secretary. He issued a royal decree on January 15, 1928, to confer on Marie-Louise Dilkes the decoration of the Cross of Chevalier in the Order of Léopold II. (Confirmation was sent from Belgian Foreign Ministry in a communication to the Belgian Cultural Officer in the Embassy of Belgium in Washington, D.C.; the confirmation was subsequently emailed to Virginia Dilkes May 7, 2009.) Prince Albert de Ligne would be a reference for MLD on her Application for Appointment as receptionist for the American Embassy in Paris. Dilkes Family Collection.

8   Richard W. Morin (1902–1988) was confirmed by the [U.S.] Senate on December 19, 1929, to serve in the American Foreign Service as a Secretary in the Diplomatic Service and as a Vice Consul of Career. (American Foreign Service Journal, Vol. VII, January 1930:24). In the *Foreign Service List,* he was assigned to the U.S. Embassy in Paris. After his career as a diplomat, Richard Morin became the librarian for Dartmouth College. He was married to Dolores Dilkes, sister of Marie-Louise Dilkes. See Papers of Richard W. Morin, Rauner Special Collections, Dartmouth College.

9   Julian Jackson in his book *France: The Dark Years 1940–1944* describes in detail the chaos that existed in the French government as the German forces entered France. For the first cabinet meeting outside Paris some cabinet members went incorrectly to the Château de Candé instead of to the agreed-upon location of the Château de Cangé. See Jackson. 118–121.

10   In a communiqué from Leland B. Morris, U.S. Chargé d'Affaires in Germany, to the U.S. Secretary State, Cordell Hull, Germany dictated the conditions required to close the U.S. Embassy in Paris yet retain a consular office. (See Morris, Leland B., Telegram 124.51/207.) The German orders stipulated a consular staff remaining of no more than 15 people, including the vice consul, Laurence Taylor. In a follow-up communication, Laurence Taylor stated the physical and staff changes that were made to the former Embassy facility in compliance with the German demands.

Introduction

1 The service record of Marie-Louise Dilkes with the U.S. Department of State assigned to the American Embassy in Paris is listed in her Application for Retirement of May 10, 1954. The Dilkes Family Collection.

Office of Military Attaché, Paris Embassy October 1919–October 1921
State Department, Paris Embassy   November 1933–July 1941
Consulate General, Portugal   July 1941–August 1941
Consulate General, Lyon   September 1941–December 1941
American Legation, Bern   December 1941–October 1944
American Embassy, Paris   October 1944–May 21, 1954

2 Pierre Audiat (1891–1961) was an accomplished French journalist, a historical works critic, and a literary scholar. He was a member of the Académie de Saintonge, a learned society of academicians of the culture and heritage of the Charente-Maritime district on the western coast of France. See "Audiat, Pierre," Saintonge Academy.

3 The preface to *Paris Pendant la Guerre* by Pierre Audiat is titled "Précisions." He expresses what his book is not before he tells the reader the purpose of his book. His words written in French are translated and summarized by MLD. *Nul, quelles que soient son erudition ou son intuition, ne saurail évoquer cette atmosphere s'il ne l'a lui-même respire.* See Audiat. 5–6.

4 Marie-Louise Dilkes' father is George R. Dilkes. George R. Dilkes (1860–1938) and Mrs. George R. (Dolores) Dilkes (1870–1929) are listed in the *Year Book of the Pennsylvania Society of New York, 1916.* See "Dilkes, George R. and Dolores Dilkes." 99, 115.

5 The Dilkes family was a prominent family in Philadelphia at the turn of the twentieth century. In the "Report of the Board of Managers of the Trades League of Philadelphia: For the Year 1904," it is recorded: "George R. Dilkes, of the firm of Messrs. George R. Dilkes & Co., they have decided to establish a steamship line between Philadelphia and Tampa, Fla., first steamship, 'Shoma,' sailing April 16th, from Pier 28, South Wharves. For the present, shippers should apply to the Southern Steamship Company, 305 Walnut Street, for freight rates and other information." See the "Report of the Board of Managers of the Trades League of Philadelphia: For the Year 1904." 47.

Chapter 1

1 D. is the author's younger sister, Dolores Dilkes Morin, married from 1928–1978 to Richard Morin, who served as Vice Consul and Diplomatic Secretary at the American Embassy in Paris, 1929–1933. Dilkes Family Collection.

2 M. (Édouard) Daladier, Prime Minister of France, signed the Munich Agreement in 1938. The Munich Conference was held September 29–30, 1938. Present were Nazi Germany (Adolf Hitler), the United Kingdom (Neville Chamberlain), France (Édouard Daladier), and the Kingdom of Italy (Benito Mussolini). To keep the peace, agreement was reached to allow Nazi Germany to take over the southern part of Czechoslovakia. See Henderson, *Failure of a Mission.* 171–175.

3 L. refers to the author, Marie-Louise Dilkes, who is most likely writing in her journal. She sometimes referred to herself as Louise Dilkes. Dilkes Family Collection.

4 World leaders responded to the world tensions created by Hitler. President Franklin D. Roosevelt expressed the opinion of the United States, King Léopold III expressed the opinion of the Belgian people, and Pope Pius XII expressed the opinion of the Catholic Church and the Vatican's request for peace. See Tolischus, "Berlin Talks Held."

5   The SS *Bremen* under Captain Ahrens continued to New York where the passengers disembarked. Upon leaving American waters, the crew camouflaged the ship and despite pursuit by British cruisers, escaped to Murmansk, Russia. By year's end it made its way to Bremerhaven, Germany. Fire later damaged the ship and rendered it no longer seaworthy; it was used for parts for the German war effort. See "A Daring Escape at the Start of WWII."

6   German–Soviet Pact of Nonaggression, aka the Molotov-Ribbentrop Pact, was signed on August 23, 1939. Nevile Henderson did not see this pact as easing tensions. See Henderson. 253–257.

7   *L'Humanité* is a Communist French newspaper (1904–present). See *l'Humanité*, Ed. Hyaric. *Le Soir* (1887–present) is a Communist French-language Belgian newspaper. See *Le Soir.be*, Ed. Delvaux.

8   Chez Francis on the Place de l'Alma is a French restaurant still serving today. See "Chez Francis," *TripAdvisor*.

9   American Field Service is an ambulance service organized by Americans to aid wounded Allied soldiers. Today it is an American organization that offers intercultural programs. See "AFS History Timeline," AFS, 2020.

10   Le Paris was a cinema house on the Champs-Élysées that showed film premières (*cinemas d'exclusivité*). It closed before the Occupation. See Smoodin, "The Paris Cinema Project."

11   *Toward His Destiny* is the French title for the American movie film *Young Mr. Lincoln* depicting the early life of Abraham Lincoln. Henry Fonda is the American actor who portrays Abraham Lincoln in the movie. "Rail splitter, tree chopper and the greatest man that history ever made" are the impressions left on the author after seeing the movie. See *Toward His Destiny*, adapt. *Young Mr. Lincoln*, by Trotti and Ford.

12   Chartres Cathedral is a medieval church with stained glass windows and sculptures from the twelfth and thirteenth centuries. See Cartwright, "The Stained Glass Windows of Chartres Cathedral."

13   Smith's Bookshop is the largest English bookshop in Paris since 1903, originally established by the Neal brothers in 1870. It is now Smith&Son Paris. See "WHSmith—The English Bookshop," *WHSmith*.

14   *Hitler's Last Year of Power* was written by the astrologer, Leonardo Blake, in 1939. Going back to the horoscope of the Bismarck Era, he tried to show there would be no great war. He examined the horoscopes of the 1930's world leaders. He believed Chamberlain's peace policy would triumph over Hitler's lust for power. See Blake, *Hitler's Last Year of Power*.

15   *Paris-midi*, afternoon edition of *Paris-soir*, published 1911–1944. The September 1, 1939, headlines read "Hitler attaque la Pologne" ('Hitler attacks Poland'). See "*Paris-midi*," *BnF Gallica*.

16   Danzig, now Gdańsk, is a seaport in Poland that was part of Germany until the end of WWI. Churchill recounts Germany's invasion of Poland and its consequences in his book, *The Second World War: The Gathering Storm*. See Churchill, *The Gathering Storm*.

17   Ledoyen Restaurant is in the gardens of the Champs-Élysées with three Michelin stars and a rich history. Taken over by Yannick Alléno in 2014, it is now known as Alléno Paris au Pavillon Ledoyen. See "Alléno Paris au Pavillon Ledoyen," *Michelin Guide*.

18   The river Seine flows from northeastern France near Dijon to the English Channel at Le Havre. It flows through Paris creating the Left Bank and Right Bank. Paris has 37 bridges that span the Seine. See Sciolino, "Ode to the Seine River, River of Romance."

19   Notre-Dame, a Catholic cathedral on the Île de la Cité in Paris, was constructed in 1163; it is known for its French Gothic architecture. A structure fire on April 15, 2019, severely damaged the Cathedral, which is currently undergoing reconstruction. See "Notre Dame Cathedral Paris," *Notre Dame Cathedral Paris 2008–2020*.

20   Pont de la Concorde bridges the Quai d'Orsay on the Left Bank with the Place de la Concorde on the Right Bank. See map of Paris with arrondissements.

21   Ange-Jacques Gabriel (1698–1782) was a French architect of the eighteenth century whose major accomplishments were the Place de la Concorde and *École Militaire* in Paris, the Petit Trianon and the Royal Opera in Versailles. See "The Gabriel Family," *Chateau de Versailles*.

22   The quoted lines "Take up the quarrel with the foe…" are from the poem "In Flanders Fields" by John McCrae, MD, who was a lieutenant colonel in the Canadian Army. He wrote the poem in 1915 after the death of his friend, Alexis Helmer, in the Second Battle of Ypres in WWI. See McCrae, "In Flanders Fields."

23   *L'Intransigeant* evolved into a right-wing newspaper that was published 1880–1940. The headline on September 4, 1939, read "LA GUERRE." The strapline read "France and England are in a state of war with Germany." See *L'Intransigeant*, Ed. Henri Rochefort.

24   V. is the author's sister, Virginia Dilkes Harrison (1903–2007). She was married (1936–1952) to John Harrison, Jr. Their residence in Philadelphia, PA, was MLD's U.S. address after their father, George R. Dilkes, died. [Note: Virginia Dilkes Harrison is the editor's namesake.] Dilkes Family Collection.

25   British ship SS *Athenia* was the first British ship torpedoed in WWII on September 3, 1939. There was a loss of 112 lives including 28 Americans. See Churchill, *The Gathering Storm*. 423.

26   Rochefort-en-Yvelines is now a commune in the Yvelines department in the Île-de-France region 33 miles southwest of Paris. The Seine-et-Oise Department was abolished and has been incorporated into the Île-de-France region. See "Rochefort-en-Yvelines," *map-france.com*.

27   Marie-Louise Dilkes most likely named her horse Picardie after the Picardy region in northern France. [Ed. Comment.]

28   In 1939 the "Daily Bulletin" was the internal news within the American Embassy and distributed to all staff members. These communications are considered historical documents and are part of the Foreign Relations of the United States (FRUS) series that are overseen by the Office of the Historian. See "Daily Bulletin," Office of the Historian.

29   *Défense Passive* groups were civil watch groups organized throughout France to defend the city or town in which it was formed. Aerial bombardments were of particular concern. The organization for *Défense Passive* was created in 1935. See "Paris at war (1939–1940)." *Paris Archives*.

30   "It is pleasant to notice everything in Paris," is from *Memoirs of My Dead Life* by George Moore (47). George Moore (1852–1933) was an Irish novelist and poet. See Moore, *Memoirs of My Dead Life*.

31   Travellers Club on the Champs-Élysées since 1904 is an elite private member's club. See Cooper, "A gentleman's guide to the Parisian members' club."

32   Marie-Louise Dilkes was a volunteer with the American Soldiers' and Sailors' Club, located at 11 rue Royale, Paris, from 1917–1919. See Preface.

33   Baron William Sylvester de Ropp (1886–1973), a British agent, had a close relationship with Hitler. He dealt with Nazi Germany before and during World War II. MLD dined with his wife, Baronne Marie Woodman de Ropp, whom he married in 1925. Baronne de Ropp lived until 1986. See Farago, *The Game of the Foxes*. 79, 84.

34   Bordeaux is in southwestern, France; Nantes in east France. Château de Candé is in Monts, France, 130 miles east of Nantes. See Glass. 60.

35   Duchesse de la Rochefoucauld is an activist in a French Catholic women's organization advocating for women's rights while appealing to women to support the war effort. See "Edmée de la Rochefoucauld," *Arllfb.be*.

36   Anthony J. D. Biddle, Jr., U.S. ambassador to Poland, was forced to flee Poland with his staff when Germany invaded Poland. His escape is recorded in *The Foreign Service Journal*. See Walser, Ray. "War Comes to Warsaw: September 1939."

37   The American Legion in Paris since 1919, Paris Post #1, has protected the memory of fallen American soldiers buried in the American military cemeteries in France (except during the period of WWII). See "American Legion," *American Legion Paris Post 1*.

38   Mr. Lord is most likely James Couper Lord of Tuxedo Park and grandson of the architect, James Brown Lord. Tuxedo Park, a New York luxury community started by Pierre Lorillard IV, is where the tuxedo for men's formal attire originated. MLD's friend, Mrs. Griswold Lorillard (née Mary V. Green of Philadelphia), was the wife of Griswold Lorillard, grandson of Pierre Lorillard IV and heir to the Lorillard tobacco fortune. See "How Mr. Lorillard Divided His Estate," *The New York Times*, July 14, 1901.

39   Hubert Renfro Knickerbocker wrote about German politics before and during WWII. Charles Glass in *Americans in Paris* notes, after the Nazi takeover of Paris, the director of the Berlin Library, Dr. Herman Fuchs, had Knickerbocker's works removed from the shelves of the American Library. See Glass. 117.

40   The *New York Herald Tribune* was published 1924–1966. (See *Lib. of Cong.* Newspaper: "*New York Herald Tribune*"). Nazi chief (Paul) Joseph Goebbels was in charge of propaganda; Hermann Wilhelm Göring was second to Hitler, marshal of the Reich, commander of the German air force (Luftwaffe), and in charge of the armament and war industry; Heinrich Himmler orchestrated the Gestapo and was the architect for the Holocaust. See Speer, *Inside the Third Reich*.

41   The American Colony in Paris was composed of Americans, mainly businessmen, who settled on the Right Bank. They distinguished themselves from the tourists. See Green, *The Other Americans in Paris*.

42   Huntington Harter, a member of the American Colony in Paris, worked for the Paris branch of Harjes and Company in 1919. See "Harter, Huntington," *Social Register for Philadelphia—1919*. 114.

43   "Madelon" (I'll Be True to the Whole Regiment) is a song from WWI. See Robert, "Madelon: 'I'll be true to the whole regiment'"; Chorale de la Promotion Laperrine sings "La Madelon," *YouTube*.

44   Edvard Beneš was President of Czechoslovakia 1935–1938 until Germany invaded Czechoslovakia in 1938. He led the government-in-exile 1939–1945. He came out of exile to lead again as President 1945–1948. Nevile Henderson wrote of the plight of Beneš in his book *The Failure of a Mission* (136–144). The French perspective is given in *Le Livre Jaune Français*, which is a book of diplomatic documents 1938–1939 offered by the French Ministry of Foreign Affairs. 13–14.

45   Vouillemont Hotel is now the Hôtel Sofitel Paris le Faubourg. See "Sofitel Paris le Faubourg." *Sofitel Paris le Faubourg*.

46   "What happened when you got back home?" is from *Wickford Point*. In Marie-Louise Dilkes' writing, she is reflecting on her own experience after WWI and how people went on with their lives as if the war never happened. See Marquand, *Wickford Point*, 238.

47   Ambassador François-Poncet was invited to the Eagle's Nest (Kehlsteinhaus), Hitler's retreat in the Bavarian Alps. Berchtesgaden is the nearest town to the Eagle's Nest. See *Le Livre Jaune Français*. 24–25.

48   Hitler became Chancellor of Germany in 1933 and Leader (Führer) and Chancellor (Reichskanzler) of Germany in 1934. Hitler's rise to power is uniquely told by Otto Strasser. See Strasser, *Hitler et Moi*.

49   "There was the hermitage perched at 1900 meters…," from *Le Livre Jaune Français*. This note refers to a letter of October 20, 1938, from M. André François-Poncet, French Ambassador to Berlin (1931–1938), to M. Georges Bonnet, [French] Minister of Foreign Affairs. The letter describes Hitler's habitat known as Eagle's Nest. Monsalvat, as told in the opera *Parsifal* by Richard Wagner, is the mystical castle in northern Spain where the Holy Grail is kept. The Holy

Grail according to legend is the cup used by Jesus at the Last Supper. It is highly sought after by the knights of the Holy Grail in Arthurian literature. Mount Athos is a mountain in Greece and an Orthodox spiritual center where monks meditate in any of the multiple monasteries located there. In the French romance drama, *Atlantide*, by Pierre Benoit, the palace of Queen Antinea has cave walls. It is the place where intruders went to signify they died of love; they were embalmed in bronze. [Note: The drama takes place in the Atlas Mountains along the coast of northern Africa.] See *Le Livre Jaune Français*, Document #18. 24.

50   MLD often went to the Garden of the Tuileries for reflection. There she found:

    o   Sculpture of Prometheus by James Pradier (1790–1852) placed in the Tuileries in 1827. See "Sculpture of Prometheus," Pradier.

    o   Statue of Alexander fighting a lion by Jacques-Augustin Dieudonné placed in the Tuileries in 1877. The statue is known as *Alexandre Combattant un Lion*. See "Paris, Tuileries, Alexandre combatant un lion (Dieudonné)."

    o   Sculpture of Cassandra by Aimé Millet (1819–1891). See "Sculpture of Cassandra," Millet.

    o   Sculpture of Bacchante by Pierre Alexandre Schoenewerk (1820–1885) now located on the northern façade of Aile Sud at Musée du Louvre. See "Sculpture of Bacchante," Schoenewerk.

51   La Côtelette restaurant was located at 41–43 rue de la Rochefoucauld. See "La Côtelette," *Documents commerciaux des restaurants de Paris et d'Ile de France.*

52   Johann Georg Elser attempted to assassinate Hitler on November 8, 1939. Elser was executed in 1945. Otto Strasser recounted the assassination attempt in his book. See Strasser, *Hitler et Moi.*

53   Georges Duhamel was a French author who wrote novels and articles on social and moral issues. He was anti-German and anti-Vichy in his writings, in which he defined French humanism. He endorsed the French culture he loved. In the inter-war years he expressed strong anti-American sentiment. See Jackson. 35–37; 315; 482.

54   G. Lenotre, pen name for Théodore Gosselin (1855–1935), is known for his historical works on the French revolution. In the six volumes of *Vieilles maisons, vieux papiers* ("Old houses, old papers") he told behind-the-scenes stories of the French Revolution through the places where historical figures of the revolution lived. See Lenotre, *Vieilles maisons, vieux papiers.*

55   "Each house, your own…" is from the Prelude to *Hampton Court: A History*. Philip Lindsay, an Australian author who wrote historical novels, published *Hampton Court: A History* in 1948. See Lindsay, Prelude.

56   "On the Quay…" MLD is referring to the Quai d'Orsay on the Left Bank in the 7th arrondissement.

57   "A great bed wide and low, 'like a battlefield'…" is from the *Memoirs of My Dead Life* by George Moore. See Moore. 143.

58   In 1939 the Allied countries included the United Kingdom and its Commonwealth of Nations, France, and Poland. Great Britain and France had a pact with Poland that they would come to the aid of Poland if Poland was invaded by Germany. Germany invaded Poland on September 1, 1939, which led to the start of WWII. See "Allies of World War II," *Wikipedia.*

59   In the 1937 British film, *Moonlight Sonata*, Ignacy Jan Paderewski, a Polish pianist, portrays himself in a recital of Romantic era works by Polish composer Frédéric Chopin and Hungarian composer Franz Liszt. See *Moonlight Sonata*, Dir. Lothar Mendes.

60   In 1939 Neville Chamberlain was Prime Minister of the United Kingdom. Winston Churchill was First Lord of the Admiralty and a member of Chamberlain's War Cabinet. The story of Winston Churchill in 1939 is told in Erik Larson's book, *The Splendid and the Vile.*

61   Lord Haw-Haw, the nickname of William Joyce, was an Irish American who broadcast Nazi propaganda to the United Kingdom from 1939–1945 on the radio show "Germany Calling." He was born in Brooklyn, New York, in 1905 and moved to England in 1921. He joined the Nazi

party in England in the mid-1930s, moved to Germany before the war broke out in 1939, and became a German citizen in 1940. He was a broadcaster for the Nazi Party Propaganda machine. William Joyce was found guilty of treason and executed in 1946. A treatment of his life can be found at the Imperial War Museum. See Charman, "The Rise and Fall of Lord Haw Haw during the Second World War."

62   "Thou must be true thyself / If thou the truth wouldst teach" is from the poem "Be True to Thyself" by the Scottish poet Horatius Bonar (1808–1889). See Bonar, "Be True to Thyself."

63   (Robert) Anthony Eden was a Conservative politician who held various positions in the British government, especially in the British foreign service. In 1939 he was Secretary of State for Dominion Affairs, which oversaw British relations with the Commonwealth. Hansard files indicate the time and substance of the radio address in November 1939 were related to one made not by Anthony Eden but by the Secretary of State for War, Mr. Hore-Belisha, who was considered to be a brilliant speaker. See "Land Warfare," *House of Common Debates* (November 22, 1939).

64   Hôtel Biron is a mansion built in 1727 that has evolved with its owners and inhabitants including the sculptor Auguste Rodin (1840–1917) and is now the *Musée Rodin*. See "The Hôtel Biron," *The Musée Rodin.*

65   In 1939 Thanksgiving was to be on the last day of November, leading to a shortened Christmas shopping season and hurting a nation coming out of the Great Depression. President Franklin Roosevelt proclaimed Thanksgiving to occur on the second to last Thursday. See "The Year We Had Two Thanksgivings," *Franklin D. Roosevelt Presidential Library and Museum.*

66   Church of the [Holy] Trinité, also known as the Église de la Sainte-Trinité, is a Roman Catholic Church in the 9th arrondissement. It was built in 1861–1867 and known for its organ and organ concerts. See "Church of the Trinité," *Paroisse de la Sainte-Trinité.*

67   Hôtel des Invalides was built in 1671 by Louis XIV as a hospital and hospice for disabled war veterans. It retains that function today along with housing other government ministries. See "Hôtel des Invalides," *World Monuments Fund.*

68   The High Command is the French military command.

69   H. G. (Herbert George) Wells was a British author known for his science fiction novels. He wrote *What Is Coming? A Forecast of Things after the War* (1916), *The War of the Worlds* (1898), and *The Time Machine* (1895). A list of his publications is maintained by the H. G. Wells Society. See "The H. G. Wells Society," *The H. G. Wells Society.*

70   After Germany invaded Poland, a Polish Army division formed in France and fought under French command. Churchill refers to the Polish soldiers that Britain evacuated from Dunkirk in the Battle of France. See Churchill, *Their Finest Hour.* 193.

71   In MLD's footnote, Winston Churchill is describing the Battle of the River Plate in South American waters and the scuttling of the *Admiral Graf Spee,* which was the first Allied naval victory in World War II. The battle took place in the harbor of the port city of Montevideo, the capital of Uruguay. See Churchill, *The Second World War: The Gathering Storm.* 526.

72   "This royal throne of kings…," is said by John Gaunt in Shakespeare's play *The Tragedy of King Richard II*: Act II, Scene I. See Shakespeare, *The Tragedy of King Richard II.*

73   La Belle Aurore Restaurant, famously seen in the movie *Casablanca,* is no longer in business. See *Casablanca.* Dir. Michael Curtiz.

74   Gaston Ernest Liébert was Consul General of France when MLD knew him. As a diplomat he worked with the U.S. to resolve political disagreements regarding Germany as a result of WWI. He died in 1944. See "Gaston Ernest Liébert," *Wikipedia.*

75   Mons. Q. is an abbreviation for *monsieurs* (misters); Q represents any anonymous person.

76   "And I said to the man who stood at the gate of the year:" is a poem by Minnie Louise Haskins (1875–1957) and is read often at royal ceremonies. The poem is referred to as "The Gate of the

Year" poem, but it was published in a collection titled *The Desert* in 1908 as "God Knows." See Haskins, "God Knows."

77   "The air bites shrewdly; it is very cold," is said by Hamlet in Shakespeare's play *Hamlet, Prince of Denmark*: Act I, Scene IV. See Shakespeare, *Hamlet, Prince of Denmark*.

78   German Messerschmitt Bf 109 is the heralded German WWII fighter plane. The plane with its history is on display at the Smithsonian National Air and Space Museum. "Messerschmitt Bf 109 G-6/R3," *Smithsonian National Air and Space Museum*.

79   The Iron Cross was a service medal given to members of the German military from the Napoléon era until 1945; it became a symbol of Nazi Germany. See "Cross of Iron," *Military History Now*.

80   The American Hospital of Paris is located at Neuilly-sur-Seine in west Paris. Originally built in 1906 to treat sick Americans, it now has dual accreditation by U.S. and French health authorities. Charles Glass's book *Americans in Paris* focuses on the Hospital and its role in the Résistance movement against Nazi Occupation.

81   MLD is comparing the wildness of the cold, windy January evening to the eeriness of the setting for the manor house in *Wuthering Heights*, a book written by Emily Brontë in 1845. See Brontë, *Wuthering Heights*.

82   "So long Thy power hast blest me" is from the hymn "Lead, Kindly Light" written by John Henry Newman in 1833. See Newman, "Lead, Kindly Light."

83   *La Batterie Triomphale* are eight Prussian cannons brought to France by Napoléon in 1805 and later to Paris in 1832. These cannons make up the Triumphal Battery. See Pommier, "The Prussian cannons of the Triumphal Battery."

84   While the Montparnasse beard was fashionable with French officers in the 1940s, the French Foreign Legion pioneers are the only French soldiers wearing beards today. See "French Foreign Legion Traditions," *French Legion Info*.

85   White Russians in general refer to Russians who supported the imperial government and opposed the Bolshevik Revolution in 1917; they typically had lived a life of nobility. Eugene Lyons wrote about the genesis of the Bolshevik Revolution.

86   "The winter is past, the rain is over and gone," from The Song of Solomon 2:11 (*KJV*).

87   The Parliament of the United Kingdom is composed of the elected members of the House of Commons and the appointed members of the House of Lords. The ministers of the government, including the Prime Minister, are required to come before Parliament to keep Parliament informed of policy decisions and to answer questions Members of Parliament (MPs) may have. Churchill used this platform effectively. See "Parliament and government," *UK Parliament*.

88   French Foreign Legion is open to soldiers from foreign countries to serve in the French Armed Forces. See "Foreign Legion," *Foreign Legion*.

89   Walter Lippmann was a well-respected political columnist noted for his column, "Today and Tomorrow," in the *New York Herald Tribune*. The European version of the *New York Herald Tribune* was the *Paris Herald Tribune* and was considered the hometown newspaper for Americans in Paris. MLD mentions Lippmann's article on hindsight and foresight. Lippmann first wrote about hindsight and foresight in 1921 in his book *Public Opinion*. See "Lippmann," *Public Opinion*.

90   Hermann Rauschning (1887–1982) supported Hitler from 1933–1935. He went into exile in 1936 and moved to the U.S. where he denounced Hitler through his writings. See Simkin, "Hermann Rauschning."

91   The game "*Bombardement de la Ligne Siegfried*" was created by the game company Jouets Vera of Paris in 1939–1940. "The game is simply a variant of the game 'Battleship.' The box cover shows a battle with artillery, tanks, and planes between a French flag and a British flag. Below, one reads the indication 'Authorized by the military censorship (17.11.39).'" See Schädler, "1945." Swiss Museum of Games. 14.

92 General Henri Gouraud (1867–1946) served in the French Army in Africa from 1894–1914 and rose to be commander of the Legion. In WWI in 1915 he was wounded in the shoulder in Argonne and again in the Dardanelles, which resulted in the amputation of his right arm. He gained fame for his leadership in the victorious Second Battle of the Somme in July–August 1918. He was active in Mideast affairs and Military Governor of Paris 1923–1937. See Pershing. 152–153, 295, 326.

93 German aggressive acts in Czechoslovakia and Poland occurred before the period known as the "Phoney war" (September 1939–May 1940) when seemingly no more Nazi aggression took place. Chamberlain and Churchill referred to this period as the Twilight War. See Churchill, *Their Finest Hour*. 302, 518, 556.

94 German participants in the March 1939 meeting were the Führer (Adolf Hitler), Hermann Göring who organized the Gestapo police state, Joachim von Ribbentrop who was Foreign Minister of Nazi Germany, and Georg Keppler who was the SS commander. See *Le Livre Jaune Français*. 101.

95 Bohemia and Moravia are in the western and eastern parts of Czechoslovakia respectively. Prague, the capital of Czechoslovakia, is in the Bohemia region of the country. On March 16, 1939, German troops occupied Czechoslovakia. Events leading up to this Occupation are documented in *Le Livre Jaune Français*. 92–99.

96 German Reich is the constitutional name for the German nation state. Historians view the First Reich as from the Roman Empire in 800 until 1806; the Second Reich from 1871 (victory in the Franco-Prussian War) until 1918 (defeat in WWI); and the Third Reich from 1933 (rise of the National-Socialism Party) to 1945 (defeat in WWII). See "Germany/ History" in the *World Book Encyclopedia*. 150–157.

97 "Our people will curse us...," from *The French Yellow Book*. Report from M. Robert Coulondre, French Ambassador to Berlin, to M. Georges Bonnet, [French] Minister of Foreign Affairs, March 17, 1939. The report describes the coercive conditions under which the Munich Agreement was signed. Minister Hácha of Czechoslovakia signed the Agreement "with death in the soul." The words "Our people will curse us" were spoken by Minister Chvalkovsky of Czechoslovakia. See *Le Livre Jaune Français*, Doc. #77. 100–102.

98 Bouffes Parisiens Theater on Rue Monsigny is open to theater-goers today. See "Théâtre des Bouffes Parisiens," *Bouffes-Parisiens Theater*.

99 *Fascicule Noir (Black Paper)*—a play written in 1939 by Louis Verneuil and performed at the Théâtre des Bouffes Parisiens starring Gaby Morlay (1893–1964) and Victor Francen. See *Fascicule Noir*, by Verveuil.

100 SS *Rochambeau* sailed 1911–1934. It was a French transatlantic ocean liner named for the commander of the French expeditionary force that helped defeat the British at Yorktown in the American Revolution. After America entered WWI, the SS *Rochambeau* carried troops in addition to its regular passengers and cargo. See McMahon, "WWI in the Passenger Lists of the U.S. Army Transport Service."

101 The play *Three Faces East* was first performed in Philadelphia before George Cohan adapted it for Broadway. See *Three Faces East* by George Cohan.

102 *Hitler et Moi* by Otto Strasser was published in French in 1940. Otto Strasser, an early member of the Nazi party, was a political idealist. He with his brother, Gregor, would take nationalism from the right and socialism from the left to form the National Socialist Party—shortened to the Nazi Party. He owned newspapers that published articles against Hitler's political ideas. He lived out his life in exile. See Strasser, *Hitler et Moi*. 9.

103 The volumes of the book(s) *Abraham Lincoln* by John George Nicolay and John Hay were published in 1914. See Nicolay, *Abraham Lincoln: a history, Vol. I–X*.

104 "Gone—glimmering through the dream of things that were..." is from "Childe Harold's Pilgrimage Canto the Second" by George Gordon Byron (Lord Byron), pub. 1812. See Byron, "Childe Harold's Pilgrimage Canto the Second."

105 "Le ciel est, par-dessus le toit, ..." (The sky is, above the roof, ...), from the poem: "*Le ciel est, par-dessus...*" by Paul Verlaine (1844–1896), a French poet and leader of the Symbolist movement. See Verlaine, "Le ciel est, par-dessus...," *Sagesse.*

106 *Louise* is a 1900 opera by Gustave Charpentier about the working-class life of Parisians. See *Louise* by Gustave Charpentier.

107 (Benjamin) Sumner Welles was U.S. Under Secretary of State who traveled to Italy and Berlin to offer the services of the United States as a peace mediator. See Knauth, *The New York Times*, March 2, 1940.

108 In 1939 Finland and the Soviet Union (MLD referred to the Soviet Union as Russia) engaged in the Winter War. By March 1940 Finland agreed to cede 9% of its territory to the Soviet Union in exchange for peace. See Upton, *Finland in Crisis 1940–1941.* 35.

109 MLD's letter to her sister in the United States was written throughout the month of March. She wrote more about the Colonel [Winslow] in her letter of April 8, 1940.

110 Paul Reynaud became Prime Minister of France on March 21, 1940. See "Change in France," *The New York Times*, March 21, 1940.

111 The Chez Elle night club in Paris is a cabaret created by popular singers such as Lucienne Boyer in the interwar years. Lucienne Boyer (1903–1983) was a French singer whose classic song was "*Parlez-moi d'amour*" ('Speak to me of love'). Chez Elle is no longer in business. See "Chez Elle–Closed," *Trip Advisor.*

112 "La Marseillaise" is the national anthem of France; "God Save the King" is the national anthem of Great Britain.

113 Chambre des Députés in 1940 is the elected legislative assembly of the French Parliament in the Third Republic of France (1870–1940); the Chambre des Députés building is located on the Left Bank. Place du Palais-Bourbon on the Left Bank is a historic square with government buildings, including the Palais Bourbon, which today houses the French National Assembly. See "National Assembly History," *National Assembly.*

114 "These people who tell us what to do…" are words translated from Hitler's address to the Hofbrauhaus in Munich on February 24, 1940 and appeared in *The New York Times* on February 25, 1940. See Hitler, "Adolf Hitler—speech for the Twentieth anniversary of the N.S.D.A.P." *Neues Europa.*

115 The tea room Boissier, founded in 1827 by Bélissaire Boissier, was a famous tea room in 1940 and sold in 2000 to Salon du Chocolat. See "Boissier." *ChocoParis.com.*

116 "Rose-red dawn" is from the sonnet, "This Was the Song," by Helen (Julia) Hay Whitney. See Whitney, "This Was the Song," *Sonnets and Songs.*

117 Grand Duchess Charlotte Wilhelmine was the monarch over Luxembourg, 1919–1964. In WWII she went into exile to France, Portugal, Great Britain, the U.S., and Canada. See Saxon, "Charlotte, Longtime Luxembourg Ruler, Dies," *The New York Times*, July 10, 1985.

118 The American Ambulance Corps was a unit of the American Field Service in WWII. Their work is recognized in the book *Americans in Paris* (see Glass, 73) and their history documented on the AFS website (see "AFS History Timeline").

119 "I have nothing to offer but blood, toil, tears and sweat," are some of Churchill's most quoted words, spoken in his first address as Britain's Prime Minister to the House of Commons: May 13, 1940. See Churchill, Address, "Blood, Toil, Tears and Sweat."

120 Gare de l'Est is a railroad station for passengers serving eastern France and beyond. Its WWII history has been preserved. See "Preserved in time: WWII bunker hidden under Paris train station." *The Local fr.*

121 Mary Astor Paul Allez (Madame Jacques Allez) was known as Pauline in the French underground. MLD knew her as a co-worker through her work with the American Aid Society; both are of Main Line society in Philadelphia, PA. Mary Astor remained in contact with MLD throughout the war including the time MLD was assigned to the U.S. Legation in Bern, Switzerland. See "Mrs. Allez Is Dead; Heroine in War, 61," *The New York Times*, July 30, 1950.

122 General Maxime Weygand (1867–1965), a French hero of WWI, was recalled from retirement in 1940 to assume command of the French armies. In an article for the *World War I: Encyclopedia*, Volume 1, Michael Neiberg wrote, "Recalled to service in 1939, Weygand commanded in the Middle East. Foch had declared before his death in 1929, 'If France is ever in trouble, call Weygand.' French Premier Paul Reynaud followed Foch's advice in 1940, recalling Weygand from Syria to replace General Maurice Gamelin as commander of French forces." See Neiberg, *World War I: Encyclopedia*, Volume 1. 1258. [Note: General Ferdinand Foch (1851–1929) commanded the Allied Forces in the closing months of WWI.] Barnett Singer in his book *Maxime Weygand: A Biography of the French General in Two World Wars* recounts Foch's respect for Weygand and Weygand's devotion to Foch. See Singer. 14–50.

123 The Tomb of the Unknown Soldier at the Arc de Triomphe commemorates a French soldier unknown but to God who gave his life fighting for France in WWI. He was buried on November 11, 1920. See Singer. 43–44.

124 In addition to national identity cards required of all foreigners and French citizens, a foreigner also had to carry a circulation card showing his movements. Jackson wrote about the authoritarian republic under French Prime Minister Daladier (1933–1940) that was anti-foreigner and one which defined who was a French citizen. See Jackson. 102–120.

125 King Léopold III of Belgium reigned 1934–1951. His surrender to Germany in 1940 was controversial. Those who opposed King Léopold III thought the King as commander of the Belgian Armies should have fought the Germans instead of surrendering. King Léopold's surrender and the subsequent life of Belgians in captivity is documented in *The Heel of the Conqueror*, Time-Life Books. 22+.

126 Suresnes American Military Cemetery and Memorial outside of Paris is the resting place for 1,541 American soldiers killed in WWI, and later those of WWII. The cemetery is maintained by the American Battle Monuments Commission. See "Suresnes American Cemetery," *American Battle Monuments Commission*.

127 "If ye break faith with us who die…" is from the poem "In Flanders Fields" by John McCrae. See Chapter 1, Note 22.

128 The battle for Belgium (May 10–28, 1940) was fought across the fields of Flanders and south Belgium. It ended in the surrender of Belgium and the withdrawal of Allied forces to Dunkirk, France, where they were evacuated. The evacuation from Dunkirk is vividly portrayed in the 2017 film *Dunkirk*, written, directed, and produced by Christopher Nolan. See Churchill, *Their Finest Hour*. 74–118.

129 "In Flanders fields the poppies weep…," is from the 1940 poem "Flanders, 1940" by D. Maitland Bushby. It is unknown where this poem first appeared in print. D. M. Bushby was elected as an honorary member of the Literary and Art Institute of France. See Bushby, D. Maitland. "Flanders, 1940."

130 During the time the U.S. was neutral, Robert Montgomery joined the American Field Service and drove ambulances in France. When the U.S. became involved, he joined the U.S. Navy and was part of the D-Day invasion aboard the destroyer USS *Barton*. He rose to the rank of lieutenant commander. See Lee, "Montgomery, Robert, LCDR," *TWS*.

131 One faction of the Belgian government in exile established itself in Limoges where King Léopold's surrender was denounced. *Vive la Belgique* ("Long Live Belgium") was the battle cry

of Belgian soldiers after Belgium surrendered to Germany. See Churchill, *Their Finest Hour* (91, 95); see Pershing (269–271).

132 "Never dreamed, though right were worsted…," from the poem "Epilogue" by Robert Browning (1812–1889). The poem appeared in 1889 in his first volume of verse, *Asolando: Fancies and Facts*, published by Smith, Elder, & Co., 1890. See Browning, Robert, "Epilogue," *King Albert's Book, 1914.*

133 Noblesse oblige is "the obligation of honorable, generous, and responsible behavior associated with high rank or birth."

134 Bordeaux was a major embarkation port in France to take American citizens fleeing political uncertainty back to America. MLD refers to the last voyage from Europe that the SS *Washington* was to make for the sole purpose of bringing American citizens back to America. The voyage originated in Genoa, Italy, ten days before Italy declared war on Great Britain and France. See "Notice to American passengers aboard SS *Washington* 07 June 1940," *ECU Libraries Digital Collections*; "Telegram Issued by the Secretary of State (Hull) to the Ambassador in France (Bullitt) on May 28, 1940," *Office of the Historian.*

135 On June 3, 1940, the Citroën automobile plant in Paris was severely damaged in a German air attack. See Green. 228.

136 George VI was king of the United Kingdom, 1936–1952. Notably portrayed in the film *The King's Speech,* Dir. Tom Hooper.

137 "We shall fight on the beaches" are words from Churchill's famous "We shall fight on the beaches" speech to the House of Commons. See Churchill, Address: "We shall fight on the beaches," June 4, 1940.

138 Moroccan Cavalry, a unit of the French Foreign Legion, was established in 1939. It took part in the Battle of France in June 1940. After the Armistice between France and Germany was signed in June, the unit stayed in France until September, returned to North Africa and disbanded. It was reactivated in 1946. See "Moroccans in the Netherlands," *Verzets Résistance Museum.*

139 History dictates Napoléon won battles through his leadership of his men and through his prowess as one who understood the battlefield. See Dean, "Napoléon as a Military Commander."

140 As the Battle of France was waging, General Weygand ordered: "Let us cling to the soil of France… Whatever are our personal anguish and our intimate sorrows, let us cling to our duty, to our daily task—let us hold with a sacred passion to the post where Destiny has placed us without any thought of retreating." However, with the onslaught of the German Army, General Weygand supported an armistice between France and Germany; he was heavily criticized for this position during and after the war. See Singer. 176–194.

141 An open city implies that the invading army will experience no resistance from the opposing force in order for the city to avoid destruction. All defensive efforts are abandoned. Weygand declared Paris an "open city" in order to preserve the beautiful cultural history of Paris. See Singer. 107.

142 "Out of defeat comes the secret of victory" is a quotation from the essay "Fidelity" by Mary Baker Eddy in her collection of Christian Science writings. MLD was a student of Christian Science, which was founded by Mary Baker Eddy. See Eddy, Mary Baker, "Fidelity." 339.

143 Ancient Chinese believed the Heavenly dog devoured the moon in a lunar eclipse. Theodore White used this folklore to describe the night of the Japanese bombing of Chungking on May 3, 1939. See White and Jacoby, *Thunder out of China.* 20.

144 "France is always saved in the eleventh hour by a miracle" is a reference to the eleventh hour in the parable of the Workers in the Vineyard (Matthew 20:1–16 *KJV*). Miraculous events that take place in the last hour still reap the full benefits of the miracle. Authors such as Antoine de Saint-Exupéry wrote, "In the spring of 1940, everybody was repeating an ancient

French saw: 'France is always saved in the eleventh hour by a miracle.'" See Saint-Exupéry, Airman's Odyssey, "Flight to Arras." 335.

145 Joan of Arc saved France in 1429 in the Hundred Years' War with England, and there was hope through prayer she would be able to save France from German aggression in 1940. See Lang. Chapters 7–9.

146 The swastika in the twentieth century going forward is seen as a symbol of pure evil. In earlier times it was a symbol of well-being in Eurasian cultures, especially India. See "The History of the Swastika," *United States Holocaust Memorial Museum*.

147 German government made its headquarters in occupied France at the Hôtel de Crillon in Paris. Glass. 37, 66.

148 Michael Neiberg, in his book *When France Fell*, refers to Secretary of War Henry L. Stimson who said that the fall of France was "the most shocking single event of the war." See Neiberg. 1.

Chapter 2

1 Dr. Thierry de Martel, a world-renowned neurosurgeon, committed suicide rather than live under Nazi rule. Much of his beliefs and his life are related in Charles Glass' book *Americans in Paris: Life and Death under Nazi Occupation*. See Glass. 66–68.

2 *Le Matin (The Morning)* is a Paris morning newspaper whose editor offered to collaborate with the Nazi government. Maurice Bunau-Varilla, owner of *Le Matin*, was anti-communism and admired Hitler. He directed his editorial staff to write pro-German articles. Over his lifetime he worked with his brother, Phillipe, on influencing major events of the time including the Dreyfus Affair and the building of the Panama Canal. See *Le Matin*. Ed. Maurice Bunau-Varilla.

3 *Les Nouveaux Temps (The New Times)* is a daily evening newspaper whose editor supported the French policy of Otto Abetz, German ambassador to Paris. See "Les Nouveaux Temps," Dir. Jean Luchaire.

4 The 1940 newspaper *Les Dernières nouvelles de Paris (The Latest News of Paris)* adopted the German point of view and was skeptical in the success of the French government. See *Lib. of Cong.*, Newspaper: *Les Dernières nouvelles de Paris*.

5 Stéphane Lauzanne left *Le Matin* in 1940 after the paper adopted a pro-Nazi stance. In 1939 he wrote about the SS *St. Louis* tragedy in which 900 Jews fled Germany to Havana only to be turned away in Havana and forced to return to Europe where 250 were killed. See Lauzanne, "Le problème des réfugiés juifs"; Goodwin. 102.

6 *La Victoire* is a Parisian publication of Gustave Hervé often thought to reflect French fascism. See Audiat. 22.

7 MLD refers to the "Earthly Paradise" poems written by the British poet William Morris (1834–1896) between the years 1868–1870. See Morris, *The Earthly Paradise*.

8 Maréchal Philippe Pétain (Marshal Pétain) became Prime Minister of France in the Vichy Regime (1940-1942). A hero of Verdun in WWI, he supported an armistice with Germany and collaborated with Nazi Germany in WWII. Staunch allies for a free France were abhorred by Pétain's armistice and thought France should have fought for its freedom from Nazi rule. After WWII Pétain was convicted of treason and sentenced to death but commuted to life in prison because of the years he served France in WWI. Pétain's role in WWII is well documented in Jackson's book *France: The Dark Years 1940–1944*.

9 Free France was the French government in exile, which was led by Charles de Gaulle from London. Free French forces were located in North Africa under General Giraud. See Jackson. 9, 398–400.

10   The 1918 armistice to end WWI hostilities was signed by Germany and the Allies in Compiègne, France. Hitler insisted France's 1940 armistice with Germany be signed in the same location. See Singer. 115.

11   Benito Mussolini was Prime Minister of Italy, 1922–1943, and dictator 1925–1943. He founded the National Fascist Party of Italy in 1919 and was known as Il Duce from 1919 until his execution in 1945. He used autocratic rule by suppressing the individual and any opposition. See Speer. 71, 308.

12   Mussolini's declaration of war against France on 10 June 1940, was seen as "a stab in the back." The words came from French Premier Paul Reynaud in a June 10 letter to U.S. President Roosevelt. In turn, FDR delivered his "stab-in-the-back" speech the same day in a commencement address to the University of Virginia. See "The Text of President Roosevelt's Address at Charlottesville," *The New York Times*, June 11, 1940.

13   The building of the Triumphal Arch, also known as the Arc de Triomphe de l'Étoile (Triumphal Arch of the Star) was requested by Napoléon in 1806. It was inaugurated in 1836 and dedicated to the armies of the French Revolution and the Empire of France. It is located at the western end of the Champs-Élysées at the center of Place Charles de Gaulle.

14   Albert Speer accompanied Hitler on his visit to Paris where Hitler requested he be shown the Opéra. The Opéra [Garnier] or the Palais Garnier is one of the most famous opera houses in the world. It was built in 1861–1875 as ordered by Emperor Napoléon III. Hitler with his artists and architects "drove past the Madeleine, down the Champs-Élysées, on to the Trocadéro, and then to the Eiffel Tower." Hitler also stopped to see the Arc de Triomphe with its Tomb of the Unknown Soldier. He then requested to go to the Invalides, "where Hitler stood for a long time at the tomb of Napoléon. Finally, Hitler inspected the Panthéon, whose proportions greatly impressed him." See Speer. 171–172.

15   MLD's reference to the Heil Hitler (Hail Hitler) salute is her statement of anguish that her beloved France should now be occupied by the fascist regime of Germany. The salute is made by raising the straightened right hand with a straightened right arm from the neck into the air. See Speer. 392.

16   The French Résistance was composed of organized activities to undermine and fight the Nazi Occupation of France. Jackson details the activities of the various resistance movements. See Jackson. 385–523.

17   General Charles de Gaulle exceled in WWI, worked with the French Résistance in WWII, led the Free French Army to regain Paris in 1944, led the French provisional government 1944–1946, and was elected President 1959–1969. See Jackson, *France: The Dark Years.*

18   Cross of Lorraine is the symbol adopted by Charles de Gaulle to represent Free France. See Glass. 279.

19   Colonies of the Third French Republic in 1940 included territories on the continents of Africa and South America and territories in the Caribbean and French Indochina. See Jackson. 94, 101–102.

20   Esthonia is an alternate form of Estonia, which is the more popular form today.

21   Super race, or superrace, is a race or nation held to be superior to others. Nazi Germans talked of being part of a master race, which is superior to other races. Speer wrote in *Inside the Third Reich* Hitler believed the Germanic people were superior to the Negro (73), the Arab (96), and the yellow race (121). He expressed hatred for the Jew (20) and wanted to subjugate the nations of the world (523).

22   "They will cheat you yet..." were words most closely uttered by the German journalist, Dr. Hermann Rosemeier, to Dr. Frank Bohn of the American Alliance for Labor and Democracy. While exiled in Switzerland his words appeared in print in the magazine *Mixer and Server*. See Rosemeier Interview, *Mixer and Server* Magazine, August 31, 1917. 45.

23 "God…, the Compassionating, the Compassionate," is from Richard F. Burton's translation of *The Book of the Thousand Nights and a Night* by John Payne. Payne's book was published in 1885, and the translation was published in 1910. The book is based on medieval fairy tales known as *One Thousand and One Nights*. See Payne, "One Thousand and One Nights."

24 MLD is referring to the Château de Candé where the American Embassy staff set up temporary quarters before moving to Vichy. Candé is today in the Department of Maine-et-Loire in western France. See Glass. 60.

25 *Le Figaro* is a French national newspaper that went into exile in 1942 and reappeared after WWII. It is now the second largest newspaper in France. See *Le Figaro 1854–1942*. Paris: *BnF Gallica* for archived editions.

26 Les Halles was Paris's central fresh food market. It has been thought of as the heart and soul of Paris. The Les Halles facility as known to MLD was demolished in 1971 and replaced with the Forum des Halles. See Kasten, "Modernization Versus Preservation in Paris During the Gaullist Era: A Tale of Two Cities."

27 Madame de Ropp, also known as Baronne de Ropp, is Marie Woodman, married to Baron William Sylvester de Ropp, a British agent. MLD often dined with Madame de Ropp.

28 General Charles Mangin's (1866–1925) legacy was created in WWI in the Second Battle of the Marne, which turned the tide of the war. See Dilkes, Charles, *Remembering World War One: An Engineer's Diary of the War*. 78.

29 Place Vauban is a semi-circular square in the 7th arrondissement by the Hôtel des Invalides where Napoléon is entombed.

30 Adrienne Monnier (1892–1955) is the French owner of the book store La Maison des Amies des Livres (The House of Friends of Books) for French writers, readers, and artists. At one point she was a lover to the American Sylvia Beach, who owned the Shakespeare and Company bookstore. The two stayed in Paris throughout WWII. See Glass. 89–97.

31 "Réveille" is played after "The Last Post" as a final honor to a soldier of France who has died. See Jarrett and Walters, "Reveille or Rouse."

32 Portugal was neutral in WWII and Lisbon found itself a major embarkation point for people trying to flee the turmoil in Europe. See Hatton. 237–244.

33 Maggy Rouff (1896–1971) was a dressmaker known for introducing ruffles into her designs. Her clientele included women from all over western Europe. Charles Glass wrote about upper class life in Paris in his book *Americans in Paris*. See Glass. 132–133, 354–355.

34 The battle of Mers-el-Kébir between Great Britain and France was controversial. Since France had signed an armistice with Germany, and since French assets were now under the control of Marshall Pétain and Nazi Germany, Great Britain did not want to risk seven French battleships falling into German hands. The British naval attack on French Navy ships at the naval base at Mers-el-Kébir took place on July 3, 1940. See Jackson, *France: The Dark Years*. 128.

35 Records of the American Export Lines' sailings to help refugees are kept by the American Jewish Joint Distribution Committee (JDC) and the U.S. Holocaust Memorial Museum. See "American Export Lines," *United States Holocaust Memorial Museum*.

36 Nazi forces were housed in people's homes in the occupied country. See Kladstrup. 45–52.

37 Gestapo was the secret police of Nazi Germany. It is a shortened form of the German word "Geheim Staatspolizei." See *The Heel of the Conqueror*. 188.

38 Chambre refers to the Chambre des Députés and the Senate to the French Senate. They constituted the National Assembly which made the laws for the Vichy Regime. The Chambre is not part of the government of today's Fifth Republic.

39 "That curious dread of life which steals through the twilight," is a quote from *Memoirs of My Dead Life* by George Moore, Chapter VIII. 99.

40   Café Viel located at 8 Boulevard de la Madeleine was known as Café Viel until it was requisitioned by the Nazi government and became "Gaststätte für Reichdeutsche" (Restaurant for Reich Germans). A photograph of the restaurant was taken by André Zucca during the Paris Occupation and is part of the Roger-Viollet collection at the Bibliothèque Historique de la Ville de Paris. See "Café Viel," André Zucca / BHVP / Roger-Viollet. The street address was printed in *Le Journal*. See *Le Journal*, January 16, 1938.

41   The great *débacle* refers to the German invasion of France and the subsequent Occupation of Paris. See Jackson. 112–136.

42   July 14 is Bastille Day, the most patriotic national holiday that honors the storming of the bastille in 1789, which was the turning point of the French Revolution. Bastille Day in France, July 14, 1940, is marked as a day of mourning. See Archambault, *The New York Times*, July 15, 1940.

43   During the Nazi era the German national anthem was the first verse of "Deutschlandlied," which included the lyrics "*Deutschland, Deutschland über Alles*", followed by "*Horst Wessel Lied*." After WWII the German national anthem became the third verse of "Deutschlandlied" with the first two verses purposely omitted because of their association with Nazi Germany. The music for "Deutschlandlied" was composed by Haydn, and the lyrics were written by the German poet August Heinrich Hoffmann von Fallersleben. See Patton, James, "Germany Gets a New National Anthem," *Roads to the Great War*, October 7, 2020.

44   Deux Magots Café carries on its reputation and traditions today as a rendezvous for artists, literary, and intellectual elites. Over the years it has transformed from a novelty shop to a café. See "Les Deux Magots," *Les Deux Magots Paris*.

45   As the German Army prepared to enter Paris, and since the United States was a neutral country in the war, American citizens with assets in France came to the Embassy to request Applications for the Protection of Property Certificates. It was understood but not always administered that the assets of citizens of a neutral country would not be commandeered. Nancy L. Green refers to these certificates in her book *The Other Americans in Paris*. 241. The U.S. Embassy seal was placed over the door to the American Library on the rue de Téhéran; the seal certified the library was American property and was not to be seized by the German government. See Glass. 115.

46   *Hôpital de la Pitié* (La Pitié-Salpêtrière Hospital) was requisitioned by the German Army in WWII; the hospital was also a place of French Résistance. Medical facilities such as hospitals played a major role in the Résistance. Charles Glass describes the resistance activities at the American Hospital of Paris in Neuilly-sur-Seine. See Glass. 136.

47   "Cowardice and cruelty amongst mankind…" is from a biography Romain Rolland wrote of Mahatma Gandhi in 1924 and translated by Catherine D. Groth. The actual words are "We have seen…the hypocrisy, the cowardice, and the cruelty of mankind. But this does not prevent us from loving mankind." Romain Rolland (1866–1944) was a French Nobel Prize novelist. See Rolland, *Mahatma Gandhi: The Man Who Became One with the Universal Being*. Chapter 5.

48   Le Bourget (officially Aeroport de Paris-Le Bourget) is an airport northeast of Paris. Hitler landed here on his visit to Paris. See Speer. 171. Today the airport hosts the annual Paris Air Show.

49   Hitler's "lonely peaks of power" is quoted in the Preface to *Nemesis? The Story of Otto Strasser* by Douglas Reed. (Note: Otto Strasser supported workers' rights as a member of the Nazi party until he was expelled by Hitler.) See Reed. 3.

50   Hitler spoke of the annihilation of Anglo-French forces in his speech to the Reichstag on July 19, 1940. This speech recognized Germany's victory over France. In this speech to his Deputies and the Men of the German Reichstag, he told them Providence has been with "all of us" and will continue to be. See Hitler, "Adolf Hitler's Address to the Reichstag (19 July 1940)."

51   President Franklin Delano Roosevelt is nominated again by the Democratic Party on July 18, 1940, to be the party's candidate for president of the U.S. for an unusual third consecutive term.

"To make America strong…," were words spoken by James Farley, chairman of the Democratic Party Convention, as a preamble to the 1940 Democratic Party Platform. See Goodwin. 125–135.

52 Hendaye is a French commune at the border with Spain on the coast of the Bay of Biscay. In 1941 MLD would pass through Hendaye after she was expelled from Paris.

53 Georges Mandel (1885–1944) was the French Minister of the Interior. As a proponent of Free France, in 1940 he fled to French North Africa, was captured, sentenced, and ultimately executed in 1944. Mandel's experience on the Massilia is well documented. Churchill thought highly of Mandel. See Churchill, *Their Finest Hour*. 179, 221.

54 "As pale and faint as the blue ash of a cigarette" is from *Memoirs of My Dead Life* by George Moore. See Moore. 42.

55 "Like a miniature in a case" is from *Memoirs of My Dead Life* by George Moore. *Memoirs of My Dead Life* is a favorite literary source of Marie-Louise Dilkes. See Moore. 44.

56 Fresnes is a French prison ten miles south of Paris that during Germany's Occupation of France was used by Germany to imprison captured British special agents and members of the French Résistance. After the war Pierre Laval, a collaborator with Nazi Germany, was held in the condemned block of Fresnes and executed there in 1945. *The Heel of the Conqueror*. 54; see Jackson. 577.

57 Sir Nevile Meyrick Henderson (1882–1942) was the Ambassador of the United Kingdom to Nazi Germany from 1937–1939. He wrote *Failure of a Mission* as an account of this tragic time. History is critical of the role he played or should have played. See Henderson, *Failure of a Mission*.

58 MLD includes in her writing one of Nevile Henderson's experiences as the UK Ambassador: Hitler's announcement he is annexing his home country of Austria into Nazi Germany (the Anschluss). See Henderson. 125–126.

59 Haus der Flieger (House of Aviators) is the building for Nazi government offices used mainly by Hermann Göring who was in charge of the Luftwaffe (the German air force). See Henderson. 124.

60 Kurt Schuschnigg was the Austrian leader forced to resign under threat of Germany's invasion of Austria. In his radio message to the Austrian people he said, "The president of the Republic of Austria has asked me to communicate to the Austrian people that we will not put up any resistance to violence." He ended his powerful address on March 11, 1938: "God protect Austria." For the actual radio broadcast, see Schuschnigg, "Last broadcast address as Austrian Chancellor." For historical perspective, see Bistrovic, "Austria's 'Anschluss' with Germany in 1938."

61 Arthur Seyss-Inquart (1892–1946) was a Nazi political appointment as Austria's Minister of the Interior. In his radio message on March 12, 1938, the day after German troops marched into Austria, as Minister of the Interior he asked the SA (brown-shirted Storm Troopers) and the SS (black-shirted protective squad) to act as auxiliary police. He gave the order to offer no resistance to the entry of the German troops. Throughout WWII Arthur Seyss-Inquart held various Nazi posts; he was tried for his war crimes at Nürnberg and executed in 1946. See "Arthur Seyss-Inquart," Propagander3.tripod.com.

62 The Hapsburg (aka Habsburg) Empire included the plains region of Europe that was divided after WWI into Romania, Hungary, Austria, Yugoslavia, and Czechoslovakia. Sir Nevile Henderson is referring to the decline of the Hapsburg Empire and the Mayerling Incident. See Henderson. 125.

63 Today Hôtel Lutetia at 45 Boulevard Raspail in the 6th arrondissement on the Left Bank is known for its architecture and WWII history. See "LVTETIA," HotelLutetia.com. Hôtel Majestic, 19 Avenue Kléber, in the 16th arrondissement is now The Peninsula Paris. In WWII it was the headquarters for the German military high command and site of the German exit permit office. See Heise, "Places where You Can Still See Evidence of the Nazi Occupation of Paris."

64 Hôtel Meurice, 228 rue de Rivoli in the 1st arrondissement, is now known as Le Meurice. In 1940 it was the Gestapo administrative offices. In 1944 it became the headquarters of General Dietrich von Choltitz, the military governor of Paris. This hotel would play a role in saving Paris from Hitler's order to destroy the city. See Kladstrup. 177–179.

65 Hôtel Matignon at 57 rue de Varenne was a section headquarters for the Gestapo. Today it is the residence of the French Prime Minister. See Abbott, "I Was Looking Forward to a Quiet Old Age," and "Hotel Matignon," EUtouring.com.

66 On one occasion the cannons were removed for the ceremony in which Hitler ordered the remains of Napoléon II be brought from Vienna to Paris to be entombed next to his father, Napoléon, in the Invalides. Reentombment took place on December 15, 1940. See "Napoléon's Tomb," *Granger Historical Picture Archive.*

67 Rond-Point des Champs-Élysées is the Champs-Élysées roundabout in the 8th arrondissement between the Place de l'Étoile (aka Place Charles de Gaulle) and the Place de la Concorde. See map of Paris with arrondissements.

68 Georges Clémenceau (1841–1929) is known as the "Tiger" for his hard-line stance against Germany. He was a statesman, Prime Minister from 1906–1909 and 1917–1920, and Minister of War. He was the hero of World War I when he negotiated the unconditional surrender of Germany. See Singer. 5, 44.

69 "*Qu'il était bleu, le ciel, et grand, l'espoir!*" is from the poem "Colloque sentimental" by Paul Verlaine (1844–1896). It is freely translated as the poem "Sentimental symposium": "How blue was the sky, and great, the hope!" See Verlaine, "Colloque sentimental," Fêtes galantes.

70 Bois de Boulogne is a public park on west side of the 16th arrondissement. See map of Paris with arrondissements.

71 The Grands Boulevards, typically tree-lined, are the favorite boulevards of Parisians for promenading. They include the Boulevard Beaumarchais, Filles-du-Calvaire, Temple, Saint-Martin, Saint-Denis, Bonne-Nouvelle, Poissonnière, Montmartre, Italiens, Capucines and the Madeleine boulevards. See "Boulevards of Paris," *Wikipedia.*

72 Peggy de Nemours, née Margaret Watson, and Prince Charles Philippe are the Duke and Duchess of Nemours. She was from Washington, D.C.; he was the great grandson of King Louis Philippe I of France. See "Franco-American Duchess: Margaret 'Golden Peggy' Watson," *The Esoteric Curiosa.*

73 Hervé Le Boterf wrote of the "Cabaret" on Avenue Victor-Emmanuel III. It is no longer in business. See Le Boterf, *La Vie Parisienne sous l'Occupation*, Vol. II. 116.

74 Victor Emmanuel III (1869–1947) was king of Italy. Italy fought with the Allies in WWI, thus a street in Paris was named in his honor. However, with Italy's support for the Axis Powers in WWII, the Avenue Victor-Emmanuel III was renamed Franklin D. Roosevelt Avenue after the end of WWII. See "Franklin D. Roosevelt (Paris Metro.), *Wikipedia.*

75 On the eve of the Battle of France, General Weygand replaced General Gamelin as commander in chief of the French Army. He criticized King Léopold III's decision to surrender to Germany and outlined an alternate strategy for which Weygand could garner no support. (Singer in *Maxime Weygand*, 103–105, thought Weygand should have replaced Gamelin years earlier; Jackson in *France: The Dark Years*, 118, thought it was a mistake to replace Gamelin.)

76 "Our raging contemporary times" is quoted from *Nemesis? The Story of Otto Strasser* by Douglas Reed. See Reed, Preface. 2.

77 *Stalin: Czar of All the Russias* is a biography of Stalin by Eugene Lyons, published in 1940. Lyons saw Russia as a country torn between European and Asiatic influences. He postulates that Asiatic influences dominated in Russia during the time of Stalin. See Lyons. 155.

78 Eugene Lyons wrote about the leaders of the Soviet Union that gave rise to Communism as the country's form of government. Vladimir Lenin (1870–1924) was leader of the Soviet movement

1917–1924. Leon Trotsky (né Lev Davidovich Bronstein: 1879–1940) was a Marxist who managed the Russian Revolution but was later disavowed by Stalin. Karl Radek (1885–1939) was a Marxist and became an international Communist leader in the Soviet Union; he was purged in 1937 and died in a labor camp. Stalin prevailed. See Lyons, *Stalin: Czar of All the Russias*.

79   MLD quoted from Lyons' book *Stalin: Czar of All the Russias*: [Stalin] "must wait for the inevitable day when the whole revolution would sag down to that level." See Lyons. 114.

80   Leningrad is known today as Saint Petersburg.

81   The Siberian desert, or the Chara Sands, is a region of sand dunes in northern Asia near the Udokan and Kodar Mountains. It is close to the Chara River. The Novaya Chara urban settlement is located there today. See "Chara Sands: mysterious Siberian desert," *56 Parallel.com*

82   First Lieutenant Edward Leopold Huffer (1886–1975) was assigned as Asst. Military Attaché in September 1918. MLD would have worked with him in 1921 when she was the code clerk for Colonel T. B. Mott, Military Attaché for the American Embassy in Paris. See "Embassies and Legations of the United States," *Congressional Directory* for the 66th Congress, July 1919. 382.

83   In the Battle of the Alps (June 10–25, 1940), a conflict between France and Italy, the French retreated from the Menton sector. An armistice was negotiated with Italy, who retained the French territory it had captured. See Churchill, *Their Finest Hour*. 129–130.

84   MLD wrote, "Those who will write the history of France under the iron heel of the conqueror will not perhaps relate the small details of this extraordinary life we are leading in Paris." The editors of Time-Life Books capture with text, essays, and illustrations what life was like under Nazi rule in their book *The Heel of the Conqueror*. See *The Heel of the Conqueror*, Time-Life Books.

85   The BBC, British Broadcasting Corporation, broadcasted Churchill's speech on August 20, 1940, to the House of Commons: "Never in the field of human conflict was so much owed by so many to so few." See Churchill, Address to the House of Commons: "The Few."

86   William Christian Bullitt, Jr. (1881–1967), U.S. Ambassador to France (1936–1940), helped negotiate the surrender of Paris to the Germans. See Beevor (117). He delivered his "America Is in Danger" speech to the American Philosophical Society in Independence Square, Philadelphia, PA, on August 18, 1940. See Bullitt, Address: "America Is in Danger."

87   "Sword of the Spirit" is part of the armor of God. (Ephesians 6:17 *KJV*)

88   Dies Committee, also known as the House Committee on Un-American Activities or HUAC (1938–1975), was chaired by Martin Dies (1901–1972), a Democratic Congressman from Texas. HUAC investigated international political ideologies operating in America that it believed were antithetical to our democratic principles including Communism and the pro-Nazi views of the German-American Bund. See "German-American Bund," *United States Holocaust Memorial Museum*.

89   Robert Daniel Murphy (1894–1978) was the U.S. Chargé d'Affaires in Paris to the Vichy government in 1940. [Note: He would become the Under Secretary of State in 1959.] See "Robert D. Murphy," *The Foreign Service Journal*, October 1940. 572.

90   Michael Neiberg saw Robert Murphy as an American diplomat "destined to sit at the center of America's French policy for the next three years." *When France Fell*, 22.

91   "Walk with Kings–nor lose the common touch...," from the poem "If" by Rudyard Kipling (1865–1936), verse 4: line 2. See Kipling, "If," *Rewards and Fairies*.

92   The All-Father is considered to be the father of all men and gods and all things that were made by him and by his might. It is commonly found in Norse and Irish mythology. MLD is most likely transferring this concept to the God of Christianity. See Skjalden, "Odin: The Allfather," *Nordic Culture*. See Ephesians 4:6.

93 A one-man power taxi is a bicycle-rickshaw. See Zucca, "Paris under German Occupation during WWII: Color Pics by Andre Zucca," *History in Images.*

94 "Envy and calumny and hate and pain…," from the poem "Adonais: An Elegy on the Death of John Keats" by Percy Bysshe Shelley (1792–1822). See Shelley, "Adonais: An Elegy on the Death of John Keats." verse XL, line 2.

95 "*Roule, roule ton flot…,*" from Verlaine's poem "*Nocturne Parisien* (Of a Paris Night)," translated, "Roll, roll your lazy stream, gloomy Seine…". See Verlaine, "*Nocturne Parisien,*" *Poèmes saturniens* (1:1).

96 The destroyers-for-bases deal was signed on September 2, 1940. The U.S. Neutrality Act of 1935 prevented the U.S. from sending troops unless attacked; it did not preclude sending ships. See Goodwin. 137–149.

97 The status today of the naval bases MLD cited that were part of the destroyers-for-bases deal:
   o   Bermuda remains a British overseas territory (see Heaton and Rushe, "Bermuda").
   o   Trinidad, now known as Trinidad and Tobago, gained independence from Great Britain in 1962 and is now its own sovereign nation (see Robinson, et al. "Trinidad and Tobago").
   o   Jamaica gained independence from Great Britain in 1962 and is now its own sovereign nation (see Ferguson and Black, "Jamaica").
   o   Saint Lucia achieved independence in 1979 and retained membership in the British Commonwealth of Nations (see Momsen and Niddrie, "Saint Lucia").
   o   British Guiana now known as Guyana became independent in 1966 and retained membership in the British Commonwealth of Nations (see Richardson and Menke, "Guyana").
   o   Newfoundland has become a Canadian province (see Harris and Hiller, "Newfoundland and Labrador").

98 The United States also gained rights to install naval bases in the Bahamas and Antigua, which were part of the destroyers-for-bases deal. See Churchill, *Their Finest Hour.* 414.

99 MLD's brother, Joseph Harold Dilkes (1898–1978), "Joe," worked for the Singer Manufacturing Company in Central and South America.

100 Church of the Madeleine is a Roman Catholic Church in the 8th arrondissement. Flowers at the foot of the Church of the Madeleine are a traditional site. See Viollet, "World War II. Flower Market, Paris, Place de la Madeleine," *Granger.*

101 In July 1940 *The New York Times* reported "Nazis Object to Statue of Edith Cavell in Paris." Edith Cavell was a British nurse in WWI who provided medical care to soldiers on both sides of the conflict without discrimination. See "Nazis Object to Statue of Edith Cavell in Paris," *The New York Times*, July 16, 1940.

102 "Sleep that knits up the ravell'd sleave of care," is said by Macbeth in Shakespeare's play, *Macbeth.* See Shakespeare, *Macbeth*, Act II, scene II.

103 "Do Not Forget Oran" refers to the Battle of Mers-el-Kébir when Britain bombed French ships. [Note: The towns of Oran and Mers-el-Kébir in Algeria are only six miles (10 km) apart.]

104 The Tricolor, or the French Tricolor, is a reference to the flag of France. See Smith, "Flag of France," *Encyclopedia Britannica.*

105 Congress passed the Selective Training and Service Act on September 16, 1940. See Borneman. 203; Goodwin. 147, 149.

106 Auteuil is an area in the 16th arrondissement of Paris. See map of Paris with arrondissements.

107 MLD wrote: "Trades people of the Jewish race must display a notice…with the sign 'Jewish Enterprise.' Most people see Judaism as a religion, ethnicity, or culture but not a race." See Rich, "What is Judaism?" *Judaism from Judaism 101.*

108 The major Axis powers were Germany, Italy, and Japan. The Axis Alliance was formally joined on September 27, 1940. Hungary joined on November 20, 1940; Romania joined on November 23,

1940; and Bulgaria joined on March 1, 1941. See "Axis Alliance in World War II," *Holocaust Encyclopedia.*

109   In 1940 Claude Pepper (1900–1989) was a Democratic U.S. Senator from Florida who supported Franklin Roosevelt and the strong defense of the U.S. See Simkin, "Claude Pepper," *Spartacus Educational.*

110   Göring committed suicide in 1946. See "High-ranking Nazi leader Hermann Göring dies," *History.* Brauchitsch died a natural death in 1948. See "Brauchtisch Dies of Heart Attack," *The New York Times,* October 20, 1948: 7. Himmler committed suicide in 1945. See "Nazi SS Chief Heinrich Himmler dies by suicide," *History.*

111   Walther von Brauchitsch (1881–1948) was the Commander in Chief of the German Army. In the Battle of France, he was the messenger between Hitler and Halder, Chief of the German General Staff. Hitler via Brauchitsch instructed Halder to withhold the armored formations for future use, which opened up the opportunity for British and French forces to retreat to Dunkirk. After the Battle of France, Brauchitsch was promoted to Field Marshal. See Speer (107); Churchill, *Their Finest Hour.* 76–77.

112   The Petit Palais is an art museum on the Avenue Alexandre-III (now Avenue Winston-Churchill) in the 8th arrondissement. Members of the Freemasons, a secret society, were persecuted under Nazi Germany rule. See Jackson. 151, 158.

113   *Le Petit Parisien* (1876–1944) was a French newspaper that became the voice of the Vichy government. In 1940 the newspaper was directed by Jean Dupuy who was a Collaborationist. He died in 1944. See "*Le Petit Parisien: 1876-1944,*" *BnF Gallica,* October 11, 1940.

114   The Trocadéro area in the 16th arrondissement is noted in Albert Speer's narrative of Hitler's visit to Paris during the Nazi Occupation as one of Hitler's requested stops. See Speer. 172.

115   Northumberland is a county in northeast England that borders Scotland to the north. See "Northumberland," *Wikipedia.*

116   "I'll lay me down and bleed a-while" are words from folksongs written about Sir Andrew Barton (1466–1511). He was a legendary privateer eulogized in song. Words attributed to him are in the English folk song "Andrew Barton," Child Ballad #167, and in the Scottish folk song "Henry Martyn," Child Ballad #250. The earliest record of these folk songs is the 1710 Roxburghe collection. Francis J. Child created an authoritative collection in his book *The English and Scottish Popular Ballads* published in 1884–1898. See "Andrew Barton, Child Ballad #167," *The English and Scottish Popular Ballads.*

117   Rumania/Romania was neutral as of October 1940. Rumania gained territory in WWI but lost it in dispute; thus, Rumania decided to join the Axis powers in November 1940.

118   The editor of *Pantagruel* is the Parisian music publisher, Raymond Deiss (1893–1943), from the Alsace region of France. He worked with two brothers, René and Robert Blanc, who were linotypists, and Roger Lescaret, printer. He printed sixteen sheets for the French Résistance before he was captured and beheaded in Cologne, Germany. See "Raymond Deiss," *Musée de la Résistance en Ligne.*

119   François Rabelais (1494–1553) was a French Renaissance writer known for the comic works *Gargantua* and *Pantagruel.* In a series of five novels Rabelais wrote of the adventures of two giants: Gargantua, the father, and Pantagruel, the son. Raymond Deiss named his clandestine information sheet after the character Pantagruel. See Rabelais, "*Rabelais: Gargantua and Pantagruel,* Book I," *gutenberg.org.*

120   Dakar, now known as Senegal, was under Vichy/Nazi control. In September 1940 British and Free French fighters attacked the strategic West Africa port of Dakar in Operation *Menace* and were defeated by Vichy loyalists. De Gaulle thought erroneously the Vichy French fighters would switch and support Free France. See Singer (138–141). *Richelieu* was a French battleship whose

crew was loyal to the Vichy government. It helped defeat the British in the Battle of Dakar (Operation *Menace*). See Churchill, *Their Finest Hour*. 473–494.

121   The American Packard Motor Company built the V-1650 Merlin airplane engine under a licensing agreement with Rolls-Royce of Great Britain. Demonstration models were available in August 1941 and mass production began in 1942. See "Packard V-1650 Merlin," *National Museum of the US Air Force*.

122   William McAdoo was Secretary of the Treasury during WWI and created the means to fund the U.S. involvement in WWI. See Pershing, vol. 1. 371.

123   "Those great men in our history who pledged their lives, their fortunes, and their honor to our new, young country" is a reference to the signers of our Declaration of Independence and to what each pledged in 1776 in our fight for independence from Great Britain. See Tourtellot, "We Mutually Pledge To Each Other Our Lives, Our Fortunes and Our Sacred Honor," *American Heritage*.

124   *The Washington Star*, a Washington, D.C. evening newspaper, was published 1852–1981. See *Lib. of Cong.*, Newspaper: "*The Washington Star*," [Washington, D.C.], *U.S. Govt. Web*.

125   *The Philadelphia Record*, a Philadelphia daily newspaper, was published 1879–1947. See "*Lib. of Cong.*, Newspaper: "*The Philadelphia Record*" [Philadelphia, Pa.], *U.S. Govt. Web*.

126   The *New York Herald Tribune*, a New York City morning newspaper, was published 1926–1966. See *Lib. of Cong.*, Newspaper: "*New York Herald Tribune*," [New York], *U.S. Govt. Web*.

127   The Consul General of Spain in Paris (1939–1943) was Bernardo Rolland de Miota. He worked to help U.S. citizens, especially Jews, leave France. See "Bernardo Rolland de Miota," *The International Raoul Wallenberg Foundation*.

128   "It's a Long, Long Way to Tipperary" is a British and/or Irish song written by Jack Judge and/or Harry Williams and popularized by John McCormack in the WWI era and carried over to WWII. See McCormack, "It's a Long Way to Tipperary," *YouTube*.

129   Café de la Paix located at 5 Place de l'Opéra was a popular hangout for Nazi troops during the Occupation. See Heritage Images, *Keystone Archives*, "Occupying German troops outside the Café de la Paix, Paris, World War II, c. 1940–c. 1944."

130   The Hôtel Ritz located at 15 Place Vendôme was the headquarters in Paris for Göring and the German air force. See "The History of The Ritz Paris Hotel and its Renovation," *EUtouring.com*.

131   Jeanne Lanvin is a famous and the oldest dressmaker establishment in France since 1889. See Reddy, "Fashion History Timeline: 1940–1949."

132   *L'Illustration*, a weekly French newspaper (1843–1944) with color pictures, was pro-Vichy during WWII. See *L'Illustration*, "The Vichy origins of modern France."

133   The Ministry of Marine building on the Place de la Concorde, where German soldiers once paraded, is being transformed into the Hôtel de la Marine in 2020. See Delorme, "The first look at the Hôtel de la Marine renovation in Paris," *Explore France*.

134   The "Punch and Judy Show" is a British slapstick comedy puppet show created in 1662 and viewed for over 350 years. See McRobbie, "Are Punch and Judy Shows Finally Outdated?" *Smithsonian Magazine*.

135   Emile Heidsieck (1881–1968) is a member of the Heidsieck family champagne establishment. Emile married the widow (second wife) of Pierre Lorillard V and step mother-in-law of Mrs. Griswold Lorillard, MLD's friend.

136   Charles Heidsieck (1822–1893), called Champagne Charlie, was known for his champagne establishment, which produced the Champagne Charlie Brut Réserve champagne. The Heidsieck House was part of the Champagne Campaign, which participated in Résistance activities. See Kladstrup. 182–187.

137 *La Toussaint*, short for "Tout les Saints (All the Saints)" on November 1 is a bank holiday. It is celebrated by practicing Catholics to remember all the saints and martyrs that do not have their own namesake day. See Pierre, "What Is la Toussaint, All Saints' Day in France?" *French Moments*.

138 "We are all impressionists today…," from the *Memoirs of My Dead Life* by George Moore. See Moore, Chapter 4. 26.

139 "Walk abroad in the darkness without stumbling" are words written by Oscar Wilde (1854–1900), an Irish poet and playwright, in his letter *Epistola: In Carcere et Vinculis*. He wrote the letter in 1897 while incarcerated in the Reading Gaol to his lover, Lord Alfred Douglas. Oscar Wilde entitled the work *Epistola: In Carcere et Vinculis* and gave it to his friend, Robert Ross, who retitled it *De Profundis*. See Wilde, *De Profundis*. 151.

140 Wendell Willkie was seen as an internationalist who supported extensive aid to Great Britain and a program to rearm America. See Neiberg, *When France Fell*, 53.

141 MLD is referring to Election Day in America, November 5, 1940. Time zone differences between Paris and New York reveal the election results one day later in Paris. Wendell Willkie was the Republican nominee for U.S. President in 1940. See Krock, "Roosevelt Elected President…," *The New York Times*, November 6, 1940.

142 "To warm itself before the fire" are words from *Swann's Way*, written by Marcel Proust (1871–1922), French novelist. He wrote *À la Recherche du Temps Perdu (In Search of Lost Time)* in seven volumes. *Swann's Way* is the first of these seven volumes. À *la Recherche du Temps Perdu* has also been translated over the years as *Remembrance of Things Past*. See Proust, *Swann's Way*, Combray, paragraph 2.

143 To be presented to the Court of St. James', the royal court for the sovereign of the United Kingdom, is an honor bestowed on ambassadors and those British subjects who have represented the UK well in foreign countries. See Olson. 27–30.

144 Armistice Day is now known as Veterans Day. In 1954 President Eisenhower signed the Congressional bill proclaiming November 11 as Veterans Day. See "Origins of Veterans Day," Celebrating America's Freedoms, *U.S. Department of Veterans Affairs*.

145 Turkey remained neutral in WWII until 1945 when it joined the Allies. Turkish troops never saw combat. See Churchill, *The Hinge of Fate*. 713, 791–792.

146 Hitler was decorated twice in WWI with the Iron Cross for bravery. In 1914 he received the Iron Cross Second Class; in 1918 he received the Iron Cross First Class. See "Cross of Iron," *Military History Now*.

147 The bookstore included vases of chrysanthemums in its display, most likely to acknowledge Hitler's love of his half-niece, Geli, whose favorite flower was the chrysanthemum. See "Hitler's Doomed Angel," *Vanity Fair*.

148 Diana FitzHerbert is the American wife of a baronet and sister of the British Minister in China. A baronet is the lowest hereditary-titled British order with the status of a commoner but able to use the prefix "Sir"; a baronet's wife can use the prefix "Lady." A baronet has precedence below that of a baron.

149 La Crémaillière is no longer in business. See Fabricant, "Menu Collection Offers a Taste of History," *The New York Times*, March 24, 1982.

150 Gallup surveys in 1940 asked the question: "Do you think Axis (Germany and Italy) or Allies (England and France) will win the war?" The respondents leaned toward the Allies two months before and after the Battle of France but leaned toward the Axis (Germany) the month of and month after the Battle of France. See "European War," *The Gallup Poll*.

151 Jean-François Houbigant founded his famous perfume house in Paris in 1775. See "The House of Houbigant," *Houbigant Paris*.

152 Aryans are of Indo-European origin, that included Germanic people. Hitler believed the Aryan race to be a superior race and that Germans were of the purest stock of that race and therefore supreme.

153 Hôtel Le Bristol Paris in 1940 became the preferred place for members of the American Embassy and American nationals living in Paris to reside. See Glass. 37.

154 On December 4, 1940, Lady Diana FitzHerbert was arrested and interned at a women's concentration camp in Besançon. She was one of the many British women and children who were rounded up. The American Embassy came to her aid since she was a U.S. citizen by birth. She was released on December 13 and made immediate arrangements to leave for New York. The Lady Diana FitzHerbert incident can also be found in Roy P. Porter's book *Uncensored France: An Eyewitness Account of France under the Occupation.* See Porter (120). [Note: Roy Porter was a former Associated Press Correspondent in France.]

155 The British Embassy Church was closed from June 1940–September 1944. See "The British Embassy Church in Paris Re-opens," *Imperial War Museums.*

156 Les Jardins du Luxembourg on the Left Bank in the 6th arrondissement were created in 1612. The Luxembourg Gardens display statues of historical figures:
o The French poet Verlaine (1844–1896).
o Polish composer Frédéric Chopin (1810–1849). See "Chopin," The Garden Guide, *gardenvisit.com.*
o French literary critic Charles Sainte-Beuve (1804–1869). See "Sainte-Beuve," *eutouring. com.*
o French sculptor Alfred Boucher (1850–1934). See "Boucher," *eutouring.com.*
o French painter Jean-Antoine Watteau (1684–1721). See "Watteau," *eutouring.com.*
o French architect Alphonse de Gisors (1796–1866) with statues representing a faun and a huntress. See "Medici Fountain," *eutouring.com.*

157 Anthony van Dyck (1599–1641), a Flemish Baroque portrait artist, was knighted and buried in St. Paul's Cathedral in London. He is known for his "Portrait of a Woman" and portraits of Charles I and his court. See "Van Dyck," *Sotheby's.*

158 Nazi *kultur* is the German native culture, assumed superior to the culture of other countries, and is founded on teachings that national interests are more important than the individual.

159 Pierre Laval, a French socialist politician turned fascist, offered his resignation as part of a collective action, and it was uniquely accepted by Pétain on December 13, 1940. Pétain asked Laval to return in April 1942 as Prime Minister. Much is written about Laval by Jackson in his book *France: The Dark Years* and Glass in his book *Americans in Paris.*

160 Duc de Nemours is legally Charles Philippe, Prince d'Orléans.

161 Duc de Reichstadt (1811–1832), Napoléon's son, is buried near his father in the Invalides.

162 *Faculté des Lettres* of the University of Paris is referring to the French educational institution based at the Sorbonne in the Latin Quarter. The University of Paris is often referred to as the Sorbonne. See Green. 28–29.

163 Italy invaded Egypt in late summer 1940. In Operation *Compass* in December, British troops from the 7th Armored Division forced the Italian 10th Army to retreat. See Churchill, *Their Finest Hour.* 542+.

164 The journalist Tucholsky wrote about some of the top cabaret artists of the time including Auguste Martini. See Burrows, *Tucholsky and France.* 166–167.

165 William D. Leahy was U.S. Ambassador to France 1941–1942. He was appointed on November 29, 1940, but not presented until January 8, 1941, when he arrived in Vichy. See Jackson (177, 185) and Singer. 160. Leahy was a Fleet Admiral in the U.S. Navy and a trusted friend of President Roosevelt. See Borneman. 5; and Goodwin. 305.

166 Assistant Secretary of State Breckinridge Long served from 1940–1944. He was a controversial member of the State Department because of his immigration policies for war refugees. See Goodwin. 100–101; 173–174.

Chapter 3

1 "That even the weariest river winds somewhere safe to sea" is from "The Garden of Proserpine" (11.7) by Algernon Charles Swinburne (1837–1909). See Swinburne, "The Garden of Proserpine," *Poems and Ballads.*

2 British troops defeated the Italian 10th Army at Bardia, Libya, on January 3, 1941, in the Battle of Bardia. See Churchill, *Their Finest Hour.* 614–616.

3 Sainte Odile (662–720 A.D.) of the Alsace region of France is known as the patron of eye patients. She was granted sainthood by Pope Pius VII on December 13, 1807. The "Prophecies of Saint Odile and the End of the War" appeared at the time of WWI and were reignited during WWII when the dry holy spring dedicated to St. Odile began to flow again. See "Prophecies of Saint Odile," Ellipsis Rare Books.

4 Musée de l'Homme (Museum of Man) is an anthropology museum established in 1937 and located at the Place du Trocadéro and Place du 11 Novembre. "The Musée de l'Homme Résistance network was one of the earliest underground organizations of the French Résistance." See "The Musée de l'Homme Résistance Network," *Musée de l'Homme.*

5 Résistance groups had names such as Résistance, The Chained Rooster, South Liberation, etc. Jackson refers to these various groups in his section entitled "The Résistance: Geography and Sociology." See Jackson. 436–439.

6 The incident took place on the evening of December 31, 1940, at the Ambassador Hotel. The British National Anthem is entitled "God Save the King" and America's patriotic anthem is entitled "My Country, 'Tis of Thee." Both songs have the same musical score. See "Un incident franco-américain à Vichy," *Le Matin,* January 15, 1941: 1.

7 MLD may be referring to the book *Medieval France* by Arthur Augustus Tilley published in 1922. See Tilley, *Medieval France: A Companion to French Studies.*

8 Sylvia Beach (1887–1962) was the owner of the Shakespeare and Company bookshop and a patron to literary artists. Shakespeare and Company bookshop (and library) was open 1919–1941. It was closed due to an altercation with a Nazi officer and never reopened. Glass' book *Americans in Paris* includes much on the life of Sylvia Beach as she chose to remain in Paris throughout the Occupation. MLD and Sylvia Beach would carry on a correspondence after the war (Ref. Princeton University Firestone Library).

9 In January 1941 British, Australian, and Indian troops took Tobruk, Libya, from Italy along with 25,000 Italian prisoners. See Churchill, *Their Finest Hour.* 616.

10 "*Chaque chose à sa place*" is a gay French tune from the 1940s. One version is on Columbia records sung by Jacques Pills with music and orchestra by Georges Van Parys and lyrics by Jean Boyer. See *Vieux Disques,* "*Chaque chose à sa place.*"

11 Édouard Alphonse James de Rothschild (1868–1949) was the male heir to the Château de Ferrières-en-Brie. The Château de Ferrières-en-Brie was confiscated by the Germans, and its art collection was looted. After the war the château remained vacant until 1959 when Guy de Rothschild refurbished it for private entertaining. In 1975 the château was donated to the University of Paris and is now open to the public. See "Château de Ferrières," *Spotting History.*

12 "Not for the sake of the enemy, but for one's own sake" are words written by Oscar Wilde in his book *De Profundis.* Oscar Wilde wrote this long love letter as *The Ballad of Reading Gaol,* which he gave to his friend, Robert Ross, who published it under the title *De Profundis.* See Wilde. 84.

13 *La Place de la Muette* is in western Paris in the 16th arrondissement.

14 The Marius on the rue de Bourgogne in the 7th arrondissement is no longer in business. The restaurant has changed names and is now the location of the Michelin-star Loiseau Rive Gauche.

15 The Biblical reference "But there was no sword in the hand of David" is from I Samuel 17:50 (*KJV*).

16 Madame Dubonnet (Jean Nash) was a society celebrity and considered to be the "world's best-dressed woman." See "Jean Nash Sailing for Son's Trial Here," *The New York Times*, March 14, 1934.

17 The rabbi was most likely wearing a rekel, a long black frock coat worn during the Jewish work week. MLD may be referring to the incident of the "grand rabbi," Isak Leifer. See Green. 193.

18 The "rosary game" is a confidence game to swindle unsuspecting individuals. A con artist would gain the confidence of gullible tourists by asking the tourists to hold some supposedly valuable item for the con artist while the con artist went on some errand. Then the con artist would have the tourists entrust the con artist with a large amount of the tourists' own money, supposedly to buy discounted jewels or some such thing. The charming con artist Frenchman would simply disappear with the tourists' money. See Levenstein. 304.

19 Deauville and Le Touquet are northern France resort towns known for the rich and famous.

20 Maxim's on the Right Bank in the 8th arrondissement in 1950 was considered the world's most famous restaurant. In WWII it was commandeered by the Nazis. See Kladstrup. 111.

21 Revillon Frères was a French fur trading company founded in Paris in 1723 as La Maison Givelet. After it was purchased by Louis-Victor Revillon in 1839, it became known for its mink coats. It now does business as Cora-Revillon. See "Revillon Frères," *Furs by Chrys*.

22 Caroline Reboux (1837–1927) was a famous French milliner known as "Queen of the Milliners." Through employment of workers who went on to establish other successful millineries, she was able to influence millinery fashion for years. Rose Valois was the name of a famous French millinery establishment in Paris from 1927–1970. It was founded by three women who used to work for Caroline Reboux. They were open for business during the Occupation. One of the three women, Vera Leigh, was active in the French Résistance, arrested, and executed in 1944. See Chico, "History of Women's Hats," *Fashion History*.

23 Queen Consort of England is the title given to the wife of King George VI. After the death of King George VI and the ascension of their daughter Elizabeth to the throne, she was known as Queen Elizabeth The Queen Mother. See "Queen Elizabeth The Queen Mother," *The Royal Household*.

24 Tickets were ration cards that functioned as a second form of currency and traded as such. See Kladstrup. 111; Glass. 163, 217.

25 "We shall not weaken or tire…" is a quote from Winston Churchill's "Give Us the Tools" broadcast on BBC Radio, February 9, 1941. See Churchill, Address: "Give Us the Tools," February 9, 1941.

26 Rumplemeyer's on rue de Rivoli is now known as Angelina's Tea House, named for the wife of the son of the founder, Antoine Rumpelmayer (1832–1914). In the memoir of Mrs. Virginia Hamill Biddle, a secretary in the Foreign Service of the U.S. in Washington, D.C., and abroad, Mrs. Biddle mentioned a lunch she had with MLD. Mrs. Biddle had just lost her brother, and "Miss Dilkes, the charming receptionist of the Embassy, took me to Rumplemeyer's for lunch and was very sympathetic." See Biddle, Virginia, "Memoir of Mrs. Virginia Hamill Biddle, 2011," *Library of Congress*.

27 Enrico Toselli (1883–1926), an Italian pianist and composer, is known for his *Serenata*, Op. 6, No. 1. See Cummings, "Enrico Toselli," *All Music*.

28 Nicolas Aubin Foucher (1780–1853) founded his chocolate factory in Paris in 1819. With the entrepreneurship of six generations, it is still in business today. See "Foucher," *Foucher Paris*.

29 Francisco Franco (1892–1975) was the general and dictator of Spain 1939–1975, who became Spain's ruler with the help of Hitler and Mussolini. Spain never joined the Axis powers. See Beevor. 143–145.

30 MLD is most likely referring to horse races at the Paris Longchamp Racecourse in the Bois de Boulogne. See Zucca, "Paris under German Occupation during WWII: Color Pics by Andre Zucca," *History in Images*.

31 The Bill for aid to England is the Lend-Lease Act, which was to provide war supplies "vital to the defense of the United States." The Bill received final House of Representatives' approval on March 11, 1941. See Goodwin. 210–215.

32 Solférino subway station in the 7th arrondissement on the Left Bank near the Musée d'Orsay is part of the Paris Metro system.

33 During the Occupation General de Gaulle established his headquarters at 4 Carlton Gardens in London. See Olson. 205.

34 Sainte-Clotilde Catholic Church on the Rue Las Cases was granted the distinction of minor basilica with accompanying privileges by Pope Leo XIII in 1896. It is known for its twin spires. See "Sainte-Clotilde," *Paroisse Sainte Clotilde*.

35 MLD wrote of the disappearance of Robert Neeser, who authored many books on the history of the U.S. Navy. Robert Wilden Neeser (1884–1940) was reported missing since September 30, 1940, Lyon, France. The Robert Wilden Neeser Collection is archived in the Yale University Library. See Fagniez, "Robert Neeser: généalogie par André Fagniez." See also "Robert Wilden Neeser," *Find a Grave*.

36 U.S. Chargé d'Affaires was S. Pinkney Tuck. See Glass (199, 275); William D. Leahy was the U.S. Ambassador to France in Paris from January–May 1941 and to France in Vichy June 1941–May 1942. See Churchill, *Their Finest Hour*. 508.

37 Rudolf Hess (1894–1987), Hitler's deputy Führer, traveled to Scotland to negotiate peace with the United Kingdom but was arrested. He committed suicide in prison at the age of 93. Hess' many travel attempts to meet with the Duke of Hamilton in Scotland is documented in *The Splendid and the Vile* by Erik Larson.

38 Queen Wilhelmina of Holland reigned 1890–1948. During WWII her radio broadcasts from England made her a symbol for Dutch resistance to Nazi Occupation. See Olson. 205–206.

39 Abyssinia refers to the Ethiopian Empire, which was composed of what are now Eritrea and the northern half of Ethiopia. In 1935 Italy invaded Abyssinia and forced its king, Haile Selassie, into exile. In 1941 with the help of British forces, Italy retreated and the King of Abyssinia returned home. See Churchill, *Their Finest Hour*. 612–626.

40 Alistair Cooke is a British writer, who became a U.S. citizen in 1941 and worked as a radio broadcaster and later as a television personality. MLD is referring to his May 10, 1941, broadcast "American Commentary." See Cooke, *American Commentary*, BBC Radio Network.

41 *Place des Pyramides* in the 1st arrondissement is the location of the famous statue of Joan of Arc.

42 *Combat* was founded in 1941 as a publication for the French Résistance. See Jackson. 439.

43 Fernand de Brinon represented the Vichy government to the German high command in occupied France. In 1942 he was Secretary of State to Laval's Vichy government. In 1944 he signed a manifesto committing to the German war effort, and in exile on German soil he exercised authority over French citizens in Germany. He was executed in 1947. See Jackson. 213, 311, 553–587.

44 Four days after the British radio reported on the flight of Rudolf Hess to Scotland, an article appeared in the May 15, 1941, edition of *Le Matin* (German controlled) with an explanation. See Les Notes Laissées en Allemagne par M. Rudolf Hess, 3.

45 Douglas Douglas-Hamilton, Duke of Hamilton, was the Scottish aviator who Deputy Führer Rudolf Hess wanted to meet to negotiate a peace settlement with the United Kingdom.

46 Cordell Hull (1871–1955) was the U.S. Secretary of State during these tumultuous times (1933–1944). Hull's words were spoken in preparation for Roosevelt's Fireside Chat. See Kluckhohn, "President Shapes Reply for Tonight to Nazis' Threats," *The New York Times.*

47 German Grand Admiral Erich Raeder developed naval plans to intercept convoys traveling between the United States and Britain. He advocated for submarines and fast cruisers to supplement the German naval fleet. See Beevor. 182.

48 The SS *Robin Moor* was a U.S. Merchant Marine ship that was sunk by the German *U-69* submarine in 1941 after ordering the crew and passengers to abandon ship. See Borneman. 200.

49 *Carte de Ravitaillement* was a program in which supply cards that contained color-coded tickets were given to people living in occupied France to purchase food and personal items.

50 Ascension Day is the day celebrated by Christians as the day Jesus ascended into heaven forty days after his resurrection (Acts 1:1–10 *KJV*).

51 "But those people—spiritually unconquered…" were words spoken by President Roosevelt in his Fireside Chat on May 27, 1941. See Roosevelt, "On an Unlimited National Emergency."

52 HMS *Hood*, the pride of the British navy, was Britain's largest battle cruiser. It was sunk by the modern German battleship *Bismarck* on May 24, 1941. The *Bismarck* was sunk by the British Royal Navy on May 27, 1941, as revenge for the sinking of the HMS *Hood.* See Borneman. 196–199.

53 The Fatherland refers to the officer's country, Germany. Hitler and patriotic Germans often referred to Germany as the Fatherland. See "Hitler Goes to Prague," *The New York Times*, March 16, 1939.

54 Iraq, led by Axis ally Rashid Ali, clashed with British forces in May 1941. By May 31 Britain had control of the oil fields, which enabled Prince 'Abd al-Ilah, an Allied ally, to return to power. See Beevor. 178.

55 The German Embassy in Paris outlined the demands of the Foreign Office in Berlin to the Foreign Missions in Paris. See telegram (now declassified) from Admiral Leahy, U.S. Ambassador to France, to Secretary of State Cordell Hull, May 28, 1941; NACP.

Chapter 4

1 From the Office of the Historian for the Department of State:
"On June 10 the Embassy was formally closed. A sign in English, French, and German was placed on the front gate which read "The American Embassy is closed. The Consulate General of the United States in Paris is at 3 rue Boissy d'Anglas." The shield over the front door was covered by a piece of sheet metal which was painted to resemble the stone of the building. The front gate and front door were closed and locked. No changes were made at the Embassy residence which had been closed for some time. Special authority was obtained from the occupying authorities to permit Forrest Pfeiffer and his wife to remain as caretakers for the residence in addition to the fifteen American employees permitted to remain as staff of the Consulate General.

"A consular seal was placed over the door of the entrance at 3 rue Boissy d'Anglas which became the main entrance and the Boissy d'Anglas entrance to the garage was placed in use.

"The Consulate General opened for business on the morning of June 6, with the newly selected staff of fifteen in order to take care of public business and permit those who were leaving to finish pending work." See Taylor, Letter from the Vice Consul to the Secretary of State on July 11, 1941, "Foreign Relations of the United States Diplomatic Papers, 1941, Europe, Volume II, Document 458."

2   Laurence W. Taylor, American Consul, was in charge of the operation in Paris that used to be the American Embassy in Paris. G. E. Morris Allen wrote in his article "Exit from Paris" that fifteen members of the staff of the American Embassy were to remain in Paris to be part of the now Consulate General of the United States in Paris. He wrote: "Fifteen were to stay on to do the work heretofore performed by about a hundred." See Allen, "Exit from Paris," *The American Foreign Service Journal*.

3   "Neither snow, nor rain, nor heat, nor gloom of night" is a version of the quote "Persian messengers…will not be hindered…either by snow, or rain, or heat, or by the darkness of night" from *Herodotus* by Herodotus of Halicarnassus, a Greek historian. The quotation tells of the fidelity of the mounted despatch couriers. The words have been adopted by the United States Postal Service, and in 1941 the words were adopted by the new Consulate in Paris for the U.S. Foreign Service. See *Herodotus of Halicarnassus*, book 8, Urania, paragraph 98.

4   Kaiser Wilhelm (1859–1941) was Emperor of Germany and King of Prussia who led Germany into WWI. He reigned from 1888–1918 and fled to Holland before the end of WWI. See Yockelson. 139.

5   Andrew Nagorski wrote that Hitler would not believe Germany could not defeat England and Russia in 1941 (303), and Stalin would not believe intelligence messages that Germany was planning to attack Russia in 1941 (118). These beliefs led to poor strategic decisions by both leaders. See Nagorski's book, *1941: The Year Germany Lost the War*. 118, 303.

6   Dorothy Thompson (1893–1961) was a U.S. journalist who used her communication skills to speak out against Nazi Germany—some called her the "First Lady of American Journalism." Her anti-Nazi rhetoric is recounted by Nagorski. See Nagorski. 168.

7   M. J. Taylor pointed out in her book *Diplomats in Turmoil* that all American consular offices in Greater Germany (Germany and all its occupied territories in Europe) closed in July 1941. This action was in response to a note of June 16, 1941, from Undersecretary of State Sumner Welles to Hans Thomsen, German Chargé d'Affaires at the German Embassy in Washington, D.C., demanding all German consulates in the U.S. and its territories be closed as of July 10. See *FRUS 1941 v02/d588*. The German State Secretary, Ernst von Weizsäcker, responded to Leland Morris, U.S. Chargé d'Affaires in Germany on June 19 and demanded all U.S. consular offices in Greater Germany be closed by July 15. See Taylor, M.J.; *FRUS 1941 v02/d590*. The U.S. Secretary of State, Cordell Hull, issued instructions that all U.S. consular offices in Greater Germany are to be closed accordingly. See *FRUS 1941 v02/d591*.

8   Letter (now declassified) of July 2, 1942, from Nathaniel P. Davis, Chief of the Division of Foreign Service Administration, to George Dilkes (MLD nephew), stating MLD is under orders to proceed to Lisbon.

9   Force majeure is a major or superior force. MLD perceived the invasion of France as one executed by a superior German force and not as an ordained event. See Beevor. 79–98.

10   Richard Strauss (1864–1949) was a German pianist, violinist, composer, and conductor, whose music was allowed to be listened to in Nazi Germany and its occupied territories. Hitler enjoyed operas and demanded his staff attend operas. See Speer. 60.

11   Wooden shoes became prevalent as materials to make leather shoes were needed for the war effort. See Sebba, "Fashion as Resistance in WWII France."

12   MLD is referring to Philip W. Whitcomb (1891–1986), a foreign correspondent who covered two world wars. Whitcomb was the Associated Press correspondent in Paris the day the German Army marched into Paris. See Glass. 2. After Germany declared war on the United States, Whitcomb was interned in southern Germany with other correspondents before being sent back to the U.S. See Glass. 205.

Chapter 5

1   Hotel Carlton in Biarritz, built in the twentieth century, is now a luxury apartment building. MLD would travel from Hendaye to Biarritz several times before the German authorities would permit her to cross into Spain. The USS *West Point (AP-23)* was converted into a troopship by the U.S. Navy in June 1941. In July the ship was to return 137 Italian citizens and 327 German citizens from their respective consulates to their home countries. FDR ordered Captain Frank H. Kelley, Jr. to return to port if American consulate employees were not allowed to cross into Spain. See "West Point II AP-23," *History Central.com.*

2   "Spies were everywhere" shows Lisbon as a hotbed of intrigue and a city described as "spyland." See Hatton. 240–241.

3   Modern book on the history of Lisbon is written by Barry Hatton, *Queen of the Sea: A History of Lisbon.* See Hatton.

4   The Avenida da Liberdade is a well-known avenue in central Lisbon famous for its restaurants and shopping. Ibid. 202–203.

5   Estoril, a town on the Portuguese Riviera, is known for its expensive real estate and its luxury style of living. Ibid. 241.

6   During WWII when Lyon, France, was within unoccupied France, members of the U.S. consulate in Lyon helped deliver news of U.S. diplomatic interests to the U.S. Embassy in Vichy. See MacArthur Interview, "An American Diplomat in Vichy France."

7   The German Army victory in the Ukraine was part of Operation *Barbarossa*, Germany's invasion into Eastern Europe. See Beevor. 186–206.

8   Telegram (now declassified) from Alexander Wilbourne Weddell, U.S. Ambassador to Spain in Madrid, to Secretary of State Cordell Hull in Washington, D.C. stating Marie-Louise Dilkes arrived in Madrid on August 29, 1941.

9   "Nothing can bring you peace but the triumph of principles" are the last words in the essay "Self-Reliance" by Ralph Waldo Emerson (1803–1882), American essayist, philosopher, and poet. See Emerson, "Self-Reliance."

10   The Hôtel Carlton in Lyon is now the Hôtel Carlton Lyon-MGallery by Sofitel. The hotel is known for its historically iconic Roux-Combaluzier elevator. See "Hôtel Carlton Lyon—MGallery," *Historic Hotels Worldwide.*

11   Lyon is the birthplace of famous French men and women:

    o   Philibert Delorme (1514–1570) was a French architect and writer known for his design of the Palace of Tuileries in Paris. See "Delorme," *Web Gallery of Art.*

    o   Antoine Coysevox (1640–1720) was a French sculptor known for his work in decorating the Palace of Versailles and its gardens. See "Coysevox," *Chateau de Versailles.*

    o   Louis-Gabriel Suchet (1770–1826) was a French marshal, the Duke of Albufera, and a commander in both the French Revolution and the Napoléonic wars. See "Suchet," *frenchempire.net.*

    o   Madame Jeanne François Julie Adélaïde Récamier (1777–1849) was a French socialite who spurned the advances of famous men and whose portrait hangs in the Louvre. See "Madame Récamier," *Louvre.*

    o   Paul Chenavard (1808–1895) was a French painter known for his work, "Divina Tragedia," in which he tried to illustrate the history of religion. See "Chenavard," *Musée d'Orsay.*

    o   Ernest Meissonier (1815–1891) was a French painter known for his paintings of military subjects and sculptures of equestrian subjects. See "Meissonier," *Art Renewal Center.*

12   The early history of Lyon with its Roman, Burgundian, Arab, German, and Huguenot influences is told in *A History of France* by André Maurois. Julius Caesar, with the expansion of the

Roman Empire into Gaul, built the city of Lyon. John Calvin in the Protestant Reformation established Calvinism in Geneva, which led to the Huguenot movement in Lyon. A traditional bond existed between Geneva and Lyon, which led to the Huguenot influence on the French middle class in Lyon. See Maurois. 10–13; 149.

13   Today La Place Bellecour is a dusty large open pedestrian square in the center of Lyon in an area known as the Presqu'ile. The Stone Watchman on the Place is a remembrance of a French Résistance bombing, which fueled harsh retaliation by the Gestapo. The Place is part of the UNESCO Heritage Site. See "Place Bellecour," *This Is Lyon*.

14   Letter (now declassified) from Monnett B. Davis, Chief of the Division of Foreign Service Administration, Washington, D.C., to Mrs. John Harrison, Jr. (MLD sister, Virginia), Meadowbrook, PA, stating Marie-Louise Dilkes arrived in Lyon on September 2, 1941.

15   In the Lyon American consulate, Marshall M. Vance was the Consul General; Dale Maher, consul; and Clark Husted, vice-consul. Lee Randall was a consul in Marseille. Alice Soelberg worked in Lyon and expressed interest in consular work in Vichy. See "The Foreign Service Personnel Changes," *Document of State Bulletin*, April 12, 1941. 456.

16   For "Marie's" restaurant MLD is most likely referring to Le Poêlon d'Or restaurant. The original owner was Marie-Danielle Rheuter. See "Marie-Danielle Rheuter and the Le Poêlon d'Or," *Les Bouchons Lyonnais*.

17   The Lyon Fair is an annual event originally held in the city located on land between the Rhône and Parc de la Tête d'Or. In 1985 the trade fair was moved to Chassieu east of Lyon. See "Fair of Lyon," *Wikipedia*.

18   Verdun was the signature battle in WWI where the French stood ground and held off the German Army for ten months. Their stand forced the German Army to retreat. See Pershing, Vol. 1. 66, 141, 301.

19   Lyon is a UNESCO World Heritage Site. In its "brief synthesis" the website describes how Lyon, despite growth over 2,000 years, has been able to preserve whole districts by expanding westward, thus saving its cultural heritage. See "Lyon," *UNESCO World Heritage List*.

20   A good description of the tour of Lyon that MLD took can be found in travel guides for France. Steves and Smith have an in-depth description of the Church of the Notre-Dame de Fourvière (938–940) and the Cathédrale of Saint-Jean-Baptiste de Lyon. See Steves and Smith. 943–944.

21   Hitler prematurely announced victory over Russia to the German people on October 3, 1941. See "Hitler Announces Victory over Russia," *The History Place*. See also James, *The New York Times*, October 5, 1941.

22   "The Résistance grows." Today Lyon has a museum dedicated to its role in the Résistance—the Résistance and Deportation History Center. Lyon was the center of French Résistance 1942–1945. See Steves and Smith. 952.

23   Representatives from the consulate in Lyon would fly to Vichy every few weeks to keep the U.S. Embassy in Vichy informed as to what was happening outside of Vichy. Douglas MacArthur II said in an interview the Lyon consulate was "keeping contact with local things and they sent one of their people up every couple of weeks to brief us." Marie-Louise Dilkes represented the Lyon consulate on a trip to Vichy in October 1941. See MacArthur Interview, "An American Diplomat in Vichy France," adst.org.

24   Louis Biddle is the great-grandson of Dr. Benjamin Rush, a founding father of the United States and a signer of the U.S. Declaration of Independence. The Biddle family is a member of Philadelphia society. See Burt. 107.

25   Penelope Royall, head librarian for the American Embassy in Paris after the war, secretly supported the French Résistance through documents inserted into diplomatic bags. She moved to Vichy with the relocation of the U.S. Embassy. MLD was to reconnect with her in Lyon.

MLD recognized Penelope Royall in her Acknowledgments for the help she gave in writing *Paris Notes*. See Royall, "Addresses of Retired Foreign Service Personnel," Foreign Service Journal, September 1962.

26 Salle Rameau, or the Rameau Room, is a theater built in 1908 in the 1st arrondissement in Lyon for symphonic music and other cultural activities. A major renovation has been delayed until 2024 due to Covid-19. See "Salle Rameau," *Wikipedia*.

27 Robert Casadesus (1899–1972) is a French pianist and composer, who is known for his classical interpretations of Mozart, Debussy, Ravel, Bach, and Beethoven. However, Robert Casadesus lived in the U.S. during the war years 1940–1946. MLD most likely attended a concert by Pablo Casals, a renown cellist, who performed in the unoccupied zone 1939–1942. See "Casadesus," *Robert Casadesus His Life*.

28 The *Gazette de Lausanne* was a French-language Swiss newspaper printed daily 1816–1991 when it was merged into *Journal de Genève*, forerunners of *Le Temps*, currently in publication. See *Lib. of Cong.*, "*Gazette de Lausanne et journal suisse.*"

29 The *Tribune de Genève* is a French-language Swiss newspaper printed daily from 1879. See *Lib. of Cong.*, "*La Tribune de Genève.*"

30 "Ivan the Terrible" in 1941 was a creative vision of the film director Sergei Eisenstein in which he adapted 1941 images of Hitler's terror to those of Ivan IV of 1547. In 1946 Eisenstein adapted "Ivan the Terrible" images to Stalin's terror. See Neuberger, "Sergei Eisenstein's *Ivan the Terrible* as History."

31 MLD is referring to General Maxime Weygand (1867–1965). In his book, *Maxine Weygand*, the author Singer recorded events leading up to Weygand's falling out with Darlan and Weygand's subsequent imprisonment. In October 1941 Weygand was Vichy's pro-consul in Africa. See Singer (160–172); see "The Vault," *Time*, June 16, 1941. 28.

32 Jean Louis Xavier François Darlan (1881–1942) was a French admiral who built the French Navy. He joined the Vichy regime to keep the French Navy whole. However, he crossed to the Allied side in the invasion of North Africa in 1942. He was assassinated three months later. See Jackson. 447–448.

33 Grenoble, Avignon, Grasse, and Nice are cities in France, south of Lyon, which offered some respite from this dismal period in France's history.

34 German Colonel Hotz was killed in Nantes on October 20, 1941. In retaliation, 50 French hostages were executed October 20–22. These incidents were reported in the Vichy-controlled newspaper *Le Matin*, October 23, 1941. See "Aidez la justice!" *Le Matin*, October 23, 1941. Historical perspective is recorded in the exhibition "The 50 Hostages" created by Château des ducs de Bretagne at the Musée Histoire de Nantes. See "The 50 Hostages," Château des ducs de Bretagne.

35 Nazi organizations in Lyon included the German Armistice Commission created on June 22, 1940, to establish supervisory regulations in conformance with the Franco-German Armistice Agreement. See Jackson (292). Germany had a consulate in Lyon with 50 employees represented by Otto Abetz. See Jackson (232); and the German Red Cross, which was subject to enquiries by the International Committee of the Red Cross, especially regarding the well-being of Jews in the concentration camps. See Bugnion. 173.

36 The French Military Mission is a French military unit loyal to the Vichy government in conformance with the Franco-German Armistice of June 1940. The unit was expected to fight alongside German soldiers. See Jackson. 183–184.

37 The Ruhr district in Germany is the urban area around Cologne, Düsseldorf, and Bonn and known for its heavy industry. Speer documents the importance of the hydroelectric plants in the Ruhr district to the armaments industry and the effect of British bombing raids on the dams. See Speer. 280–281, 414.

38 "Life is in ourselves and not in the external" are words written by Fyodor Dostoevsky (1821–1881) in a letter to his brother, Mikhail, on December 22, 1849. These words are found in the introduction to *The Brothers Karamazov* as translated by Richard Pevear and Larissa Volokhonsky. See Dostoevsky, Letter to Mikhail, in Introduction to *The Brothers Karamazov* translated by Pevear. xii.

39 Maître Marcel de Gallaix was a Parisian lawyer who represented the interests of the winegrowers during the Occupation and was a patron of the arts. More stories of Marcel de Gallaix and his family can be found in *Wine & War* by Don & Petie Kladstrup (106) and *Americans in Paris* by Charles Glass (94).

40 MLD's American friend is Gertrude de Gallaix, who was active in FAWCO (Federation of American Women's Clubs Overseas). FAWCO addressed issues of children of marriages of an American to a foreign spouse and the education thereof. FAWCO became recognized as an NGO by the United Nations. See Kladstrup. 106–112+.

41 The battle of Rostov in 1941 took place around the city of Rostov-on-Don in Russia. The Soviet 37th Army drove out the German 1st Tank Division resulting in a Russian victory. Germany recaptured Rostov in 1942; Soviet Russia recaptured it in 1943. See Beevor. 238.

42 *Marie Stuart* refers to Mary, Queen of Scotland (1542–1587), and the story of her relationship with Elizabeth, her first cousin once removed. The movie had an alternate title, *Das Herz der Königin (The Heart of a Queen)*. According to Trivia, the film was ordered by Goebbels as part of his anti-British propaganda campaign. See *Marie Stuart*, Dir. Carl Froelich.

43 Pearl Harbor, December 7, 1941: Japan attacked the United States and declared war on the United States an hour after the attack. See Beevor (249) and Goodwin (283). The United States declared war on Japan on December 8, 1941. See Goodwin. 295.

44 On December 11, 1941, Germany and Italy declared war on the United States, which prompted the United States to declare war on Germany and Italy on the same day. See Beevor. 257; Goodwin. 298.

45 The attack on Pearl Harbor had global rippling effects on America's foreign policy, especially on its relationship with Vichy. See Neiberg, *When France Fell*, 135+.

46 Japan captured and occupied the island of Guam, December 12, 1941–July 21, 1944. See Goodwin. 295, 303, 531; Beevor. 253, 564–565.

47 "When we think of the insane ambition…" are words from Winston Churchill's BBC broadcast on the war with Japan. He spoke these words on December 8, 1941, the day after Japan's attack on the United States. See Churchill, Address: "Broadcast on War with Japan."

48 Operation *Crusader* was a North African campaign in November–December 1941 with the British Eighth Army against German General Erwin Rommel's Afrika Korps. The British successfully fended off the siege on Tobruk forcing Rommel back to Gazala. See Beevor. 224–228.

49 German General Erwin Rommel (1891–1944) was a highly respected military commander known for his Afrika Korps. See Churchill, *The Hinge of Fate* (67). He was implicated in the attempted assassination of Hitler. See Beevor (603). He committed suicide shortly thereafter. See "Nazis Reveal Rommel's Death," *The New York Times*, October 16, 1944.

50 Russell H. Porter's experience of leaving Paris and his dramatic exit for unoccupied France is also told in *The Other Americans in Paris* by Nancy L. Green. 244–247.

51 The story of Elijah is recorded in I Kings 19: 3–13 (*KJV*)

52 Telegram (now declassified) from Admiral William D. Leahy, U.S. Ambassador to France, Vichy, France, stating Marie-Louise Dilkes is assigned to Bern with the approval of (Marshall M.) Vance, Consul General in Lyon, December 22, 1941; File 123 Dilkes, Marie-Louise/31; File 124.513/1676; NACP.

53   Japan captured the Wake Islands; American forces surrendered on December 23, 1941. See Beevor (252–253).

54   Japan captured Hong Kong on December 25, 1941. See Beevor. 259–262.

55   Clark Husted (1915–1944) was vice consul at Lyon before being transferred to Bern on December 12, 1941. At twenty-nine years of age, he died of pneumonia and is buried in France. See "Husted, Clark," *Find a Grave*.

56   "Nature, whose sweet rains fall…" are words from Oscar Wilde's *De Profundis*. See Wilde. 150–151.

Epilogue

1   The U.S. Legation presented its papers to the Political Federal Department of Switzerland in Bern on December 29, 1941. Swiss Federal Archives, E2001D#1000/1553#1131*, B.22.21, Unterlagen 0000003, "Dilkes, Marie-Louise, Stenotypistin," 1942–1945.

2   Letter (now declassified) from Harry A. Havens, Assistant Chief of the Division of Foreign Service Administration, Washington, D.C., to Augustus M. Dilkes (MLD brother), La Mesa, California, stated Marie-Louise Dilkes is now at her post at Bern, Switzerland. Sent December 31, 1941.

3   Switzerland was officially neutral in WWII, but its citizens retreated to the Swiss National Redoubt in the high Alps as a defensive measure. See *The Heels of the Conqueror*. 8; Singer. 125.

4   These newspapers were French-language Swiss newspapers no longer in publication unless merged:
    o   *Gazette de Lausanne* 1816–1991, when it merged with *Journal de Genève*. See Lib. of Cong., Newspaper: *Gazette de Lausanne*.
    o   *Tribune de Lausanne* 1893–1984. See Lib. Of Cong., Newspaper: *Tribune de Lausanne*.
    o   *Journal de Genève* 1826–1991. See Lib. Of Cong., Newspaper: *Journal de Genève*.
    o   *La Tribune de Genève*, published since 1879, still in publication today. See *Lib. Of Cong.*, Newspaper: *La Tribune de Genève*.

5   *La Suisse* magazine is part of an exhibit of the Valais-Martigny Media Library featuring the photoreporting of Max Kettel from 1926–1960 in *La Suisse*. Research is unable to confirm an anti-Anglo-Saxon bias.

6   *Le Courrier* is a French-language Swiss newspaper published in Geneva since 1868. From 1868 to 1995 it was supported by the Roman Catholic Church; however, it has been independent since then. It is still in publication. See *Le Courrier, Wikipedia*.

7   *Die Nation* was a German-language Swiss newspaper published from 1933–1952. A reference was found in the archives of the Los Angeles Museum of the Holocaust. "RG-46.08.34, From Swiss newspaper *Die Nation*, Theresienstadt, a propaganda trick, May 1945, translation | Los Angeles Museum of the Holocaust." The description of Theresienstadt, a transit concentration camp for Czech Jews, illustrates the pro-Allies bias. See "RG-46.08.34, From Swiss newspaper *Die Nation*," Holocaust Museum LA.

8   *Das Vaterland* is a German-language Catholic newspaper founded in Austria around 1868 by Leopold Graf von Thun und Hohenstein. *Das Vaterland* saw different forms of totalitarianism, whether Communism or Nazism, as equal threats to a social democracy. See Imhof, et al., "Swiss Refugee and Foreign Economic Policies seen within the context of Press Publications on Politics 1938–1950."

9   *Neue Zürcher Zeitung* is a German-language Swiss newspaper published since 1780. Although the newspaper tried to remain neutral, it told its readers that the Nazi government in Germany showed the Swiss needed to be aware of "the need for 'the spiritual defense of our country [Switzerland].'" See Halbrook, "Target Switzerland: Swiss Armed Neutrality in World War II."

Also see Imhof, et al., "Swiss Refugee and Foreign Economic Policies seen within the context of Press Publications on Politics 1938–1950."

10   International Command was established in a Stanmore suburb northwest of London, England, to command the RAF. It was known as RAF Bentley Priory. In 1943 International Command was moved to Camp Griffiss, which was the headquarters for SHAEF (Supreme Headquarters for the Allied Expeditionary Force); it was built in a Teddington suburb southwest of London. See Beevor. 323; Olson. 253–254.

11   Singapore was captured by Japan on February 15, 1942, which was the largest British surrender ever. Churchill speaks of the fall of Singapore in a BBC address. See Churchill, Address: "The Text of Premier Churchill's Broadcast on Singapore," *The New York Times*, February 16, 1942.

12   Leland Harrison (1883–1951) led the American consulate in Bern from 1937–1947. In his obituary *The New York Times* included the words of Secretary of State Dean Acheson who said, "All those who have intimately known Mr. Harrison, and especially those who have had the good fortune to serve with him in the Foreign Service, will always remember him for his outstanding ability in the performance of his duties." See "Leland Harrison Ex-Diplomat, Dies," *The New York Times*, June 8, 1951.

13   In the Battle of the Atlantic, January 28, 1942, U.S. Navy pilot Donald Francis Mason sighted a U-boat and dropped depth charges. The U-boat disappeared, which led Mason to send the triumphant signal "Sighted sub sank same." "Navy Flier Cited for Sinking 'Sub,'" *The New York Times*, February 27, 1942.

14   *Il Giornale d'Italia* is an Italian newspaper published 1901–1976. In 1942 and 1943 the newspaper published articles indicating that the Italians were ready to "fight until victory" with an "undiminished will to win." Articles are in the Los Angeles Museum of the Holocaust collections. See "RG-79.04.04" and "RG-79.04.05," *Il Giornale d'Italia, The Italian Journal*.

15   Bernese Oberland is the higher part of the Bern canton, an administrative region in the country of Switzerland. See "Overview of the Bernese Oberland," *Earth Trekkers*.

16   Pierre Laval was asked to resign from the Pétain government and was arrested on December 13, 1940; Pétain asked him to come back in April 1942 as prime minister. See Glass. 159–164; 224–227.

17   Neuchâtel *L'Express* is the oldest Swiss French-language daily newspaper (1738–) still in publication. The historical archives have been digitized for access by the general public. Ref. 1942-08-04 to 1942-08-06. See "The Archives of the Neuchâteloise Press from 1738 to the Present Day," Neuchâtel *l'Express*.

18   Lugano, Switzerland, is a resort in Italian-speaking southern Switzerland, which shares a border with Italy. It is known for its Lake Lugano. See Pozzoli and Luchessa, "Lugano: 1939–1945."

19   Locarno, Switzerland, is an Italian-speaking city in southern Switzerland on Lake [Lago] Maggiore. Locarno was the scene of international treaties. The 1925 Pact of Locarno generated the "Spirit of Locarno" that reinforced peace after WWI until Hitler reoccupied the Rhineland and disavowed the Pact of Locarno. See *Le Livre Jaune Français*. 420.

20   Neiberg gives a detailed account of the deterioration in America's relationship with Vichy. *When France Fell*, 162+.

21   As a result of Operation *Torch*, Algiers surrendered to the Allies in November 1942. Events leading up to Operation *Torch* are well-documented in Singer's book *Maxime Weygand*. 158–172. The military maneuvers are detailed in Churchill's book *The Hinge of Fate* (614–626). The political fallout is told in Glass's book *Americans in Paris*. 271–273.

22   Vichy France severed diplomatic relations with the U.S. on November 8, 1942. The White House issued the statement by the President, "Nevertheless, no act of Hitler, or of any of his puppets, can sever relations between the American people and the people of France. We have

not broken relations with the French. We never will." See "Press Release Issued by the White House on November 9, 1942." *Office of the Historian.*

23   On November 12, 1942, the American diplomatic corps in Vichy was arrested. They were first escorted to Lourdes, France, before internment in Baden-Baden, Germany. In a web posting by the Association for Diplomatic Studies & Training, U.S. diplomats were interviewed on their travails: Paul Du Vivier was interviewed by Charles S. Kennedy, and Constance R. Harvey was interviewed by Dr. Milton Colvin. See "Guests of the Gestapo," Association for Diplomatic Studies & Training, July 9, 2013.

24   The French fleet of 77 ships at Toulon was scuttled on November 27, 1942, by the French Navy to avoid the ships getting into German hands. Weygand addressed options for the French fleet off of Toulon before the decision was made for the French to scuttle their own fleet. See Singer. 171.

25   Admiral François Darlan was a French naval officer who initially sided with the Vichy Government. Two years later he switched to a pro-Ally position, which led to thoughts of conspiracies and jealousies with Generals Giraud and de Gaulle. Darlan was assassinated in Algiers December 24, 1942. Beevor. 113+.

26   *Maquis* is the underground and a part of the French Résistance movement outside of urban areas. Julian Jackson in his book *France: The Dark Years* covers the *Maquis* in detail. 482–580.

27   The *Los Angeles Times* newspaper (1881–) has the largest circulation on the U.S. West Coast.

28   The British raids on Berlin in January 1943 are documented on the website *Chronology of Aviation History—1940 to 1949.* See "Chronology of Aviation History—1940 to 1949," *Skytamer Images.*

29   The tenth anniversary of Nazi rule was celebrated in Berlin on January 30, 1943. An article in *The New York Times* emphasized "the absence of any mention of either Britain or the United States, and the exclusive concentration on Russia." See "Fear-Haunted Anniversary," *The New York Times,* February 1, 1943.

30   German General Friedrich von Paulus (1890–1957) surrendered to Russia at Stalingrad January 31, 1943. Stalingrad, now called Volvograd, was the site of the Battle of Stalingrad, a major German loss in WWII. The Battle of Stalingrad is well-documented in Beevor's book *The Second World War.* 337+.

31   General Barnwell Rhett Legge (1891–1949) was with the U.S. Legation in Bern, Switzerland, as the U.S. military attaché. He arranged the escape of interned U.S. flyers and established an elaborate communications network to keep Washington informed as to the progress of the war. His escapades are recorded in the *ADST Journal* interview with Constance Ray Harvey. See Colvin and Morin, "Interview with Constance Ray Harvey," July 11, 1988.

32   In February 1943 the Allies were victorious in the battle of Guadalcanal, a nation in the Solomon Islands. See Borneman, *The Admirals.* 310–313.

33   In November 1943 the Allies were victorious in the battle for Tarawa in the Gilbert Islands where the U.S. suffered many casualties (Holloway, *Pacific War Marine.* 67–90).

34   In July 1943 the Allies successfully launched Operation *Husky* to liberate Sicily. This military operation is well-documented in the movie *Patton.* Mussolini was deposed and a new Italian government under Pietro Badoglio immediately sought peace terms with the Allies. President Roosevelt's reaction is recorded in Goodwin's book *No Ordinary Time.* See Goodwin. 449, 460, 468.

35   Reggio Calabria is in southern Italy across the Strait of Messina from Sicily. It was the site of the British Eighth Army invasion of the Italian peninsula in September 1943. See Beevor. 501.

36   In September 1943 Nazis evacuated Sardinia, the second largest Italian island in the Mediterranean, and retreated to the French island of Corsica. See *Axis History Forum,* "Seeking info about Corsica's and Sardinia's position in WWII," alias Lupo Solitario.

37   French General Henri Honoré Giraud (1879–1949) organized support for the French Résistance on Corsica and arrived there on September 20 to participate in the campaign. In October 1943 Corsica was the first French Department liberated in WWII. See Varley, "History of Modern France at War," *FranceHistory.wordpress.com.*

38   General Mark Clark and his U.S. 5th Army along with Lucien Truscott's VI Corps took Rome on June 4, 1944, which was two days before D-Day. Egos clashed as General Clark desired recognition for his capture of Rome but was overshadowed by the scope of the D-Day invasion. See Beevor. 569–573.

39   The D-Day landings on the Normandy beaches were a combination of the largest air and amphibious operations ever attempted.

40   Caen, France, in the northern Normandy region commemorates WWII in its Mémorial de Caen with a focus on the D-Day invasion, the Cold War, and the pursuit for peace. Caen was liberated on August 6, 1944. See Beevor. 580–601.

41   German General Dietrich von Choltitz (1894–1966), who surrendered Paris to French General Leclerc, is credited for saving Paris by disobeying Hitler's order to destroy Paris. See Kladstrup. 177–179.

42   General Philippe François Marie Leclerc de Hauteclocque (1902–1947) received the surrender of Paris at Gare Montparnasse on August 25, 1944. See Jackson. 565.

43   After Germany surrendered Paris to Free French forces, French General Marie-Pierre Kœnig (1898–1970), appointed by General Charles de Gaulle as military governor of Paris, arrived on August 26, 1944, to restore law and order. See Audiat. 328.

44   *"Aux armes, citoyens…"* are lyrics to the chorus of "La Marseillaise," the French national anthem. The joy for the liberation of Paris is described by Audiat. See Audiat. 327.

45   Telegram (now declassified) sent from Cordell Hull, Secretary of State, on September 8, 1944, to the U.S. Legation in Bern, Switzerland, stated contemplation to transfer six members, including Marie-Louise Dilkes, to Paris "as soon as communications are open."

46   Telegram (now declassified) from Selden Chapin, Chargé d'Affaires in the American Embassy in Paris in the absence of an ambassador, expressed concern for lack of urgency in securing experienced personnel urgently needed to help reestablish the American Embassy in Paris. "We are unable to cash drafts or personal checks and consequently cannot pay bills coming due the end of this month or make salary payments…Overland travel to Bern is now feasible and I suggest that the Misses Dilkes, Perret, and Royall be ordered here at once from Bern. I will make necessary arrangements for their clearance and transportation from the Swiss border." The telegram was sent to [Cordell Hull] Secretary of State, Washington, D.C., September 27, 1944. See Chapin, Selden.

47   Telegram (now declassified) from Leland Harrison, U.S. Minister in Bern, Switzerland, to Secretary of State, Washington, D.C., indicated he should be glad to release Misses Dilkes and Perret for return to Paris upon receipt of their orders with transport to the Swiss border, September 22, 1944. See Harrison, Leland.

48   Telegram (now declassified) sent on September 20, 1944, from Cordell Hull, Secretary of State, to the American Legation in Bern, Switzerland, formally assigned five members of the Legation to Paris. He requested Marie-Louise Dilkes and Lydia Perret "be released as soon as travel instructions are received as they are most urgently needed particularly owing to a large number of Americans from concentration camps requiring urgent services."

49   In a telegram (now declassified) Leland Harrison, U.S. Minister in Bern, Switzerland, asked the State Department to "please request War Department to instruct Army Headquarters Paris and Seventh Army Headquarters to facilitate…transportation to Paris of American Foreign Service

personnel [Dilkes and Perret] traveling under official orders…I am greatly appreciative of aid already received from General Patch." September 24, 1944. See Harrison, Leland.

50 Several telegrams (since declassified) were exchanged. Cordell Hull rejected Leland Harrison's request (September 28, 1944). Chapin indicated no requests for travel arrangements have been received at SHAEF; he suggests the State Department arrange with the War Department to have the Joint Chiefs of Staff initiate action by cable to SHAEF which will forward request to the European Theater of Operations and the reply to be returned through the same channels (Sept. 28, 1944). Harrison telegrammed that it was impracticable to send Dilkes and Perret on September 29 trip to Seventh Army Headquarters. See Dilkes, Marie-Louise.

51 The Seventh Army under the command of General Alexander McCarrell Patch (1889–1945) was under orders to move northward through the Rhône Valley, liberating much of France and routing German forces. See Turner and Jackson, chapters IV–XII, and Bonn, "Most Underrated General of World War II: Alexander Patch."

52 Some Paris members of the American Legation in Bern, Switzerland, including Marie-Louise Dilkes left Bern on October 10, 1944. Swiss Federal Archives, E2001D#1000/1553#1131*, B.22.21, Unterlagen 0000002, "Dilkes, Marie-Louise, Stenotypistin," 1942–1945.

53 A telegram (now declassified) from Leland Harrison, Bern, Switzerland, to the Secretary of State, Washington, D.C., announced that "Dilkes, etc. left this morning for Paris accompanying Communications Officer Clark." See Harrison, Leland, October 10, 1944.

54 A telegram (now declassified) from Cordell Hull to the U.S. Legation in Bern, Switzerland, announced the clerks, including Marie-Louise Dilkes, who are "transferred to Paris for duty with Office of the Representative of the United States to the French Committee of National Liberation…These transfers not made at their request nor convenience." See Hull, Cordell, October 2, 1944.

55 While members of the U.S. Legation in Bern arrived in Paris to reopen the American Embassy facility on October 11, the ceremonial reopening occurred on October 14, 1944. This reopening was restricted to diplomatic purposes only. See "Reopening of the American Embassy, Paris," *The American Foreign Service Journal*, December 1944. 655.

56 The Seventh Army provided the vehicles for the U.S. Legation in Bern, Switzerland, to go back to Paris to reopen the American Embassy in Paris. The presence of the Seventh Army in the Rhône Valley lent itself to help the American Legation address the urgent request to reopen the American Embassy.

57 In a telegram (now declassified) from John Gilbert Winant, U.S. Ambassador to the Court of St. James, Winant wrote to the Secretary of State that he had made "careful inspection of the Paris Embassy property, both the chancery and the residence. With the exception of a few bullets which scratched the façade and the plaster of some inner walls and broken window panes, the premises are in excellent condition…The excellent condition of the Embassy is due to the continued devotion and care taken by the guardian, M. Bizet, and by Mme. Blanchard who remained faithfully at their posts throughout the entire period." See Winant, John G., September 7, 1944.

58 Kenneth C. Krentz, Assistant Chief of the Division of Foreign Service Administration, Washington, D.C., wrote a letter to Augustus M. Dilkes (MLD brother) stating Marie-Louise Dilkes, who recently transferred from Bern, arrived at the American Mission at Paris on October 11, 1944. See Krentz, Kenneth, October 16, 1944.

59 "Romantic love, to…dreams of glory…" are excerpts from Thomas Wolfe's book *You Can't Go Home Again,* Book VII, *"A Wind is Rising and the Rivers Flow"* (1940). See Wolfe. 706.

Glossary

À bas Hitler!; À bas les Boches!
Down with Hitler! Down with the Germans!

Abri
Shelter

Accrochons nous au sol de France.
Let us cling to the soil of France.

   Quels que soient nos angoisses personnelles
   Whatever are our personal anguish

   et nos douleurs intimes,
   and our intimate sorrows,

   accrochons nous à notre devoir,
   let us cling to our duty,

   à notre tâche quotidienne—
   to our daily task—

   accrochons nous avec une fureur sacrée au poste
   let us hold with a sacred passion to the post

   ou le destin nous à places sans pensées de recul.
   where destiny has placed us without thoughts of retreating.

Achetez les journaux des mensonges!
Buy these lying newspapers!

Adieu
Farewell

Agent de police
Police agent

Anciens Combattants
War veterans

Apéritif
A drink, typically alcoholic, served before a meal

Arrondissement
District within a city

Aux armes, citoyens
To arms, citizens

   Marchons, marchons
   Let's march, let's march

Berlin est comme ça
Berlin is like that

Biscottes
Biscuits; crusty bread

Blocus
Blockade

Boche
Derogatory name for a German soldier

Bombardement de la Ligne Siegfried
Bombardment of the Siegfried Line (German line of fortification)

Bonsoir
Good evening

Bonsoir, Monsieur l'Agent, et grand merci
Good night, Mr. Policemen, and many thanks

C'est curieux
It is curious

C'est vrai, n'est-ce pas?
It is true, isn't it?

Ce n'est pas vraie
It isn't true

Café national
What was served as coffee when ingredients were in short supply, typically made from acorns and chickpeas

Camion
Cart or wagon for transporting heavy loads, such as military supplies

Camouflage
Disguise

Canaille
Scoundrel

Capitaine
Captain, as in one in command of a unit of soldiers

Carte de Ravitaillement	Supply (ration) card
Carte d'Identité, s'il vous plaît	Identification card, please
Cave	Wine cellar
Cenobite	Member of a monastic community; a monk
Chaque chose à sa place	Everything in its place
Les vaches dans le pré	Cows in the meadow
Le chat sur le toit	The cat on the roof
Les oiseaux dans leurs nids	Birds in their nests
Et vous, Madame, dans mon lit…	And you, Madam, in my bed…
Mais, oui!	But, yes!
Chancery	In England office for diplomatic proceedings
Chargé d'affaires	Diplomatic official who temporarily takes the place of an ambassador
Châtelaine	Mistress of a castle
Clairvoyant	Someone who claims to be able to see things in the future
Coat of mail	A mesh of metal rings worn as a type of armor
Cocher	Coachman
Coiffeur	Hairdresser
Commissaire	Commissioner
Commissariat	Police station that deals with criminal activity
Complaissance	Complacency; a satisfaction with oneself
Contre-espionnage	Counter intelligence
Coup d'état	Overthrow of a state government
Coupés	Front part of a vehicle where passengers sit
Crétins	Idiot
Débâcle	Disaster
Défense Passive	Citizens' Defense Force
Dépêchez-vous	Hurry up
Deutschland Über Alles	Germany Over All (German National Anthem)
Dimanche	Sunday
Duce	Leader or dictator; Italian leader Benito Mussolini called himself Il Duce, meaning The Leader
Éclairs	Dessert with a cream filling
École Militaire	Military academy for various military training
Eh bien, mon vieux. Il faut te coucher ce soir ce soir à dix heures.	Well, old man. You must go to bed tonight at ten o'clock.
Élan	French pride and spirit from within, one of duty or high purpose; it is what motivates a Frenchman; unique to France
Élégance	Elegance
Elles sont jolies, n'est-ce pas?	They are pretty, aren't they?
En fraude	Secretly; illegally
En permission	On leave from military service
En poste	Position, employment
En rapport	Connected
En route	On the way to a location

Épaulettes	Shoulder piece; material ornamentation worn on the shoulder
Éteignez vos lumières	Put out your lights
Étoile	Star; junction of 12 roads in Paris at Place Charles de Gaulle
Faculté des Lettres	School of the Arts
Faculté de Médecine	School of Medicine in Paris where physicians are trained
Fainéants	Ne're-do-wells; people who are thought never to do any good
Fascicule Noir	Black book
Fatherland	Refers to Germany
Faux brouillard	False fog
Fifth column	French citizens who are Nazi sympathizers
Finns	People who are native to Finland
Force majeure	Force or tragedy unexpected and beyond control
Fous le camp	Get out; leave (slang)
Foyers du Soldat	A club for soldiers on leave or waiting for orders
France, debout!	France, stand up!
Fritz	French term for a German soldier
Führer	Leader in German, bordering on tyrant
Funiculaire	Cable car that typically runs on an incline
Garde Mobile	A French force created to maintain public order and provide general security before, during, and after the Occupation
Gauleiter	Leader of a political district under Nazi rule
Gendarmerie	An armed police force organized to maintain public order
Hitler et Moi	Hitler and I
Hun	A German military aggressor
Ici s'élevait la statue du Général Mangin détruite par Hitler le 18 juin, 1940	Here the statue of General Mangin was raised, destroyed by Hitler June 18, 1940
Il faut être belle pour sa permission	It is necessary to be beautiful for his leave
Jap	Derogatory term for a Japanese soldier; used to characterize people of Japanese descent
Kiosques	Kiosks; vendor stands on the streets
Kommandantur	Officer in charge of the police force; commander in the German military
La Batterie Triomphale	The cannons that surround the Hôtel des Invalides
La Légion Étrangère Française	French Foreign Legion
"La Marseillaise"	French national anthem
La Patrie	France—the homeland as known to a loyal French person
La vie de Bohème	The Bohemian life; an unconventional lifestyle with the like-minded
Laissez-passer	A travel document giving permission to "let me pass."

Lavabo	Wash stand
Le ciel est, par-dessus le toit, *Si bleu, si calme!*	The sky is, above the roof top, So blue, so calm!
Le Livre Jaune Français	The French Yellow Book
Locataire	Tenant
Lumière au premier	Light on the first (floor)
Lycées	High schools
Ma belle petite espionne	My beautiful little spy
Madame	A woman, typically an older or married woman
Mademoiselle	A miss, typically a young girl
Maginot Line	Series of fortresses France built along its border with Germany
Mairie	Town hall; the place where the mayor manages a town's affairs
Maître	Professional who expresses authority
Maître d'hôtel	One who manages the front of a formal restaurant
Manœuvres	Military movements or movements that require skill
Maquis	Underground Resistance that was part of the French Resistance movement outside of urban areas
Marchand d'habits	Clothes merchant
Marchez	March
Maréchal	Marshal
Marionette	Puppet
Matières grasses	Fat or fatty substances
Médecines	Medicines
Merci, sale boche; Mon sale boche	Thank you, dirty German; My dirty German
Midinettes	Salesgirls
Milliard	One billion or one thousand million
Ministère des Affaires Étrangères	Minister for Foreign Affairs
Moi, c'est moi	I, it is I
Monsieur, mons.	Mister; typically a grown man
Monsieur Bœuf	Butcher
Mort aux Juifs	Death to the Jews as dictated by Nazi policy
Naiveté	Showing a lack of understanding, such as it relates to ideology
Nazi	Germans who pledged allegiance to the Third Reich
Nazi kultur	The German native culture, assumed superior to the culture of other countries, with teachings that national interests are more important than those of the individual
Noblesse oblige	The referred responsibility of privileged people to act with generosity and nobility toward those less privileged; high position justifies great expectations
Objets d'art	Objects of art other than paintings

Open city	An open city implies that the invading army will experience no resistance in order for the city to avoid destruction. All defensive efforts have been abandoned.
Oursins	Sea urchins
Parlez-moi d'amour	Speak to me of love
Pas de bavardages	No prattling or useless conversation; no gossip
Pas de savon	No soap
Petites Françaises, nous danserons avec vous le 14 juillet	Little French ladies, we shall dance with you on the 14th of July
Poilu	Name given to a French soldier in WWI
Population abandonée, avez confiance dans le soldat Allemand	Abandoned population, have confidence in the German soldier
Porto	Fortified wine from the Porto region in northern Portugal
Pourriture	Rottenness
Préfecture de Police	Provides public security to maintain law and order
Préfet de Police	State representative of a police station
Promeneurs	Strollers
Pucelle	Maid—Joan of Arc referred to herself as a maid at her trial
Quand même	Even so; all the same; anyway
Qu'il était bleu, le ciel, et grand, l'espoir!	How blue was the sky, and great, the hope!
Quelques Fleurs	Some flowers
Rauchen verboten	Smoking forbidden
Regardez, c'est beau, n'est-ce pas?	Look, it is beautiful, isn't it?
Roule, roule ton flot— indolent, morne Seine	Roll, roll your stream— lazy, gloomy Seine
Sale macaroni	Dirty pasta; dirty Italian
Salon	Living room
Saucisses	Barrage balloons that looked like sausages
Sens unique	One way
Serieux	Serious
Soirée	Evening party
Sortie	Exit
Soutane	An ankle-length piece of Christian clerical clothing such as typically worn by a Roman Catholic priest
Switzer cheese	Emmental cheese also known as Swiss cheese in the U.S.
Taisez vous	Keep quiet
Tapissier	Upholsterer or interior decorator
Tiens!	Look at this!
Toilette	Restroom; toilet
Tracts	Leaflet propaganda
Traveller's checks	Method to travel safely with money without carrying cash

Tricolor	The flag of France
Tutoiement	Saying "thou" and "thee"
Un de plus disparu—un de moins	One more gone, one less
Veronal	Barbital available over the counter in France in 1939; veronal poisoning has been cited in suicide cases
Victoire	Victory
Vieilles maisons, vieux papiers	Old houses, old papers
Vision fugitif	Fleeting vision
Vive de Gaulle; Pétain	Long live de Gaulle; Pétain
Vive l'Angleterre; Belgique; France	Long live England; Belgium; France
Voiturette	A two-seated car run by electricity
Wehrmacht	Collective name for Germany's armed forces 1935–1945
Yaourt	Yogurt

Bibliography

Primary Sources

Audiat, Pierre. *Paris Pendant la Guerre*. Paris: Librarie Hachette, 1946.

Biddle, Virginia Hamill. "Memoir of Mrs. Virginia Hamill Biddle, 2011." Frontline Diplomacy, Manuscript Division, Library of Congress, Washington, D.C. Accessed June 9, 2022.https://memory.loc.gov/service/mss/mfdip/2011/2011bid01/2011bid01.pdf.

Chapin, Selden. Declassified telegram from the Chargé d'Affaires in the American Embassy in Paris (in the absence of an ambassador) via the War Department suggesting that Marie-Louise Dilkes, among others, be ordered to Paris at once from Bern. The telegram was sent to [Cordell Hull] Secretary of State, Washington, D.C., September 27, 1944. RG 59, File 124.51/9–2744; NACP.

Churchill, Winston. Address. "Blood, Toil, Tears and Sweat." To Cabinet and to House of Commons, London. May 13, 1940. Accessed June 9, 2022. https://winstonchurchill.org/resources/speeches/1940-the-finest-hour/blood-toil-tears-sweat.

——. Address. "We Shall Fight on the Beaches." House of Commons of the Parliament of the United Kingdom, London. June 4, 1940. Accessed June 9, 2022. https://winstonchurchill.org/resources/speeches/1940-the-finest-hour/we-shall-fight-on-the-beaches.

——. Address. "The Few." House of Commons, London. 20 August 1940. Accessed June 9, 2022. https://winstonchurchill.org/resources/speeches/1940-the-finest-hour/the-few.

——. Address. "Give Us the Tools." BBC radio broadcast, London. 09 February 1941. Accessed June 9, 2022. https://winstonchurchill.org/resources/speeches/1941–1945-war-leader/give-us-the-tools.

——. Address. "Broadcast on War with Japan." BBC radio broadcast, London. 08 December 1941. Accessed June 9, 2022. http://www.ibiblio.org/pha/policy/1941/411208e.html.

——. Address. "The Text of Premier Churchill's Broadcast on Singapore." *The New York Times*, February 16, 1942: 6. Retrieved October 12, 2020.

——. *The Second World War: The Gathering Storm*. Cambridge: Houghton Mifflin Company, 1948.

——. *The Second World War: Their Finest Hour*. Cambridge: Houghton Mifflin Company, 1949.

——. *The Second World War: The Hinge of Fate*. Cambridge: Houghton Mifflin Company, 1950.

Davis, Monnett B. Declassified letter to Mrs. John Harrison, Jr. (MLD sister), Meadowbrook, PA, September 12, 1941; RG 59, file 123 Dilkes, Marie-Louise/29; NACP.

Davis, Nathaniel P., Declassified letter to George Dilkes (MLD nephew), New York, NY, July 2, 1941; RG 59, file 123 Dilkes, Marie-Louise/22; NACP.

Deiss, Raymond. *Pantagruel*. Ed. Raymond Deiss. Published by René and Robert Blanc. October 1940.

Dilkes, Charles Edward. *Remembering World War One: An Engineer's Diary of the War*. Atlanta: Juliet Publishing, 2014.

Dilkes, Marie-Louise. "Application for Appointment," Form 205a. U.S. Consular Service. Paris: November 8, 1933, Dilkes Family Collection.

——. "Application for Retirement," Form SF 101. Department of State—American Embassy, Paris. Paris: May 10, 1954, Dilkes Family Collection.

——. Original Manuscript of *Paris Notes* written by Marie-Louise Dilkes for the years 1939–1944. Dilkes Family Collection.

——. Picture of Marie-Louise Dilkes. Paris, France, 1936. Personal photograph by unknown photographer. Dilkes Family Collection.

——. "Several telegrams (since declassified) were exchanged..." referenced in Note 270. RG59, File 123 Dilkes, Marie-Louise; and File 124.513/9–2844; NACP.

Harrison, Leland. Declassified telegram from Bern, Switzerland, to Secretary of State, Washington, D.C., glad to release MLD for return to Paris, September 22, 1944. RG 59, File 123 Dilkes, Marie-Louise; NACP.

——. Declassified telegram from Bern, Switzerland, to Secretary of State asking the State Department to request the War Department to instruct Army Headquarters Paris to facilitate transportation for Dilkes and Perret for return to Paris, September 24, 1944. RG59, File 124.513/9–2444; NACP.

——. Declassified telegram from Bern, Switzerland, to Secretary of State announcing Dilkes, etc. had left Bern this morning, October 10, 1944. RG 59, File 123 Dilkes, Marie-Louise; NACP.

Havens, Harry A. Declassified letter, Washington, D.C., to Augustus M. Dilkes (MLD brother), La Mesa, CA, December 31, 1941. RG 59, File 123 Dilkes, Marie-Louise/38; NACP.

Henderson, Sir Nevile Meyrick. *Failure of a Mission: Berlin 1937–1939*. New York: G.P. Putnam's Sons, 1940.

Hitler, Adolf. Address. "Adolf Hitler–speech for the Twentieth anniversary of the N.S.D.A.P. in the Hofbrauhaus." Munich. February 24, 1940. *Neues Europa*. Accessed November 6, 2020. http://der-fuehrer.org/reden/english/40–02–24.htm.

——. Address. "Adolf Hitler's Great speech to the German Reichstag," Berlin. July 19, 1940. *Neues Europa*. Accessed October 25, 2020. http://der-fuehrer.org/reden/english/40–07–19.htm.

Holloway, Clyde. *Pacific War Marine*. Vancouver, Washington: So Many Books..., Inc., 2005.

Huddle, J. (Jerome) Klahr. Declassified telegram #455 sent from Bern, Switzerland, most likely sent to the Secretary of State's office, Washington, D.C., December 27, 1941; File 123 Dilkes, Marie-Louise/33; NACP.

Hull, Cordell. Declassified telegram from the U.S. Secretary of State to U.S. Ambassador William Bullitt concerning extracting American citizens from France in light of advancing German Army, Washington, May 28, 1940. Foreign Relations of the United States Diplomatic Papers, 1940, General and Europe, Volume II. Accessed November 20, 2020. https://history.state.gov/historicaldocuments/frus1940v02/d130.

——. Declassified telegram #2443 from the U.S. Secretary of State to Leland Morris, U.S. *Chargé* in Germany acknowledging that all U.S. consular offices in Greater Germany would be closed, Washington, June 20, 1941. "Foreign Relations of the United States Diplomatic Papers, 1941, Europe, Volume II." Accessed December 22, 2021. https://history.state.gov/historicaldocuments/frus1941v02/d591.

——. Declassified telegrams from the Secretary of State, Washington, D.C., to the American Legation in Bern, Switzerland, contemplating the transfer of six personnel to Paris, September 8, 1944; assigning five personnel to Paris with Dilkes and Perret leaving ASAP, September 20, 1944; and officially transferring them, October 2, 1944. RG 59, File 123 Dilkes, Marie-Louise; NACP.

Krentz, Kenneth C. Declassified telegram from the Assistant Chief of the Division of Foreign Service Administration, Washington, D.C., to Augustus M. Dilkes (MLD brother), La Mesa, CA, announcing MLD had arrived on October 11, 1944, at the American Mission at Paris, October 16, 1944. RG 59, File 123 Dilkes, Marie-Louise; NACP.

Leahy, Admiral William D. Declassified telegram from the U.S. Ambassador in France, Vichy, France, to Cordell Hull, Washington, D.C., outlining demands of the Foreign Office in Berlin on Foreign Missions in Paris, May 28, 1941. File 124.51/200; NACP.

——. Declassified telegram #1588 assigning Marie-Louise Dilkes to Bern, December 22, 1941; File 123 Dilkes, Marie-Louise/31; File 124.513/1676; NACP.

Ministry of Foreign Affairs. *Le Livre Jaune Français: Documents Diplomatiques 1938–1939.* Paris: National Printing, 1939.

——. *Le Livre Jaune Français: Documents Diplomatiques 1938–1939.* Traité de Locarno entre la France et la Pologne du 16 Octobre 1925. 420.

Morris, Leland B. Telegram 124.51/207 from the U.S. *Chargé* in Germany (Morris) to the Secretary of State: Department's instructions concerning the closing of the Embassy at Paris and the establishment of the Consulate General of the United States in Paris as a separate office, Berlin, May 30, 1941. "Foreign Relations of the United States Diplomatic Papers, 1941, Europe, Volume II." Accessed June 9, 2022. https://history.state.gov/historicaldocuments/frus1941v02/d456>

——. Telegram 125.0062/299 from the U.S. *Chargé* in Germany to the U.S. Secretary of State concerning Germany's demands that all U.S. consular offices in Greater Germany be closed, Berlin, June 19, 1941. "Foreign Relations of the United States Diplomatic Papers, 1941, Europe, Volume II." Accessed December 22, 2021. https://history.state.gov/historicaldocuments/frus1941v02/d590>

Pershing, John J. *My Experiences in the World War* Vol. I and II. New York: Frederick A. Stokes Company, 1931.

Peters, C. Brooks, "Germans Furious at Britain's Coup." *The New York Times*, July 5, 1940: 4. Retrieved August 18, 2020.

Philadelphia in the World War, 1914–1919. New York: Wynkoop Hallenbeck Crawford Co., 1922.

Report of the Board of Managers of The Trades League of Philadelphia: For the year 1904, Horace T. Potts. "Fourteenth Annual Report of Board of Directors, The Trades League of Philadelphia, for the Year 1904." Philadelphia, 1905. *Google Books.*

Roosevelt, Franklin D. "The Text of President Roosevelt's Address at Charlottesville," Commencement Address, University of Virginia Law School, Charlottesville, VA, June 10, 1940. *The New York Times*, June 11, 1940: 6. Retrieved November 6, 2020.

——. "On an unlimited national emergency," Fireside Chat. White House, Washington, D.C., May 27, 1941. Accessed June 9, 2022. https://millercenter.org/the-presidency/presidential-speeches/may-27-1941-fireside-chat-17-unlimited-national-emergency.

Rousseau, Andrea. "Re: Marie-Louise Dilkes." E-mail to Virginia Dilkes confirming Cross of Chevalier in the Order of Léopold II was presented to Marie-Louise Dilkes," May 7, 2009.

Schuschnigg, Kurt. "Last broadcast address as Austrian Chancellor." Radio broadcast, Vienna. March 11, 1938. Accessed November 10, 2020. https://www.mediathek.at/atom/015C6FC2–2C9–0036F-00000D00–015B7F64.

Speer, Albert. *Inside the Third Reich.* Trans. by Richard and Clara Winston. New York: The Macmillan Company, 1970.

Strasser, Otto. *Hitler et Moi,* Trans. by Gwenda David and Eric Mosbacher. New York: AMS Press, 1940.

Swiss Federal Archives, E2001D#1000/1553#1131*, B.22.21, Unterlagen 0000002, "Dilkes, Marie-Louise, Stenotypistin," 1942–1945.

Taylor, Laurence W. Letter from the Vice Consul at Paris (Taylor) to the Secretary of State: Department's instructions…concerning the closing of the Embassy at Paris and the establishment of the Consulate General at Paris as a separate office, Paris, 11 July 1941. "Foreign Relations of the United States Diplomatic Papers, 1941, Europe, Volume II, Document 458." Accessed November 11, 2020. https://history.state.gov/historicaldocuments/frus1941v02/d458.

The Holy Bible, *King James Version.* Great Britain: The Westminster Book Stores, 1949.

Weddell, Alexander Wilbourne. Declassified letter from Weddell, Madrid, Spain, to Cordell Hull, Washington, D.C., August 29, 1941; RG 59, File 125.8553/211; NACP.

Welles, Sumner. Note from the Undersecretary of State to the German *Chargé d'affaires* demanding the closure of German consulates in the U.S. and its territories, June 16, 1941. "Foreign Relations of the United States Diplomatic Papers, Europe, Volume II, Document 588." Accessed December 22, 2021. https://history.state.gov/historicaldocuments/frus1941v02/d588.

Winant, John G. Declassified telegram from the Office of European Affairs, London, England, to the Secretary of State, Washington, D.C., on the excellent condition of the American Embassy in Paris property, September 7, 1944. File 124.511/9–744; NACP.

Secondary Sources

"The 50 Hostages." Exhibition. Created by Château des ducs de Bretagne. *Musée Histoire de Nantes*. Accessed November 12, 2020. https://artsandculture.google.com/exhibit/the-50-hostages-ch%C3% A2teau-des-ducs-de-bretagne/jAJCHONt4id3JQ?hl=en.

Abbott, Karen. "I Was Looking Forward to a Quiet Old Age." Smithsonian Magazine, May 25, 2012. Accessed January 18, 2021. https://www.smithsonianmag.com/history/i-was-looking-forward-to-a-quiet-old-age-106393195.

"AFS History Timeline." *AFS*. 2020. AFS Intercultural Programs 2020. Accessed June 9, 2022. https://afs.org/archives/timeline.

"Aidez la justice! Adjure le Maréchal après l'abominable crime de Nantes." *Le Matin*, October 23, 1941. Retrieved November 12, 2020. https://gallica.bnf.fr/ark:/12148/bpt6k587242m.item.

Allen, G.E. Morris. "Exit from Paris." *The American Foreign Service Journal*. Vol. 18 No. 9, September 1941. 500. Accessed June 9, 2022. http://www.afsa.org/sites/default/files/fsj-1941–09-september_0. pdf.

Alléno Paris au Pavillon Ledoyen." *Michelin Guide France 2020*. Michelin Guide. Accessed October 16, 2020. https://guide.michelin.com/en/ile-de-france/paris/restaurant/alleno-paris-au-pavillon-ledoyen.

"Allies of World War II." *Wikipedia*. Wikipedia Foundation. Accessed October 15, 2020. https://en.wikipedia.org/wiki/Allies_of_World_War_II.

"American Export Lines." *United States Holocaust Memorial Museum*. Accessed October 24, 2020. https://www.ushmm.org/search/results/?q=American+Export+Lines+in+1940.

American Foreign Service Journal. Vol. VII. "Executive Nominations Confirmed by the Senate December 19, 1929." Washington, D.C.: American Foreign Service Assn., January 1930. Accessed June 9, 2022. http://www.afsa.org/sites/default/files/fsj-1930–01-january_0.pdf.

"American Legion." *American Legion Paris Post 1*. Accessed November 8, 2020. http://www.parispost1.com.

Archambault, G.H. "Bastille Day Marked by Mourning in France." *The New York Times*. July 15, 1940: 1, 4. Retrieved October 24, 2020.

"The Archives of the Neuchâteloise Press from 1738 to the Present Day." Neuchâtel *l'Express*, 05 August 1942: 1. Accessed October 13, 2020. http://www.lexpressarchives.ch/olive/apa/swissnp_fr/#panel=home.

"Arthur Seyss-Inquart." *Propagander3.tripod.com*. Accessed November 10, 2020. http://propagander3.tripod.com/nur17.html.

"Audiat, Pierre." Saintonge Academy. Accessed October 15, 2020. http://academie-saintonge.org/?p=210.

"Axis Alliance in World War II." United States Holocaust Memorial Museum. *Holocaust Encyclopedia*. Accessed October 27, 2020. https://encyclopedia.ushmm.org/content/en/article/axis-alliance-in-world-war-ii.

Axis History Forum. "Seeking info about Corsica's and Sardinia's position in WWII," alias Lupo Solitario. Updated June 3, 2006. Accessed November 7, 2020. https://forum.axishistory.com/viewtopic.php?t=102442.

Beevor, Antony. *The Second World War*. New York: Little, Brown Company Hatchette Book Group, 2012.

"Bernardo Rolland de Miota." *The International Raoul Wallenberg Foundation*. Accessed October 29, 2020. https://www.raoulwallenberg.net/saviors/diplomats/spanish/diplomats-52/bernardo-rolland-de-miota.

Bistrovic, Miriam. "Austria's 'Anschluss' with Germany in 1938." Deutsches Historisches Museum. Accessed November 10, 2020. https://www.dhm.de/blog/2018/03/12/stories-austrias-anschluss-with-germany-in-1938.

Blake, Leonardo. *Hitler's Last Year of Power*. London: Andrew Dakers Limited, 1939.

"Boissier." *ChocoParis.com*. Updated 2020. Accessed October 22, 2020. http://www.chocoparis.com/boissier.

Bonn, Keith E. "Most Underrated General of World War II: Alexander Patch." July 2003. Accessed October 13, 2020. https://www.marshallfoundation.org/100th-infantry/wp-content/uploads/sites/27/2014/06/Bonn_Most_Underrated_General_of_World_War_II.pdf.

Borneman, Walter R. *The Admirals*. New York: Little, Brown and Company, 2012.

"Boucher, Jean. (La Comtesse de Segur monument by Jean Boucher)." *EUtouring.com*. Accessed November 1, 2020. https://www.eutouring.com/images_paris_statues_339.html.

"Boulevards of Paris." *Wikipedia*. Wikipedia Foundation. Updated August 25, 2020. Accessed October 25, 2020. https://en.wikipedia.org/wiki/Boulevards_of_Paris.

"Brauchitsch Dies of Heart Attack." *The New York Times*, October 20, 1948: 7. Retrieved November 18, 2020.

"British Embassy Church in Paris Re-opens." *Imperial War Museums*. Accessed October 31, 2020. https://www.iwm.org.uk/collections/item/object/1060024130.

Bugnion, François. *The International Committee of the Red Cross and the Protection of War Victims*. Oxford, England: Macmillan, 2003. Accessed June 10, 2022. http://icrcndresourcecentre.org/wp-content/uploads/2016/03/X_0503–002_ICRC_The_proctection_of_war_victims_WEB_09–2014.pdf.

Bullitt, Jr., William C. Address. "America Is in Danger." American Philosophical Society. Independence Square, Philadelphia, 18 August 1940. *The New York Times*, 19 August 1940: 4. Retrieved October 25, 2020.

Burrows, Stephanie. *Tucholsky and France*. Abingdon, Oxfordshire, UK: Routledge Publishers, 2001.

Burt, Nathaniel. *The Perennial Philadelphians*. Boston: Little, Brown and Company, 1963.

"Café Viel," André Zucca, Bibliothèque Historique de la Ville de Paris, Roger-Viollet collection. (Reference no. 37809–3). Accessed June 10, 2022. https://www.roger-viollet.fr/image-photo/guerre-1939–1945-boulevard-de-madeleine-le-restaurant-viel-requisitionne-devient-andre-zucca-bhvp-roger-viollet-1004791.

Cartwright, Mark. "The Stained Glass Windows of Chartres Cathedral." *Ancient History Encyclopedia*. Ancient History Encyclopedia, October 16, 2018. Accessed October 15, 2020. https://www.ancient.eu/article/1277/the-stained-glass-windows-of-chartres-cathedral.

"Casadesus, Robert." *Robert Casadesus His Life*. Accessed November 5, 2020 http://www.robertcasadesus.com/index_savie.php.

"Change in France." *The New York Times*, March 21, 1940: 23. Retrieved November 4, 2020.

"Chara Sands: mysterious Siberian desert." *56 Parallel.com*. Accessed October 25, 2020. https://www.56thparallel.com/chara-sands/.

Charman, Terry. "The Rise and Fall of Lord Haw Haw during the Second World War." *Imperial War Museums*. Updated 22 June 2018. Accessed November 16, 2020. https://www.iwm.org.uk/history/the-rise-and-fall-of-lord-haw-haw-during-the-second-world-war.

"Château de Ferrières," *Spotting History*. Accessed August 31, 2020. https://www.spottinghistory.com/view/5940/chateau-de-ferrieres.

"Chenavard, Paul." *Musée d'Orsay*. Accessed November 4, 2020. https://www.musee-orsay.fr/en/collections/works-in-focus/painting/commentaire_id/divina-tragedia-16858.html?cHash=a28610.

"Chez Elle–Closed." *Trip Advisor*. Accessed October 21, 2020. https://www.tripadvisor.com/Restaurant_Review-g187147-d7686293-Reviews-Chez_Elle-Paris_Ile_de_France.html.

"Chez Francis." *Trip Advisor*. Accessed October 15, 2020. https://www.tripadvisor.com/Restaurant_Review-g187147-d714958-Reviews-Chez_Francis-Paris_Ile_de_France.html.

Chico, Beverly. "History of Women's Hats." *Fashion History*. Accessed November 2, 2020. https://fashion-history.lovetoknow.com/fashion-clothing-industry/history-milliners.

"Chopin." The Garden Guide. Accessed November 1, 2020. https://www.gardenvisit.com/gardens/jardin_du_luxembourg.

"Chronology of Aviation History–1940 to 1949." *Skytamer Images*. Accessed October 13, 2020. https://www.skytamer.com/1943.html.

"Church of the Trinité." *Paroisse de la Sainte-Trinité*, Paris. Accessed October 19, 2020. https://latriniteparis.com/pages/arts-culture/.

Colvin, Milton, and Ann Miller Morin. Interview with Constance Ray Harvey. *Association for Diplomatic Studies & Training*. 11 July 1988. Accessed November 7, 2020. https://adst.org/oral-history/fascinating-figures/constance-ray-harvey-diplomat-and-world-war-ii-heroine.

Cooke, Alistair. *American Commentary*. BBC Radio Network. London, May 10, 1941. Accessed August 11, 2023.

Cooper, Edward. "A gentleman's guide to the Parisian members' club." *Gentleman's Journal*. Accessed October 17, 2020. https://www.thegentlemansjournal.com/article/gentlemans-guide-parisian-members-club.

"Coysevox, Antoine." *Chateau de Versailles*. Accessed November 4, 2020. http://en.chateauversailles.fr/discover/history/great-characters/antoine-coysevox.

"Cross of Iron." *Military History Now*. Updated January 3, 2016. Accessed October 19, 2020. https://militaryhistorynow.com/2016/01/03/cross-of-iron-11-amazing-facts-about-germanys-best-known-military-medal.

Cummings, Robert. "Enrico Toselli." *AllMusic.com*. Accessed November 3, 2020. https://www.allmusic.com/artist/enrico-toselli-mn0002153966/biography.

"Daily Bulletin." *Office of the Historian*. Office of the Historian, Foreign Service Institute, U.S. Department of State. Accessed October 17, 2020. https://history.state.gov/historicaldocuments/frus1941v02/d458.

"Daring Escape at the Start of WWII." *Greatoceanliners.com*. Accessed February 1, 2023. https://greatoceanliners.com/ss-bremen.

"Dean Frederick Beekman Dies; Served at Holy Trinity in Paris." *The New York Times*, March 22, 1964: 29. Retrieved October 25, 2020.

Dean, Peter J. "Napoleon as a Military Commander." *Research Subjects: Napoleon Himself*. Accessed October 23, 2020. https://www.napoleon-series.org/research/napoleon/c_genius.html.

Delorme, Anne-Claire. "The first look at the Hôtel de la Marine renovation in Paris." *Explore France*. Updated November 5, 2019. Accessed October 30, 2020. https://us.france.fr/en/paris/moodboard/hotel-de-la-marine-renovation.

"Delorme, Philibert." *Web Gallery of Art*. Accessed November 4, 2020. https://www.wga.hu/bio_m/d/delorme/biograph.html.

"Dilkes, George R., and Dolores Dilkes." *Year Book of the Pennsylvania Society of New York, 1916*. Internet Archive. Accessed October 15, 2020. https://archive.org/stream/yearbookpennsyl00yorkgoog/yearbookpennsyl00yorkgoog_djvu.txt.

Dostoevsky, Fyodor. *The Brothers Karamazov*. Trans. Richard Pevear and Larissa Volokhonsky. New York: Macmillan, 2002. Reference to letter to Mikhail Dostoevsky, December 22, 1849, included in the Introduction translated by Richard Pevear.

Eddy, Mary Baker. "Fidelity." *Miscellaneous Writings 1883–1896*. Chapter IX. Boston: Trustees under the Will of Mary Baker G. Eddy, 1896. Accessed August 11, 2023. https://www.gutenberg.org/files/31427/31427-h/31427-h.html.

"Edmée de la Rochefoucauld." *Arllfb.be*. Académie Royale de Langue et de Littérature Françaises de Belgique. Accessed October 17, 2020. https://www.arllfb.be/composition/membres/delarochefoucauld.html.

"Embassies and Legations of the United States." *Congressional Directory*. Washington, D.C.: United States 66th Congress, July 1919. Accessed June 10, 2022. https://babel.hathitrust.org/cgi/pt?id=mdp.39015022758612&view=1up&seq=408.

Emergency Aid of Penna. Foundation, Inc. "A Small Sampling of 100 Years of the Emergency Aid." Accessed May 16, 2020. https://www.eafoundation.org/a-small-sampling-of-100-years-of-the-emergency-aid.

Emerson, Ralph Waldo. "Self-Reliance," Essays, 1841. Accessed June 10, 2022. https://archive.vcu.edu/english/engweb/transcendentalism/authors/emerson/essays/selfreliance.html.

"European War." *The Gallup Poll*. Accessed October 31, 2020. http://ibiblio.org/pha/Gallup/Gallup%201940.htm.

Fabricant, Florence. "Menu Collection Offers a Taste of History," *The New York Times*, March 24, 1982: C15. Retrieved October 31, 2020.

Fagniez, André. "Robert Neeser: généalogie par André Fagniez." Accessed August 28, 2020. https://gw.geneanet.org/afag?lang=fr&n=neeser&oc=0&p=robert.

"Fair of Lyon." *Wikipedia*. Wikipedia Foundation. Updated January 7, 2020. Accessed November 5, 2020. https://en.wikipedia.org/wiki/Fair_of_Lyon#:~:text=The%20Fair%20of%20Lyon%20(French,center%20in%20Chassieu%20since%201985.

Farago, Ladislas. *The Game of the Foxes*. New York: Bantam Books, 1971.

Farley, James. Address. 1940 Democratic Party Platform. Chicago Stadium. Chicago. July 15–18, 1940. Accessed August 11, 2023. https://www.presidency.ucsb.edu/documents/1940-democratic-party-platform.

"Fear-Haunted Anniversary." *The New York Times*, February 1, 1943: 14. Retrieved August 18, 2020.

Ferguson, James A., et al. "Jamaica." *Encyclopedia Britannica*. Updated September 10, 2020. Accessed October 27, 2020. https://www.britannica.com/place/Jamaica.

"Foreign Legion." *Foreign Legion*. Accessed October 20, 2020. https://www.legion-etrangere.com.

Foreign Service List. "Classification of Foreign Service Officers 01 July 1931." Washington, D.C.: U.S. Printing Office, 1931. Accessed June 10, 2022. http://www.afsa.org/sites/default/files/fsj-1930-01-january_0.pdf.

"Foreign Service Personnel Changes." *Department of State Bulletin*, Vol. 4.2, April 12, 1941. Accessed June 10, 2022. https://babel.hathitrust.org/cgi/pt?id=uc1.c061075713&view=1up&seq=46&q1=Vanc.

"Foucher." Foucher Paris. *Chocolat-Foucher.com*. Accessed November 3, 2020. https://www.chocolat-foucher.com/content/7-la-maison-foucher.

"Franco-American Duchess: Margaret 'Golden Peggy' Watson." The Esoteric Curiosa: Knowledge Is Power. September 2, 2020. Accessed October 25, 2020. http://theesotericcuriosa.blogspot.com/2009/12/franco-american-duchess-marguerite.html.

"Franklin D. Roosevelt (Paris Metro.) *Wikipedia*. Wikipedia Foundation. Updated August 19, 2020. Accessed October 25, 2020. https://en.wikipedia.org/wiki/Franklin_D._Roosevelt_(Paris_M%C3%A9tro).

"French Foreign Legion Traditions." *French Legion Info*. Updated July 18, 2019. Accessed October 19, 2020. http://foreignlegion.info/traditions.

"The Gabriel Family." *Chateau de Versailles*. Chateau of Versailles. Accessed October 17, 2020. http://en.chateauversailles.fr/discover/history/great-characters/gabriel-family.

"G.A. Lorillard to Marry." *The New York Times*, July 14, 1915: 9. Retrieved September 1, 2020.

"Gaston Ernest Liébert." *Wikipedia*, Wikipedia Foundation. Accessed June 22, 2021. https://fr.wikipedia.org/wiki/Gaston_Ernest_Liébert.

"German American Bund." United States Holocaust Memorial Museum. Accessed October 27, 2020. https://encyclopedia.ushmm.org/content/en/article/german-american-bund.

Glass, Charles. *Americans in Paris: Life and Death under Nazi Occupation 1940–1944*. London: Penguin Books, 2011 Accessed June 10, 2022 https://erenow.net/ww/americans-in-paris-life-and-death-under-nazi-occupation-1940–1944/2.php.

Goodwin, Doris Kearns. *No Ordinary Time*. New York: Simon & Schuster, 1994.

Green, Nancy L. *The Other Americans in Paris*. Chicago: University of Chicago Press, 2014.

"Guests of the Gestapo." *Association for Diplomatic Studies & Training*. 09 July 2013. Accessed October 13, 2020. https://adst.org/2013/07/guests-of-the-gestapo.

Halbrook, Stephen. "Target Switzerland: Swiss Armed Neutrality in World War 2," Chapter I. *American Swiss Foundation*. Accessed October 12, 2020. https://www.americanswiss.org/resources_and_publications/target-switzerland-swiss-armed-neutrality-in-world-war-2.

Harris, Leslie, and James Hiller. "Newfoundland and Labrador." *Encyclopedia Britannica*. Updated September 20, 2019. Accessed October 27, 2020. https://www.britannica.com/place/Newfoundland-and-Labrador.

"Harter, Huntington." Social Register Association (U.S.) *Social Register, Philadelphia, including Wilmington … 1919*. New York: Social Register Association Accessed June 10, 2022. https://babel.hathitrust.org/cgi/pt?id=njp.32101077272092&view=1up&seq=118&q1=Harter.

Hatton, Barry. *Queen of the Sea: A History of Lisbon*. London: C. Hurst & Co., 2018.

Heaton, Pauline, and George J. Rushe. "Bermuda." *Encyclopedia Britannica*. Updated November 27, 2019. Accessed October 27, 2020. https://www.britannica.com/place/Bermuda.

The Heel of the Conqueror, Editors of Time-Life Books. Alexandria, Virginia: The Time Inc. Book Company, 1991.

Heise, Lily. "Places where You Can Still See Evidence of the Nazi Occupation of Paris." Frommer's. Accessed November 20, 2020. https://www.frommers.com/slideshows/848347-places-where-you-can-still-see-evidence-of-the-nazi-occupation-of-paris.

Heritage Images / Keystone Archives / akg-images. "Occupying German troops outside the Café de la Paix, Paris, World War II, c1940–c1944." Accessed October 30, 2020. https://www.akg-images.co.uk/archive/-2UMEBMYS15NEX.html.

Herodotus of Halicarnassus. *Herodotus,* Book 8 "Urania," paragraph 98. Trans. George Rawlinson. University of Chicago Press, 1952. *Great Books of the Western World*, Vol. 6.

"The H. G. Wells Society." *The H. G. Wells Society*. Accessed October 19, 2020. http://hgwellssociety.com.

"High-ranking Nazi leader Hermann Göring dies." *History*. Updated October 14, 2020. Accessed October 29, 2020. https://www.history.com/this-day-in-history/hermann-goering-dies.

"The History of The Ritz Hotel and its Renovation." *EUtouring.com*. Accessed October 30, 2020. https://www.eutouring.com/the_ritz_paris_hotel_history.html.

"The History of the Swastika." United States Holocaust Memorial Museum. Updated August 7, 2017. Accessed October 23, 2020. https://encyclopedia.ushmm.org/content/en/article/history-of-the-swastika.

"Hitler Announces Victory over Russia." *The History Place*. Accessed November 5, 2020. http://www.historyplace.com/worldwar2/defeat/attack-russia.htm.

"Hitler Goes to Prague." *The New York Times*, March 16, 1939: 21. Retrieved November 4, 2020.

"Hitler reoccupies the Rhineland, violating the Treaty of Versailles." *History* Ed. History.com. March 7, 1936. Accessed October 13, 2020. https://www.history.com/this-day-in-history/hitler-reoccupies-the-rhineland.

"Hitler's Doomed Angel," *Vanity Fair*. Accessed October 31, 2020. https://www.vanityfair.com/news/1992/04/hitlers-doomed-angel.

"The Hôtel Biron," *The Musée Rodin*. Accessed October 19, 2020. http://www.musee-rodin.fr/en/museum/musee-rodin-paris/hotel-biron.

"Hôtel Carlton Lyon-MGallery." *Historic Hotels Worldwide*. Accessed November 4, 2020. https://www.historichotels.org/hotels-resorts/hotel-carlton-lyon-mgallery-by-sofitel/history.php.

"Hôtel des Invalides." *World Monuments Fund*. Accessed October 19, 2020. https://www.wmf.org/project/h%C3%B4tel-des-invalides.

"Hotel Matignon–the Official French Prime Minister's Residence in Paris." EUtouring.com. Accessed January 18, 2021. https://www.eutouring.com/hotel_matignon.html.

"House of Houbigant." *Houbigant Paris*. Accessed October 31, 2020. https://www.houbigant-parfum.com/eu_en/the-house-of-houbigant.html.

"How Mr. Lorillard Divided His Estate." *The New York Times*, July 14, 1901: 10. Retrieved September 30, 2020.

Husted, Clark. *Find A Grave*, memorial page for Clark E. Husted, Jr. (1915–1944), Find A Grave Memorial, no. 56373176, citing Epinal American Cemetery and Memorial, Epinal, Departement des Vosges, Lorraine, France. Accessed October 10, 2020. https://www.findagrave.com/memorial/56373176/clark-e-husted.

Imhof, Kurt, et al. "Swiss Refugee and Foreign Economic Policies seen within the context of Press Publications on Politics 1938–1950." Vol. 8. *Publications of the Independent Commission of Experts Switzerland–Second World War*. Accessed October 12, 2020. https://www.uek.ch/en/schlussbericht/Publikationen/zusammenfassungen/08poloeff.htm.

Jackson, Julian. *France: The Dark Years 1940–1944*. New York: Oxford University Press, 2003.

James, Edwin L. "Hitler Finishes Reds before His Army Does." *The New York Times*, October 5, 1941: 107. Retrieved November 5, 2020.

Jarrett, John, and Peter Walters. "Reveille or Rouse." Accessed November 10, 2020. https://youngdiggers.com.au/reveille-or-rouse.

"Jean Nash Sailing for Son's Trial Here." *The New York Times*, March 14, 1934: 14. Retrieved November 2, 2020.

Kasten, Scott. "Modernization Versus Preservation in Paris During the Gaullist Era: A Tale of Two Cities." *Essays in History*, 2013. Accessed November 22, 2020. http://www.essaysinhistory.com/modernization-versus-preservation-in-paris-during-the-gaullist-era-a-tale-of-two-cities/.

Kladstrup, Don and Petie Kladstrup. *Wine & War*. New York: Broadway Books, 2002.

Kluckhohn, Frank L. "President Shapes Reply for Tonight to Nazis' Threats." *The New York Times*, May 27, 1941: 1,4. Retrieved November 4, 2020.

Knauth, Percival. "Berlin Seeks to End Rift with US." *The New York Times*, March 2, 1940: 70. Retrieved October 15, 2020.

Krock, Arthur, "Roosevelt Elected President…" *The New York Times*, November 6, 1940: 1. Retrieved October 30, 2020.

"La Côlette." *Documents commerciaux des restaurants de Paris et d'Ile de France*, Accessed June 17, 2021. https://bibliotheques-specialisees.paris.fr/ark:/73873/FRCGMSUP-751045102-EP02/BHPEP022060/v0001.simple.selectedTab=otherdocs.

"La Suisse Magazine. Max Kettel. Reports from 1926 to 1960." *Kultur Wallis Culture Valais*. Valais Media Library–Martigny. Accessed October 11, 2020. https://agenda.culturevalais.ch/fr/event/show/17401.

"*La Victoire*." Dir. Gustave Hervé. *La Victoire*, June 17, 1940: 1. Accessed November 9, 2020. https://www.ebay.fr/itm/FAC-SIMILE-JOURNAL-LA-VICTOIRE-G-HERVE-17-JUIN-1940-ARMISTICE-PARIS-OCCUPE-/153785122231.

"Land Warfare." *House of Commons Debates* (November 22, 1939) vol 353 cc1265–366. Accessed October 19, 2020. https://api.parliament.uk/historic-hansard/commons/1939/nov/22/land-warfare.

Lang, Andrew. *The Story of Joan of Arc*, 1906. Project Gutenberg. Updated December 17, 2016. Accessed October 23, 2020. https://www.gutenberg.org/files/48470/48470-h/48470-h.htm.

Larson, Erik. *The Splendid and the Vile*. New York: Crown Publishing Group, 2020.

Lauzanne, Stéphane. "Le problème des réfugiés juifs." *Le Matin*, June 17, 1939: 1. Accessed November 9, 2020. https://gallica.bnf.fr/ark:/12148/bpt6k5863520?rk=3390574;4.

Le Boterf, Hervé. *La vie parisienne sous l'occupation, 1940–1944*, Tome II, Paris: Éditions France-Empire, 1975.

Le Courrier. Wikipedia, Wikimedia Foundation, Updated April 27, 2020. Accessed August 12, 2023. https://en.wikipedia.org/wiki/Le_Courrier.

Le Figaro 1854–1942. Paris: *BnF Gallica*. Updated October 15, 2007. Accessed August 12, 2023. https://gallica.bnf.fr/ark:/12148/cb34355551z/date.

Le Journal 1892–1944. Paris: BnF Gallica. Accessed August 12, 2023. https://gallica.bnf.fr/ark:/12148/bpt6k76326093/f7.item.

Le Matin. Ed. Maurice Bunau-Varilla. 1882–1944. BnF Gallica. Accessed October 23, 2020. https://gallica.bnf.fr/html/und/presse-et-revues/les-principaux-quotidiens?mode=desktop.

Le Petit Parisien 1876–1944. Le Petit Parisien. Ed. Jean Dupuy. Paris: *BnF Gallica*. Accessed October 29, 2020. https://gallica.bnf.fr/html/und/presse-et-revues/les-principaux-quotidiens?mode=desktop.

Le Soir.be. Ed. Béatrice Delvaux. Brussels: *Le Soir.be*. Accessed August 12, 2023. https://www.lesoir.be.

Levenstein, Harvey. *We'll Always Have Paris: American Tourists in France since 1930*. Chicago: University of Chicago Press, 2004. Google Books.

"L'Humanité." Ed. Patrick Le Hyaric. Paris: *L'Humanité*. Accessed October 15, 2020. https://www.humanite.fr.

L'Illustration. "The Vichy origins of modern France." Accessed October 30, 2020. https://lefroggydotcom.wordpress.com/vichy/the-vichy-origins-of-modern-france-how-the-vichy-government-superseded-traditionalism-and-promoted-modernity.

"*L'Intransigeant*." L'Intransigeant. Ed. Henri Rochefort. September 4, 1939. Accessed August 12, 2023. https://gallica.bnf.fr/ark:/12148/bpt6k796315d.item.

Lee, R. E. "Montgomery, Robert, LCDR." *TWS*. Accessed October 22, 2020. https://navy.togetherweserved.com/usn/servlet/tws.webapp.WebApps?cmd=ShadowBoxProfile&type=Person&ID=386022.

"Leland Harrison Ex-Diplomat, Dies," *The New York Times*, June 8, 1951: 27. Retrieved October 12, 2020.

"Les Deux Magots." *Les Deux Magots–Paris*. Accessed August 12, 2023. http ://www.lesdeuxmagots.fr/en/history-restaurant-paris.html.

"Les Notes Laisées en Allemagne par M. Rudolf Hess." *Le Matin*, May 15, 1941. Retrieved February 5, 2023. https://gallica.bnf.fr/ark:/12148/bpt6k587101j/f3.item.

"Les Nouveaux Temps. "Dir. Jean Luchaire. *Wikipédia*. Wikipédia Foundation. February 2020. Accessed October 23, 2020. https://fr.m.wikipedia.org/wiki/Les_Nouveaux_Temps.

Lib. of Cong. Newspaper: *Gazette de Laussane et journal suisse*. [Lausanne, Switzerland] *U.S. Govt. Web.* Accessed October 11, 2020. https://www.loc.gov/item/sn91020845.

——. Newspaper: *Journal de Genève*. [Geneva, Switzerland] *U.S. Govt. Web.* Accessed October 11, 2020. https://www.loc.gov/item/sn95046950.

——. Newspaper: *La Tribune de Genève*. [Geneva, Switzerland] *U.S. Govt. Web.* Accessed October 11, 2020. https://www.loc.gov/item/sn95058026.

——. Newspaper: *Les Dernieres nouvelles de Paris*. [Paris, France] *U.S. Govt. Web.* Accessed October 23, 2020. https://www.loc.gov/item/sn90048725.

——. Newspaper: *New York Herald Tribune*. [New York, N.Y.] *U.S. Govt. Web.* Accessed October 29, 2020. https://www.loc.gov/item/sn83030216.

——. Newspaper: *The Philadelphia Record.* [Philadelphia, Pa.] 1879–1947. Pub. W.M. Singerly. *U.S. Govt. Web.* Accessed October 29, 2020. https://chroniclingamerica.loc.gov/lccn/sn83045563.

——. Newspaper: *Tribune de Lausanne.* [Lausanne, Switzerland] *U.S. Govt. Web.* Accessed October 11, 2020. https://www.loc.gov/item/sn94048439.

——. Newspaper: *The Washington Star.* [Washington, D.C.] 1854–1972. Pub. W.D. Wallach & Hope. *U.S. Govt. Web.* Accessed October 29, 2020. https://chroniclingamerica.loc.gov/lccn/sn83045462.

Lindsay, Philip. *Hampton Court: A History.* London: Meridian Books, 1948.

Lippmann, Walter. *Public Opinion.* New York: Harcourt, Brace & Co., 1922. Accessed November 20, 2020. https://wps.pearsoncustom.com/wps/media/objects/2429/2487430/pdfs/lippmann.pdf.

"LVTETIA." *HotelLutetia.com.* Accessed October 25, 2020. https://www.hotellutetia.com/history.

"Lyon." *UNESCO World Heritage List.* Accessed November 5, 2020. https://whc.unesco.org/en/list/872.

Lyons, Eugene. *Stalin: Czar of All the Russias.* Philadelphia: J. B. Lippincott Company, 1940.

MacArthur, Douglas II. Interview (beginning in 1986) by Charles Stuart Kennedy and conducted as a Moment in U.S. Diplomatic History for the Association for Diplomatic Studies & Training, published as "An American Diplomat in Vichy France," July 18, 2013. Accessed August 12, 2023. https://adst.org/2013/07/an-american-diplomat-in-vichy-france.

"Madame Récamier." *Louvre.* Written by De Vergnette François. Accessed November 4, 2020. https://www.louvre.fr/en/oeuvre-notices/madame-recamier.

"Marie-Danielle Rheuter and Le Poêlon d'Or." *Les Bouchons Lyonnais.* Accessed November 5, 2020. http://lesbouchonslyonnais.org/en/restaurants/le-poelon-dor.

Marquand, John. *Wickford Point.* Boston: Little, Brown and Company, 1939. Accessed June 11, 2022. https://www.fadedpage.com/books/20121202/html.php.

Maurois, André. *A History of France.* Trans. By Henry L. Binsse. New York: Farrar, Straus and Cudahy, 1956.

McMahon, Margaret. "WWI in the Passenger Lists of the U.S. Army Transport Service." *A Week of Genealogy,* July 4, 2017. Accessed November 21, 2020. https://aweekofgenealogy.com/wwi-in-the-passenger-lists-of-the-u-s-army-transport-service-part-ii/.

McRobbie, Linda Rodriquez. "Are Punch and Judy Shows Finally Outdated?" *Smithsonianmag.com.* Updated February 4, 2013. Accessed October 30, 2020. https://www.smithsonianmag.com/arts-culture/are-punch-and-judy-shows-finally-outdated-10599519.

"Medici Fountain." *EUtouring.com.* Accessed November 1, 2020. https://www.eutouring.com/fontaine_medicis.html.

"Meissonier, Jean-Louis Ernest." *Art Renewal Center.* Accessed November 4, 2020. https://www.artrenewal.org/artists/jean-louis-ernest-meissonier/84.

"Messerschmitt Bf 109 G-6/R3." *Smithsonian National Air and Space Museum.* Accessed October 19, 2020. https://airandspace.si.edu/collection-objects/messerschmitt-bf-109-g-6-r3/nasm_A19600327000.

"Model is….in front of Marius restaurant," Image. Accessed November 2, 2020. https://www.pinterest.com/pin/432486370435703177.

Momsen, Janet D., et al. "Saint Lucia." *Encyclopedia Britannica.* Updated September 10, 2020. Accessed October 27, 2020. https://www.britannica.com/place/Saint-Lucia.

Moore, George. *Memoirs of My Dead Life.* London: William Heinemann Ltd., 1936Accessed August 12, 2023. http://www.gutenberg.org/files/7789/7789-h/7789-h.htm.

"Moroccans in the Netherlands," *Verzets Résistance Museum.* Accessed November 9, 2020. https://www.verzetsmuseum.org/museum/en/tweede-wereldoorlog/digiexpo/marocco/marocco-netherlands.

"Mott, T. Bentley: Colonel in the U.S. Army." *Prabook.,* Version 2.0.45.1040, 2020. Accessed October 15,v2020. https://prabook.com/web/t.bentley.mott/936380.

"Mrs. Allez Is Dead; Heroine in War, 61," *The New York Times,* July 30, 1950: 60. Retrieved August 18, 2020.

"Musée de l'Homme Résistance Network." *The musée de l'Homme*. Accessed November 1, 2020. http://www.museedelhomme.fr/en/museum/museums-history/musee-lhomme-resistance-network-3921.

Nagorski, Andrew. *1941: The Year Germany Lost the War*. New York: Simon & Schuster, 2019.

"Napoleon's Tomb." *Granger Historical Picture Archive*. Accessed October 25, 2020. https://granger.com/results.asp?inline=true&image=0407801&wwwflag=1&itemx=40.

"National Assembly History." *National Assembly*. Updated 2019. Accessed October 22, 2020. http://wWWII.assemblee-nationale.fr/decouvrir-l-assemblee/histoire.

"Navy Flier Cited for Sinking 'Sub'," *The New York Times*, February 27, 1942: 3. Retrieved December 20, 2020.

"Nazi SS Chief Heinrich Himmler dies by suicide." *History*. Updated May 26, 2020. Accessed October 29, 2020. https://www.history.com/this-day-in-history/himmler-commits-suicide.

"Nazis Object to Statue of Edith Cavell in Paris," *The New York Times*, July 16, 1940: 11. Retrieved October 4, 2020.

"Nazis Reveal Rommel's Death." *The New York Times*, October 15, 1944: 1,8. Retrieved November 6, 2020.

Neiberg, Michael. *When France Fell*. Cambridge, MA: Harvard University Press, 2021.

——. *World War I: Encyclopedia*, Volume 1. Ed. Spencer Tucker and Priscilla Mary Roberts. ABC-CLIO, Santa Barbara, 2005.

Neuberger, Joan. "Sergei Eisenstein's *Ivan the Terrible* as History." *The Journal of Modern History*, vol. 86, no. 2, 2014. 295–334. JSTOR. Accessed November 5, 2020. https://www.jstor.org/stable/10.1086/675483.

New International French Dictionary. Chicago: Wilcox & Follett Co., 1943.

"Northumberland." *Wikipedia*. Wikipedia Foundation. 25 October 2020. Accessed 29 October 2020. https://en.wikipedia.org/wiki/Northumberland.

"Notice to American passengers aboard *SS Washington*." June 7, 1940." *ECU Libraries Digital Collections*. Accessed August 17, 2023. https://digital.lib.ecu.edu/36375#.

"Notre Dame Cathedral Paris." *Notre Dame Cathedral Paris 2008–2020*. Accessed October 16, 2020. https://notredamecathedralparis.com.

Olson, Lynne. *Citizens of London*. New York: Random House, 2010.

"Origins of Veterans Day," Celebrating America's Freedoms, *U.S. Department of Veterans Affairs*. Accessed November 11, 2020. https://www.va.gov/opa/publications/celebrate/vetday.pdf.

"Overview of the Bernese Oberland." *Earth Trekkers*. Accessed October 12, 2020. https://www.earthtrekkers.com/bernese-oberland-travel-guide-jungfrau-region/#overview.

"Packard V-1650 Merlin." National Museum of the U.S. Air Force. Published April 21, 2015. Accessed June 11, 2022. https://www.nationalmuseum.af.mil/Visit/Museum-Exhibits/Fact-Sheets/Display/Article/196239/packard-v-1650-merlin/.

The Papers of Richard W. Morin, Rauner Special Collections, Dartmouth College Library. Dartmouth College, Hanover, New Hampshire.

"Paris at war (1939–1940)." *Paris Archives*. Accessed October 17, 2020. http://archives.paris.fr/r/249/paris-en-guerre-1939-1940.

"*Paris-Midi*." Ed. Maurice de Waleffe. *BnF Gallica*. "Hitler attaque la Pologne," September 1, 1939. Accessed October 16, 2020. https://gallica.bnf.fr/ark:/12148/bpt6k4738101j.item.

"Paris, Tuileries, Alexandre combattant un lion (Dieudonné)." *Europeana*. Accessed February 1, 2021. https://classic.europeana.eu/portal/en/record/9200495/yoolib_inha_2364.html?utm_source=new-website&utm_medium=button.

"Parliament and government." *UK Parliament*. Accessed October 20, 2020. https://www.parliament.uk/about/how/role/parliament-government.

"The Partial Text of Chancellor Adolf Hitler's Address on the Nazi Party's Anniversary." *The New York Times*, February 25, 1940: 32. Retrieved August 18, 2020.

Patton, James. "Germany Gets a New National Anthem," *Roads to the Great War,* October 7, 2020. Accessed June 11, 2022. http://roadstothegreatwar-WWI.blogspot.com/2020/10/germany-gets-new-national-anthem.html.

Payne, John. "One Thousand and One Nights." Trans. Richard Burton. *The Book of the Thousand Nights and a Night.* Burton: Burton Club. 1910. Accessed June 11, 2022. https://ia902700.us.archive.org/19/items/arabiantranslat01burtuoft/arabiantranslat01burtuoft.pdf.

"The Peninsula Paris." *Wikipedia.* Wikipedia Foundation. Updated September 28, 2020. Accessed October 25, 2020. https://en.wikipedia.org/wiki/The_Peninsula_Paris.

"Phila. Emergency Aid Girl Goes to France." *Philadelphia Inquirer,* September 18, 1918.

Philadelphia War History Committee. *Philadelphia in the world war, 1914–1919.* Albany, New York: Wynkoop Hallenbeck Crawford Co., 1922. Accessed November 8, 2020. https://archive.org/stream/philadelphiainwo00philrich?ref=ol#page/566/mode/2up.

Pierre. "What Is la Toussaint, All Saints' Day in France." *Frenchmoments.eu.* Updated 28 November. Accessed October 30, 2020. https://frenchmoments.eu/all-saints-day-in-france-la-toussaint.

"Place Bellecour." *This Is Lyon.* Accessed November 12, 2020. https://thisislyon.fr/things-to-do/historical-monuments/place-bellecour.

Pommier, Christophe. "The Prussian cannons of the Triumphal Battery." *Musée de l'Armée Invalides.* March 6, 2013. Accessed October 19, 2020. https://collections.musee-armee.fr/les-canons-prussiens-de-la-batterie-triomphale.

Porter, Roy P. *Uncensored France: An Eyewitness Account of France under the Occupation.* New York: The Dial Press, 1942. Accessed June 11, 2022 https://babel.hathitrust.org/cgi/pt?id=inu.32000013335890&view=1up&seq=7.

Pozzoli, Francesca, and Christian Luchessa. "Lugano: 1939–1945." *Interreg IIIA Project.* Taiana, Muzzano, Switzerland: La memoria delle Alpi, 2008. 288. Accessed August 12, 2023. https://silo.tips/download/lugano-guida-ai-luoghi-ai-personaggi-e-agli-avvenimenti-della-citta-e-dei-suoi-d."Preserved in time: WWII bunker hidden under Paris train station." *The Local fr.* Updated February 5, 2018. Accessed October 22, 2020. https://www.thelocal.fr/20180205/preserved-in-time-wwii-bunker-hidden-under-paris-train-station.

"Press Release Issued by the White House on November 9, 1942." *Office of the Historian.* Foreign Service Institute, United States Department of State. Accessed October 13, 2020. https://history.state.gov/historicaldocuments/frus1942v02/d204.

"Prophesies of Saint Odile" c. 1940. Ellipsis Rare Books. Accessed November 1, 2020. https://www.ellipsisrarebooks.com/product/handwritten-prophecies-of-saint-odile-c-1940.

Proust, Marcel. *Swann's Way.* Trans. C.K. Scott Moncrieff. The Project Gutenberg eBook of *Swann's Way. Remembrance of Things Past* Vol. I. New York: Henry Holt and Co, 1922. Accessed August 12, 2023. https://www.gutenberg.org/files/7178/7178-h/7178-h.htm.

"Queen Elizabeth The Queen Mother." The Royal Household. Accessed November 2, 2020. https://www.royal.uk/queen-elizabeth-queen-mother.

Rabelais, François. *"Rabelais: Gargantua and Pantagruel, Book I." Gargantua and Pantagruel, Book I.* Updated August 8, 2004. Accessed October 29, 2020. https://www.gutenberg.org/files/8166/8166-h/8166-h.htm.

"Raymond Deiss." Musée de le Résistance en Ligne. Updated January 13, 2019. Accessed August 29, 2020. http://museedelaresistanceenligne.org/media10439-Raymond-Deiss.

Reddy, Karina. "Fashion History Timeline: 1940–1949." *Fashion History.* Updated August 18, 2020. Accessed October 30, 2020. https://fashionhistory.fitnyc.edu/1940–1949.

Reed, Douglas. *Nemesis? The Story of Otto Strasser.* London: Jonathan Cape, 1940. Accessed June 11, 2022. https://www.resist.com/Onlinebooks/Nemesis-DouglasReed.pdf.

"Reopening of the American Embassy, Paris: October 14, 1944." *The American Foreign Service Journal,* December 1944. 655 Accessed June 11, 2022 https://www.afsa.org/sites/default/files/fsj-1944–12-december_0.pdf.

"Report of the Board of Managers of the Trades League of Philadelphia: For the Year 1904." *Fourteenth Annual Report of the Board of Directors, The Trades League of Philadelphia: For the Year 1904.* Philadelphia: The Trades League of Philadelphia, 1905. 47. *Google Books.*

"Revillon Frères." *Furs by Chrys.* Accessed November 2, 2020. https://fursbychrys.com/ranch_mink_coat_RM546.htm.

"RG-46.08.34, From Swiss newspaper *Die Nation,* Theresienstadt, a propaganda trick, May 1945, translation | Los Angeles Museum of the Holocaust." *Holocaust Museum LA.* Accessed October 11, 2020. http://www.lamoth.info/?p=digitallibrary/digitalcontent&id=8521.

"RG-79.04.04. Il Giornale d'Italia, The Italian Journal, December 3, 1942, No 288, 3 December 1942." European periodicals of the wartime period, 1939–1945, 1933–1945 | Los Angeles Museum of the Holocaust. Holocaust Museum LA. Accessed August 12, 2023 http://www.lamoth.info/?p=collections/findingaid&id=88&q=&rootcontentid=10884#id10884.

"RG-79.04.05. Il Giornale d'Italia, The Italian Journal, June 10, 1943, No 138, 10 June 1943." European periodicals of the wartime period, 1939–1945, 1933–1945 | Los Angeles Museum of the Holocaust. Holocaust Museum LA. Accessed August 12, 2023. http://www.lamoth.info/?p=collections/findingaid&id=88&q=&rootcontentid=10884#id10884.

Rich, Tracey R. "What Is Judaism?" *Judaism from Judaism 101.* Accessed October 5, 2020. https://www.jewfaq.org/judaism.htm.

Richardson, Bonham C., and Kack K. Menke. "Guyana." *Encyclopedia Britannica.* Updated September 8, 2020. Accessed October 27, 2020. https://www.britannica.com/place/Guyana.

"Robert D. Murphy." *The Foreign Service Journal,* October 1940. Accessed October 27, 2020. https://www.afsa.org/foreign-service-journal-october-1940.

"Robert Wilden Neeser." *Find a Grave.* Memorial no. 196124801. Created January 17, 2019 and maintained by Squadron A Association. Accessed November 3, 2020. https://www.findagrave.com/memorial/196124801/robert-wilden-neeser.

Robinson, Arthur N.R., et al. "Trinidad and Tobago." *Encyclopedia Britannica.* Updated October 25, 2020. Accessed October 27, 2020. https://www.britannica.com/place/Trinidad-and-Tobago.

"Rochefort-en-Yvelines," *Map-France.com.* Accessed November 8, 2020. https://www.map-france.com/Rochefort-en-Yvelines-78730.

Rolland, Romain. *Mahatma Gandhi—The Man Who Became One with the Universal Being.* Trans. Catherine D. Groth. The Project Gutenberg eBook of Mahatma Gandhi. New York: The Century Company, 1924. Accessed 11 June 2022. http://www.gutenberg.org/files/61575/61575-h/61575-h.htm.

Rosemeier, Dr. Hermann. Interview by Dr. Frank Bohn and published as "German Exiles Demand Crushing of Prussian Militarism by Force" in Mixer and Server magazine. 45. August 31, 1917. Google Books.

Royall, Penelope. "Addresses of Retired Foreign Service Personnel." Foreign Service Journal, September 1962–Part 2. 13A. Accessed November 17, 2020. https://www.afsa.org/foreign-service-journal-september-1962.

Saint-Exupéry, Antoine de. *Airman's Odyssey,* "Flight to Arras." New York: Reynal and Hitchcock, 1939. Accessed June 11, 2022. https://www.google.com/books/edition/Airman_s_Odyssey/9JSQUG74tFgC?hl=en&gbpv=1&dq=France+is+always+saved+in+the+eleventh+hour+by+a+miracle&pg=PT346&printsec=frontcover.

"Sainte-Beuve." *EUtouring.com.* Accessed November 1, 2020. https://www.eutouring.com/images_paris_statues_285.html.

"Sainte-Clotilde." *Paroisse Sainte Clotilde.* Accessed November 3, 2020. http://www.sainte-clotilde.com/v2/index.php/qui-sommes-nous.html.

"Salle Rameau." *Wikipedia.* Wikipedia Foundation. Accessed February 10, 2023. https ://fr.wikipedia.org/wiki/Salle_Rameau.

Saxon, Wolfgang. "Charlotte, Longtime Luxembourg Ruler, Dies." *The New York Times*, July 10, 1985: 29. Retrieved October 22, 2020.

Schädler, Ulrich. "1945." Swiss Museum of Games, Dossier "75 years ago…" *Swiss Museum of Games*. Accessed October 20, 2020. http://museedujeu.ch/wp-content/uploads/2020/06/WWII_Dossier_GB_-75-years-ago.pdf.

Sciolino, Elaine. "Ode to the Seine River, River of Romance." *Literary Hub*. Updated October 31, 2019. Accessed November 19, 2020. https://lithub.com/ode-to-the-seine-river-of-romance.

"Sculpture of Bacchante." Pierre Alexandre Schoenewerk. HD photographs of Bacchante statue on Aile Sud at Musée du Louvre. *EUtouuring.com*. Accessed November 13, 2020. https://www.eutouring.com/images_paris_statues_908.html.

"Sculpture of Cassandra." Aimé Millet. HD photographs of Cassandre se met sous la protection de Pallas inside Tuileries Gardens. *EUtouring.com*. Accessed October 18, 2020. https://www.eutouring.com/images_paris_statues_30.html.

"Sculpture of Prometheus." James Pradier, Garden Tuileries. *Alamy*. Accessed June 11, 2022. https://www.alamy.com/2B97YX3.

Sebba, Anne "Fashion as Resistance in WWII France." *Wonders & Marvels*. Accessed November 12, 2020. https://www.wondersandmarvels.com/2017/01/fashion-resistance-wwii-france.html.

Shakespeare, William. *Hamlet, Prince of Denmark,* Vol. II, Ed. William George Clarke and William Aldis Wright. University of Chicago Press, 1952. *Great Books of the Western World*, Vol. 27.

Simkin, John. "Claude Pepper." *Spartacus Educational*. January 2020. Accessed October 27, 2020. https://spartacus-educational.com/NDclaude_pepper.htm.

——. "Hermann Rauschning." *Spartacus Educational*. January 2020. Accessed October 20, 2020. https://spartacus-educational.com/Herman_Rauschning.htm.

Singer, Barnett. *Maxime Weygand: A Biography of the French General in Two World Wars*. Jefferson, North Carolina: McFarland & Company, Inc., 2008.

Skjalden. "Odin: The Allfather." *Nordic Culture*. Updated June 1, 2011. Accessed October 27, 2020. https://norse-mythology.net/odin-the-allfather-of-the-aesir-in-norse-mythology.

Smith, Whitney. "Flag of France." *Encyclopedia Britannica*. Updated July 11, 2018. Accessed October 27, 2020. https://www.britannica.com/topic/flag-of-France.

Smoodin, Eric. "The Paris Cinema Project." *Paris Cinema Blog*, WordPress, September 1, 2017. Accessed June 11, 2022. https://pariscinemablog.wordpress.com.

"Sofitel Paris le Faubourg." *Sofitel Paris le Faubourg*. Accessed October 18, 2020. https://www.sofitel-paris-lefaubourg.com/en/discover-the-hotel/history.

Steves, Rick, and Steve Smith. *France*. Brentwood, Tennessee: Hachette Book Group, 2019.

"Suchet, Marshal Louis-Gabriel." *Frenchempire.net*. Accessed November 4, 2020. https://www.frenchempire.net/biographies/suchet.

"Suresnes American Cemetery." *American Battle Monuments Commission*. Accessed October 22, 2020. https://www.abmc.gov/cemeteries-memorials/europe/suresnes-american-cemetery.

Taylor, Melissa Jane. "Diplomats in Turmoil: Creating a Middle Ground in Post-Anschluss Austria." *Diplomatic History*, vol. 32, no.5, Oxford University Press, 2008. 812.

Testelmans, Eddy. "de Cartier de Marchienne, Baron Emile-Ernest." *Ars-Moriendi*. Accessed October 15, 2020. http://www.ars-moriendi.be/DE_CARTIER_DE_MARCHIENNE.HTM.

"Théâtre des Bouffes Parisiens." *Bouffes-Parisiens Theater*. Updated October 17, 2020. Accessed October 20, 2020. https://www.bouffesparisiens.com/fr_FR.

Tolischus, Otto D. "Berlin Talks Held." *The New York Times*, August 26, 1939: 1,2. Retrieved November 8, 2020.

Tourtellot, Arthur Bernon. "We Mutually Pledge to Each Other Our Lives, Our Fortunes and Our Sacred Honor," American Heritage. Vol. 14. Issue 1. Updated December 1962. Accessed October 29,

2020. https://www.americanheritage.com/we-mutually-pledge-each-other-our-lives-our-fortunes-and-our-sacred-honor#3.

Turner, John Frayn and Jackson, Robert. *Destination Berchtesgaden*. New York: Charles Scribner's Sons, 1975.

"Tuxedo Park History." *Tuxedo Park Fine Homes*. Accessed September 1, 2020. https://tuxedoparkfinehomes.com/?page_id=88.

"Un incident franco-américain à Vichy." *Le Matin* 15 janvier 1941: 1. Retrieved November 1, 2020. https://gallica.bnf.fr/ark:/12148/bpt6k5869851.item.

Upton, Anthony F. *Finland in Crisis 1940–1941: A Study in Small-Power Politics*. Ithaca, NY, Cornell University Press, 1965.

"Van Dyck." *Sotheby's*. Accessed November 1, 2020. https://www.sothebys.com/en/artists/anthony-van-dyck.

Varley, Karine. "History of Modern France at War." *Francehistory.wordpress.com*. Updated May 31, 2014. Accessed November 7, 2020. https://francehistory.wordpress.com/2014/05/31/laboratory-of-liberation-lessons-for-france-from-the-liberation-of-corsica.

"The Vault." *Time Magazine*. June 16, 1941. Accessed November 17, 2020. https://time.com/vault/issue/1941–06–16/page/28/.

Viollet, Roger. "World War II. Flower Market, Paris, Place de la Madeleine." *Granger*. Accessed November 11, 2020. https://www.granger.com/results.asp?image=0764589&itemw=4&itemf=0001&itemstep=1&itemx=20.

Walser, Ray. "War Comes to Warsaw: September 1939," *The Foreign Service Journal*, September 2019. Accessed June 11, 2022. https://www.afsa.org/war-comes-warsaw-september-1939.

"Watteau." *EUtouring.com*. Accessed November 1, 2020 https://www.eutouring.com/images_paris_statues_319.html.

"West Point II AP-23." *History Central*. Accessed November 4, 2020. https://www.historycentral.com/navy/ap/West%20Point%20II.html.

White, Theodore, and Annalee Jacoby. *Thunder out of China*. New York: William Sloane Associates, 1946. Accessed June 11, 2022. https://archive.org/stream/thunderoutofchin031761mbp/thunderoutofchin031761mbp_djvu.txt.

"WHSmith–The English Bookshop." *WHSmith*. Now known as Smith&Son Paris. Accessed June 13, 2022. https://www.smithandson.com/.

Wilde, Oscar. *De Profundis*. London: Methuen & Company, 1911. Accessed June 11, 2022. https://ia802705.us.archive.org/2/items/deprofundis00wildiala/deprofundis00wildiala.pdf.

Wolfe, Thomas. *You Can't Go Home Again*. Book VII, "A Wind Is Rising and the Rivers Flow." New York: Grosset & Dunlap, 1940. Accessed June 11, 2022. http://gutenberg.net.au/ebooks07/0700231h.html#book7.

The World Book Encyclopedia, Chicago: Field Enterprises Educational Corporation, 1976.

"WWII British Command Centres." *Sky History*. Accessed October 12, 2020. https://www.history.co.uk/article/WWII-british-command-centres.

"The Year We Had Two Thanksgivings." *Franklin D. Roosevelt Presidential Library and Museum*. Accessed October 20, 2020. http://docs.fdrlibrary.marist.edu/thanksg.html.

Yockelson, Mitchell. *Forty-Seven Days*. New York: New American Library, 2016.

Zucca, André. "Paris under German Occupation during WWII: Color Pics by Andre Zucca." *History in Images*. Accessed November 3, 2020. https://historyimages.blogspot.com/2012/02/paris-german-occupation-WWII-color-images.html.

Poetry Cited

Bonar, Horatius. "Be True to Thyself." *Poeticous*. Accessed April 24, 2020. http://www.poeticous.com/horatius-bonar/be-true-to-thyself.

Browning, Robert. "Epilogue." *King Albert's Book, 1914*. London: The Daily Telegraph. 1914. Accessed June 11, 2022. https://poets.org/poem/epilogue-1.

Bushby, D. Maitland. "Flanders, 1940." Humboldt, AZ. May 4, 1940. [Note: MLD footnote]

Byron, Lord (George Gordon), "Childe Harold's Pilgrimage Canto the Second." London: John Murray Publishing Company, 1812. Accessed June 11, 2022. https://www.gutenberg.org/files/5131/5131-h/5131-h.htm#link2H_4_0004.

Haskins, Minnie Louise. "God Knows" also known as "The Gate of the Year." *The Desert* collection. 1912. Accessed June 11, 2022. https://blogs.lse.ac.uk/lsehistory/2013/12/10/the-gate-of-the-year-minnie-louise-haskins-1875–1957.

Kipling, Rudyard. "If," *Rewards and Fairies*. 1910. Accessed October 21, 2020. https://www.poetryfoundation.org/poems/46473/if---.

McCrae, John. "In Flanders Fields," 1915. *Arlington National Cemetery*. Updated November 12, 2008. Accessed April 24, 2020. http://www.arlingtoncemetery.net/flanders.htm.

Morris, William. *The Earthly Paradise*. London: F.S. Ellis. 1868–1870. Accessed June 11, 2022. https://www.gutenberg.org/files/30332/30332-h/30332-h.htm.

Newman, John Henry. "Lead, Kindly Light" also known as "The Pillar of the Cloud." *Lyra Apostolica*. London: Rivingtons, 1836. Accessed June 11, 2022. http://www.newmanreader.org/works/verses/verse90.html.

Shakespeare, William. *The Tragedy of King Richard II*, Vol. I, Ed. William George Clarke and William Aldis Wright. University of Chicago Press, 1952. *Great Books of the Western World*, Vol. 26.

——. *Macbeth*, Act II. Ed. William George Clarke and William Aldis Wright. University of Chicago Press, 1952. *Great Books of the Western World*, Vol. 27.

Shelley, Percy Blythe. "Adonais: An Elegy on the Death of John Keats." Charles Ollier, 1821. Accessed June 11, 2022. https://www.poetryfoundation.org/poems/45112/adonais-an-elegy-on-the-death-of-John-Keats.

Swinburne, Algernon Charles. "The Garden of Proserpine," *Poems and Ballads*. 1866. Accessed June 11, 2022 https://www.poetryfoundation.org/poems/45288/the-garden-of-proserpine.

Verlaine, Paul. "Nocturne Parisien," *Poèmes saturniens*. 1866. Accessed October 21, 2020 https://eternels-eclairs.fr/Poeme-Paul-Verlaine-Nocturne-parisien.

——. "Colloque sentimental," Fêtes galantes. 1869 Accessed October 21, 2020. https://www.poetica.fr/poeme-505/paul-verlaine-colloque-sentimental.

——. "Le ciel est, par-dessus…". *Sagesse*. 1881. Accessed October 21, 2020 https://www.poetica.fr/poeme-756/paul-verlaine-le-ciel-est-par-dessus.

Whitney, Helen [Julia] Hay. "This Was the Song." Sonnets and Songs. New York: Harper & Brothers, 1905. Accessed June 11, 2022. http://www.archive.org/stream/sonnetssongs00whitrich/sonnetssongs00whitrich_djvu.txt.

Books Cited

Adler, Irving. *Then and Now*. Self-published, Irving M. Adler, 2021.

Brontë, Emily. *Wuthering Heights*. London: Thomas Cautley Newby, 1847.

Hall, Melvin Adams. *Journey to the End of an Era*. New York: Charles Scribner's Sons, 1947.

——. *Bird of Time*. New York: Charles Scribner's Sons, 1949.

Lenotre, G. *Vielles maisons, vieux papiers*. Sydney, Australia: Wentworth Press, 2019.

Nicolay, John George, and John Hay. *Abraham Lincoln: A History, Vol. I–X*. New York: The Century Co., 1914.

Tilley, Arthur Augustus (Ed.). *Medieval France: A Companion to French studies*. Cambridge, UK: Dalcassian Publishing Company, 1922.

Performances Cited

"Andrew Barton, Child Ballad #167." *The English and Scottish Popular Ballads*. Ed. Francis J. Child. 1884–1898. Accessed June 11, 2022. https://www.contemplator.com/child/abartin.html.

Casablanca. Dir. Michael Curtiz. Perf. Humphrey Bogart, Ingrid Bergman, Paul Henreid, Claude Reins, etc. Warner Brothers, 1942.

Chorale de la Promotion Laperrine. "La Madelon." *YouTube*. Chants des Armees Française, 2016. Accessed 11 June 2022. https://www.youtube.com/watch?v=5aASoaP1hhs.

Dunkirk. Dir. Christopher Nolan. Perf. Fionn Whitehead, Tom Glynn-Carney, Jack Lowden, etc. Warner Brothers, 2017.

Fascicule Noir. By Louis Verveuil. Perf. Gaby Morlay and Vincent Francen. Théâtre des Bouffes-Parisiens, Paris. February 23, 1940.

The King's Speech. Dir. Tom Hooper. Perf. Colin Firth, Geoffrey Rush, Helena Bonham Carter, Guy Pearce, etc. Distributed by Momentum Pictures, 2010.

Lenoir, Jean. "Parlez-moi d'amour." Perf. Lucienne Boyer. Chez Elle, Paris. April 8, 1940. Accessed June 11, 2022. https://www.youtube.com/watch?v=rIAQWr34De0.

Louise. By Gustave Charpentier. National Theater of the Opera Comique, Paris. February 1900.

Marie Stuart. Based on the novel by Harald Braun. Dir. Carl Froelich. Perf. Zarah Leander, Willy Birgel, Maria Koppenhöfer, et al. Universus Film AG (UFA), 1940. Accessed August 12, 2023. https://www.imdb.com/title/tt0032587/?ref_=fn_al_tt_6.

McCormack, John. "It's A Long Way to Tipperary." *YouTube*, uploaded by jack11anbar, 2008 Accessed June 11, 2022 https://www.youtube.com/watch?v=XVM-tFAdADg.

Moonlight Sonata. Dir. Lothar Mendes. Written by E. M. Delafield and Edward Knoblock. Perf. Ignacy Jan Paderewski. United Artists, 1937.

Patton. Dir. Franklin J. Schaffner and Delbert Mann. Perf. George C. Scott, Karl Malden, Stephen Young, et al. 20th Century Studios, 1970.

Robert, Camille, "Madelon: 'I'll be true to the whole regiment': English version of the celebrated French soldier's song Quand Madelon: song" (1918). *World War I Sheet Music*. Brown Digital Repository. Brown University Library. Accessed June 11, 2022. https://repository.library.brown.edu/studio/item/bdr:96571.

Rouget de Lisle, Claude-Joseph. "La Marseillaise". Strasbourg, 1792. Accessed June 11, 2022. http://www.marseillaise.org/english/francais.html.

Three Faces East. By George Cohan. Perf. Emmett Corrigan and Violet Heming. Cohan and Harris Theatre, New York. October 1918.

Toward His Destiny, adapt. *Young Mr. Lincoln*. Screenplay by Lamar Trotti. Dir. John Ford. Perf. Henry Fonda. Le Paris, 1939.

Vieux Disques. "*Chaque chose à sa place.*" Recorded [Paris, October 1940]. YouTube video, 3:05. Posted December 21, 2014. Accessed June 11, 2022. https://www.youtube.com/watch?v=FE5AQHi9OI4.

Williams, Henry James (Harry), and Judge, Jack. "It's a Long, Long Way to Tipperary." Stalybridge music hall, Greater Manchester, England, 1912.

Acknowledgments

"I wish to acknowledge with gratitude the kind help I have received from the many friends whose encouragement has spurred me on to assembling these notes. Especially I would like to thank Colonel Melvin Hall, author of *Journey to the End of an Era* and *Bird of Time*, for his valuable help in critiquing my manuscript; Miss Penelope Royall, in charge of the Library of the United States of America at Paris, who not only loaned me books that were of great assistance but who indicated and found for me those that would be most beneficial in my work; and Mr. Morgan Heiskell, who was so kind as to show me photographs he took during the German Occupation."

Marie-Louise Dilkes, Paris, 1955

The publication of the World War II experiences of my Aunt Marie-Louise Dilkes has required a good deal of family support. Foremost I need to thank my Aunt Marie-Louise for her foresight in writing about her WWII experiences so that generations to come will understand the global yet personal impact of the war. Although she had a front row seat to this time in our country's history, she would never know the extent of her impact because she died before classified documents were made available for my research into her experiences.

I would like to thank my brother, Charles Edward Dilkes, Jr., for providing me with the typewritten copy of her manuscript. An original unpublished manuscript was given to our father by his sister, our Aunt Marie-Louise. Upon his death in 1968, it was given to our mother. When she died in 1984, it was passed to my brother who shared a copy with each of his siblings. I would also like to thank my daughter, Anne, who helped me digitize my aunt's manuscript and gave clarity to its presentation. My siblings followed me in the creative process and offered moral support when I needed it.

Staff members at several universities and libraries have been instrumental in helping me find information on places and events that Marie-Louise Dilkes mentioned in her manuscript. Dr. Kenneth Mouré at the University of Alberta suggested resources to help me locate some WWII restaurants in Paris that she had frequented. He directed me to the Bibliothèque Historique de la Ville de Paris where the curator, Vincent Bruand, and the conservator, Séverine Montigny, helped me. Monsieur Bruand identified the La Côtelette restaurant where Marie-Louise Dilkes dined with a secretary of the South African Legation in Paris. Ms. Montigny provided me with references to the life of former French foreign minister Gaston Liébert (1866–1944). These references are consistent with Marie-Louise Dilkes having dined with M. Liébert on Christmas 1939 at Le Relais de la Belle Aurore restaurant.

Dr. Mouré also directed me to SINDBAD Bibliothèque nationale de France, where staff person, Marianne Arnold, provided me with references to the café Viel on the Boulevard de la Madeleine where Marie-Louise Dilkes met Mico of Guatemala for an apéritif. Shortly after their meeting in July 1940, the café Viel was requisitioned by Nazi Germany and renamed. Thank you to Dr. Mouré at the University of Alberta and the staff at the Bibliothèque Historique de la Ville de Paris and the SINDBAD Bibliothèque nationale de France for their help.

Mr. Guido Koller of the Swiss Federal Archives was instrumental in helping me find documents on Marie-Louise Dilkes while she served with the U.S. Legation in Bern, Switzerland. From these documents I was able to ascertain the date of arrival and the date of departure for her assignment with the U.S. Legation in Bern. I would like to thank him and his staff for their support.

I would like to acknowledge the help of Wesley Lucas, Librarian at the National World War II Museum Library; Linda K. Smith, Archives Specialist at the Dwight D. Eisenhower Presidential Library; Thomas Buffenbarger, Library Technician at the U.S. Army Heritage and Education Center; and David Langbart, Archivist with the National Archives in College Park, Maryland. Each of these individuals added a piece to the puzzle as to how Marie-Louise Dilkes was able to return to Paris to help reestablish the American Embassy in Paris after it had been closed from 1941–1944. The documents at the National Archives were particularly valuable.

Special thanks to Dr. Michael Neiberg, Chair of War Studies at the U.S. Army War College, and Dr. Monique Seefried, both of whom I came to know through work on the commemoration of the WWI Centennial. Monique Seefriend, whose parents lived in France during the Nazi Occupation, knew about my project to publish my aunt's WWII experiences and told me of the book Michael Neiberg was in the process of writing. She suggested I contact him because both efforts involved work between the U.S. State Department and France. Michael Neiberg cited the manuscript of Marie-Louise Dilkes several times in his book: *When France Fell* (2021), which I appreciated.

Many friends supported me in my research. I would like to thank Dr. Irving Adler, a longtime friend who shared some of his research on his book *Then and Now* (2021), particularly as related to the closing of the United States consulates in Greater Germany in 1941. I would like to acknowledge Amy Bailey, librarian with the Sequoyah Regional Libraries; the Reverend Don Jordan, WWII amateur historian whom I came to know through the Peachtree Presbyterian Church in Atlanta; and Col. William Woodcock, WWII historian.

Online support from websites was invaluable. During the COVID-19 pandemic, access to libraries and museums was difficult and travel to France was restricted. I relied heavily on the internet: literature——gutenberg.org and archive.org; poetry——the poetryfoundation.org, poets.org, and poetica.fr; speeches——winstonchurchill.org, ibiblio.org, and youtube.com; maps——Wikimedia Commons for the maps of Western Europe and d-maps.com for the map of Paris; and general information——the Wikipedia Foundation and its lists of resources. In the Notes and Bibliography, I have included links to the online source. Also, online vendors of used books supplied me with inexpensive resource material. Access to the internet allowed me to do some of the editorial research while sheltering in place.

Virginia A. Dilkes, 2023

Index